AMERICA'S ORIGINAL SIN

AMERICA'S ORIGINAL SIN

White Supremacy, John Wilkes Booth,

and the Lincoln Assassination

JOHN RHODEHAMEL

Johns Hopkins University Press

BALTIMORE

Johns Hopkins University Press
2715 North Charles Street
Baltimore, Maryland 21218-4363
www.press.jhu.edu

Library of Congress Cataloging-in-Publication Data
Names: Rhodehamel, John H., author.
Title: America's original sin : white supremacy, John Wilkes Booth,
and the Lincoln assassination / John Rhodehamel.
Description: Baltimore : Johns Hopkins University Press, 2021. |
Includes bibliographical references and index.
Identifiers: LCCN 2020045988 | ISBN 9781421441610 (hardcover) |
ISBN 9781421441627 (ebook)
Subjects: LCSH: Lincoln, Abraham, 1809–1865—Assassination. | Booth, John
Wilkes, 1838–1865. | White supremacy movements—United States. | United
States—Race relations—History. | United States—History—1849–1877.
Classification: LCC E457.5 .R525 2021 | DDC 973.7092—dc23
LC record available at https://lccn.loc.gov/2020045988

A catalog record for this book is available from the British Library.

Frontispiece: Abraham Lincoln, February 5, 1865. Alexander Gardner.
Huntington Library, photOV10681.

*Special discounts are available for bulk purchases of this book. For more
information, please contact Special Sales at specialsales@jh.edu.*

Johns Hopkins University Press uses environmentally friendly
book materials, including recycled text paper that is composed of
at least 30 percent post-consumer waste, whenever possible.

Typeset in Dante by Amy Ruth Buchanan / 3rd sister design.

CONTENTS

AMERICA'S ORIGINAL SIN

PROLOGUE

There's a story of what never happened that's been told thousands of times, a story of political murder and revenge, sorrow and crippling doubt. A family of famous American actors named Booth all knew this story by heart. Father and sons, they'd played it many times. This story is William Shakespeare's tragical history of Hamlet, Prince of Denmark. The father of the acting family, the "mad tragedian" Junius Brutus Booth, had moved two generations of theatergoers on two continents with his portrayal of the melancholy prince. The older son, Edwin Booth, won enduring fame as the finest Hamlet of them all—becoming the "standard to which all actors aspired and none reached"—with his hundred-night run in the title role in New York City during the last winter of the Civil War.[1] The younger son, John Wilkes Booth, had played Hamlet, too. But he won far more fame for his spectacular, violent portrayal of the murderous tyrant Richard III in another of Shakespeare's tragedies.

Prince Hamlet has sworn to avenge the murder of his father, King Hamlet. The killer is none other than the dead king's brother, Claudius, Hamlet's uncle, who has elevated himself to the Danish throne by his crime and in the bargain has incestuously taken his brother's widow, Gertrude, the prince's mother, as his wife. But doubt drains away Hamlet's native resolution. He cannot bring himself to kill. Then in the third act the hesitant avenger comes upon his guilty uncle alone and vulnerable. On his knees, his back turned and his eyes closed, Claudius will be easy to dispatch. Hamlet bares his sword.

But then the prince, who has thought long and hard about the geographies of the undiscovered country of the dead, is stricken again by doubt. He decides that this is not the time to strike. For Claudius is on his knees in prayer, and to kill him thus clean-souled will be to send him straight to heaven, hardly a fitting punishment for his cold-blooded murder of his own brother, all the more so when Hamlet reflects that his father's own unshriven ghost is consigned to a purgatory of fearful punishment. Hamlet sheathes his sword. Two more acts remain before the stage is strewn with corpses and the prince perceives that the rest is silence.

The irony is that the usurper had been unable to shed his guilt. Claudius remained unforgiven, with no hope of salvation. He couldn't pray; he couldn't repent his crime so long as he continued to enjoy the fruits of that crime—"My crown, mine own ambition and my queen" (act 3, scene 3). Had Hamlet run Claudius through on the spot, his uncle's soul would have been hell-bound after all, and Hamlet would have freed himself from the treble-sworn promise of vengeance he had made to his father's perturbed spirit.

Another character well acquainted with sorrow and sometimes troubled by doubt, one Abraham Lincoln of Kentucky, Indiana, and Illinois, was among William Shakespeare's most devoted American admirers. Like the Booths, Lincoln knew Shakespeare by heart. He judged *Macbeth* Shakespeare's greatest play. But he thought the despairing Claudius's speech here in act 3 of *Hamlet* the finest passage in all the tragedies. Lincoln said that Claudius's soliloquy "always struck me as one of the finest touches of nature in the world."[2]

Hamlet had let his doubts cancel his resolution when striking out boldly would have given him his revenge. Like the fictional Hamlet, the actual Abraham Lincoln had known heartache and had often been mired in doubt, particularly in his youth and particularly in matters of faith.

Unlike the fictional Hamlet, the actual John Wilkes Booth knew no doubt. Booth was a true believer in a time when millions of American men were proving themselves willing to kill and to die for what they believed. For when his own chance for vengeance came, at the performance of a very different kind of play, Booth never doubted. He knew he was killing for his country and for the white race, and he killed with the expectation that the killing would make him a hero, in the North as well as the South.

The actual Booth didn't hesitate like the fictional Hamlet. Instead, rigid with a terrible certainty, he stepped forward and raised the small pistol in his right hand. Inches separated the muzzle from the back of Lincoln's head. Booth squeezed the trigger. When a few pounds' pressure from his index finger tripped the sear, mechanical energy stored in the pistol's mainspring pulled the hammer down onto the copper percussion cap mounted on the steel nipple with its touchhole through the barrel into the firing chamber. A dab of mercury fulminate in the cap exploded. A tiny spark jetted through the touchhole to detonate the gunpowder packed behind the bullet. Chemical energy stored in the black powder instantly became fiery gases expanding to pressures of thousands of pounds per square inch. The trapped gases shoved mightily against the only movable part of the firing chamber's enclosure—the bullet itself—driving it down the bore and out the muzzle at four hundred miles per hour.

Unburned powder igniting on contact with oxygen flared in

a dazzling muzzle flash, briefly illuminating the presidential box before dissipating as smoke. The explosion rang through the theater. The half-inch leaden sphere crossed the intervening space in a time too short for the instrumentalities of that century to measure and crashed through the back of Abraham Lincoln's skull, slightly off center and just above the left lateral sinus.

The bullet punched a disc out of the occipital bone and plowed a bloody .44-caliber tunnel strewn with bone chips through the soft tissue of the left posterior lobe of the cerebrum before coming to rest somewhere behind the right eye. The impact cracked the thin bone at the back of Lincoln's eye sockets like eggshell, and blood suffused the sockets. As he lay dying, his eyeballs would bulge out and his face darken with deep bruises, more work for the undertakers. As many as one million Americans would look on the president's decaying face in the days that followed.

Lincoln raised his right arm convulsively from the armrest. His head dropped forward. He looked as though he were asleep in the big rocking chair. Mary Lincoln screamed. Blue gun smoke drifted lazily out of the box. Booth dropped the pistol and slashed out with his Bowie knife, botched the twelve-foot leap to the stage and broke his leg, shouted his last lines, and made his final exit, stage right. It had been, Walt Whitman later said, "one brief flash of lightning-illumination—one simple, fierce deed."[3]

Although his lungs continued to breathe and his heart to beat until 7:22 the next morning, Abraham Lincoln was a dead man the instant Booth pulled the trigger. As Carl Sandburg would put it near the end of the sixth and final volume of his sprawling Lincoln biography, "For Abraham Lincoln it was lights out."[4] So it was, while holding his wife's hand on the happiest day of his life.

RICHMOND, VIRGINIA, APRIL 4, 1865

Surely the most extraordinary month in American history, April 1865 brought the succession of spectacular events that signaled the final collapse of Southern fortunes in the Civil War. Day by day, April presented new prodigies to an astonished people. For four years, America had been locked in a war that sometimes seemed like it might end in the independence of the insurgent slave republic. Now, in the space of just a week, Northern victory came on swiftly as one triumph followed another. The North was delirious with joy. The white South was speechless with despair.

Washington City celebrated with bands and fireworks, songs and speeches, beer and whiskey, and citywide "Grand Illuminations" with "one million candles" and countless lamps and gas jets burning in every window of every house and every public building up and down every street on every block in every neighborhood until the whole city seemed ablaze. Bonfires burned on every corner. Giant transparent banners bearing patriotic slogans were illuminated from behind like lantern slides. An array of brilliant gas jets spelled out "UNION" in huge letters across the facade of the Patent Office. "PEACE," said the lights on the Treasury. "GRANT," replied the War Department. Rockets arced across the sky. Thousands of drunks stumbled through the streets singing, shouting, and laughing, intoxicated by sheer happiness as much as by alcohol. A reporter did comment on the "strange affinity between patriotism and whiskey."[1]

To the east loomed the great white-painted iron dome of the US Capitol, completed just two years before, now illuminated by tiers of lights in the misty night air, seeming to float on the horizon like a full moon. The window-shattering thunder of the eight-hundred-gun salute on Monday, April 3, for the capture of Richmond was topped a week later on Monday, April 10, by the roar of nine hundred cannon celebrating the surrender of Robert E. Lee's Army of Northern Virginia—the final giving-way that marked the effective end of the war. Perhaps Walt Whitman captured best the indescribable emotions stirring the Northern people when he wrote that "over all, and saturating all, that vast, vague wonder, *Victory*, the nation's victory, the triumph of the Union, [was] filling the air, the thought, the sense, with exhilaration."[2]

Between those two signal victories had appeared the otherworldly vision of President Abraham Lincoln's risky walking tour through the still-burning Southern capital, where he was greeted as a modern-day savior by the hosannas of newly freed people wild with joy as white Virginians watched the end of their world from behind shuttered windows. After rowing miles up the James River, skirting shipwrecks, dead horses, and mines packed with hundreds of pounds of gunpowder, Admiral David Dixon Porter's barge nosed up to the Richmond landing, and Abraham Lincoln stepped out. The enemy's government had evacuated its capital city just a day before—on the night and morning of Sunday–Monday, April 2–3. They had fled because U. S. Grant had finally pried Robert E. Lee out of his trenches, ending the long siege of Petersburg. Also ended was any hope of holding Richmond.

Now the rebellion's champion army was disintegrating in its final retreat—hemorrhaging thousands of dead and wounded, prisoners and deserters, as the Army of Northern Virginia went reeling west toward collapse at Appomattox, aggressively pursued by Grant's exultant regiments. Lee's grim survivors were starving, barefoot, and profoundly discouraged. What remained of the enslavers' government, still headed by Jefferson Davis, was also in flight, jammed aboard the passenger cars of a single train that rattled slowly south along the decrepit tracks of the last remaining railroad out of Richmond.

Before fleeing the city on the windy night of April 2, the retreating Southerners had torched tobacco warehouses, ammunition depots, and bridges, setting off the conflagration that consumed Richmond's business district. More than 750,000 artillery shells exploded as the ordnance dumps went up, creating spectacular pyrotechnic displays and showering the city with shrapnel and flaming debris. Just before dawn, the last ironclad warships of the rebel navy were blown up in the river with earth-shaking detonations.

Union soldiers—including the regiments of the United States Colored Troops that had been among the first to enter the fallen city—were still fighting the flames when the president came ashore about midday Tuesday, April 4. The sailors whose strong arms had propelled the barge upriver presently laid aside their oars and shouldered carbines to become a meager presidential bodyguard. Six marched in front of him, four behind. Flanked by officers, the president walked along in the middle holding the hand of his younger son, Tad. It happened to be Tad's twelfth birthday.

If Lincoln had imprudently risked his safety on the voyage up the James River, the mile-and-a-half trek from the shore to the center of the city represented an even more irresponsible exposure of a life that was so precious to the nation. Mobs of wildly excited people, white and Black, had ruled the streets of Richmond for thirty-six hours. There were crowds of the formerly enslaved, delirious with their new freedom. There were drunken rebel deserters and stragglers, still in their gray uniforms. Escaped inmates from the penitentiary—"leaping, shouting demons"—were running wild with their shaved heads and bold-striped prisoners' suits. Hungry for months, many Richmonders hurried along, carrying bags of flour and sides of bacon stolen from government warehouses. Every store and warehouse that escaped the flames had been broken open and looted. The air was thick with smoke and dust and the stink of burning tobacco and gunpowder. Into this maelstrom the president set off on foot with his young son. As he said himself, "I walked alone on the street, and anyone could have shot me from a second-story window."[3]

Abraham Lincoln was the most photographed and caricatured president in history. Even here, in the city that had so recently been the seat of the rebellion, his was an unmistakable figure. Dressed in black, his gaunt, six-foot-four frame stretched even taller by the iconic stovepipe hat, he was recognized instantly as the little party made its way into the city.

The Black people of Richmond, most of them suddenly free for the first time in their lives, proclaimed him their savior. "Glory! Hallelujah!" they shouted. "Massa Lincoln has come! The great Messiah! I knowed him as soon as I seed him. Come to free his children from bondage."[4] A reporter for a Boston newspaper called it "a spectacle. . . . Such wild, indescribable, ecstatic joy I never before have witnessed."[5] "Thank you, dear Jesus, for this!" shouted one freed woman. Another declared, "I know that I am free, for I have seen father Abraham and touched him."[6]

The journalist continued: "It was the great deliverer meeting the delivered. Yesterday morning the majority of the thousands who crowded the streets and hindered our advance were slaves. Now they were free, beholding him who had given them liberty."[7] Throngs of them crowded forward to grasp or touch his hands or brush against his clothing. As Lincoln acknowledged the acclamations, the reporter thought he saw tears in the president's eyes.

When a white-haired Black man doffed his ragged straw hat, bowed low, and said, "May the good Lord bless you and keep you safe, Master Lincoln," the president lifted his own hat and bowed in return. Lincoln was stern, however, when some of the freed people knelt down before him. "Don't kneel to me," he said. "That is not right. You must kneel to God only, and thank him for the liberty you will enjoy hereafter."[8]

Lincoln's bow to the old man had been a stunning rebuke to white supremacy. Witnessing it, one white woman had angrily turned away, snorting in disgust.[9] The next issue of the *Atlantic Monthly* did not exaggerate in its assertion that Lincoln's bow "upset the forms, laws, customs, and ceremonies of centuries. It was a death-shock to chivalry, and a mortal wound to caste."[10]

Finally, a squad of cavalry galloped up to accompany the presidential party the rest of the way to Union army headquarters in Jefferson Davis's home—the mansion known as the "White House of the Confederacy." There Lincoln, who had been sweating freely on the hike up from the river, collapsed wearily into Davis's chair and asked for a glass of water. When officers offered him a celebratory shot of whiskey, the president, who didn't drink alcohol, quietly declined. The reporter thought that he wore a "look of unutterable weariness, as if his spirit, energy and animating force were wholly exhausted."[11] Lincoln had lost thirty pounds and aged a good decade in the four years since taking office. Throughout those years of killing, the president had been haunted by the ghostly presence of the ever-growing battalions of the dead, fallen in a war his election had touched off. "If there is a worse place than hell I am in it," he told one friend. "If there is a man out of perdition who suffers more than

Alexander Gardner took one of the last photographs of Abraham Lincoln on February 5, 1865. The president had lost thirty pounds and aged a good decade in the four years since taking office. The bitter years of war had punished the president, cut deep lines in his face, and left him profoundly weary. "Sometimes I think I am the tiredest man on earth," he said.

Library of Congress, Prints and Photographs Division,
LC-DIG-ppmsca-19469.

I do, I pity him."[12] He was worn out by the never-ending work and the lonely burden of leadership. "Sometimes I think I am the tiredest man on earth," he said.[13]

Later, after lunch, the president toured the city in an open carriage. The freed people renewed their displays of irrepressible joy and affection. A Black reporter for a Philadelphia paper wrote that "the colored population was wild with enthusiasm. Old men thanked God in a very boisterous manner, and old women shouted upon the pavement."[14]

A twelve-acre square enclosed the venerable Virginia State Capitol, the neoclassical pile Thomas Jefferson had designed at the end of the Revolutionary War. An American flag now flew again over the building that two days before had been the seat of the insurgents' government. Lincoln passed through Jefferson's old Capitol, walking through hastily abandoned chambers strewn with worthless currency and government documents. Presiding in the rotunda was Houdon's magnificent 1792 marble statue of George Washington, a slaveholding Virginian who would have opposed secession with all his heart.

The square outside was filled to overflowing with freed people and refugees with the pathetic heaps of furniture and belongings they'd managed to pull from their burning homes. Until the day before, no African American had been allowed to enter Capitol Square. Now the grounds were crowded with them. Lincoln spoke to them: "My poor friends, you are free—as free as air. You can cast off the name of slave and trample upon it; it will come to you no more. Liberty is your birthright. God gave it to you as he gave it to others and it is a sin that you have been deprived of it for so many years."[15]

Then he made his exit in a most dramatic fashion. The Boston newspaperman told how Lincoln drove away:

Slowly his vehicle moved as he bowed and threw his salutations to those who were ready to worship him. The carriage

RICHMOND, VIRGINIA, APRIL 4, 1865

crossed the open space and halted in the street beyond. Mr. Lincoln arose from the back seat, on which he had been sitting, turned half around, faced the great multitude of blacks who thronged the area behind his carriage, and reached out his hands till he stood in the attitude of a minister pronouncing the benediction. Thus he remained, without speaking a word, for more than a minute, while the carriage stood still; and, when the horses moved forward, in the same attitude he was driven out of sight.[16]

Richmond's racial divide had never been more starkly evident than on the streets of the city the day of Lincoln's visit. After he came, the jubilant crowds were almost entirely Black. White residents had shut themselves up in their homes. Nothing about the fall of Richmond, not even the fire that burned some seven hundred buildings, was as stunning to people as the sight of the United States Colored Troops—a vision of a new reality that white and Black Virginians greeted with markedly different feelings.

For Blacks, soldiers of their own race coming to rescue their people from slavery was the millennium itself, the long-awaited Day of Jubilee. For most white Virginians, it was the ultimate nightmare—armed slaves in full revolt—but one that came with a surprising twist: for generations, Southern whites had dreaded a mass slave rebellion like the horror show in the French colony of Haiti in the 1790s. They had envisioned a merciless race war, darkened by murder, rapine, and arson. The great American slave rebellion finally came to pass in the Civil War. But instead of coming as midnight assassins, the rebels came as regulars, just as Frederick Douglass had predicted, the brass letters *US* glinting on their collars, the American eagle screaming from the gold-gilt buttons on their blue tunics, and .58-caliber rifle muskets across their shoulders.

The colored regiments entered the city singing "John Brown's

*During his risky walking tour through the still-burning rebel capital,
President Lincoln was greeted as a modern-day savior by the hosannas
of newly freed people as white Virginians watched the end of
their world from behind shuttered windows.*

"President Lincoln Riding through Richmond, April 4," *Frank Leslie's
Illustrated Newspaper*, April 22, 1865. Huntington Library, RB 762274.

Body"—a hymn to the abolitionist bogeyman whose example
was so feared and detested by the enslavers. Then the men turned
out of their ranks to begin fighting the fires. In its comprehensive
repudiation of the old order of white supremacy and Black subordination, the scene in Richmond that day was the Dixie Arma-
geddon, a Southern Götterdämmerung. Nearly as disturbing to

the enslavers as the sight of armed Blacks was the joyous welcome given the hated enemy by the enslaved people of Richmond, who many whites had fooled themselves into believing were loyal and grateful servants, content in their lives of bondage.

The first Union regiment to enter the fallen city the day before Lincoln's visit had been the Fifth Massachusetts Cavalry, a unit of mounted Black troopers commanded by Colonel Charles Francis Adams Jr., grandson of President John Quincy Adams and son of Lincoln's minister to Great Britain. The troopers' appearance excited surges of wild enthusiasm among Richmond's newly freed people.

Black joy was paired with white despair. As Lincoln's presidential secretaries John G. Nicolay and John Hay later reflected in their ten-volume court history of the administration:

> The arrival of these black soldiers was to the people of Richmond the visible realization of the new order to which four years of rebellion and war had brought them. The prejudices of a lifetime cannot be instantly overcome, and the rebels of Richmond doubtless felt that this was the final drop in their cup of misery and that their "subjugation" was complete. It is related that about this time, as by a common impulse, the white people of Richmond disappeared from the streets, and the black population streamed forth with an apparent instinctive recognition that their day of jubilee had at last arrived. To see this compact, organized body of men of their own color, on horseback, in neat uniforms, with flashing sabers, with the gleam of confidence and triumph in their eyes, was a palpable living reality to which their hope and pride, long repressed, gave instant response. They greeted them with expressions of welcome in every form—cheers, shouts, laughter, and a rattle of exclamations—as they rushed along the sides of the streets to keep pace with the advancing column and feast their eyes on the incredible sight; while the black Union soldiers rose

high in their stirrups and with waving swords and deafening huzzas acknowledged the fraternal reception.[17]

"You've come at last," the crowds shouted; "we've been looking for you these many days."[18]

Indeed, the provision of President Lincoln's Emancipation Proclamation for enlisting African Americans in the Union army in 1863 had been almost as radical as emancipation itself. Fielding Black soldiers was a true revolution. As historian James McPherson has written, the policy "marked the transformation of a war to save the union into a war to overthrow the old order," the old order of slavery and white supremacy.[19]

By war's end, some 180,000 Black soldiers, about 135,000 of them formerly enslaved, had marched in the ranks. They did much more than merely "garrison forts, positions, and stations," as the proclamation had originally mandated. They fought in some of the bloodiest battles of the war. Their foes often gave them no quarter, slaughtering them when they tried to surrender. Another nineteen thousand Black men served in the US Navy. About forty thousand men, approximately 20 percent of the total number of Black warriors, gave their lives. These men killed slavery. Lincoln said the North could not have won the war without them.

Yet to the millions of America's white supremacists—men like the famous young actor John Wilkes Booth—emancipation and the fielding of Black regiments were despicable acts of barbarism, as well as an explicit invitation to the apocalyptic race war Southerners had so long dreaded. Jefferson Davis, the so-called president of the rebellion that had styled itself a nation, quickly denounced the Emancipation Proclamation as "the most execrable measure recorded in the history of guilty man."[20] Yet his words seemed almost restrained alongside the howls of execration that greeted news that the Union army was being strengthened by tens of thousands of Black men.

RICHMOND, VIRGINIA, APRIL 4, 1865

15

The Black fighters presented a living, breathing refutation of some of white supremacy's most cherished beliefs—that whites would always dominate nonwhites, that the enslaved people were content in their bondage, and that African American men lacked the character, intelligence, devotion, and discipline to make good soldiers.

In the most perverse of ironies, by the end of 1864 their military fortunes had fallen so low that Jefferson Davis and Robert E. Lee decided to start forcing enslaved soldiers to fight for the preservation of slavery. When denouncing the plan, one Southern statesman had objected: "If slaves make good soldiers our whole theory of slavery is wrong."[21] At places like Battery Wagner and Port Hudson, the good soldiers of the United States Colored Troops soon succeeded in proving that the enslavers' theories were indeed wrong.

Today the label *white supremacist* calls to mind radical extremists, wild-eyed fanatics with shaved heads and swastika tattoos, characters most Americans abhor. In the Civil War era, to the contrary, to hold white supremacist beliefs was anything but radical. Such opinions were then both respectable and utterly conventional, commonly shared by statesmen and politicians, journalists, scientists, educators, and clergymen—indeed, by almost all white people, in the North as well as the South. Racist pseudo-science had "proved" that nonwhite people were inferior to Northern Europeans.

According to its nineteenth-century proponents, white supremacy rested on two related premises: first, that Blacks were born inferior to whites—inferior intellectually, morally, and, in some respects, physically. Second, white supremacists thought that whenever two peoples of differing capabilities inhabit a single nation, the superior race must dominate the inferior. Without such a system of race control, warfare will inevitably break out between the two different peoples, ending in death or exile for the losers. Slavery provided such a system of social control in the Old South. Jefferson Davis claimed that "a superior race" had used the institution of slavery to mold "brutal savages into docile, intelligent, and civilized agricultural laborers."[22]

In the words of that shining avatar of Southern defiance John C. Calhoun of South Carolina, "Where two races of different origin, and distinguished by color, and other physical differences, as well as intellectual, are brought together, the relation now existing in the slaveholding states between the two is, instead of an evil, a good—a positive good." The end of slavery, Calhoun maintained, "would substitute for the existing relation a deadly strife between the two races, to end in the subjection, expulsion, or extirpation of one or the other."[23]

Despite the ominous talk of "one or the other" surviving a race war, the defenders of slavery never doubted that the whites would prevail and the Blacks go under. The former slaves would be destroyed by the more numerous, better armed, and superior whites. So, the argument went, keeping these people enslaved protected them and assured their survival. Even before Thomas Jefferson had presented the proposition in his 1785 *Notes on the State of Virginia*, it had been an article of faith among the defenders of slavery that emancipation would inevitably lead to the extinction of Blacks. The freed people, furious to revenge generations of injustices visited on them, would attack the white masters who had harmed them. "Deep rooted prejudices entertained by the whites," Jefferson argued, as well as "ten thousand recollections, by the blacks, of injuries they have sustained . . . will divide us into parties, and produce convulsions."[24] Those convulsions could only end in Black annihilation.

Another founder and president, John Adams, no defender of slavery himself, had envisioned the same grim outcome: "I can see nothing but insurrections of the blacks against the whites and massacres by the whites in their turn of the blacks . . . till at last the whites exasperated to madness shall be wicked enough to exterminate the negroes."[25] Years later, denouncing the Emancipation Proclamation, Jefferson Davis echoed Jefferson and Adams when he said that by Lincoln's provisions, "several millions of human beings of an inferior race, peaceful and contented laborers in their sphere, are doomed to extinction."[26]

Moreover, the defenders of slavery—statesmen and writers like Edmund Ruffin, James Henry Hammond, John C. Calhoun, and George Fitzhugh—agreed that true republican liberty was possible only in a slave society governed by white supremacy. The South, not the North, was the real home of republican equality among white citizens. Jefferson Davis explained how white supremacy raised even the lowliest Southern white to equality with the upper classes:

> The lower race of human beings that constitute the substratum of what is termed the slave population of the South, elevates every white man in our community. . . . Hence it is that the mechanic in our southern States is admitted to the table of his employer, converses with him on terms of equality—not merely political equality, but an actual equality—wherever the two men come in contact. . . . It is the presence of a lower caste, those lower by their mental and physical organization, controlled by the higher intellect of the white man, that gives this superiority to the white laborer. Menial services are not there performed by the white man. We have none of our brethren sunk to the degradation of being menials. That belongs to the lower race—the descendants of Ham, who, under the judgement of God speaking to the prophet Noah, were condemned to be servants.[27]

The fiction of racial superiority provided a gratifying inspiration to many discouraged whites. W. J. Cash, a historian of the American South writing in 1941, remarked on how the poor Southern white man, who owned no slaves himself, would take his stand as a strong defender of the institution that had awarded him the "dear treasure of his superiority as a white man, which has been conferred on him by slavery; and so was determined to keep the black man in chains."[28] Some have continued to cling to this comforting illusion a century and a half after the Thirteenth Amendment destroyed slavery forever. As President Lyndon B. Johnson once observed: "If you can convince the lowest white man he's better than the best colored man, he won't notice you're picking his pocket. Hell, give him somebody to look down on, and he'll empty his pockets for you."[29]

Back in Richmond that day, the commander-in-chief's military excursion presently came to an end. Lincoln took leave of his generals and admirals. He spent a few hours in the vast hospitals at City Point, shaking hands with seven thousand sick and wounded soldiers, rebels and Yanks alike, going at it, he said, "like a man sawing wood."[30]

The president finally left the war front on Sunday, April 9. He wouldn't learn until late in the evening that Lee had surrendered that day to Grant at Appomattox Court House. The surrender ceremony had been taking place even as the president's steamship, the *River Queen*, pushed its way up the broad tidewater Potomac. Aboard the ship, probably to forestall unwelcome discussions of reconstruction policy, the president chose to pass the time by reading Shakespeare aloud for hours to his shipboard companions—his wife, Mary, and a little collection of officers, politicians, diplomats, and reporters. He read twice for emphasis a favorite passage from *Macbeth*:

> Duncan is in his grave;
> After life's fitful fever he sleeps well;
> Treason has done his worst; not steel, nor poison,
> Malice domestic, foreign levy, nothing
> Can touch him further.[31]

So Abraham Lincoln and his friends steamed up the Potomac to the White House, where he would live out the five days of life remaining to him.

RICHMOND, VIRGINIA, APRIL 4, 1865

"ALL THOSE GODDAMNED BOOTHS"

"All those goddamned Booths are crazy," muttered the famous comedian Joseph Jefferson when he heard that John Wilkes Booth had murdered President Lincoln.[1] This is not, however, an altogether satisfactory explanation for the first American presidential assassination, indeed, the first political murder of any significance in the seventy-six years of the young republic's history.

The story begins in the London winter of 1820–21, when the brilliant young actor Junius Brutus Booth joined his life with that of Mary Ann Holmes. Mr. Booth was twenty-four, Miss Holmes only eighteen. Theirs was a love match; the couple would be parted only by the death of Junius thirty-one years later. And their love gifted them ten children, six of whom lived to adulthood. The ninth of the ten babies was a son, born in Harford County, Maryland, on May 10, 1838. Mary Ann and Junius named their little boy John Wilkes Booth.

There is ample evidence that Junius, though an accomplished seducer from the age of twelve, remained faithful to his pretty Covent Garden flower girl. Twenty years after the couple ran off to America, Junius was still signing his letters "Your husband and worshiper."[2] It was not an entirely accurate subscription, however. That he worshiped her is not to be doubted, but Junius was not Mary's husband. For any wedding vows they may have exchanged (the Booth children were taught that their parents were married in January 1821) had been a legal fiction—Booth already had a wife and child.[3] Years later, Asia Booth Clarke tried to dismiss her father's first marriage as "a boyish *mésalliance*, contracted in Brussels in the year 1814."[4]

The record shows, however, that Junius Brutus Booth was in fact a bigamist, an attribute that would find its place in a catalog that eventually included genius, madman, drunk, polyglot scholar, farmer, animal lover and vegetarian, homicidal maniac, and—in the words of the *Dictionary of American Biography*— "easily the foremost tragedian of his day."[5]

His father, Richard Booth, was a hard-drinking London lawyer and something of a fanatic on the subject of the Great Republic. In 1777, when he was barely more than a boy, Richard Booth and a cousin, utterly "infatuated with republicanism," had seized on the idea of going to America and taking up arms against their native Britain in the Revolutionary War, then raging on that distant continent. They got as far as Paris. There an American diplomat to whom they applied for Continental Army commissions demanded they first produce letters of recommendation from some notable British friend of American liberty. The two boys went straight back to their hotel and wrote to the foremost English radical of the day, John Wilkes, an ardent supporter of the American cause. The Booths were related by marriage to the famous agitator.[6]

The letter's recipient may have been mildly gratified to learn that the two young men were spurred by an "ardent desire to serve the Glorious cause of Freedom." But whatever he thought, John Wilkes was not about to vouch for a pair of strangers he suspected to be minors. He wrote at once to young Booth's father, who speedily dispatched agents to Paris to catch the runaway and bring him back to London. It was the last truly rebellious act of Richard Booth's life. He returned to the legal apprenticeship he had fled. By 1790, London directories listed him as a lawyer practicing in the city.[7]

But there was more than a nod to rebellion in the name that the lawyer Booth gave his son. "Junius Brutus Booth" fairly sang with republican music, with the heady notion that rebellion to tyrants is obedience to God. It was a name that called to mind the legendary founders of the Roman republic, the heroes who threw out the last kings of the ancient city-state and fought to prevent the restoration of a Roman monarchy. In eighteenth-century England, "Junius" had also been the pen name adopted by a well-known antigovernment pamphleteer.[8]

The most famous namesake of all was, of course, Marcus Junius Brutus, the assassin-hero of the dying Roman republic. Brutus was one of the killers of Julius Caesar, the would-be autocrat whose name itself became the root-word for royal titles, like *czar* and *kaiser*, that bespoke the most swollen tyranny. Brutus, "the noblest Roman of them all," was one of the principal roles in Shakespeare's *Julius Caesar*, a play the Booths, father and sons, would act in many times.

The name of Brutus would echo down the generations of the Booth family, resonating in the highest tragedy ever enacted in the American republic the young Richard Booth had so longed to serve. In the last words he scribbled into his little pocket diary, the despairing, hunted, injured, death-bound John Wilkes Booth would identify himself a final time with Roman Brutus, the tyrant-killer. One of the assassin's theatrical friends even claimed that the actor's admiration for the classical Brutus was the "mainspring" of the assassination.[9] "Sic semper tyrannis!" Booth would shout like a Roman the moment he sent his bullet crashing through Lincoln's head. "Thus always to tyrants," translated of the defiant motto that adorned the obverse of the great seal of the Commonwealth of Virginia. After his death, an anonymous poem that circulated through the South eulogized Booth as "Our Brutus."

If Richard Booth had expected better from John Wilkes in 1777, he clearly never lost his admiration for the old republican stalwart. Sixty years after he sent his fruitless appeal from Paris, Richard Booth persuaded his son Junius to bestow the English agitator's name on Richard's infant grandson, John Wilkes Booth. (The boy was proud of his middle name. "It means liberty," he would explain.)[10]

After Junius Brutus Booth had learned and abandoned printing; mastered Latin, Greek, French, Spanish, and Hebrew; toyed with painting, sculpture, and literature; and had almost gone to sea, he studied law for a while in his father's office. He found the law "dry and turgid." Nor were he and his father particularly happy with each other. Richard Booth's legal skills were of little use when Junius was guilty as charged in two paternity suits—the first the result of his "acquaintance" with a servant girl named Molly when he was only twelve. The second came five years later, when another girl accused Junius of a "deed of darkness that her situation could no longer conceal."[11] His father had to pay up.

But the moment he first stood on a stage, Junius Brutus Booth knew that he had found his calling. He saw at once that "the actor's higher art" transcended poetry, painting, and sculpture. He had already fallen in love with the theater. *Othello* was the first play he saw. Inspired, he devoured Shakespeare and a host of other dramatists, memorized speeches, and ran through parts in his head.

From the beginning, the aspirant's favorite character was the hunchbacked royal villain in Colley Cibber's popular adaptation of Shakespeare's *Richard III*. As he repeated Richard's lines to himself, he dreamed of one day projecting Shakespeare's mighty words to hundreds of upturned faces. Much against his father's wishes, he joined a company of roving players as an extra, earning one pound a week.

He made his debut in 1813, in the undistinguished comedy *John Bull*, before an undistinguished audience in a converted cow barn on London's Pancras Street. Junius Brutus Booth was seventeen years old. He would follow the actor's road, with fits and starts, with odd excursions, episodes of intoxication and madness, and flashes of sublime artistry, for all of the thirty-nine years that remained to him.

A player's calling in the nineteenth century meant a life of travel. The year of 1814 found Booth performing on the Continent. In Brussels he made another female acquaintance—Adelaide Delannoy, his landlady's daughter. Booth was now eighteen, Adelaide three or four years his senior. Before long, Adelaide was scaling her mother's garden wall to meet the lover waiting in the darkness. The two eloped—or rather, ran off together, since they were not to be married for several months. They eluded pursuit by the young lady's angry family. Madame Delannoy's still-unmarried daughter was pregnant.

The lovers went to London and moved in with Richard Booth. Late in May 1815 Adelaide could write her mother, "Very Dear Mother—It is with the greatest pleasure in the world that I inform you I am married to Booth since the 8th of May, and am the happiest of women. I am as well as I can be, and I am getting as fat as a great beast."[12] In October, Adelaide gave birth to a daughter, Amelia.

For the next two years Booth paid his dues with circuits of provincial engagements, building his strength and learning some of the roles that would make him famous. His big break came in 1817, when a stage manager drafted him to stand in for Edmund Kean, the preeminent English actor of the day. That night the twenty-one-year-old played the role of Sir Giles Overreach in *A New Way to Pay Old Debts*. Striding from the stage in a storm of applause after the final curtain fell, the young actor boasted that he'd just given his audience "the god-damnedest show" they had ever seen. Waking the next morning, he discovered he was a star.[13] (The Oxford English Dictionary informs us that as early as 1779, the term *star* has been used to mean "an actor, singer, etc., of exceptional celebrity.")

The critical and popular acclaim the young actor won with that single performance was the making of him. He soon opened as Richard III at the Covent Garden, one of London's two principal theaters. At a thousand pounds a year, the young actor who had so recently been earning a pound a week now made more than his lawyer father, who may have taken some pride in his son for the first time.

But Junius was still not satisfied. He had success but not preeminent stardom; the established veteran Kean still held that crown. The rivalry with other actors was embittering. And Booth was erratic. His performances remained uneven, yet any response from an audience that fell short of worshipful rapture hurt him into thinking that the ignorant public failed to grasp the true range of his genius. He was not above manifesting his disdain for the unappreciative. He was chased out of a Manchester theater by an angry mob of textile workers he had insulted as "low-lived button-makers."[14] His earnings sometimes disappointed him. He also found to his disgust that any theatrical career was likely to be entangled in lawsuits, feuds, unpaid fees, and contractual fights.

More than anything else, however, it was probably his soured marriage that made him so ready for a change. Little Amelia had died in infancy, but a second child, Richard Junius, was born to the Booths in 1819. Still, it may be surmised that it was not a happy marriage. He was ready to throw over his entire life. In the fall of 1820, he tripped over what he had been looking for in the person of Mary Ann Holmes, a teenage flower girl who sold her wares in Covent Garden, the shopping neighborhood that surrounded the theaters.

Mary Ann's history is obscure. She was the daughter of a "seedsman" named Robert Holmes, a pious shopkeeper who sold grain, seeds, bulbs, and flowers. The shopkeeper's girl was a rung or two below the lawyer's boy on the English social ladder, but she was beautiful. Booth was handsome. His sublime and astonishing interpretation of *King Lear* was then the sensation of all London. Mary Ann had seen him in the role. Both were smitten.

Students of the Booth family once advanced the notion that Junius practiced a double deception on the two women in his life. He told Adelaide his stage career would benefit from an American tour that would mean the temporary separation of husband from wife and child, while going through the charade of a fake marriage to fool Mary Ann. The man was, after all, a gifted actor. But the diary of a London theater manager preserved in the Huntington Library reveals that Mary Ann's parents knew that their daughter had run off with a married man.[15] Mary Ann obviously knew it, too.

It is more plausible that Adelaide Delannoy Booth really did not yet know that her husband had deserted her for another woman. Events would show that Adelaide had no intention of renouncing her claim to be Booth's only lawful wedded wife.

Either way, Booth found himself in a tight spot. He decided to leave England. (His daughter Asia Booth Clarke later claimed with a straight face that a desire "to visit the West Indies professionally" prompted the journey.)[16] The couple departed Britain for Madeira. From there they caught a clipper ship that carried them to America in forty-four days. The merchantman had no berths for passengers, but Booth rented the captain's own cabin.

They took along Junius's favorite pet, a little horse named Peacock. Mary Ann was also carrying their first child, to be named Junius Brutus Booth Jr., who would be born the first of the American Booths in Charleston, South Carolina, several months later. The tour turned out to be more than a professional visit: like so many who made the westward passage, the Booths became Americans.

Booth stepped ashore at Norfolk, Virginia, on June 30, 1821. He appeared on an American stage for the first time a week later in Richmond, the nearby Virginia capital. Some there were doubtful that this little stranger really was, as he claimed, the celebrated English tragedian Junius Brutus Booth. But the manager of Richmond's Marshall Theater was willing to risk booking the boy (twenty-five, Booth looked about sixteen) in that actor's most famous role—*Richard III*.

The player the audience saw that night was a small man of about five foot three with dark hair and piercing gray-blue eyes that could look black in the stage lights. He was possessed of a splendid voice he had learned to wield with both preternatural precision and impassioned feeling. He also possessed fire and conviction, a wide-ranging intellect nurtured by much reading, and a prodigious memory for lines that even alcohol could not often overthrow. His reputation had preceded him. The Virginians already knew him as one of the foremost dramatic actors in the English-speaking world.

The eager actor, probably short on funds, immediately arranged to repeat *Richard III* the following evening in nearby Petersburg. Unlike his first performance in Richmond, in Petersburg there were observers, both on the stage and among the audience, who left accounts that hint at the powers Booth had brought with him across the Atlantic. The Petersburg theater manager and his players had also greeted with a certain skepticism the unprepossessing stranger's claim to be the famous London actor. He arrived late for rehearsal and covered with dust from the twenty-five-mile trek from Richmond. (He'd missed the stagecoach.) He ran through the rehearsal like an apathetic student reciting a lesson. "That will do," he said.[17]

After the curtain went up, the young Briton listlessly mumbled his way through the opening scenes. Skepticism became conviction: the man was an imposter. Then, without warning, Booth revealed himself, stepping into character as the gloating killer. Eyes widened and hairs pricked up on the backs of arms and necks. Almost against their will, the Virginians found themselves thrilled and terrified as Booth bestirred himself to turn on them his raw, inexplicable power.

These were only the first of countless American audiences to be so moved. Booth's performances could be so riveting that his fellow actors sometimes forgot their lines. Struck dumb, they stood frozen in place, staring at the prodigy. Sometimes he had the entire cast, extras and all, as well as the audience, in tears. He scared some of his leading ladies right off the stage. His combat scenes were so ferocious he might knock his stage opponents out cold or leave them covered with blood. As Othello, he once came close to smothering the actress playing Desdemona.

Richard III was always his most celebrated role. And of the whole tragedy, the actor's most celebrated scene was the final fight to the death, the swordplay that kills King Richard and ends the play. Junius Brutus Booth sometimes refused to follow Shakespeare's stage directions to die by the sword of the upright Henry Tudor, Earl of Richmond, the ancestor of Shakespeare's reigning monarch, Queen Elizabeth. One night, heatedly exchanging blows with an unfortunate fellow actor playing Richmond, the eminent tragedian decided that he was not ready to die just yet. A storm of blows from his stage sword drove this Richmond off the stage, up the aisle past the audience, out onto the sidewalk, and finally into the tavern next door. The drinkers there disarmed the distracted man.[18]

One of the actor's most devoted admirers was the poet Walt Whitman. He could never forget Booth's Richard III:

> I can see again Booth's quiet entrance from the side, as, with head bent, he slowly and in silence, (amid the tempest of bois-

terous hand-clapping,) walks down the stage to the footlights with that peculiar and abstracted gesture, musingly kicking his sword, which he holds off from him by its sash. Though fifty years have pass'd since then, I can still hear the clank, and feel the perfect following hush of perhaps three thousand people waiting. (I never saw an actor who could make more of the said hush or wait, and hold the audience in an indescribable, half-delicious, half-irritating suspense.) . . . A shudder went through every nervous system in the audience. . . .

. . . His genius was to me one of the grandest revelations of my life, a lesson of artistic expression. The words, fire, energy, *abandon* found in him unprecedented meanings. I never heard a speaker or actor who could give such a sting to hauteur or the taunt. I never heard from any other the charm of unswervingly perfect vocalization.[19]

To Whitman, Booth was simply "the grandest histrion of modern times. . . . For though those brilliant years had many fine and even magnificent actors, undoubtedly at Booth's death (in 1852) went the last and by far the noblest Roman of them all."[20]

At the same time, Whitman said that Junius Brutus Booth "illustrated Plato's rule that to the forming [of] an artist of the very highest rank a dash of insanity, or what the world calls insanity, is indispensable."[21] The actor's daughter Asia alluded to her father's "slight aberrations of mind which mark that exquisite turning point between genius and madness." In her father's case, Asia continued, these aberrations "seemed to increase in strength and frequency with maturer years."[22]

Within a few months of his arrival, Booth had played New York, Norfolk, Richmond, Petersburg, New Orleans, and Savannah. Mary Ann remained hidden away in Charleston during her confinement and delivery. Booth didn't want news of his domestic arrangements appearing in the press and reaching back across the Atlantic. Success came quickly. "His travels," Asia Booth

Clarke later claimed, constituted "one long ovation."[23] From his first night, then, Junius Brutus Booth found on American stages the preeminence that had eluded him in London. The United States was still a cultural backwater. However Booth may have ranked against Edmund Kean, there was not another actor in America who even came close. Embedded in a stanza of indifferent verse cut into the obelisk that rises above his grave in a Baltimore cemetery is a five-word tag that sums up Booth's career in his new country: "Of Tragedy the mighty chief."[24] So he was for more than thirty years.

But it was not to be an entirely unbroken train of ovations. One sketch explains that "owing to his attacks of madness, his intemperance, and his general irresponsibility, Booth broke his theatrical engagements with reckless frequency, and on more than one occasion, when irritated, came forward to the footlights and expressed his contempt for the audience. But the public always forgave him because of his unquestioned ability."[25]

Coming to America, Booth had succeeded in leaving behind his old life and his old wife, his enemies, creditors, and rivals, but he could not escape his demons. By 1824, the demons were growing bolder. There was a sudden flaring of madness on a New York street, ignited by a false report of Mary Ann's death. (The report was some sixty years premature.) Booth attacked a fellow actor with a knife. He almost killed him. Restrained, he was soon himself again. The newspapers reported the episode.

With increasing frequency, Booth's life would be punctuated by spells of derangement, self-destruction, and inexplicable homicidal fury. It was a mercy that he never actually killed anyone. Or himself. "By the time John was born," John Wilkes Booth's biographer Terry Alford has written, "Junius had compiled an unenviable resume of trouble. He had shot one man in the face, assaulted others, attempted suicide on three occasions, and been jailed in four states."[26] His long-suffering wife once had to cut him down when she discovered him hanging from a noose.

While some journalists accused him of staging his "mad freaks" to titillate the public and swell his box office, there is no doubt that Junius Brutus Booth was authentically, if only episodically, crazy. There are many stories about him, about his acting, his drinking, his violence, and his sheer craziness. And a good many of these stories were very likely true. John Wilkes Booth once complained to his sister Asia, "I cannot see why sensible people will trouble themselves to concoct ridiculous stories of their great actors. We know that two-thirds of the funny anecdotes about our own father are disgraceful falsehoods."[27] Johnny hardly seemed to notice that he was conceding that a third of the wild stories were quite true. Junius's sons had theatrical ambitions of their own, but if they were to be heir to their father's disorder as well as his talent, it promised to be a fearsome legacy indeed.

Booth's eccentricities were so well known that the papers started billing him as the "mad tragedian." In April 1838, his hometown paper, the *Baltimore Sun*, reported that "Mr. Booth, the mad tragedian, has arrived in our city."[28] Then on May 3, the *Sun* blasted the actor, who had stood up another audience: "BOOTH AGAIN. Is this man a maniac? or is he not more fool than madman? 'Booth is a genius,' is the cry; and he has heard it reiterated so often, that he imagines his vagaries will be overlooked; but we can inform him that in this city he is eternally disgraced."

Exactly one week after this notice appeared, on May 10, 1838, John Wilkes Booth was born at the farm north of Baltimore. Years later, when Americans were trying to explain away the white supremacist's politically motivated murder of Abraham Lincoln as a meaningless aberration, as "one mad act" somehow outside of history, the father's reputation made it easy to claim that the son had been crazy, too. This persistent charge of insanity became part of the legend that has attached itself to the person of the republic's first presidential assassin. For although he was certainly extremely angry, John Wilkes Booth was never mad.

*The assassin's father, "the mad tragedian," Junius Brutus Booth,
for decades the preeminent tragic actor in the Unites States.*

The gunfire that has disfigured our public life in the years since John Wilkes Booth's murderous encounter with Abraham Lincoln has made Americans all too familiar with assassination. There remains, however, a longing to deny that the violence is purposeful; we see this denial in the tendency to ignore the political dimensions of assassination in the United States. One study prepared by a governmental commission concluded that assassins of American presidents, including Booth, were for the most part "mentally disturbed persons, who did not kill in advance of any rational political plan."[29] That judgment is simply mistaken;

most attacks on presidents and presidential candidates have been politically motivated.

John Wilkes Booth set the pattern when he killed Abraham Lincoln for clearly articulated political motives. Yet Booth has often been dismissed as a crazy, drunken actor—the son, after all, of a famously crazy, drunken actor. Some have enlarged their condemnations. In the final volume of his massive Lincoln biography, Carl Sandburg was compelled to reach deep into the supernatural to find words charged with evil sufficient for his portrait of the assassin. If the Good Friday murder had worked to transform Abraham Lincoln into a sort of American Christ-figure, a hero who gave his own life so that his nation might live, it wasn't hard to figure what that made of Booth himself: "the American Judas." "But who was this Booth?" Sandburg asked:

> In what kind of green-poison pool of brain and personality had the amazing and hideous crime arisen? . . . [H]e had now wrapped the letters of his name with a weird infamy synony- mous with Enemy of Mankind. His name on a thousand oc- casions was to go unspoken with loathing for the unspeakable and untouchable: a pitiless, dripping, carnivorous, slathered, subhuman and antihuman beast mingling snake and tiger; the unmentionable . . . a lunatic . . . with an unstrung imagina- tion, a mind deranged, a brain that was [a] haunted house of monsters of vanity, of vampires and bats of hallucination.[30]

In recent years, however, there has been increasing recog- nition that the shot from Booth's little pocket pistol was not a bolt out of the pathological blue, neither an act of psychosis or drunken frenzy nor the monomaniacal bid of a failed actor to win for himself a name that would belong to the ages, and not an act driven by rivalry to overshadow his more famous brother Edwin, but rather a political murder that can be understood only in the context of the most violent period in American history. However misguided he may have been, John Wilkes Booth was not a monster. He was a highly successful actor and a rebel secret agent. He was also an impulsive young man who shared the conviction of millions, in the North as well as the South, that Abraham Lincoln was a malignant tyrant whose policies threatened to expunge the liberties that had long been the birthright of free white Americans. Booth believed that he acted for his country and for the so-called white race, and he did so with the expectation that the killing would make him a hero.

While it is uncertain how much drink contributed to the unhappy man's deterioration, it is clear that Junius Brutus Booth was an alcoholic. (One acquaintance offered the not-very-helpful observation that Junius Brutus Booth was only crazy when he was drunk but that he was drunk nearly all the time.)[31] Alcoholism is a disease that grows progressively worse. Booth's case followed this familiar, dreary, and ultimately terrifying course. Alcoholism also tends to run in families. Junius's father, Richard, was a veteran boozer. All his sons would battle their own thirsts. In the weeks before the assassination, many noticed that John Wilkes Booth was putting away brandy "by the quart."

"Intemperance" was an occupational hazard of the nineteenth-century stage. As one actor wrote of the American theater in midcentury, "These were days when liquor drenched the stage and few there were who escaped the flood." Junius Brutus Booth spoke for himself when he said that among actors, "the temptations to Drunkenness here are too common and too powerful for many weak beings."[32] He tried to stay sober. As he once wrote Mary Ann, "to avoid drinking I make every effort."[33] But all too often, his resolution dissolved in a flood of liquor.

Stage managers soon learned what to expect when they booked the great Junius Brutus Booth: a sold-out house and the chance of an absent or incapacitated star—surely a theatrical nightmare of the first order. They began taking extraordinary measures, with varying degrees of success, to keep the tragedian sober enough to make his curtain calls. (One of the better stories concerns the time a manager locked Booth in a hotel room to keep him off the bottle until the curtain went up. The ingenious star bribed a bellboy to fetch a bowl of liquor that Booth proceeded to inhale through a pipe stem stuck through the keyhole of the door behind which he was imprisoned.)

Before long, Booth could no longer be trusted to go on tour alone. So his sons were drafted as his traveling guardians. First to serve was the eldest, Junius Brutus Jr. ("June"). As the son's own theatrical career began to take off, however, he cut himself free from his father. The job passed to the next son, Edwin Thomas Booth. Edwin was a middle child. Born in 1833 on the night of a spectacular meteor shower, Edwin was three years older than Asia and five years older than John Wilkes. He went on the road with his father when he was only fourteen. Edwin Booth would one day be acknowledged as America's greatest actor. He learned much of his art by touring with his father, but protecting the afflicted man was surely a sad and lonely duty to impose on a child.

CASTE

Junius Brutus Booth had been able to win himself a measure of peace when, about a year after arriving in America, he found a place to settle. "The Farm," about twenty-five miles north of Baltimore, would be his welcome retreat from the world and the beloved childhood home of the brood of little Booths the couple hastened to produce. The rural obscurity also held out the hope of keeping the actor's second, illegitimate family from prying eyes. All the Booth children except Junius Brutus Jr., the first, and Joseph, the tenth and final child, were born on the farm hidden in the northern Maryland countryside a mile or two from the little rural hamlet of Bel Air in Harford County.

The two Britons who settled there were city people. Their London, with its 1.5 million inhabitants, was the biggest city in the world. The farm was a different world, not wilderness but a still-wild place where paths dwindled away in a vast forest, where ancient frogs croaked mightily in swamps, and fallen leaves hid a scattering of stone projectile points lost by aboriginal hunters. The Booth children would be creatures of both urban and rural worlds, growing up on the farm in an enchanted, timeless place. The farm remained a summer home for the Booths until after

Tudor Hall was the Booth family's home on their farm near the little village of Bel Air, Maryland, about twenty-five miles north of Baltimore.

Library of Congress, Prints and Photographs Division,
HABS MD, 13-Bela, 2–1.

Junius's death. The family also kept a townhouse in Baltimore, where they usually passed the winters so the children could attend city schools. During their childhoods, Baltimore was successively the second and third largest city in the United States.

The Londoners may have found the adjustment to country life challenging. There were other differences. Were Booth and Mary Ann surprised by the contrast between the democratic equality white people in the United States enjoyed and the rigidly hierarchical class system that ruled society in the constitutional monarchy they had left behind? They didn't say, but both seemed content to stay in America for the rest of their lives. Except for a few brief visits, they never considered returning to Europe. Of course Booth had other reasons to stay in his new country—the wife and son he'd abandoned when he ran off with his flower girl.

Yet there remained a fundamental difference between class-conscious England and the egalitarian Maryland that was of far greater significance: the presence of African slavery. The American way of fixing the value of people was more rigid and pervasive than all the hierarchies of social class that obtained in Europe. The republic's boasted equality of free white men was a reality, the consummation of the noblest ideals birthed by the world-changing American Revolution. This egalitarianism was unmatched in any of the nations of the Old World. At the same time, the ultimate worth of individuals in the United States was immutably determined, not by wealth or high birth, or the lack thereof, but by artificial distinctions of physical appearance—standards that derived from the unscientific concept of race.

Journalist Isabel Wilkerson has recently suggested that the American model is best understood as a caste system, analogous to the social system that has persisted for millennia in India. The most important pillar of any caste system, Wilkerson maintains, is the preservation of the purity of the dominant caste by confining marriage and childbearing to other members of that caste alone.[1] In America, the dominant caste is the so-called white race. So the most reprehensible of all crimes was any pollution of the purity of whiteness by the admixture with the blood of lesser races. Most white Americans, and particularly most Southern enslavers, were unutterably opposed to what they called amalgamation—that is, race mixing or interracial marriage. The enslavers' ultimate and, they believed, most persuasive argument in their defense of slavery, was the conviction that enslavement prevented race mixing. So slavery was most important not primarily as a labor system but as a means of preserving white racial purity.

Junius Brutus Booth himself refused to become an enslaver,

though he could easily have afforded such purchases. Still, John Wilkes Booth grew up from infancy in a slave society. There were no real plantations in the area, but many of his neighbors owned small numbers of people. These people generally considered human bondage a natural and unremarkable part of their world. Young Booth absorbed such attitudes.

Many of the African Americans the Booths lived among were free people. A free Black woman helped raise the Booth children. When they were grown, she stayed on as a cook and housekeeper, virtually a member of the family for decades. Other Blacks, mostly those who labored on the farm, were enslaved men leased from owners who had no need of their labor. So Junius Brutus Booth, although he rejected human bondage, participated in the slave system by paying rent to slaveholding neighbors. This leasing arrangement, common in Maryland and the upper South, was rare in the Deep South cotton states, where the plantation regime was based on torture and the threat of torture and enslaved people were much more tightly controlled. Some upper South enslavers even allowed the workers they leased out to keep some fraction of their wages. Many of these workers saved their pay for years to buy their own freedom or the freedom of family members.

Indeed, slavery in the Booths' region of northern Maryland, bordering the free state of Pennsylvania, was perhaps the least harsh example of the institution that could be found in America. The reasons were largely demographic: there were fewer African Americans in the state. Moreover, a great many Maryland Blacks were free people. When farming for grain crops had eclipsed the labor-intensive planting of tobacco in the upper South during the eighteenth century, the labor of enslaved people was needed less. Some surplus slaves were emancipated by their owners. Many more were sold out of the old Chesapeake tobacco colonies— sold south down the Mississippi to the booming cotton states. There, the cultivation of that export crop was making millionaires out of some big planters at a time when $1 million was a truly prodigious amount. The big cotton lords worked hundreds of enslaved people on vast plantations that could be defined as labor camps. They were eager to buy more laborers. So the vast fortunes made by cotton planting in the Deep South swelled the prices of the surplus people owned by upper South enslavers. The sale of people remained a significant source of revenue for enslavers in the upper South and border slave states throughout the antebellum period. Each of these sales shattered a family—separating, almost certainly forever, husbands from wives, parents from children. Tearing apart loved ones was the cruelest of the many wrongs inflicted by slavery. The unending grief brought on by this sundering of family ties was a kind of emotional death suffered by people still among the living. The defenders of slavery tended to ignore this atrocious practice.

Maryland was unique among the fifteen slaveholding states at midcentury. Free Blacks there were almost as numerous as the enslaved—representing 41 percent of the Black population—a ratio greatly surpassing that of any other slave state. The second-highest proportion of the free to enslaved was neighboring Virginia's much smaller 10 percent. There were virtually no free Blacks in the seven Deep South states that would one day be the first to declare their secession. Fully 99.7 percent of the African Americans in Mississippi, for example, were enslaved. Also unlike Maryland, in the Deep South states, Black population was nearly equal, equal, or greater than the white population. In some regions, enslaved Blacks greatly outnumbered whites. Yet in Maryland at midcentury, African Americans, free and enslaved, constituted only 28 percent of the state's population.[2]

As a boy, John Wilkes Booth had come to regard African Americans with contempt—"nigs" and "niggers" he called them—and to believe that their ancestral degradation was the happiest condition to which they could aspire. With most white Americans of his time, Booth shared the conviction that Blacks were an inferior people, incapable of living alongside whites as free men and women. In the wild speech Booth wrote but never delivered during the 1860 secession crisis he declared: "I hold [enslavement] to be a happiness for themselves and a social & political blessing for us. . . . I have been through the whole South and have marked the happiness of master & of man. Take every individual and you will find the happiness greater there than here. True I have seen the Black man whipped but only when he deserved much more than he received."[3]

The young actor lived among Blacks all his life, interacting with them on a daily basis. After he left his mother's house, he had no home. He lived in hotels and boardinghouses, ate in restaurants, drank in saloons, and spent days in steamboat parlors and railway carriages. Black people carried out most of the menial tasks in such venues. Most of the waiters who served his meals, the chambermaids who made his bed, the bellboys who carried his bags, the servants who pressed his clothes and shined his boots were Black people. Daily experience thus confirmed and reinforced the white supremacist beliefs Booth had already embraced. The lives African Americans were forced to live in the nineteenth-century United States marked them unmistakably as members of the subordinate caste.

Booth encountered those who were enslaved and lacking any human rights whatsoever. Less numerous, the free Blacks he knew owned their own bodies but little else. Whites had pushed the freed people down to the very bottom of the social ladder. Free or slave, most Blacks were impoverished, uneducated, and struggling to get by, working hard at the most menial and unpleasant tasks. They perched on the lowest rung as domestic servants, barbers, muckers of stables, and performers of other low-status, poorly paid jobs that most white men would be ashamed to take. Booth's preconceptions of Black inferiority were bolstered by their obligatory subordinate status.

Prudent self-preservation also required American Blacks,

both slave and free, to conduct themselves with extreme caution in their interactions with dangerous white men. A misstep could quite literally be fatal. They became practiced actors skilled at portraying a persona that would be pleasing to people of the dominant caste who held such power over their lives. So most African Americans presented themselves to whites as docile, contented, humble, and passive. Most Black people were illiterate; their masters made every effort to assure that they remained so. Whites generally believed them inferior in native intelligence. The science of the era had supposedly demonstrated their intellectual imbecilities. For their part, the enslaved people had always known that feigning stupidity could be an excellent tactic for baffling tyrants too powerful to resist openly. If an overseer had to explain a task repeatedly to apparently uncomprehending enslaved workers, the time spent explaining was time when work was suspended. Other "stupid" actions like breaking tools, misunderstanding orders, procrastinating, moving slowly, botching simple jobs, and a host of other tricks tended to make enslaved labor inefficient in many work environments. In contrast, on the big cotton plantations where the most severe discipline was imposed, the workers' regime was highly profitable.

Defending slavery as an adult, John Wilkes Booth would run through all the familiar arguments of the enslavers. Many of these notions he must have learned during his Maryland boyhood. Other ideas he picked up a little later in Richmond saloons and drawing rooms during his time as an apprentice actor in the city that would soon become the capital of the enslavers' four-year rebellion. Booth claimed that the South's peculiar institution was a benign, paternalistic arrangement that improved the lives of both the white enslavers and their human property. The United States was a white man's country, founded by white men to be governed by white men for the benefit of white people. The founders never intended Blacks to gain citizenship, a point emphasized by Supreme Court Chief Justice Roger Taney, a Maryland slaveholder, in his brief for the notorious Dred Scott decision in 1857. Enslavement was a distinct blessing to African Americans, Booth said, echoing the writings of the South's political theorists: Blacks were far better off in Dixie than were their distant cousins then living in West Africa.

Whatever discipline enslavers might be obliged to impose on their charges, the young man claimed, was generally mild, based on principles of justice, and necessary to improve the character and conduct of "half-civilized Africans." The treatment of the enslaved was no different, Booth contended, than the kind of widely approved discipline, often involving physical punishment, that parents used to correct the behavior of their children. Moreover, enslavement assured African Americans survival; these feckless people would surely perish by war or famine if emancipated. Although he had never read their books, John Wilkes Booth was simply repeating the arguments of slavery's leading political theorists—writers and politicians such as James Henry Hammond, Thomas R. Dew, William Harper, George Fitzhugh, and Edmund Ruffin.

In November 1864, half a year before the assassination, Booth would lay it all out in the uncharacteristically well-written declaration he composed to justify his conspiracy. He expected it to be made public after the consummation—as indeed it was, being widely published in the press in April 1865. Regarding slavery, he wrote:

> This country was formed for the *white* not for the black man.
> And looking upon *African slavery* from the same stand-point,
> held by those noble framers of our Constitution. I for one,
> have ever considered *it*, one of the greatest blessings (both for
> themselves and us,) that God even bestowed upon a favored
> nation. Witness heretofore our wealth and power. Witness
> their elevation in happiness and enlightment above their race,
> elsewhere. I have lived among it most of my life and have seen

less harsh treatment from Master to Man than I have beheld in the north from father to son. Yet Heaven knows *no one* would be willing to do, *more* for the negro race than I. Could I but see a way to still better their condition, But Lincoln's policy is only preparing the way for their total annihilation.[4]

It is notable that Booth seemed far less concerned about the whole issue of interracial marriage than most other white Southerners, many of whom, as we have seen, tended to make the purity of the white race the cornerstone of their justification of slavery. The accepted formula was that the end of slavery would inevitably result in racial equality, and racial equality would inevitably result in interracial marriage and a nation of "half-breeds" and "mongrels." Yet Booth never raised this point.

Moreover, since he was also not particularly religious, he did not celebrate, as did many pious advocates of slavery, the inestimable value of the Christian faith. Others singled out religious faith as the most precious gift bondage had bestowed on the benighted Africans. As slaves in America, they argued, Blacks could embrace Christianity, and, if they conducted themselves as virtuous and obedient servants, they might, through the grace of God, have a chance to attain eternal salvation. What mattered a fleeting human lifetime of deprivation, suffering, and hard labor if it purchased an eternity of bliss? Yet this particular blessing Booth never mentioned.

Although Junius Brutus Booth had achieved his greatest stage success in portraying the cruelties of murderous villains, he was a singularly merciful man. He was a strict vegetarian. (Some carnivores speculated that vegetarianism was the root-cause of Booth's madness.) He slept on a mattress stuffed with straw instead of feathers, refused to read by the light of whale oil or tallow candles, and wouldn't let his farm animals be branded. He wouldn't allow even insects or venomous snakes to be killed.

In 1833, an outbreak of cholera swiftly carried off three of the Booths' six little children. Mary Ann herself was pushed to the brink of madness by the shock. Junius went over the edge. He had rushed back from a tour after death took the third child, his wife's six-year-old namesake, Mary Ann. Crazy with grief, he had the little girl's body dug out of its grave and carried into the house, where he tried desperately to bring her back to life. Convinced that his own sins had brought on Mary Ann's death, Booth did penance by making himself a pair of shoes with soles of lead, filling them with dried peas, and walking in them from Baltimore to Washington.[5] The Booths lost another child three years later during a London theatrical tour when eleven-year-old Henry Byron died of smallpox. Junius had loved this little boy more than any of his other children. "So proud as I was of him above all the others," the brokenhearted father lamented.[6]

So Junius may have been ready to fill the void by lavishing an especial love on his next child, also a son, born a year and a half after Henry's death. But there was more to it than that. By all accounts John Wilkes was a singularly lovely, joyful, winning, and good-natured child. He was his mother's, as well as his father's, favorite. Edwin remembered that Wilkes was "his father's favorite child." Booth family historian Stanley Kimmel also maintained that John Wilkes "was the darling of his father's heart. Indeed, both his parents so idolized and spoiled him that by comparison they seemed indifferent to the older children."[7] The other children did not resent their parents' preference for their brother; he was their favorite, too. Sometimes they called him Johnny, sometimes Wilkes.

The child would carry the charms that won over his family into adulthood. His radiant personality captivated almost everyone he met. He was passionate, sentimental, and romantic. He loved children, and they loved him. He was called "the handsomest man in America" by his admirers, who also agreed that he was kind and generous, a brilliant conversationalist, helpful to fellow actors on the stage, a most fashionable dresser, brave, athletic, compassionate, and, all in all, one of the most attractive characters imaginable. His friends reacted with absolute incredulity to word that the young actor had killed Abraham Lincoln. Edwin said that getting the news was like being hit in the forehead with a hammer.[8]

4

"THERE ARE NO MORE ACTORS!"

Most of John Wilkes Booth's opinions on race and slavery came, probably in the form of barroom hearsay, from the theories of the peculiar institution's intellectual champions. The prominent South Carolina politician James Henry Hammond was best known for his "Cotton Is King" theory of the South's economic and military invincibility. Also much admired by Southern whites as a literary and polemical gem was Hammond's famous and widely reprinted 1845 letter refuting an English abolitionist's attacks on slavery.

Booth would extoll the circumstances of enslaved African Americans in the South as superior to the lives led by their distant relatives in Africa. The young actor spoke of "their elevation in happiness and enlightment above their race, elsewhere."[1] His words were simply an abbreviated paraphrase of Hammond's argument in his 1845 letter that those whose kidnapped ancestors had been taken from pagan Africa had been given a blessing: "Though they might be perpetual bondsmen, still they would emerge from darkness to light—from barbarism into civilization—from idolatry to Christianity—in short from death to life."[2]

Stylistically impeccable, his letter was held up as an example of literary virtuosity and a telling blow against abolitionist hypocrisy. Yet Hammond's opinions were not based on reason or evidence. His principal rhetorical tool was deceit. His depiction of slavery as an enlightened and benevolent feature of the distinctive civilization of the South relied heavily on lies. On page after page, Hammond lied brazenly and unceasingly, resorting to what we might call today "alternative facts." He had the audacity to claim that the reports of widespread sexual predation by white men were nothing but the breathless pornographic fantasies of sex-starved maiden abolitionists. Hammond said it was a "subject on which ladies of eminent virtue so much delight to dwell, and on which in especial learned old maids . . . linger with such an insatiable relish. . . . The constant recurrence of the female abolitionists to this topic, and their bitterness in regard to it, cannot fail to suggest to even the most charitable mind, that 'Such rage without betrays the fires within.'"[3]

Hammond believed it imprudent to discuss the repulsive topic at all. It might give people ideas. He did feel obligated, nevertheless, to state the bedrock truth that exonerated the Southern white man: "I will not deny that some intercourse of the sort does take place. Its character and extent, however, are grossly and atrociously exaggerated."[4] But what of the many biracial people living in the slave states, the hundreds of thousands of residents identified as "mulatto" in successive US censuses? They were not the children of white men, Hammond explained. They were the result of couplings in which both partners were mulattoes, a trend he called "the prolific propagation of these mongrels among themselves."[5] This lie denying centuries of rape was stunning in its mendacity.

Hammond climbed to even loftier heights of deception when he tried to talk down the well-known fact that enslavers broke up families by sales and inheritance. He compounded his shameful words with a heartless lie that Black people, whose attachment to their families, he asserted, was weak, were not troubled by such separations: "Negroes are themselves both perverse and comparatively indifferent about this matter." He added that sometimes "it happens that a negro prefers to give up his family rather than separate from his master."[6] His final lie of lies was his pronouncement that "our slaves are the happiest three millions of human beings on whom the sun shines." Unfortunately, he continued, now "into their Eden is coming Satan in the guise of an abolitionist."[7]

It is conceivable, though not likely, that John Wilkes Booth really believed that the violent discipline that undergirded slavery was not overly harsh because he had never personally witnessed the kind of shocking atrocities that were routinely inflicted on enslaved workers, not only on the cotton plantations of the Deep South but also in his native Maryland. Except for a brief visit to a few Deep South cities during the great secession winter of 1860–61, Booth didn't spend time in the region. He never saw a cotton plantation. Maybe he also never witnessed punishments of local slaves.

It is more likely, however, that when Booth insisted that the enslavers did not employ brutality, he was simply protecting himself from unwelcome recognition of slavery's hideous cruelty by resorting to the primitive but powerful psychological defense mechanism of denial. He believed enslavement to be a moral institution because that is what he wanted to believe. Even in relatively lenient Maryland, it is hard to imagine he could have escaped knowledge of the white Southerners' crimes.

No one described the pathological inhumanity of those crimes more powerfully than another boy who came of age in rural Maryland about a generation earlier than John Wilkes Booth. That Maryland native, who would assume the name Frederick Douglass, had been born in 1818, making him eighteen years older than Booth. While Booth left no account of his short life, Frederick Douglass would become one of the most gifted practitioners of the art of autobiography in American history. His creation of compelling life stories would one day help him capture the attention of much of the English-speaking world.

The enslaved youngster, whose given name was Frederick Bailey, was born on Maryland's Eastern Shore—those counties cut off from the rest of the state and the whole of the continent by Chesapeake Bay. In the mulatto boy's Talbot County, as in the Booths' Harford County in northern Maryland, slavery was less common and free Blacks more numerous than in the more southerly slave states.[8] So the future abolitionist and the future assassin shared similar environments as boys. They certainly had nothing else in common. There could be no social distance in America greater than the one that stretched down from the dominant caste of the free, white John Wilkes Booth to the subordinate caste of the enslaved, mixed-race Frederick Bailey.

Though he lived in Baltimore at times, Frederick spent enough time on plantations to witness the many sadistic tortures that he would later describe in his autobiographies. He told how whites used or threatened to use the infliction of severe pain to terrorize enslaved people into unhesitating obedience. A single disturbing example should suffice here: As a boy of five, Frederick's sleeping quarters were a little closet that opened into the kitchen of the big plantation house. Early one morning, before the household was astir, "shrieks and piteous cries" from the kitchen woke the boy. Peering through the cracks in the crude door, the "terrified and horror-stricken" child watched a waking nightmare unfold. The master of the plantation, Aaron Anthony, was torturing little Frederick's aunt, fifteen-year-old Hester Bailey. He'd hung her up by her arms from a ceiling beam, stripped her to the waist, and was flogging her with a stiff, three-foot-long cowhide whip.

In *Narrative of the Life of Frederick Douglass, an American Slave*, the fugitive author explained that his former owner, Aaron Anthony, the man some whispered was his natural father, "was a cruel man, hardened by a long life of slaveholding. He would seem at times to take great pleasure in whipping a slave." That morning Frederick had watched the old man whip Hester Bailey "upon her naked back till she was literally covered with blood. No words, no tears, no prayers, from his gory victim, seemed to move his iron heart from its bloody purpose. The louder she screamed, the harder he whipped; and where the blood ran fastest, there he whipped the hardest . . . and not until overcome by fatigue, would he cease to swing the blood-clotted cowskin."[9]

A strong sense of sexual violation informed the whole ugly episode. Hester Bailey was unlucky: she was a most fetching young woman. Her beauty had attracted an enslaved man her own age who wanted to marry her. That was fine; Hester wanted to marry him, too. Much less welcome was the lust the teenage girl had stirred in her fifty-five-year-old owner. He didn't rape her, but he hurt her severely for spurning him and for disobeying his orders never again to see the young man she loved. Frustrated sexual desire powered the blows that lacerated the poor girl's bare back. Frederick Douglass's biographer David Blight suspects that as he grew older, Aaron Anthony "may have descended into mental instability and increased sexual aggression."[10]

The three autobiographies Douglass wrote are lengthy catalogs of the suffering, violence, and even murder he witnessed during the years before he escaped enslavement. He told the story of a brutal overseer who actually shot a young man to death. The monetary value of such a prime hand would have equaled several years of the overseer's salary. Yet, despite the heavy loss, the slave owner approved the murder since it conveyed to other enslaved people so blunt a warning about the consequences of defiance.

In 1846 the reeling tragedian was hit with new troubles. The long silent Adelaide Delannoy Booth finally came looking for her husband. As early as 1821, the year Junius and Mary Ann Holmes ran off to America together, the claim was made that Junius had reached an agreement of "separate maintenance" with Adelaide and had promised to provide her with fifty pounds a year. He abided by this pledge. A pair of parallel fictions had long obtained, fictions maintained for the sake of the children and the purposes of polite society. Adelaide, who knew her husband had abandoned her for another woman, pretended that she was only temporarily separated from him by a wide ocean and the exigencies of an actor's life. Mary Ann, who knew she had run off with a married man, pretended to be an innocent bride. Junius Brutus Booth simply continued to be married to the woman everyone called "Mrs. Booth," the mother of all but one of his eleven children.

Adelaide's arrival in Baltimore in 1846 exploded all the fictions. In 1843, Junius and Adelaide's son Richard Junius Booth, by then a young man in his twenties, had sailed to America to join his father. Junius had approved of the idea and sent his son eighty pounds to make the trip. Inevitably, Richard learned of the brood of illegitimate half-brothers and -sisters thriving in the Maryland countryside. He wrote his mother about her husband's second family. She immediately determined to cross the Atlantic to set things right.

Surviving a shipwreck on the Irish coast, Adelaide finally reached America at the end of 1846. Shortly after her arrival, she wrote her sister:

> Booth was playing in New York when I arrived. He is just about to commence his winter tour. I don't want to do anything to prevent him from making money, so I will wait until he comes to Baltimore, and as soon as he arrives my lawyer will fall on his back like a bomb. Nobody here has any notion that I am the wife of the famous tragedian. My lawyer tells me that, considering the fortune which remains to him, I may demand 5,000 francs.[11]

A few weeks later Adelaide confronted Junius, whom she had not seen since a London theatrical tour twenty-two years earlier, in 1825. It is hardly surprising that the reunion was "very stormy."[12] Junius demanded she go back to Brussels. Adelaide had no intention of leaving. She had learned that she would have to be a resident of Maryland for two years before she could bring divorce proceedings against Booth and cash in on his success. So she and Richard settled down to wait, in a miserable flat in a poor section of Baltimore. There was little money. No longer did the eminent tragedian favor them with an annual stipend.

After a life of sorrows, Adelaide had evidently become a drunkard herself. Booth was often in Baltimore selling his vegetables at the farmers' markets. Adelaide, probably in her cups, persisted in "falling on his back like a bomb" in a series of noisy, public confrontations on the city's streets. Once Adelaide even made the twenty-five-mile trip out to the farm at Bel Air to continue the argument, attacking Mary Ann viciously. If the older Booth children did not know that their mother's last name was still Holmes and that they were all of them bastards, they would certainly have relinquished their innocence at this point. Even Wilkes, though just a boy of eight when Adelaide first appeared, would have known something was wrong.

Not until 1851 did Adelaide file for divorce in Baltimore County Court, charging Booth with acts of desertion and adultery he did not bother to contest. The divorce was promptly granted, ending a marriage of thirty-six years, almost thirty of which husband and wife had lived on different continents. Adelaide got a substantial settlement. Not long after, Junius Brutus Booth married Mary Ann Holmes in a private ceremony that none of their children ever mentioned. The date of their wedding, May 10, 1851, was coincidentally the birthday of the couple's favorite child, Johnny, who had been born a bastard thirteen years before.

Illegitimacy—"bastardy"—could be a major social impairment in the nineteenth century, a kind of moral leprosy. (Abraham Lincoln, for example, was deeply shamed by the likelihood that his own mother had been born out of wedlock.) How heavily the disgrace of illegitimacy weighed on the Booths, particularly on John Wilkes, cannot be known. One biographer has gone so far as to suggest that the initials "JWB" that Johnny crudely tattooed on the back of his left hand in India ink as a boy were another attempt to prove that he was a real, *legitimate* Booth.[13] (The bold letters would help identify the assassin's nearly unrecognizable corpse in 1865.)

In 1852, Junius Brutus Booth made his final tour. With Edwin in tow, the aging actor traveled for weeks by land and sea to reach golden California, where the discovery of vast quantities of the noble metal had thrilled the world four years earlier. But Booth didn't strike it rich. He missed his wife. Before long, he decided to go home. Edwin elected to stay behind in San Francisco.

Booth crossed the Isthmus of Panama and, with the most dangerous part of his journey behind him, paused in New Orleans to stage several lucrative engagements. Then he headed north aboard a Mississippi River steamboat. But the actor incautiously drank of the great river's murky, pathogenic waters. He was soon overtaken by fatal sickness of the bowels, perhaps typhoid or cholera. Unable to move and almost unable to speak, he perished miserably in his cabin as the boat chugged up the Ohio River, attended only by a compassionate stranger. The date was November 30, 1852. He was fifty-six, the same age that death had taken William Shakespeare and would one day take Abraham Lincoln. Offered a drink of brandy near the end, Booth declined: "No more in this world."[14]

The actor's body was brought ashore at Cincinnati, where Mary Ann came to fetch him home in an airtight iron coffin with a little glass window through which the dead man seemed to peer out through half-opened eyes. Back in snowy Baltimore, a procession of mourners passed silently through the Booths' white-draped parlor for a last look at the sacred mask that two generations of theatergoers had seen transformed into myriad human souls. A bust of Shakespeare presided.

Though her father had been dead several days, Asia remembered that "the face under the glass plate was very calm. . . . The lips retaining their lifelike color were smilingly closed [and this] naturalness occasioned doubt in many minds and [so] physicians were sent for to satisfy us whether this was really death."[15] But her father's final role was no performance. Junius Brutus Booth had become death. Presently, a band playing "a solemn dirge" led a procession bearing the coffin to the vault of the Baltimore Cemetery to await burial when the ground thawed in the spring.[16] Though the streets were glazed in ice and a heavy snow was falling, a thousand mourners followed him to the graveyard.

"There are no more actors!" one critic exclaimed on hearing the news.[17] But, of course, the world was full of actors. There was even a whole new generation of Booths waiting in the wings. Two of them would become actors of high distinction. The first was already a star. Edwin Booth, whose cool, intellectual art was so unlike that of his father, would nevertheless dominate tragic theater in America during the second half of the nineteenth century, much as the older man had done during the first. The second was still awaiting his first curtain call. Before long, however, the spectacular stagecraft of the young action hero J. Wilkes Booth would thrill theatergoers and call to mind the terrifying mastery with which the mad tragedian Junius Brutus Booth had once bestrode the stage. But Johnny was still a boy, just fourteen years old when his father came home in a box.

5

"I USED TO BE A SLAVE"

"I am naturally anti-slavery," Abraham Lincoln would say. "If slavery is not wrong, nothing is wrong. I cannot remember when I did not so think, and feel."[1] Lincoln's hatred for slavery extended back before the beginnings of memory because his earliest memories were of a kind of personal slavery—an enslavement to poverty and ignorance, to cold and hunger and backbreaking labor.

"I used to be a slave" was how Lincoln recalled the squalor and travail of his impoverished boyhood in Kentucky and Indiana.[2] Reviewing his early years, it's hard to disagree with the scholar who concluded that the boy lived "amid want, poverty and discomfort that was about on the plane of the slaves he was destined to emancipate."[3] (Of course, to speak of Lincoln's youthful suffering and deprivation as enslavement is to speak metaphorically. As a free white male, his prospects were vastly superior to those of enslaved African Americans.)

Abraham Lincoln's preeminent biographer, Michael Burlingame, has speculated that the man's "deep aversion to the way his father treated him made him sensitive to the injustice suffered by slaves, with whom he probably felt a bond of identity. Just as slaveowners robbed their bondsmen of the fruits of their labor, thwarted their attempts to gain an education, and abused them physically, so too did Thomas Lincoln rob Abraham of the fruits of his labor, hinder his efforts to educate himself, and occasionally beat him for no good reason."[4]

The young Lincoln's poverty had been foreordained in part by a family tragedy that had taken place a generation before he was born: in May 1786, a forty-two-year-old Revolutionary War veteran and Indian fighter, Captain Abraham Lincoln, was putting in a crop of Indian corn on his farm in Jefferson County, Virginia, on the newly independent state's far western frontier.

Within a decade, Jefferson County would become part of the new state of Kentucky. Slavery had been a cornerstone of Virginia society ever since a ship laden with enslaved people had brought the first captive Africans to the colony's shores in 1619. Naturally Kentucky, too, would enter the Union as a slave state.

Americans claimed this region south of the Ohio River by virtue of Virginia's ancient colonial charter and the 1783 Treaty of Paris. That agreement had recognized the independence of the former British colonies and fixed the Mississippi River as the new republic's western boundary. But the native inhabitants repudiated European diplomacy. They maintained the land was theirs by right of long use. Tribes living north of the Ohio had always depended on Kentucky as a hunting ground. Farming the land would ruin the hunting. It was once again the primordial conflict between hunter-gatherers and agriculturalists. The Indians were determined to drive out the white interlopers by force of arms. Not for nothing did frontiersmen call Kentucky "dark and bloody ground."

Helping Captain Lincoln with the corn planting that day were his three young sons—Mordecai, thirteen; Josiah, eleven; and Thomas, only six. Suddenly a shot rang out from the forest. Father Lincoln fell. Mordecai ran back to the cabin to fetch a loaded rifle. Josiah took off for the nearby fort to summon help. Little Thomas stood frozen and sobbing over his dying father, stunned into shock. The killer emerged from the trees, a bare-chested Shawnee warrior with a gleaming medal hanging from his neck and musket and tomahawk in his hands. He approached the paralyzed six-year-old, ready to split the boy's skull or carry him off into the forest.

Brother Mordecai aimed carefully, drawing a bead on the shining medal hanging on the Indian's chest and squeezed the trigger. Mordecai's bullet killed his father's killer. Little Thomas, fatherless now at six, would one day become a father himself. He would name his only surviving son Abraham, after the father he had seen murdered that day.

Under Virginia's primogeniture laws, all Captain Lincoln's property went to first-born Mordecai. The consequences for Thomas were dire. Mordecai dealt harshly with his youngest brother. One relative said that "the reason why Thomas Lincoln grew up unlettered was that his brother Mordecai, having all the land in his possession, turned Thomas out of the house when the latter was 12 years old."[5]

As Abraham Lincoln himself explained in 1848, "Owing to my father being left an orphan at the age of six years, in poverty, in a new country, he became a wholly uneducated man."[6] He elaborated years later in an autobiographical sketch composed while he was seeking the 1860 presidential nomination: "Thomas, the youngest son, and father of the present subject, by the early death of his father, and very narrow circumstances of his mother, even in childhood was a wandering laboring boy, and grew up litterally without education. He never did more in the way of writing than to bunglingly sign his own name."[7]

So when Abraham Lincoln was born, in 1809 at Kentucky's Sinking Spring farm, he came into his father's world of poverty and ignorance. More than bad luck was involved, however, for Thomas Lincoln, a subsistence farmer and semiskilled carpenter, showed no inclination to better his condition. He was conspicuously lacking in ambition, a quality his son would later display in supreme measure. People praised Thomas for his honesty and witty storytelling—attributes he would pass on to his son—but they also said that he wasn't much of a worker. Family members, as well as neighbors in Kentucky and Indiana, agreed that Thomas "was a man who took the world Easy."[8]

He moved restlessly from one meager farm to another, losing money on each transaction. An "indolent" farmer with an "aversion to work," he cleared only enough land to grow what he needed to meet his own needs rather than getting ahead by raising surplus crops to sell at market. He could have used such cash to buy more land to expand his farm, as many of his neighbors were doing. But he much preferred roaming the woods and hunting game to farmwork. One relative believed that "Thomas Lincoln did not improve with age nor with increasing responsibilities. He . . . grew more and more shiftless as the years rolled on."[9]

In a time and place where everyone was appallingly poor by contemporary standards, the Lincolns stood out for their greater poverty. Their low-ceilinged Kentucky cabin was a hut with a dirt floor. They had no real furniture and only a skillet for cooking. They were "the very poorest people" living in "abject poverty." More than most families, the Lincolns experienced "the terrible hardships, the stark crudeness and even abject squalor that prevailed on the fringe of the settlements."[10] It is hardly possible to exaggerate the crudity of frontier life. The adolescent Lincoln's idea of a hilarious prank was relieving himself in a friend's hat. (But turnabout is fair play: the friend fooled him, quickly making a switch so that it was Lincoln's own hat that "caught the whole Charge.")[11]

The Lincoln family's situation inevitably brings to mind the well-worn slur applied to impoverished rural whites near the bottom of the social ladder. The African American scholar W. E. B. Du Bois is only the most distinguished of the many writers who have characterized Lincoln's family as "poor white trash."[12]

The deprivation was emotional as well as material. No love

was lost between father and son. Abraham Lincoln's law partner, William Herndon, concluded that the boy had been deeply wounded by his father's "cold and inhuman treatment."[13] The older man beat and whipped his son for little reason, threw things at him, and constantly belittled him. His boy's uncanny precociousness apparently irritated him. Proudly illiterate himself, he condemned education as time wasted. "Now I hain't got no eddication," he bragged, "but I get along far better than ef I had."[14] He was baffled by his son's fanatical determination to educate himself and by his constant reading. It's hard to imagine two people more opposed in character, outlook, and temperament.

Less is known about Lincoln's relationship with his mother, Nancy Hanks. Like her husband, Nancy Hanks Lincoln had been born a Virginian. It's significant that both Lincoln's parents were from Virginia, the oldest, largest, and richest of the slaveholding states, its enslaved population far greater than that of any other state. Abraham Lincoln's Southern roots went deep. Nancy Hanks Lincoln died, aged about thirty-four, in Indiana in 1818, when Abraham was only nine. To her son's intense shame, Nancy Hanks was "base-born" (born out of wedlock). The bastard girl's father was said to have been a Virginia aristocrat, a "large farmer of the highest & best blood."[15] The seduction couldn't have been difficult: Lucey, Nancy's mother, was a "halfway prostitute."[16]

Though it was openly talked about in Indiana, to Abraham Lincoln his mother's illegitimacy was a dark, humiliating secret. He almost never spoke of it. Apparently, she was a loving mother, but her approach to housekeeping, cooking, and child-rearing was likely as casual as was her husband's toward farming. Nancy also couldn't write, but she could read a little. She read Bible stories to her young son, starting him on his way to becoming a lifelong student of scripture. Her death precipitated the nine-year-old into a period of the most intense suffering he ever endured.

Thomas Lincoln had moved his family north across the Ohio

River in 1816, from the slave state of Kentucky to the free state of Indiana, part of the old Northwest Territory. "This removal," Abraham Lincoln would explain, "was partly on account of slavery; but chiefly on account of the difficulty in land titles in K[entuck]y."[17] It was true that Thomas Lincoln disliked slavery. He probably thought that it limited opportunities for poor white farmers like himself. Slavery was certainly a central feature of Kentucky frontier society then. In the Lincolns' Hardin County at the time of Abraham's birth, some 1,007 enslaved people mingled with 1,627 adult white males.[18]

The Lincolns had religious objections as well. They were members of the Separate Baptist Church, a Baptist subdenomination that opposed slavery. They were "just steep full of . . . notions about the wrong of slavery and the rights of man as explained by Thomas Jefferson and Thomas Paine."[19] Abraham must have picked up these antislavery sentiments as a child.

In their new Indiana home in the wilderness of dense woods and thickets at Little Pigeon Creek, life was even more grim. For the first several months, they lived in a "half-faced camp," a flimsy, three-sided hut made of poles and brush and completely open to the weather on one side, where the fire was kindled. It must have been unbearably cold in winter. Moreover, the gigantic eruption of Mount Tambora the year before had blasted dust into the sky, cutting sunlight enough to make 1816 the "Year without a Summer," the year people called "Eighteen Hundred and Froze to Death," when it snowed in July and crops failed throughout the Northern Hemisphere as temperatures set record lows.[20] The Lincolns endured this extreme weather in a shelter that was little better than a tent. The family's winter of 1816–17 was described as a "Valley Forge, of suffering, discomfort and self-denial."[21] Lincoln "remembered when my toes stuck out through my broken shoes in winter; when my arms were out at the elbows; when I shivered with the cold."[22]

During their first year in Indiana, the family built an eighteen-by-twenty-foot dirt-floored log cabin, a single windowless room with a loft. Though still a boy of eight, Abraham was immediately put to work. He would recall that his family had "settled in an unbroken forest; and the clearing away of surplus wood was the great task ahead. A. though very young, was large for his age, and had an axe put into his hands at once; and from that till within his twenty third year, he was almost constantly handling that most useful instrument—less, of course, in plowing and harvesting seasons."[23]

Immensely strong after he attained his full stature of six feet, four inches—he once hoisted a thousand-pound load over his shoulders—Lincoln would win a reputation as the most powerful axeman in the country. Until he came of age, he labored at a series of rural jobs—farmwork, clearing trees, grubbing and digging, plowing fields, sowing and reaping, hauling produce, slaughtering hogs, tending livestock, working at a gristmill and a river ferry, and, most famously, splitting rails for fences.

When he was nineteen, he took a flatboat loaded with pork and corn down the Ohio and Mississippi Rivers all the way to New Orleans. There he watched a slave auction and told his friend, "Allen, that's a disgrace."[24] He made a second trip to New Orleans a few years later. Lincoln was again dismayed by slavery. John Hanks, his cousin and companion on part of the trip, said Lincoln "saw Negroes Chained-maltreated-whipt & scourged." Lincoln's "heart bled," "was Sad-looked bad." Hanks said that "it was on this trip that he formed his opinions of Slavery; it ran its iron in him then & there." At another slave sale, Lincoln "saw a beautiful mulatto girl, sold at auction. She was *felt over, pinched, trotted* around to show bidders that said article was sound, etc. Lincoln walked away from the sad, inhuman scene with a deep feeling of *unsmotherable* hate."[25]

Until he reached twenty-one, the law demanded he give all his earnings to his father. He chaffed under this quasi enslavement. It probably seemed to him a "monstrous injustice," the words with which he would later describe the enslavement of African people. He managed to grasp only about one year of schooling "by littles"—a month or two here and there. But he soon taught himself to read and write and proceeded to borrow and read every book he could lay his hands on.

The year after his mother's death, in 1818, had been the worst of the bad times. Though he never spoke of it, the nine-year-old boy had been devastated by the loss. Bereft and lonely, he felt himself deliberately abandoned by his better parent. He was left in the care of his eleven-year-old sister, Sarah, under the desultory supervision of his often-absent father. Thomas Lincoln left the two siblings alone for as much as three months at a time.

The neglected children were often hungry and cold, dressed in rags, and filthy, fiercely clinging to life like a pair of wild animals. They were finally redeemed when their father's remarriage to Sarah Bush Johnston provided a loving and hardworking stepmother. But Lincoln never healed entirely. He was deeply wounded again when his beloved big sister died in childbirth in 1828. When he got word, Lincoln "sat down on a log and hid his face in his hands while the tears rolled down through his long bony fingers."[26] A few years later, the death of his teenaged sweetheart, Ann Rutledge, wounded him again. For the rest of his life, Abraham Lincoln felt abandoned in an indifferent universe. And as much as he may have wanted to, he was not able to take comfort in the belief in a providential God.

Lincoln was permanently scarred by his harsh childhood. "I have seen a good deal of the backside of the world," he said. The experience predisposed him to spells of savage depression. It also gave him a lifelong sympathy for the downtrodden.[27] He apparently never entirely forgave his parents. Thomas Lincoln lived to be an old man of seventy-three, dying in 1851. By that time, his son was a distinguished and prosperous lawyer living in Springfield, the Illinois state capital. He had recently finished serving a term in the US House of Representatives. He'd been married for about a decade and was father to three sons. But Thomas Lincoln never met his grandsons or his daughter-in-law, Mary Todd Lincoln. He was never invited to Springfield. The son's visits to the old folks had been few and far between.

In 1851, when the dying father sent a plea for a last meeting, the son declined to make the eighty-mile trip. He sent a message instead: "Say to him that if we could meet now, it is doubtful whether it would not be more painful than pleasant."[28] He didn't attend the funeral. Before he left Springfield for Washington, Lincoln would occasionally talk about putting tombstones on his parents' unmarked graves. Somehow he never got around to it.

In 1830, Thomas Lincoln had moved his family yet again, from his Indiana home to Macon County, Illinois. They set out just three weeks after Abraham turned twenty-one, finally escaping his father's guardianship. Though free now to go his own way, he elected to help with the move. He stayed with his family for a while in their new Illinois home to help his father build a cabin. Then he set off alone to begin his new life. The young man went into the world, he said, "a stranger, friendless, uneducated, penniless boy."[29]

Penniless or not, Abraham Lincoln had become a remarkable young man, set apart by superior intelligence and impressive physical strength and stature. He would one day describe his formal education with a single word: *defective*. But Lincoln managed to educate himself. He eventually attained a mastery of language unsurpassed by any other American statesman except Thomas Jefferson. Indeed, Lincoln's gifts as a stylist were surpassed by few literary artists. He stands with great American writers of the nineteenth century. The foundations of his sublime and distinctive prose poetry were the two Elizabethan masterworks he knew and loved the best—the 1611 King James Bible and the plays of Shakespeare. Lincoln's ability to affirm political principles in soaring eloquence would one day constitute a vital element of his leadership.

The young Lincoln's most essential attribute, however, was his driving, relentless ambition to rise in the world. Encompassing more than merely a desire for his own success, Lincoln's brand of ambition was also the principle that became the foundation of his political philosophy. He called it "the right to rise." For Abraham Lincoln, an equal chance to succeed in life was the great promise of America. He said, "I want every man to have the chance—and I believe a black man is entitled to it—in which he *can* better his condition."[30]

He believed such equality of opportunity was possible only in a democratic nation. Like so many patriots before him, Lincoln was convinced of the universality of the American promise. The United States had a special mission to demonstrate the success of popular government based on human equality in a world still largely ruled by hereditary despotism. American slavery stood as the antithesis, the very contradiction of the nation's professed ideals. Slavery threatened Lincoln's most deeply held beliefs. So of course he was "naturally anti-slavery." As he put it in a famous speech in 1854: "I hate it because of the monstrous injustice of slavery itself. I hate it because it deprives our republican example of its just influence in the world—enables the enemies of free institutions, with plausibility, to taunt us as hypocrites—causes the real friends of freedom to doubt our sincerity."[31]

It was the hardship of his early years that made him so passionately devoted to the principle of equality and to the success of the American experiment, the endeavor he would one day extol as "the last, best hope of earth."[32]

A YOUNG SOUTHERN GENTLEMAN

Junius Brutus Booth's acting had brought his family a steady $5,000 a year, the equivalent of as much as $150,000 today. But he had spent recklessly and was often swindled by sharpers. He had saved little. "His monetary affairs," daughter Asia admitted, "were pitiable failures; and by trusting to the honor and probity of others, his wealth . . . was easily diverted into other channels."[1]

His loss challenged his survivors with a major retrenchment. There was now no source of sufficient income. The two older brothers, Junius Jr. and Edwin, were struggling to make it as actors and theater managers in distant California. Often they were flat broke. About as often they were flush with cash and gold dust, only to pour it away on liquor and women. It wasn't often they were able to send help back to their mother and siblings in Maryland.

Wilkes, a boy just entering adolescence, was now the man of the house—when he was home, that is. He was still away at St. Timothy's Hall, his military boarding school in the Maryland countryside, with his little brother, Joseph. Joe, the tenth and youngest of the brood, would soon begin slipping in and out of madness. Doctors called his disorder "melancholy insanity." At the farm, Wilkes's beloved sister and constant companion, Asia, was seventeen. The oldest Booth daughter, Rosalie, already thirty, may have been autistic. She was strange and reclusive, an "invalid" the family called her. She would cling to her mother all her life.

By the time his father died, John Wilkes had gotten the rudiments of an education at a series of private schools.[2] At St. Timothy's Hall, he wore a gray artillery cadet's uniform and mingled with the sons of some of the upper South's most distinguished slaveholding families. His sister remembered him as a slow but tenacious student. Classmates recalled a frustrated striver, gripping his head with both hands as though trying to keep his brain from exploding. His marks were poor, his teachers exasperated. He certainly never distinguished himself as a writer. His schoolboy orthography was defective, though he could write effectively as an adult. He apologized for his poor writing in most of the fifty-odd letters from his pen that survive.[3] He blamed bad lighting, bad pens, distractions, and, more forthrightly, his own deficiencies.

Asia said that though he learned with difficulty, he rarely forgot what he had mastered. Guided by his sister, he grew to love novels and poetry. And since he knew Shakespeare by heart, he was already intimate with the most glorious passages in the language. He had mastered voice. He had been declaiming Shakespeare and delivering juvenile political speeches since he was a little boy.

Johnny was always popular with his classmates and would continue to be well-liked wherever he went in life. A loyal and generous friend, Booth liked to sign his schoolboy letters "Thine till Death" or "Yours Forever." He would bring two of his boyhood friends into his plot against Abraham Lincoln. Both went to prison, and one died there.

He left school for good six months after his father's death, failing to finish high school. Maybe there was no money for tuition;

maybe his mother needed him at home. Hard times had forced Mary Ann Booth to rent out the convenient Baltimore townhouse and retreat to the Bel Air farm full time. She needed a man around the place, and the fifteen-year-old was the best she could do. June was still in California. Edwin was touring Australia.

For the next three years, the Booths tried unsuccessfully to make a living farming, an occupation John Wilkes called "trying to starve respectably by torturing the barren earth."[4] The Booths held 180 acres, eighty of them under cultivation. The main burden fell on Johnny. Asia reported that he was up at dawn, clearing trees, grubbing fields, plowing and planting and harvesting—that is, when there were any crops to gather, for the worn-out fields yielded only meager produce. He was aided by tenant farmers, hired laborers, and enslaved people leased from slaveholding neighbors.

The task of managing the workers did not go smoothly for the young scion of theatrical greatness. Young as he was, Wilkes had taken a supercilious, almost aristocratic, stance toward these hirelings, an attitude completely out of step with the democratic instincts of his father and grandfather. Wilkes, his sister would approvingly explain, held to "that reservation that jealously kept the white laborer from free association with his employer or his superior."[5]

It is little surprise that the animosity was reciprocated. Many of the laborers were recent immigrants from Ireland. They hated the Booths for their Englishness and bridled at John Wilkes's pretensions of gentility. "We were not a popular family with our white laborers," Asia continued, "because, as they said, 'They'd heer'd we had dirty British blood, and being mixed up with Southern ideas and niggers made it dirtier.' "[6] The workers finally complained so bitterly about being excluded from family meals that Wilkes had to invite them into the kitchen. He shared the midday meal with these "sons of the soil . . . [who] were not the most delightsome guests to entertain, particularly in a hot kitchen in the scorching days of August."[7] Even then, however, a patriarch at fifteen, the man of the house refused to let his womenfolk eat with the menials.

If his arrogance was at odds with family tradition, it went along nicely with the core values of the society that white Southerners had created over the past several decades. Asia explained: "The difference between the impassioned self-made Republican and the native-born southern American is wide. One overleaps restraint by his enthusiasm . . . and is over eager to fraternize with all men," while, unlike the Northerners, the Southern gentleman "cautiously creates for himself a barrier called respect, with which he fences off familiarity and its concomitant evils. This made the master a god in the South, to be either loved or feared. There are no 'Masters' and 'Mistresses' in the North."[8]

John Wilkes Booth had already come to think of himself as a Southern gentleman. A Southern gentleman was a man of honor, generous and proud, patriarchal and conscious of his superior station, gracious in company but always quick to use violence in defense of his honor. He customarily went armed in public—with a knife, a gun, or both. He wasn't afraid to use his weapons, for he admired courage above all virtues. Even as late as the Civil War, fatal duels still took place in the South.

Booth would comport himself on this model for the rest of his short life. It is hardly surprising that a Southern gentleman like Booth would come to despise the common, vulgar, lowborn prairie buffoon Abraham Lincoln. Gentlemen were composed of finer materials. He told his sister that Lincoln's "appearance, his pedigree, his coarse low jokes and anecdotes, his vulgar similes, and his policy are a disgrace to the seat he holds."[9]

Honor and violence were two sides of the same coin. Each upheld the other. Violence purified tarnished honor.[10] When the fifteen-year-old Wilkes learned in July 1853 that a tenant farmer had insulted his mother, he armed himself with a "stout stick" and marched off to confront the churl. When the man refused to come up to the house to apologize, he shouted, "Then I'll whip you like the scoundrel you are," bringing his club down on the farmer's head. A friend stopped the beating but not before, Booth boasted, "I knocked him down, which made him bleed like a butcher."[11]

This obscure incident seemed to foreshadow the infamous beating another Southern gentleman would inflict on the Massachusetts abolitionist senator Charles Sumner on the floor of the Senate in 1856. That gentleman, too, would be striking for Southern honor. The enslavers' adherence to this code of honor and violence was one of the reasons they were so confident they could defeat the pusillanimous Yankees if it actually came to war. In 1856, one Southern statesman, Louis Wigfall of Texas, "alluded to the assault on Senator Sumner as a type of the manner in which Southerners would deal with the Northerners generally."[12] The "Southrons" knew they would be invincible in battle.

Rural life gave the young man a chance to indulge his love of gunplay. He was a dead shot—drilling cans and smashing bottles and nailing flying birds and small animals. He was certainly not averse to shedding blood. He shot neighbors' livestock that strayed onto the Booths' fields. He killed a dog that belonged to a nearby family of free Blacks. He conceived a virulent hatred for all things feline. He hated cats for hunting and killing songbirds. Before long, he had succeeded in exterminating all of them in the vicinity of the farm. As Booth biographer Terry Alford has noted, such cruelty to animals in a young person is distinctly alarming, likely predictive of future violence directed at people, a judgment endorsed by the *Diagnostic and Statistical Manual of Mental Disorders*.[13]

Booth remained a gunman all his life, armed when out in public. By the time of his theatrical apprenticeship in Richmond, from 1858 to 1860, he had begun carrying a little single-shot pocket pistol called a derringer, probably the same weapon he would wield in the presidential box at Ford's Theatre on the fatal night of April 14, 1865.[14]

Farming soon lost its charms, if indeed it had any to lose. Acting had never been far from John Wilkes's mind. Though Junius Brutus Booth had talked down any ideas of theatrical careers for his sons and had tried to steer them into more conventional occupations, like surgery or cabinetmaking, three of the Booth boys followed the old man onto the stage. Two won high distinction. Edwin would one day be acknowledged the finest actor in America, while John Wilkes would thrill the nation with his spectacular stagecraft.

But for the three years after his father's death, the young man was thwarted. He had always dreamed big dreams. "I must have fame! fame!" he cried.[15] He longed to become a great actor like his father. He talked of winning undying glory with some prodigious feat. He despaired at the prospect of being marooned in the countryside with his mother and sisters and little brother. He envied the two older brothers, who had toured with the "Elder Booth" and seen the actor's craft illuminated by their father's genius. Wilkes could only practice his elocution by declaiming to the field hands passages he had memorized from *Julius Caesar*.

Still, by August 1855, the seventeen-year-old felt confident enough to make his stage debut, playing the Earl of Richmond in Colley Cibber's popular adaptation of Shakespeare's *Richard III* at the St. Charles Theatre in Baltimore. Brother Edwin, already a star, who played the title role, had invited Wilkes to join him. The novice was billed under his own name and as the son of the great tragedian.

Asia remembered that after his first performance, the young actor's "face shone with enthusiasm, and by the exultant tone of his voice it was plain that he had passed the test night. Mother was not so pleased as we to hear of this adventure; she thought it premature, and that he had been influenced by others who wished to gain notoriety and money by the use of his name."[16] (Later, when he acted in Philadelphia and Richmond from 1857 to 1860, Booth appeared under stage names.)

However the performance may have gone that night in 1855, it is notable that Booth's first stage role was that of a hero who kills a murderous tyrant, for that is exactly what he thought he was doing in Ford's Theatre ten years later when he squeezed the trigger of his derringer. Throughout Booth's short life, the line between the drama and the world was always a little blurred, and many of the plays he acted were bloody spectacles, studded with killings.

Finally, the Booths gave up on agriculture. They leased the farm and moved back into the Baltimore townhouse. Two years passed before Wilkes performed on the stage again. His career really began in August 1857, when he hired on as a supporting player in the stock company of the Arch, Philadelphia's leading theater. The Arch's owner and manager was William Wheatley, an old actor who still mounted the boards himself. He had been a friend and admirer of the great tragedian. He may have hired the untried son to honor the father's memory. Wilkes had also been recommended by his brother Edwin and by Edwin's friend John Sleeper Clarke, the Arch's resident "low comedian." Before long, Clarke would join the family when, against John's wishes, he became Asia Booth's husband.

Like every big-city American theater of the day, the Arch had its own troupe, its resident company of professional actors, typecast for the appropriate roles in whatever play was being presented. There was always a leading man, the hero or protagonist, a capable actor not quite of star quality. He was supported by the leading lady. There was always a villain. There was an old man and an old woman, perhaps a child or two. The professionals were supported by the dispensable extras, the "supernumeraries," and the "walking gentlemen," like Booth, who sometimes got a few lines to speak. As a walking gentleman, Wilkes earned eight dollars a week.

The managers' most lucrative strategy was to book a touring star, a big name, to visit the theater for a week or two, boosting ticket sales. The star would choose the plays. He or she would get top billing at the head of the playbill posters, above the name of the playwright and the title of the play itself. The resident company would take direction from the star and support him or her on the stage.

Stardom was where the real money lay. The stock company players, even the leads, were paid a fixed wage. A star, in contrast, traveling from town to town, was entitled to a substantial share of ticket sales and was guaranteed at least one "benefit" performance during his stay. In a benefit, the star claimed the entire evening's box office after expenses. Every member of the stock company dreamed of becoming a star. Few succeeded. Though he started out inauspiciously, such were his natural gifts that the novice Booth would make the ascent from mere walking gentleman to a star touring the country after just three seasons.

The star system dominated American theater at midcentury, a circumstance not all observers have regarded as a happy one. A twentieth-century theatrical dictionary defines the star system as "the custom of selling a play by exploiting a prominent actor whose name is a guarantee of good box-office business. The play is diminished in importance and less care is exercised in selecting and producing it. In production, the consideration of the star takes precedence over dramatic considerations. As a system it is an evil, deleterious of the drama."[17] A cynical journalist described the star as "an actor who belongs to no one theatre, but travels from each to all, playing a few weeks at a time, and is sustained in his chief character by the regular or stock actors. A stock actor is a good actor and a poor fool. A Star is an advertisement in tights, who grows rich and corrupts the public taste."[18]

During the time that Booth was on the road as a star himself—from October 1860 until May 1864—some critics praised him for accomplished, even brilliant, acting. Others, however, maintained that J. Wilkes Booth (the billing he customarily used during his acting career) was mostly hype—a big name, rare good looks, acrobatic moves, and thrilling fight scenes, along with plenty of bombastic ranting—in other words, an "advertisement in tights." What no one doubted, though, was his fame and his resounding popular success.

"I AM MYSELF ALONE!"

The Booth name was an imposing property in the American theater at midcentury. Unwilling to sully that shining name with poor showings or risk being accused of trading on the reputations of his father and brothers, the beginner was careful to bill himself as Mr. J. B. Wilkes or plain J. Wilkes. This was probably a wise move; the young player's early efforts were greeted with mixed reviews. He missed cues, forgot his lines, was struck dumb by stage fright, and, on at least one occasion, was laughed and hooted from the stage. But the theater was in his blood. Mr. Wilkes persevered, playing stock in Philadelphia for a year. His last performance there was in June 1858.

Nineteenth-century theaters closed over the summer, when the galleries were too hot for comfort. When fall returned, Booth signed on as a supporting player at Richmond's Marshall Theatre. His first performance there was on the steaming hot evening of August 15, 1858. Billed as John Wilkes, he was now making eleven dollars a week. Edwin Booth made a star visit to the Marshall that fall. John Wilkes played Richmond again to Edwin's Richard III. "I don't think he will startle the world," Edwin reported to their mother, "but he is improving fast, and looks beautiful on the platform."[1]

After an adolescence marked by exuberant boozing, the worried young man had decided to sober up. He knew what alcohol had done to his father and brothers. In Richmond he shared a hotel room with the famous actor Harry Langdon, the Marshall's popular leading man. Heavy drinking was damaging Langdon's performances, and he, too, was determined to reform. The two friends rode the water wagon together for some months, encouraging each other in their sobriety. Unfortunately, neither could stay off the sauce for long. Langdon would eventually die of cirrhosis of the liver, although, surprisingly, not until the year 1910.[2] Booth's own drinking only accelerated over the next several years. Langdon also mentored the beginner. "I taught John Booth the rudiments of acting," he later boasted.[3]

During his two years in Richmond, Booth supported the leading actors in *Hamlet*, *Macbeth*, and *Richard III*, as well as in such long-forgotten dramas as *Satan in Paris*; *Wanted, 1000 Spirited Milliners for the Gold Diggings*; *Milly, the Maid with the Milking Pail*; *De Soto, Hero of the Mississippi*; *A Kiss in the Dark*; *The French Spy*; and many others. Nine back-to-back performances made him thoroughly familiar with the popular comedy *Our American Cousin*, the play President Lincoln would come to see at Ford's in April 1865.[4] At the Marshall, seats went for twenty-five and fifty cents, while places in the "Eastern Gallery for Colored Persons" were 37.5 cents.[5]

John Wilkes Booth came of age as an actor in Richmond, Virginia, and it was living there that confirmed his determination to be recognized as "of the South." He wanted, he said, "to be loved of the Southern people above all things. He would work to make himself essentially a Southern actor."[6] Whatever kind of actor he might be, no one had the slightest doubt about the presence Booth brought to the stage. By the time he turned twenty, the dark-eyed mother's darling had grown into a figure many called "the handsomest man in America." Of Booth it was said that "women spoiled him," and it was small wonder that few of the female persuasion were proof against the glamour and self-assured charm of the performer who could move an audience to tears with his readings of the maudlin poem "Beautiful Snow."

One acquaintance concluded that "John Wilkes Booth cast a spell over most men and I believe over all women without exception," while the actress Clara Morris resorted to a tender metaphor to suggest Booth's power over women when she recalled that "at the theater, as the sunflowers turn upon their stalks to follow the beloved sun, so old and young, our faces smiling turned to him."[7] She also said that Booth

> had more than mere talent as an actor. In his soul the fire of genius burned brightly, and he promised to top them all in the profession to which he was born. He had by inheritance the fire, the dash, the impetuosity, the temperament, and the genius of his great father, and he more nearly resembled the elder Booth in those qualities which go to make up a great actor than any of the other sons of the eminent sire. . . . It was impossible to see him and not admire him; it was equally impossible to know him and not love him.[8]

"Seldom has the stage seen a more impressive, or a more handsome, or a more impassioned actor," remembered another who knew him. "Picture to yourself Adonis, with high forehead, ascetic face corrected by rather full lips, sweeping black hair, a figure of perfect proportions and the most wonderful black eyes in the world. . . . At all times his eyes were his striking features but when his emotions were aroused they were like living jewels. Flames shot from them. His one physical defect was his height, but he made up for the lack by his extraordinary presence and magnetism."[9]

Nearly everyone agreed that the young man was also charming, generous, and instinctively kind. He was a most fashionable

A carte de visite portrait of "the handsomest man in the United States," by Silsbee and Case, Boston, Dec. 3, 1862.

dresser. He had a splendid voice. And Booth possessed the gifts of a natural athlete: he was a fine horseman, a marksman, an acrobat, an expert fencer, and a body builder. With these formidable resources joined to his own hungering ambition, John Wilkes Booth would soon fashion himself into one of the most successful actors in the United States.

As he grew in stature as an actor and as a dashing, much-admired figure in the streets and drawing rooms of the city that would soon be the capital of the so-called Confederacy, Booth was growing as well in his passionate, even fanatical, love for the South and its institutions, a love that was fully requited by both theater audiences and Richmond society. Virginians had embraced Booth as one of their own. One of them remembered that when

> John Wilkes Booth was in the Richmond Stock Company, he was very young. In his early twenties he weighed about 175 pounds, was a little taller than his brother Edwin, possessed his marvelously intellectual and beautiful eyes, with great symmetry of features, an especially fine forehead, and curly, black hair. He was a great social favorite, knowing all the best men and many of the finest women. With men John Wilkes was most dignified in demeanor, bearing himself with insouciant care and grace, and was a brilliant talker. With women he was a man of irresistible fascination by reason of his superbly handsome face, conversational brilliancy . . . and a peculiar halo of romance. His ability was unquestionable and his success assured.[10]

The young man took full advantage of his power over women. One friend claimed that Booth was "a very slave to his almost insatiable amorous propensities."[11] Given the assets he brought to the game, it is no surprise that his conquests were said to be beyond number. He was more often the pursued than the pursuer. His mail was full of missives the senders should have known better than to write. Many an ardent aspirant was turned away ungratified, from motives of pity or chivalry or simply Booth's lack of interest. But many others got exactly what they were looking for. The actor warned one infatuated young woman that, before things went any further, she should know that he had no affection for her, though he did feel "a sufficient desire." She assured him that his admission did not present the slightest obstacle to their budding friendship.[12]

Clara Morris remembered that "there were many handsome, well-bred and wealthy ladies in the land, married as well as unmarried, who would have given much for one of his kisses. Booth's striking beauty was something that thousands of silly women could not withstand. His mail each day brought letters from women weak and frivolous, who periled their happiness and their reputations by committing to paper words of love and admiration which they could not, apparently, refrain from writing."[13]

Booth played stock in Richmond for two years. By the fall of 1860—the beginning of only his fourth year on the stage—he was ready to make his first tour as a star. Success came quickly. Before long, the playbills were hailing "J. Wilkes Booth" in bold capitals as "A STAR OF THE FIRST MAGNITUDE! THE YOUNGEST TRAGEDIAN IN THE WORLD!" When comparisons to his father and brothers persisted, he added to his playbills the defiant motto "I am Myself Alone!"—a line from *Richard III*.

Critics praised him while theatergoers voted with their pocketbooks. Booth played to packed houses across the North and Midwest. Within a short time, the young actor could boast of earning more than $20,000 a year, then an altogether spectacular sum. It was four times what his father had earned at the height of his career, the equivalent of upwards of $750,000 today. (At the time, the president of the United States earned $25,000 a year.)

After his first star tour, Booth acted as his own agent. Most of his letters that escaped the great burning that followed the assassination concern the actor's own management of his flourishing career. Booth negotiated with theater owners for his share of the box office. He set the dates of his engagements and picked the plays. A theater of the period might seat fifteen hundred, but some were big enough to accommodate two to three thousand. With tickets ranging from twenty-five to fifty cents and up, a popular favorite could pocket hundreds of dollars a night.

Actors worked for their money. An evening's performance—a five act tragedy or drama followed by a shorter comedy—began at seven o'clock and rarely ended before midnight. A different program was usually staged each night. When not playing to an audience, the company was therefore probably in rehearsal. Plays were drawn from the star's repertoire. The star would often assume the role of stage director as well. The play was, after all, presented chiefly as a vehicle for the star. Rehearsals gave the stock company a chance to learn how best to support the star. Booth was said to possess considerable talent as a director. By most accounts, he was also considerate in working with the supporting actors, something that could not be said of many other stars. His letters also show how he devised stratagems to extract more money from managers.

He revealed an intense interest in the success of other actors and rival theaters. He begged for plenty of promotion, urging that a *"big thing* be made of" his engagements.[14] He exulted in his success: "My goose does indeed hang high (long may she wave.)"[15] By the beginning of 1863, his correspondence contained hard proof of that success: Booth was making more money than he knew what to do with. He was investing substantial sums in real estate and stocks.

But a star's lot was not all applause. Booth experienced the grinding hardship and monotony of an actor's life on the road. There was danger as well. Trains derailed with alarming frequency. The boilers of steamboats exploded. The boats caught fire or sank when they tore their bottoms out on snags and sandbars. (The average Mississippi River steamboat had a life span of just five years.)[16]

Booth nearly lost his life traveling in an open sleigh at twenty-five degrees below zero through a midwestern blizzard in January 1864. The injury the extreme cold did to his throat and voice troubled him onstage for months. The United States was an enormous country in a time when a hundred-mile trip could take as much as a day. Booth once spent fifty-one wearisome hours on a train ride from Boston to Chicago.

Some of his appearances were as short as a night or two. The longest—at the Boston Museum in the spring of 1864—ran for two months. Although some have charged that he played so many western towns because of poor receptions in the big cities of the East, touring the provinces was actually good business. "The star system," one theater historian has written, "was unequivocally aided by this western expansion, for western managers paid higher salaries than in the East to attract the best talent available."[17]

The picture that emerges from Booth's fleeting stardom is of a confident, ambitious, and highly successful young actor who, many of his peers predicted, would one day surpass them all. The paradox was all the more striking, then, when, at the height of his powers in the summer of 1864, he abruptly abandoned acting to devote all his energies to the conspiracy against Abraham Lincoln.

The twenty-year-old novice actor who arrived in Richmond in 1858 was still politically unsophisticated, though he certainly possessed strong beliefs and prejudices, deep loves and hatreds. He was already, of course, a convinced white supremacist and an advocate of slavery. As a teenager, he flirted briefly with the Know-Nothings in 1854 and 1856; however, he never engaged in any serious political activity or supported any party. Shunning such pursuits was family tradition. The Booths had never been partisan people. As a foreign national Junius Brutus Booth had not been eligible to vote. Moreover, he eschewed politics altogether, arguing that theater people should never vote, support a party, or stoop to political argument. Most of his family followed his lead. By 1864, the stakes had grown so high that Edwin Booth broke down and voted for Lincoln's reelection. We don't know if John Wilkes Booth himself ever cast a ballot.

His earliest known political allegiance had been to the American Party—the "Know-Nothing" Party—whose nativist platform had been erected on the fear that the flood of Irish and German Catholic immigrants threatened to degrade the republican institutions and Anglo-Saxon culture of the United States. The sixteen-year-old supported the Know-Nothings in the elections of November 1854, serving as a steward at an American Party rally near Bel Air. Two years later, during the 1856 presidential election, Asia wrote that "men are all gone deranged over their politics. We have two small flags crossed over the door, Know Nothingism of course." Asia described the "Know-Nothing meetings" as "a so-called 'debating society,' where the question of putting a limit on white labor was contested. This, it was feared, would eventually supersede that of the blacks, and great privileges were falling too easily into the hands of the unnaturalized Irish immigrants."[18] Despite young Booth's trifling allegiance, the party was strongest in the North and was considered by some an antislavery organization.

Though the American Party had virtually disappeared by 1860, nativist doctrines remained an important element in John Wilkes Booth's political thinking. He sounded very much like a Know-Nothing when he declared in 1864 that the supporters of Abraham Lincoln were "false-hearted, unloyal foreigners who would glory in the downfall of the Republic."[19]

Booth's nativism was in keeping with his Southern sympathies. Mass immigration was a Northern phenomenon. The South was a land of native-born Americans, Black and white. Newcomers looking for work flocked largely to the big cities of the North, not to the plantation South, where most labor fell on the ranks of the enslaved. Booth's hatred for the foreign-born would only grow as the war turned against the South. He was enraged that so many of them took their places in the ranks of the Union armies. There were whole Irish and German brigades. Booth believed that if the North would only fight the South "man to man," the white Southerners were sure to win. "If the North conquers us it will be by numbers only, not by native grit, not pluck, and not by devotion."[20]

JOHN BROWN'S BODY

During his days as an apprentice actor in Richmond, John Wilkes Booth had an adventure that impressed him deeply. In December 1859, he took part in the hanging of the abolitionist revolutionary John Brown. Brown had already gained notoriety as a terrorist in the Kansas brawls by hacking apart enslavers with a broadsword.

In October 1859, he led his little band of Black and white freedom fighters on the famous raid on the federal arsenal at Harpers Ferry, Virginia. Overwhelmed, wounded, and captured with his survivors by a squad of US Marines commanded by Colonel Robert E. Lee, Brown was swiftly tried and condemned to hang for murder and for treason against the Commonwealth of Virginia.

His ostensible purpose had been to spark a slave rebellion. He had brought along a cargo of fearsome iron-tipped pikes to arm the rebels. He hoped to seize plenty of muskets at the arsenal. The local Blacks, however, were far too wise to join in such a hairbrained suicide pact. "It was not a slave insurrection," Abraham Lincoln would say four months later in his Cooper Union Address. "It was an attempt by white men to get up a revolt among slaves, in which the slaves refused to participate."[1] But John

Brown did succeed in what may have been his true purpose—to make civil war all but inevitable.

Harpers Ferry electrified America as had no political event since Benedict Arnold's 1780 treason. Despite its utter failure as a military venture, the raid was of immense significance in ratcheting up the escalating sectional crisis. Hysteria prevailed in the North, as well as the South. The contrasting reactions to the raid in the two sections—geography mainly determined whether citizens regarded Brown as bloodthirsty monster or holy martyr—showed that America had become two distinct and antagonistic nations. More alarming to Southerners than the raid itself was the praise lavished by many in the North on John Brown, a man who, as they saw it, had come to slaughter women and children in their beds. Yet some antislavery Northerners now compared him to Moses and Jesus of Nazareth.

In John Brown's "streaming beard," Herman Melville discerned "the meteor of war."[2] The South came so close to leaving the Union after Harpers Ferry that secession was all but inevitable when Abraham Lincoln was elected in November of 1860. Frederick Douglass went so far as to say that Harpers Ferry, not Fort Sumter, was actually the first battle of the Civil War.[3] If so, and if Abraham Lincoln's murder was indeed the war's last battle, then John Wilkes Booth played his part in both the beginning and the end.

The court had ordered Brown's hanging in Charles Town, the county seat, to take place on December 2, 1859. Then, on November 19, a warning supposedly came to Virginia's fire-eating governor, Henry Wise, that an army of eight hundred men, armed with pikes and revolvers, was marching on Charles Town from Ohio and Pennsylvania. They could only be militant abolitionists, determined to free the traitor.

The rumor had no basis in fact. It may even have been promulgated by Governor Wise himself. He lusted after the 1860 Democratic presidential nomination and would have welcomed

the chance to perform some military heroics to boost his candidacy. This was in keeping with the man's character. During the presidential campaign of 1856, Wise had threatened that, should the Republican candidate, John C. Frémont, win the election, Wise would in response occupy the national capital with Virginia militia to forestall the inauguration of an antislavery president.

More warnings of attempts to rescue Brown poured in, Wise claimed. He averred that "information from all quarters came of organized conspiracies to obstruct our laws, to rescue and seize hostages, to commit rapine and burning along our borders on Maryland, Pennsylvania, Ohio, and Indiana, proceeding from these states and from New York, Massachusetts and other states and Canada."[4] It was a full-scale Yankee invasion, with a Canadian contingent thrown in for good measure! Wise said that whatever the source of the rumors, the widespread public sympathy for Brown in the North convinced him of their truth.

"Spitting tobacco and invective" against the "d—d Yankees," the governor sprang into action. Alarm bells rang, telegraph lines vibrated, and members of the militias ran to the armories for their rifles. "Realization that something momentous was happening spread through Richmond and in just a few minutes the entire city would be in pandemonium."[5] Charles Town was miles away, it was true, but the Old Dominion was threatened with invasion, and Richmond was the state's capital. A mob of ten thousand—fully a third of Richmond's population—gathered in the square surrounding Thomas Jefferson's imposing Virginia State Capitol. Many in the crowd were carrying rifles. They were "awash with patriotic indignation and surging with State pride."[6]

Booth and the rest of the Marshall's company were performing *The Filibuster* and *The Toodles*. It was a bad night for ticket sales. People preferred the real excitement in the streets to make-believe on the stage. When Governor Wise's military train, a locomotive hauling nine cars, pulled up at the depot across from the Marshall and came to a stop with a great hiss of escaping steam, the show was over. Audience and players alike ran out of the theater to see what was happening.

What was happening was that Governor Wise and about four hundred members of the Richmond Grays, Richmond's leading militia company, were boarding the train that would take them off to war against the abolitionist hordes. "All expected a fight and were fired up for one."[7] It was as though civil war had actually begun. Many other armed Virginians volunteered their services, eager to join up. None were accepted. Despite all the pleading, Wise was adamant that only enrolled members of the Richmond Grays could join the expedition. With one exception: John Wilkes Booth, somehow outfitted with uniform and musket, climbed aboard with the approval of the governor, at whose side he would march through the streets of Washington, DC, early the next morning. Booth was certainly a favored character in Richmond.

The train chugged north at twelve miles an hour, the maximum nighttime speed, arriving at Acquia Creek landing on the Potomac in the dark of morning. There the Grays boarded a steamer that took them on to the nation's capital by daybreak. They marched two miles down Pennsylvania Avenue, provocatively passing the White House, to the depot, where they caught the special train that took them on to Charles Town.

The Richmond Grays and hundreds of other armed men garrisoned the town for the two weeks before Brown's hanging. Of course, no invading abolitionists appeared, but rampant paranoia prevailed. The men stood watch all night. The *Richmond Enquirer* reported on November 28, 1859: "The Richmond Grays and Company F which seem to vie with each other in the handsome appearance they present, remind one of caged birds, so wild and gleesome they appear. Amongst them I notice Mr. J. Wilkes Booth, a son of Junius Brutus Booth, who, though not a member, as soon as he heard the tap of the drum, threw down the sock and buskin, and shouldered his musket with the Grays to the scene of deadly conflict."

Booth's Southern patriotism was heartily applauded by the people of Virginia. A journalist later wrote that "from his connection with the militia on this occasion he was wont to trace his fealty to Virginia."[8] He "proclaimed himself a champion of the South."[9] At the time of his brief enlistment, Wilkes's family was worried that he might actually throw over his acting career to become a professional soldier. His sister wrote a friend that "John is crazy or enthusiastic about going for a soldier. I think he will get off. It has been his dearest ambition, or perhaps it is his true vocation."[10]

At one point during his two weeks in Charles Town, Booth managed to charm his way into the jail for a personal visit with John Brown himself.[11] No account of their conversation survives, but the young actor apparently found much to admire in the condemned man's heroic character. In 1864, he would rage that Lincoln was "walking in the footprints of old John Brown, but no more fit to stand with that rugged old hero—Great God! no. John Brown was a man inspired, the grandest character of the century!"[12] And though he often declared himself proud of the small part he had played in the battle against abolitionism, Booth never forgot John Brown's courage or the old man's bold gamble at changing history with a single violent act. Five years later, in April 1865, the memory of seeing Brown die a criminal's death on the gallows strengthened the assassin's resolve not to be taken alive by the bluecoat cavalry who had brought him to bay in a Virginia tobacco barn.

On the day of Brown's hanging, commanders arrayed their troops in an open, three-sided square around the gallows. Booth stood to the right. He was seeing Brown in right profile from just fifty feet away. They had driven the condemned man, his arms pinioned, from the jail in a wagon. He sat on the coffin he would soon occupy. He mounted the gallows calmly. On the brink of eternity, Brown bore himself with a courage that awed all the onlookers. When the sheriff finally sprang the trap, Brown's emaciated body fell with a force too slight to break his neck. He strangled painfully on the noose, struggling for several minutes.[13]

Overcome by the spectacle, Booth paled and nearly fainted. He said he'd give anything for a good slug of whiskey. But he would later boast that "I may say I helped to hang John Brown and while I live, I shall think with joy upon the day when I saw the sun go down upon one traitor *less* within our land."[14] Back in Richmond, the actor learned that he'd been fired for deserting the theater company in the middle of a performance. Presently, a menacing crowd of militiamen gathered in front of the Marshall, demanding their friend's reinstatement. Management backed down and rehired him.

John Wilkes Booth's first starring tour took him to Georgia and Alabama at the time of Abraham Lincoln's November 1860 election. There he must have breathed the fiery atmosphere of the secession winter in the lower South. But in Booth, the fire-eaters were preaching to the converted. He already believed, as he was to write six months before he killed Lincoln, "that the abolitionists, *were the only traitors* in the land."[15]

While spending the 1860 Christmas holidays with his family in Philadelphia, Booth wrote a passionate twenty-page speech in which he blamed all of the country's troubles on the abolitionists. Edwin Booth found the manuscript of this speech many years later. He chose to preserve it rather than consign it to the flames that consumed much of the assassin's writings.[16]

One can only guess at Edwin Booth's motives for saving his brother's speech. In 1881, Edwin, who was always most reluctant to speak of Wilkes, wrote that the Booth family regarded him

> as a good-hearted, harmless, though wild-brained boy, and
> [we] used to laugh at his patriotic froth whenever secession

was discussed. That he was insane on that one point, no one who knew him can well doubt. When I told him I had voted for Lincoln's re-election he expressed deep regret, and declared his belief that Lincoln would be made king of America; and this, I believe, drove him beyond the limits of reason. All his theatrical friends speak of him as a poor, crazy boy, and such his family think of him.[17]

By revealing the almost hysterical fervency of John Wilkes Booth's passion for the South and that passion's wild, often disordered, expression in the speech, Edwin Booth may have hoped that someday the people would be able to see his brother as one misguided, unlucky, or insane, rather than as a figure of unalloyed evil.

Booth wrote the speech while staying with his mother and sister Rose in a Philadelphia boardinghouse. Edwin and Asia both lived nearby. He had just made the all-important advance from a stock player to star, but his first star tour had been marred by an accident. His agent, Matthew Canning, had arranged for Booth to appear in Columbus, Georgia, and Montgomery, Alabama, supported by Canning's New York stock company. Booth would star in roles that included the titular heroes in *Romeo and Juliet*, *Hamlet*, and *Richard III*. But on October 16, 1860, in the dressing room of the Columbus Theatre, Canning and Booth were horsing around with a revolver. The gun went off, seriously wounding the star.

The point at which the projectile transected Booth's body has been variously described as "in the side," "in the fleshy part of the leg," "in the thigh," and "in the rear." Wherever it struck, the bullet inflicted an injury severe enough to prevent Booth's playing most of the roles scheduled for the rest of the tour. He wouldn't fully recover for more than three months. The bullet was never cut out of him. Five years later, when the whole North was seeking Abraham Lincoln's fugitive killer, Canning tried to help with identification by telling the authorities that the 1860 wound "left a large scar on his person, not to be mistaken."[18]

After the shooting, the actor spent more than a week recuperating in his hotel in Columbus. Then he continued on to rejoin the company in Montgomery, Alabama, on October 23. Booth remained laid up in Montgomery for more than a month, all through the intense excitement over the 1860 presidential election. In Alabama, the actor was caught up in the secession furor. He may have read this editorial opinion of the *Montgomery Daily Mail* of October 25, 1860: "If the South could be stupid enough to submit to such an administration as Lincoln's, for one moment, it ought to be plundered and mulattoized, both—made no better than the North! But the white people of the South are very different from those of Massachusetts, and we think they will resist free Negro rule at all hazards." The neologism *mulattoized* shows that the enslavers' obsession with so-called race mixing persisted, even though they themselves were by far the most prolific progenitors of biracial children in America.

Montgomery was the home of former congressman William L. Yancey, the silver-tongued fire-eater known as "the Orator of Secession." (In its sketch of Yancey's career, written in the 1930s, the *Dictionary of American Biography* ventured that "without him there would have been no Confederate States of America.") Yancey's fiery call for secession to a Montgomery audience on November 5, the day before Lincoln's election, enraptured the young man. Booth would echo Yancey's views in his own 1860 speech.

THE "CORNER-STONE"

John Wilkes Booth wrote his twenty-page speech of December
1860 in a gathering of leaves stitched together into a thin book-
let, a form in which stationers sold writing paper then. The main
body of the speech is followed by several pages of roughed-out
material to be inserted into the running text and some fragments
that Booth must have meant to work into additional text. At
more than five thousand words, the manuscript is by far the longest document he ever wrote. It is also the earliest, the most dramatic, and one of the most revealing of the handful of political
testaments that the assassin left behind.

The manuscript is clearly a rough draft, ending abruptly in
midsentence. Behind the soaring wildness of its words is the lofty
presumption of a man who seems to have believed in 1860, as he
would believe in 1865, that he, acting alone, could change history.
But the views he expressed were shared by almost all of the white
population of the slave states, where so many were then raging,
like Booth, for "eaqual rights and justice for the South."

There were also many in the North who, though they opposed
secession, believed that the crisis had been brought by Northern

antislavery forces. First among those so convinced was the out-going president, Pennsylvania Democrat James Buchanan, who would remain in the White House until Lincoln was sworn in on March 4, 1861.

President Buchanan's last major state paper, his December 3, 1860, Annual Message to Congress—what we now call the State of the Union Address—could have served as an outline for portions of Booth's speech.[1] Buchanan declared that antislavery agitation had driven the South to secession. Secession was unconstitutional, Buchanan conceded, but the unbridled extremism of abolitionists had pushed the enslavers over the brink. And to coerce the seceded states back into the Union, concluded the fifteenth president, was itself unconstitutional.

The actor dramatically structured his address with a chorus of questions followed by responses from his imaginary audience. "Gentlemen," he boldly began, "Alow me a few words! You every-where permit freedom of speech. You must not deny me now."[2] Booth would have had little trouble imagining himself addressing a crowd. He had, after all, appeared before a good many large audiences over the past three years. The audience he imagined addressing had been suggested to him by the "Grand Union meeting" held in Philadelphia on December 13, 1860, a few days before Booth drafted his speech. The speech also shows the influence of the plays of Shakespeare. The words are sometimes ordered in Elizabethan cadences and are driven by the furious, ranting delivery typical of the mid-nineteenth-century American theater.

Although self-conscious about his limitations as a writer (he often appended to his letters the apology "excuse this hasty scrawl"), Booth was sometimes willing to try for powerful, even poetic, language. There are such attempts in his 1860 speech. The speech has been described as Booth's plea for the preservation of the Union, but it is in actuality a call for counterrevolution:

he was demanding the restoration of the traditional supremacy of the white Southern enslavers' power in the American government that had prevailed until the 1850s.

Southern slaveholders, some prominent abolitionists, and certain present-day historians have maintained that the Constitution of 1787 was a proslavery document. Antislavery leaders such as Frederick Douglass and Abraham Lincoln, as well as certain other contemporary historians, have argued that the Constitution was actually antislavery in its implications. Whichever the case may be, there can be no doubt that the federal government had long been dominated by enslavers and that its conduct had been decidedly proslavery throughout the nation's history.

That stance began to change with the rise of the new Republican Party in the mid-1850s, and it was this change that so angered the enslavers and those who thought like them, including John Wilkes Booth. They wanted a return to the old state of affairs, where the protection of slavery had guided American domestic politics and foreign policy.

Philadelphia, like the rest of the nation, was in turmoil over the extraordinary constitutional crisis provoked by Abraham Lincoln's election and the looming secession of the lower South slave states. Pennsylvania bordered two upper South slave states, Maryland and Delaware. Many Pennsylvanians regarded their state as a sort of bridge between the country's two antagonistic sections. Philadelphia was also a mercantile city with long-standing economic ties to the South. Although Lincoln had carried both the city and the state in the presidential election the month before, there remained considerable sympathy for the South among white Philadelphians.

Most white Philadelphians despised the abolitionists, whose ideology threatened to destroy trade, as well as national unity. By the end of 1860, Philadelphia merchants were already losing Southern customers. They feared worse to come. When an antislavery leader proposed making a speech in Philadelphia, the threat of riots canceled his appearance. Instead, Philadelphia mayor Alexander Henry called for a "Grand Union demonstration" on December 13 in Independence Square outside Independence Hall, the venerable building that had been the scene of the signing of the Declaration of Independence and the drafting of the Constitution. Now the Great Republic framed by those documents was breaking apart.[3]

Outraged by Lincoln's election, the first state to go, South Carolina, declared its independence on December 20, a week after the Philadelphia rally. Since Booth refers to the "cesession of South Carolina," we know his speech was written shortly after December 20.[4] Six other Deep South states would quickly follow. Hoping to forestall such an outcome, the organizers of the December 13 Philadelphia rally had called the mass meeting to address the "serious peril of the dissolution of the union of these states."

Businesses and stores would close for two hours. Delegations of factory workers would march. As many as forty thousand people showed up. Booth must have been among them. He would have heard the speakers condemning Northern antislavery extremists for driving the Southern states out of the Union. A banner reading "Concession before Secession" summed up the aim of the rally and the tone of the speeches. "Many good citizens still believed that Philadelphia's duty was that of an arbitrator between the extremists of both North and South," one writer explained.[5]

The rally's speakers, though, seemed to believe that it was mostly the South that had been wronged. They pushed through a series of resolutions that amounted to a repudiation of the Republican Party platform on which Abraham Lincoln had just been elected. These called for strict enforcement of the Fugitive Slave law, the opening of federal territories to slavery, and an end to "all denunciations of slavery" as "inconsistent with the spirit of brotherhood and kindness."[6] The resolutions were forwarded to South Carolina, but the citizens of that state, by then mad for secession, took no notice.

Some of those attending the rally were disgusted by the pro-Southern tone of the speeches. Some must also have been puzzled to hear that the approbation of slavery was in keeping "with the spirit of brotherhood and kindness." John Wilkes Booth, however, would have been well pleased. It must have appeared to him that most white Philadelphians agreed with him in blaming the secession crisis on the abolitionists.

When he wrote his own speech a few days later, Booth used many of the ideas and some of the language of the speakers on the platform that day. It is easy to imagine that the twenty-two-year-old actor was inspired by the notion of himself addressing a mass rally like the December 13 meeting. It was a time in which oratory was much admired. Young men studied the master speeches of American statesmen like Webster, Clay, and Calhoun. Booth's sister remembered that "the oratorical powers of the cadets at St. Timothy's [the boarding school Booth had attended] were, without doubt, encouraged and cultivated; stump-speaking was the delight of those youths who longed to make their voices heard throughout the country. It was almost a bad school for fostering the wild ambition born in Wilkes Booth."[7]

Booth also had personal knowledge of two of the most divisive episodes of the decade of growing sectional conflict that preceded the Civil War—the fugitive slave "riot" in Christiana, Pennsylvania, in 1851, and John Brown's raid on Harpers Ferry in 1859. Both these violent events had sharpened Booth's indignation over the injustices he believed the North was visiting on the South. He referred to both events in his speech.

The Christiana riot flared when a band of abolitionists and escaped slaves defied the federal Fugitive Slave Act of 1850 by violently resisting a US marshal and a posse of slave-catchers. The posse had pursued four Maryland fugitives into Pennsylvania. Confronting them, Maryland farmer Edward Gorsuch, owner of the four, vowed that "my property is here, and I will have it or perish in the attempt."[8]

Perish he did, for the armed and defiant Black men he confronted insisted that human beings could not be property. They were prepared to defend that proposition with their lives. Presently Edward Gorsuch lay dead—shot, stabbed, and bludgeoned. When the men who did the killing were brought to trial for treason by federal authorities and then acquitted by a local Pennsylvania jury, the South was outraged.

Edward Gorsuch's youngest son, Thomas, was a schoolmate and friend of John Wilkes Booth. Young Booth must have heard his friend tell how a gang of Black abolitionists had murdered his father, only to be set free by a Yankee jury. To Booth, the acquittal of the guilty was an injustice that called out for revenge. Throughout his speech, Booth called again and again for "justice for the South." Among other things, justice meant the strict enforcement in the North of the Fugitive Slave law and the speedy return of fugitives to their Southern masters.

As we have seen, Booth's involvement with John Brown's raid was more personal still. In his speech, Booth fiercely insisted that all abolitionists were traitors like John Brown and that if they did not cease their agitation against slavery, they all deserved Brown's fate.

He argued that abolitionists were perverting the Bill of Right's guarantee of free speech to broadcast lies that were tearing America apart:

Then what are they who preach the Abolition doctrine who have in doing so nigh destroyed our country. I call them traitors. . . . So deep is my hatred for such men that I could wish I had them in my grasp And I the power to crush. I'd grind them into dust! . . . Now that we have found the serpent that madens us, we should crush it in its birth. . . . You all feel the fire now raging in the nations heart. It is a fire lighted and faned by Northern fanaticism. . . . I tell you the Abolition doctrine is the fire which if alowed to rage—will consume the house and crush us all beneath its ruins.[9]

Nowhere in his five-thousand-word speech did Booth so much as mention Abraham Lincoln, the one figure whose election had provoked the crisis that was tearing the Union apart. Apparently, the actor had yet to come to regard Lincoln as either a leading abolitionist or an important enemy of white supremacy. This was soon to change. Lincoln presently became in Booth's eyes the very personification of Black Republican wickedness, of an unjust aggressive war against the South, as the champion of negro equality and the perfidious enemy of white America. During the final months of the Civil War, many observers commented on the astonishing ferocity and vividly personal nature of the actor's hatred for Lincoln. He was a "monomaniac" on the subject, his brother said, unable to stop talking about his enemy's crimes.

Booth's sister Asia had noticed early on her brother's habit of personifying issues, making certain problems into personal enemies or friends. He began doing this with his schoolwork. "He had a singular way of surmounting a difficulty," Asia wrote. "This was by individualizing his task or his work. He would imagine a column of spelling so many foes in a line, and attacked them with a vigor he declared nothing else could inspire." Wilkes admired John Bunyan's allegory *Pilgrim's Progress*, maintaining that "Bunyan understood exactly how small minds would grasp the abstract ideas when portrayed as men and women."[10] Of course, Abraham Lincoln was a living person, not an abstract idea, but in a parallel transformation Booth made his nemesis the personification of everything he hated about the Union and its war policies. By April 1865, the young man was hysterical with rage and longing for revenge.

Despite all his frantic scribbling, Booth probably never had a chance to deliver his 1860 speech. Presently the nation's attention was consumed by the secession of one cotton state after another—Mississippi, Florida, Alabama, Georgia, and Louisiana—all in January 1861—followed by Texas on February 1. The time for concessions had passed.

The seceded states sent delegates to Montgomery, Alabama. With remarkable rapidity, those men drafted a constitution and elected a provisional president, Jefferson Davis of Mississippi. Though their actions were illegal and unconstitutional, the delegates claimed to have founded a new nation that they styled "the Confederate States of America." All this before the legitimate president-elect had even arrived in the nation's capital.

The enslavers' new constitution was for the most part a direct copy of the US Constitution. They did see fit to insert into their otherwise identical preamble the phrase "invoking the favor and guidance of Almighty God."[11] For unlike the deist founders of 1787, the slaveholding patriarchs of 1861 were pious men. Theirs was a religious charter of government.

The Confederate Constitution did differ from the original document in two important respects: its approach to state sovereignty and its treatment of the institution of slavery. The US Constitution of 1787 had replaced the inadequate Articles of Confederation. Unlike the US Constitution, the Articles of Confederation did not create a supreme national government. Rather, it framed a loose coalition of independent states that had agreed to cooperate in a limited range of governmental functions. It remained only "a firm league of friendship" in which "each state retains its sovereignty, freedom and independence."[12] The opening paragraph of the Articles of Confederation named the states themselves as the framers of this charter of government, listing them in geographical order from north to south: "New-Hampshire, Massachusetts-Bay, Rhode-Island and Providence Plantations, Connecticut, New-York, New-Jersey, Pennsylvania,

Delaware, Maryland, Virginia, North-Carolina, South-Carolina and Georgia." There was no mention of any such authority as "we the people."

At the Constitutional Convention in 1787, the first draft of the Constitution, known as "The Report of the Committee of Detail," followed the Articles, again naming as the sovereign creators of the charter all the American states listed in geographical order from north to south. By the end of that summer, however, the delegates, united in a new vision of nationhood, made an important change. In its first sentence, the Constitution now took its authority not from the states but from "We the People of the United States." It was an avowal of a supreme national identity that transcended the states. Unlike the Articles of Confederation that it replaced, nowhere does the Constitution recognize the "sovereignty, freedom and independence" of the states.

In regard to state sovereignty, the slaveholders' new constitution followed the Articles of Confederation, not the US Constitution, stating that in coming together to form their new confederacy "each State [was] acting in its sovereign and independent character."[13]

Of course, the peculiar institution of African slavery required a few other changes and additions to the document. Written into the law of the land was the stipulation that the central government could never tamper with slavery in any way. Moreover, "no bill of attainder, ex post facto law, or law denying or impairing the right to property in negro slaves shall be passed" (art. 1, sec. 9.4). Should their new confederacy acquire additional territory, "the institution of negro slavery, as it now exists in the Confederate States, shall be recognized and protected . . . and the inhabitants . . . shall have the right to take to such territory any slaves lawfully held by them" (art. 4, sec. 3.3). (The words *slave* and *slavery*, of course, appear nowhere in the Constitution of 1787, their place being taken by such circumlocutions as "persons held to service or labor." Antislavery leaders like Abraham Lincoln regarded this significant omission as evidence that the framers had hoped and expected that slavery would gradually disappear from the United States.)

The new Southern government was, in fact, founded on slavery, and slavery was founded on white supremacy. Alexander Stephens of Georgia, the first and only vice president of the rebellion that called itself a nation, laid out the underlying principle that the enslavers had made their political foundation in his famous "corner-stone speech." He delivered it in Savannah, Georgia, on March 21, 1861, about two weeks after Lincoln's inauguration.

Stephens began by lamenting the failings of the republic's founding generation, those eighteenth-century statesmen whose sad infatuation with natural rights and human equality had introduced such errors into the Declaration of Independence and the Constitution. The founders of 1861 had put aside childish things. They had "discarded the pestilent heresy of fancy politicians, that all men, of all races, were equal, and we have made African *inequality* and subordination, and the *equality* of white men, the chief cornerstone of the Southern Republic."[14] The secessionists had forthrightly repudiated the founding fathers' antique and fallacious proposition that all people are created equal.

"The prevailing ideas entertained by [Thomas Jefferson] and most of the leading statesmen at the time of the formation of the old constitution," Stephens told his audience, "were that the enslavement of the African was in violation of the laws of nature; that it was wrong in *principle*, socially, morally, and politically. . . . Those ideas, however, were fundamentally wrong. They rested on the idea of the equality of races. This was an error. . . . Our new government," he continued, "is founded upon exactly the opposite idea; its foundations are laid, its corner-stone rests, upon the great truth that the negro is not equal to the white man; that slavery, subordination to the superior race is his natural and nor-

Alexander Stephens of Georgia, vice president of the insurgency.
In his notorious "corner-stone" speech, Stephens affirmed what he called
the "great physical, philosophical, and moral truth" that "the negro is
not equal to the white man; that slavery, subordination to the
superior race is his natural and normal condition."

mal condition. This, our new government, is the first, in the history of the world, based upon this great physical, philosophical, and moral truth."[15]

Given the core values of this "our new government," it is hardly surprising that white nationalists and reactionaries everywhere have always regarded the Southern enslavers' defeat as a matter of profound regret. Indeed, Adolf Hitler himself exclaimed: "If only Britain had supported the Southern States in the American Civil War! And what a tragedy that God allowed Germans to put Lincoln firmly in the saddle!"[16] Der Führer assumed that British support would have ensured Southern independence and the preservation of slavery, as well it might have. By "Germans," he probably meant the German American voters and soldiers who supported the Union.

When white nationalists gather on American streets today, wearing body armor and bearing black rifles, above their helmeted heads fly the two flags they revere as emblems of brave experiments at building an ideal white supremacist nation state. The first is the red, white, and black Nazi swastika flag. The second is the Confederate battle flag.

THE RISE OF ABRAHAM LINCOLN

By 1849, the political career of the Honorable Abraham Lincoln, Esq., of Springfield, Illinois, had hit a dead end. His high ambitions had been thwarted. The forty-year-old had served a single, undistinguished term in the US House of Representatives and, before that, four two-year terms in the Illinois legislature. He had no way of winning another term in Congress, and he had no desire to go back to the Illinois House.

He remained fiercely loyal to his Whig Party, but the Whigs, never dominant, had become a moribund minority party in Illinois and throughout the nation, further limiting Lincoln's options. Soon the Whigs would dissolve altogether, pulled apart when the Kansas-Nebraska Act intensified the slavery controversy in 1854. "The Democracy," the venerable Democratic Party of Thomas Jefferson and Andrew Jackson, had long dominated state and national politics. Before long, however, sectional conflict would split the Democracy into Northern and Southern parties.

Above all else, Lincoln had always dreamed of serving in the US Senate. His idol, Henry Clay of Kentucky, Lincoln's "beau ideal of a statesman," had been one of the titans of the Senate

Chamber for more than a generation. But no Whig could hope to win a Senate race in Illinois. So after his two years in Congress ended in 1849, Lincoln had no choice but to turn his back on politics and devote himself to his increasingly successful law practice. Before long, he was making as much as $5,000 a year, the same handsome salary enjoyed by the famous tragedian, Junius Brutus Booth.[1] Lincoln was also a highly respected and popular figure in his hometown of Springfield.

But he was deeply dissatisfied. Often, he was sunk in abysmal depression, so despondent that he could not speak. He had always been supremely ambitious for political success. His law partner, William Herndon, would famously call Lincoln's ambition "a little engine that knew no rest."[2] Lincoln's was not an egotistical ambition for high office merely for the sake of exalted standing. As he put it in 1858: "I have never professed an indifference to the honors of official station; and were I to do so now, I should only make myself ridiculous. Yet I have never failed—do not now fail—to remember that in the republican cause there is a higher aim than that of mere office."[3]

Lincoln's higher aim was to win an honored reputation as a benefactor of his country. Like the founding fathers themselves— like Washington and Adams and Hamilton before him—Lincoln longed to win lasting fame as a leader who had worked to better the lives of others. That was the "spur of fame" that drove him, just as it had once driven the founders. As he had said when seeking his first elective office, "I have no other [ambition] so great as that of being truly esteemed of my fellow men, by rendering myself worthy of their esteem."[4] Was that chance now out of reach? "How hard, oh how hard," he lamented, "it is to die and leave one's Country no better than if one had never lived for it."[5]

Since starting out in New Salem as a young man, Lincoln had remained a skeptic in matters of faith—actually an atheist, some of his friends thought. (He would change his mind when the great war raged.) Though he could take no comfort in notions of life everlasting, there was a kind of personal survival beyond death that Lincoln did believe in. What he yearned for has been described by historian Robert V. Bruce as "immortality through remembrance, eternal consciousness by proxy in the mind of posterity."[6] Lincoln had sometimes spoken of this notion of immortality by proxy—the chance to live on in the collective memory of the species. Putting it as a question, Bruce asked: "if Lincoln found the total annihilation of the self an intolerable prospect, and if he could not achieve abiding faith in a literal afterlife, what alternative might he have taken refuge in?"[7] The answer was that persistence in the historical record was the best alternative. Lincoln longed to win as much of immortality as fame can ever give.

The darkest depression of Lincoln's life descended on him in January 1841 after he broke off his engagement to Mary Todd. His friends feared he might kill himself. In this moment of his greatest despair, the reflection that tormented Lincoln the most was knowing that if he died, he'd be forgotten. He'd achieved nothing in the political realm worthy of remembrance. He grieved "that he had done nothing to make any human being remember that he had lived—and that to connect his name with the events transpiring in his day & generation and so impress himself upon them so as to link his name with something that would redound to the interest of his fellow man was what he desired to live for."[8] Lincoln would eventually decide that the one achievement that would "redound" most nobly "to the interest of his fellow man" was the emancipation of the enslaved people of America.

In 1854, the Kansas-Nebraska Act upset the political equilibrium that had prevailed since the Compromise of 1850. Senator Stephen A. Douglas, an old Illinois rival of Lincoln's, was Nebraska's parent. He had introduced and pushed through Congress the precedent-shattering legislation. Slavery had been banned from most of the western US territories since the Missouri Compromise of 1820. The Nebraska Act overturned that ban by opening a vast new region of the West to the spread of slavery. Southern enslavers were elated by the prospect. Much of the North was outraged. Antislavery leaders called the Nebraska Act an "atrocious plot" to turn the West into a "dreary region of despotism, inhabited by masters and slaves."[9]

Douglas, once Lincoln's political peer in Illinois, was now a national figure—one of America's foremost statesmen, both the most powerful figure in the US Senate and a leading Democratic candidate for president. The thwarted Lincoln agonized over the contrast between the two Illinoisans' trajectories, unable to conceal his envy. "Twenty-two years ago," he reflected in a private memorandum, "Judge Douglas and I first became acquainted. We were both young then; he a trifle younger than I. Even then, we were both ambitious; I, perhaps, quite as much so as he. With *me*, the race of ambition has been a failure—flat failure; with *him* it has been one of splendid success. His name fills the nation; and is not unknown, even, in foreign lands."[10] (The rivalry was all the more personal since Douglas had once been an avid suitor pursuing Miss Mary Todd, the woman Lincoln married.)

What Lincoln couldn't know was that the turmoil Douglas's Kansas-Nebraska Act unleashed by overturning the old two-party system would propel Lincoln back into the political arena and open up an unexpected path that would carry him all the way to the White House.

Abraham Lincoln revered the founders of the American republic. The creation of the United States, however, had left a contradictory legacy of freedom and slavery. In 1776, the year the revolutionaries declared their independence and named equality their guiding principle, about a sixth of the population of the thirteen colonies was enslaved. Captive Africans had already been laboring in America for more than a century by then. The founders themselves deplored the paradox that had made the United States—a nation dedicated to the proposition that all people were created equal—also home to a system of chattel slavery, based on race, that condemned millions to lives of harsh captivity. The statesmen who drafted the Constitution and conducted the new government through its infancy could comfort themselves with the hope that their descendants would somehow achieve a gradual, peaceful emancipation. Instead, as the United States grew, slavery spread and flourished. The peculiar institution became the acknowledged "cornerstone" of Southern society. No longer did white Southerners lament slavery as a "necessary evil." They began to celebrate it as a "positive good."

By the outbreak of the Civil War, this violent enslavement of four million people was the foundation on which the entire American economy rested, as it had for decades. The monetary value of the enslaved, then about $3 to $4 billion, surpassed the value of all the factories and railroads in the United States. And it must be remembered that this was $4 billion at a time when an ounce of gold went for nineteen dollars, not today's $1,900. Economic historians have placed the equivalent figure in 2016 dollars at something like 13 *trillion*.[11] Equity in "slave property" represented at least half of the total wealth of the South. The cotton fields of the Deep South had created more millionaires than all the factories of New England. The annual cotton crop, produced entirely by enslaved people, was by far the nation's most valuable export. More money came into the United States in exchange for Southern cotton than from any other source.

Although only about a quarter of the white Southern population owned slaves, those who did not were fully committed to the defense of slavery as a means of boosting their own status by creating a race-based underclass and preserving the white supremacy to which they were so devoted. Many of them also hoped to become slaveholders themselves someday. More important than the labor system itself was the conviction that slavery served to maintain white supremacy—what one Alabama secessionist in 1860 called "the heaven-ordained superiority of the white over the black race."[12] Southern white men who owned no slaves would soon prove themselves just as ready as the enslavers to die in battle for their race. An aged veteran from Georgia, interviewed in the twentieth century, recalled in the present tense his motivation for dying for slavery: "I'd rather git killed than have these niggers freed and claiming they's as good as I is."[13]

At the same time, American white supremacists were no more monolithic than were the various antislavery factions. Some wanted to preserve the status quo. Some wanted to reopen the African slave trade so more white men could become enslavers. Some wanted to deport all Blacks. Some would be satisfied if the African Americans could merely be confined to the existing slave states so that the North and the western territories would remain "white man's country." Some thought the Dred Scott decision meant that slavery was actually legal in all the states, North as well as South. Certain theorists even advocated expanding the peculiar institution to enslave poor white people along with Blacks. They'd be better off under the South's kind and paternalistic system of bondage than to continue to suffer misery as downtrodden, poorly paid, slum-dwelling factory workers in the North.[14]

The prominent South Carolina theorist of slavery and Southern nationalism James Henry Hammond was successively elected congressman, governor, and senator by his state. Famous as the author of the "Cotton Is King" thesis of Southern invincibility and notorious as the uncle who had raped his four teenage nieces, Hammond had defiantly proclaimed on the floor of the House of Representatives in 1836:

> Slavery is said to be an evil. . . . But [it] is no evil. On the contrary, I believe it to be the greatest of all the great blessings which a kind Providence has bestowed upon our glorious region. . . . As a class, I say it boldly; there is not a happier, more contented race upon the face of the earth. . . . Lightly tasked, well clothed, well fed—far better than the free laborers of any country in the world . . . their lives and persons protected by

the law, all their sufferings alleviated by the kindest and most interested care . . . I do firmly believe that domestic slavery regulated as ours is produces the highest toned, the purest, best organization of society that has ever existed on the face of the earth.[15]

One wonders if Hammond even knew that nearly every word in that passage was a damnable lie?

After touring industrial regions in Europe and New England, Hammond concluded that free laborers were no more than "*scantily* compensated slaves" who possessed the "liberty only to starve." Their condition compared most unfavorably to the contented bondspeople of the South, he claimed, whose benevolent enslavers treated them with the same kind of care and affection they lavished on their own children.[16] These obscene lies would not have convinced anyone familiar with the descriptions of horrific torture and widespread abuse of enslaved people that abolitionists had documented and published.

In any event, it was abundantly clear that white Southerners would never give up their economic system and their way of life without a fight. Another obstacle to emancipation was the whole issue of "racial adjustment," the question of the future status of the formerly enslaved people if freedom came. What place would they hold in America's transformed society? It was unthinkable to most whites that Blacks would become equal citizens.

So central, so entrenched, and so strongly defended did slavery ultimately prove that its destruction required a second and more sweeping American Revolution—a vast civil war of unprecedented scale and catastrophic violence that killed 750,000 Americans from a population of a little over thirty million while also destroying the Old South forever.[17] (An equivalent "butcher's bill" in the early twenty-first-century United States would be seven to eight million dead.)

It seems that nothing less sweeping than the great war of the

1860s could have sufficed. A program of compensated emancipation by the federal government, like the one Great Britain imposed on Caribbean enslavers in 1833, would have been angrily rejected by white Southerners. Abraham Lincoln had nevertheless advocated emancipation with compensation for his entire political career. He was still arguing for it in February 1865, two months before his death.

As much as Lincoln detested the immorality of slavery, he was no abolitionist. The abolitionists, who had begun their campaign in the 1830s, demanded the immediate and unconditional end of slavery. They also called for racial equality in an intensely racist nation. A small minority, abolitionists were almost universally despised, in the North as well as the South. Nearly everyone hated them as fanatics out to overturn white supremacy and break up the Union. Historian William W. Freehling calculated that in 1840, support for abolition "peaked at around 2 percent of the northern voting population. The other 98 percent of northern citizens considered immediate abolition as too extreme to be American, too problack to be tolerable, too keen on seizing property to be capitalistic, and too antisouthern to be safe for the Union. Antiabolitionists preferred saving the Union, saving white supremacy, [and] saving property values."[18]

And this, of course, was in the North. No one could speak in favor of abolition in the South without exposing himself to immediate risk of violent death. Even in the North, club-wielding ruffians broke up abolitionist meetings. Their speakers were shouted down and pelted with debris. Mobs dumped their printing presses into rivers. Their leaders were lynched or assassinated. Postmasters were forbidden to deliver abolitionist literature and even Northern newspapers in the slave states.

Abraham Lincoln said slavery was wrong, but at the same time, he bluntly called abolitionism a greater danger to the survival of the republic than slavery itself. He also stuck to the "federal consensus" that all understood that the Constitution gave the federal government no power whatsoever over slavery in the states where it existed. Lincoln first gained national prominence as a determined opponent of the spread of slavery into the US territories in the West. Never did he so much as hint, however, that the government should move against slavery in the South or that the institution should be immediately ended. "If all earthly power were given me," he said, he still wouldn't know how to solve the ugly riddle of American slavery.[19]

Lincoln's personal journey toward emancipation can stand as a kind of recapitulation of the progress of the nation as a whole toward freedom and equality. Lincoln himself embodied the paradox of the slaveholding republic; he lived the American dilemma. He believed that slavery was wicked, backward, and an offense to the nation's republican ideals. At the same time, he saw no peaceful way to alter such a monumental and seemingly permanent feature of the American political landscape. He knew slavery was evil, but he believed that a direct attack on the institution could result in an even greater evil: the breakup of the Union and the destruction of the only significant democratic nation in the world—the nation that he believed was "the last, best hope of earth."

He said he hated slavery "as much as any abolitionist." Yet before the war, he could never bring himself to embrace the abolitionists' uncompromising demand for an immediate end to the centuries-old evil. Abolitionists also insisted that the freed people be taken into the American body politic as equal citizens, a position Lincoln was only beginning to approach at the end of his life. In the eyes of radical opponents of slavery, Lincoln in the mid-1850s was no more than a moderate who gave lip service to the cause.

Lincoln also continued to cling to the retrograde strategy of colonization. Colonization was a way of getting rid of slavery by getting rid of Black people. They would all be shipped to an overseas colony in Africa or the Caribbean. Lincoln's hero, Henry

Clay, had been a major backer of the preposterous notion that four and a half million African Americans (about four million slaves and a half million free Blacks by 1860) could be persuaded to leave their native land and, more preposterous still, that a means of transporting them all overseas actually existed. (At the time, the African American population of the United States was growing at a rate of some fifty thousand souls a year.)

Lincoln would continue to promote colonization right up until the moment he issued the Emancipation Proclamation. Scholars have long argued whether his advocacy of colonization represented a policy he actually believed in or was rather a political tactic to persuade white Americans to accept emancipation by assuring them that it would not result in a large population of free Blacks living in their midst.[20]

THE TRIUMPH OF
THE "BLACK" REPUBLICANS

So, like the founders, like the very slaveholding constitutional republic that he believed could by its example promote the future happiness of all people everywhere, Abraham Lincoln accepted the continuation of the inhuman tyranny of chattel slavery. He could only hope that, confined to the South, it would eventually die away. He had even reconciled himself to the possibility that the end might not come before the mid-twentieth century. In the Lincoln-Douglas debates in 1858, he declared that he would be satisfied just to know that slavery was "on a course to ultimate extinction," even if that process took one hundred years to complete.[1] (One hundred years from 1858 is 1958, yielding a bizarre hallucination of an Eisenhower administration in which the US dollar could buy human beings, as well as Cadillacs with forty-eight-inch tailfins.)

Then suddenly the Kansas-Nebraska Act changed everything, dispelling all Lincoln's comforting dreams of peaceful gradualism. "Aroused as he had never been before," he threw himself back onto the political battleground.[2] In this fight to contain slavery, historian Eric Foner has written, "Lincoln had finally found a subject worthy of his intellectual talent and political ambition."[3]

Kansas-Nebraska left Lincoln "thunderstruck and stunned."[4] This great betrayal transformed his life and his political philosophy.

Before 1854, slavery had occupied a relatively small place in Abraham Lincoln's political thinking. It was true that he had always described himself as antislavery. He had made gestures against slavery in the Illinois legislature and in the House of Representatives. But as a politician he had been much more dedicated to promoting such Whig Party concerns as individual opportunity, economic development, social progress, and Henry Clay's "American System." That was the Whig program of tariffs on imports to foster American industry and the creation of internal improvements—roads, canals, railroads, ports, and other public works—undertaken by an energetic federal government to grow the economy. (The Democrats adamantly opposed such innovations. They opposed any augmentation of the powers of the federal government, to assure that the government could never undertake emancipation.)

After Nebraska, however, Lincoln became a single-issue politician. That issue was stopping the spread of slavery into the West. In the years between 1854 and the outbreak of the war, Lincoln gave roughly 175 speeches. The central message of almost all of them was that slavery must be excluded from the territories as a way eventually to bring about its "ultimate extinction" throughout the nation.[5] These addresses were new in tone as well as substance. They were framed in striking eloquence and distinguished by a kind of moral grandeur as he affirmed the world-altering promise of the American experiment and the humanity of the enslaved people. He began to exhibit for the first time in his anti-Nebraska speeches the lofty eloquence for which he would be celebrated. He was becoming a leader that other opponents of slavery admired and that white supremacists everywhere hated. It would be interesting to know when Abraham Lincoln first caught the attention of John Wilkes Booth.

Congress passed the Kansas-Nebraska Act in 1854, after

months of acrimonious debate. Northern Whigs voted against the act. Southern Whigs voted for it. The Whig Party was thereby dismantled, and former Whigs went looking for a new political home. Southern Democrats all supported the Nebraska bill. Northern Democrats split over it. Many of them, rejecting party orthodoxy, voted against the legislation, spawning a whole new faction known as anti-Nebraska or independent Democrats.

Despite their former antipathy, an alliance of anti-Nebraska Democrats and disaffected Whigs now seemed a logical next step. Over the next year, with additions from various minority parties, this fusion of former opponents, now united by their shared determination to arrest the spread of slavery, resulted in the creation of the new Republican Party. Lincoln moved slowly, joining the Republicans in 1855 only after months of cautious consideration.

In the presidential contest of 1856, the first Republican contender ever fielded, John C. Frémont, did remarkably well for the candidate of a brand-new third party, carrying the upper North, but Democrat James Buchanan, who had won only 45 percent of the popular vote, carried the South and beat Frémont in the Electoral College. Though he hailed from Pennsylvania, Buchanan, elected by Southern votes and controlled by Southerners in his cabinet, would govern as the most proslavery president in history. Buchanan and the Democrats campaigned as the party of white supremacy: "The White Man's Party." During the 1856 campaign, Indiana Democrats at a Buchanan rally paraded a troupe of girls in white dresses carrying a banner reading, "Fathers, Save Us from Nigger Husbands."[6]

Immediately after Buchanan's 1857 inauguration, the nation was stunned by the Supreme Court's notorious Dred Scott decision. Dred Scott was a blatant attempt to settle the slavery controversy once and for all in favor of the enslavers. The Court, dominated by slaveholders, ruled that Blacks could never be citizens and that Congress had no authority to bar slavery from the territories. Indeed, no governmental authority, federal, state, or territorial, could lawfully prohibit the enslavers from taking their chattel into all the federal territories.

Dred Scott was naked white supremacy. One infamous passage of the fifty-five-page decision written by Chief Justice Roger Taney, a Maryland slaveholder, ruled that African Americans were "beings of an inferior order, and altogether unfit to associate with the white race, either in social or political relations, and so far inferior, that they had no rights which a white man was bound to respect." African Americans, the Court claimed, were not included in the Declaration of Independence's assertion that all people are created equal.[7] Lincoln had been insisting for years that they were included in the Declaration. Dred Scott delighted the South and most Northern Democrats. They smugly declared that the slavery issue had been settled forever and in their favor. "Southern opinion upon the subject of Southern slavery," they asserted, "was now the supreme law of the land."[8] Northerners and antislavery leaders were outraged. They vowed to defy a decision they deemed unconstitutional.

Meanwhile, actual civil war, a ferocious, bloody, take-no-prisoners fight between slaveholding and free-soil settlers continued to rage in the Kansas territory. (One of the free-soil guerrillas was a grim, sword-wielding true believer named John Brown.) Kansas was set to join the Union as a new state. But would Kansas come in slave or free? Free-soil settlers outnumbered enslavers, but through fraud, rigged elections, and the connivance of the Buchanan administration, proslavery Kansans gained the upper hand for a time, provoking intense anger among Republicans.

Free-soil men rushed in heavily armed reinforcements. Ambushes, massacres, arson, and the violent expulsion of opponents continued. The egregious Buchanan did all he could to make Kansas a slave state. The large majority of free-soil settlers in the territory and determined antislavery forces in the nation's capital eventually prevailed, however. Kansas would come in as a free state in January 1861, just as the Civil War was about to break out. The Kansas bloodshed did much to intensify animosities on both sides. Slavery extension was clearly an issue worth killing and dying for.

In the 1858 Illinois campaign for the US Senate, Lincoln ran to unseat his old rival, the incumbent Stephen A. Douglas, and to win for himself the place he had always desired above all others. The famous Lincoln-Douglas debates in the fall of that year made Abraham Lincoln a national figure for the first time and set the stage for his presidential nomination in 1860.

Race was really the only issue in the seven debates. Race underlay other questions, such as the extension of slavery or the authority of the Supreme Court. The Democratic Party had long been the party of white supremacy. Though Democrats extolled the Jacksonian equality of the common man, African Americans were not included. As historian James McPherson has written "The Democratic party's professed egalitarianism was for whites only. Its commitment to slavery and racism was blatant in the North as well as the South."[9]

Douglas played the white supremacy card for a winning hand throughout the debates. "This government," Douglas intoned, "was made by white men, for the benefit of white men and their posterity, to be executed and managed by white men."[10] He attacked Lincoln constantly as a proponent of "negro equality." Douglas's definition of negro equality was the complete political and social equivalence of the two races. He never failed to refer to his opponent's political party as the "Black" Republicans. (Indeed, Democrats and secessionists attached the adjective so consistently that many probably believed that "Black Republican" was the party's actual, official name.)

As much as possible, Douglas tried to create a false dichotomy between himself, the champion of white men, and Lincoln, a man, he charged, devoted only to promoting the equality and advancement of African Americans. "This new republican party,"

Douglas insisted, "abjures and ignores every question which has for its object the welfare and happiness of the white man—every question that does not propose to put the negro on an equality with the white man, politically and socially."[11] This was, of course, a complete lie. The Republican Party had been organized by white men; its membership was composed almost entirely of white men; and its platform consisted of policy objectives designed for the benefit of white men. Banning slavery from the territories was one Republican policy for the benefit of white men. In the long term, so long as it could be accomplished most carefully and gradually and peacefully, the eventual abolition of slavery in the remote future was another goal for the benefit of whites that many Republicans embraced. At the same time, abolitionists who wanted immediate emancipation also tended to vote Republican, but they remained a minority in the party.

Of course, Douglas also hammered away in every debate on the white supremacists' favorite bogeyman: amalgamation or race mixing. Republican victory, Senator Douglas claimed, would usher in the widespread horror of the marriage of Black men to white women and flood Illinois with mulatto children, "mongrelizing" the white race. Lincoln liked to counter by pointing out that most of the mixed-race people in America were born in the South, where white men could easily exploit enslaved women and girls sexually.

Lincoln's white supremacist opponents would level such charges against him throughout his presidency. The racists outdid themselves for vile obscenity in the presidential election of 1864. They even coined a new word, *miscegenation*, to describe the Republican Party's supposed campaign to defile the purity of the white race through interracial marriage.

Advocating abolition or negro equality would have amounted to political suicide for any candidate in Illinois in 1858. Lincoln had to deny that he favored negro equality. But he went on to damn slavery as a "vast moral evil." He emphasized the Declaration of

Independence's affirmation that "all men are created equal" as the foundation of American nationhood. Lincoln denied that he advocated equality but went on to affirm that "I think the negro is included in the word 'men' used in the Declaration of Independence—I believe the declaration that 'all men are created equal' is the great fundamental principle upon which our free institutions rest."[12] African Americans were "entitled to all the natural rights enumerated in the Declaration of Independence, the right to life, liberty, and the pursuit of happiness," Lincoln maintained. "I hold that he is as much entitled to these as the white man."[13] Douglas countered that Blacks weren't included in the statement since they weren't equal to white men, being rather another, lower order of humanity.

This was an argument Southern enslavers had been making for at least a generation. It was that long ago that one of slavery's most ferocious defenders, John C. Calhoun of South Carolina, had denounced the Declaration's assertion of equality as "the most false and dangerous of all political error."[14] Another prominent South Carolina politician, James Henry Hammond, echoed Calhoun: "I repudiate, as ridiculously absurd, that much lauded but nowhere accredited dogma of Mr. Jefferson that 'all men are born equal.'"[15] In the debates, Douglas agreed with his fellow Democrats that when the signers of the Declaration of Independence spoke of men, they had meant white men only. To say otherwise was a "monstrous heresy."[16] The founders "did not mean negro, nor the savage Indians, nor the Fejee Islanders, nor any other barbarous race."[17] Senator Douglas was an alcoholic, suffering from an affliction that would kill him a few years later at the age of forty-eight. He was apparently drunk during some of the debates, intoxication magnifying his racist savagery. Lincoln Biographer Michael Burlingame has written that many in his audiences "thought that Douglas was under the influence of liquor, for a sober man would hardly talk and act as he did."[18]

Given a choice between "a negro and crocodile," Senator

Douglas reckoned he'd probably favor the negro, but that was about as far as he'd go. He contrasted his own convictions of white superiority with those he attributed to his opponent. "I do not question Mr. Lincoln's conscientious belief that the negro was made his equal, and hence his brother; but for my own part, I do not regard the negro as my equal, and positively deny that he is my brother or any kin to me whatsoever. . . . Now, I do not believe the Almighty ever intended the negro to be the equal of the white man. If He did, He has been a long time demonstrating the fact. For thousands of years the negro has been a race upon the earth, and during all that time, in all latitudes and climates, wherever he has wandered or been taken, he has been inferior to the race he has there met. He belongs to an inferior race, and must always occupy an inferior position."[19] The contemporary newspaper transcripts on which our texts of the Lincoln-Douglas debates are based give *negro* as the word the incumbent senator used to designate Black Americans. He may have actually used another, far less respectful, term. Douglas harangued the crowds with rhetorical questions that brought forth predictable answers shouted out by his supporters: "Are you in favor of conferring upon the negro the rights and privileges of citizenship? ['No, no.'] . . . Do you desire to turn this beautiful State into a free negro colony? ['no, no'], in order that when Missouri shall abolish slavery, she can send these emancipated slaves to become citizens and voters on an equality with you? ['Never, no.']." Those who wanted such an outcome should vote the Republican ticket. As for himself, Douglas averred, "I am opposed to negro citizenship in any form. [Cheers.]."[20] Candidate Lincoln was obliged to affirm that he also opposed Black citizenship.

Lincoln and the Republicans probably took the popular vote that fall, but that wasn't enough to win Lincoln a place in the Senate. Before ratification of the Seventeenth Amendment in 1913, US senators were not elected directly by the people but rather by the state legislatures. The Democrats had retained their former

The Republican nominee for president: Abraham Lincoln, June 3, 1860.

Library of Congress, Prints and Photographs Division,
LC-DIG-ppmsca-19200.

edge in the Illinois legislature. Douglas got another term. But Lincoln had won what turned out to be the greater victory. The prominence he gained in 1858 put him on the road to the White House.

It was his relative obscurity and reputation for moderation, however, that allowed him to snatch the Republican presidential nomination away from the several more famous contenders in 1860. As it turned out, the slavery controversy had handed the presidency to this unlikely candidate, a moderate former Whig with no executive experience and little prior claim to national prominence.

By 1860, the slavery fight had sundered the Democracy into antagonistic Northern and Southern parties. The Northern Democrats ran Douglas for president. The Southerners picked John C. Breckinridge of Kentucky, Buchanan's vice president. A coalition of conservative Whigs, seemingly risen from the dead, ran their own Union ticket, headed by John C. Bell. In the four-way race that followed, which has been called "the most fateful in American history," Lincoln's election was assured.[21]

Ominously, though, he came in as a minority president, winning only 39 percent of the popular vote. More ominous still was the stark sectional divide. Lincoln carried no slave states. Of the fifteen slave states, eleven would presently declare themselves out of the Union. In ten of those eleven states, the Republican Party was not even on the ballot in 1860, and Abraham Lincoln received not one single vote.

The white South reacted with incandescent rage. It was not just a political defeat that threatened dire consequences; it was a deadly insult to the honor of all Southern whites, deliberately inflicted by the Northern people. To be forced to live under the government of a man who thought slavery was wrong was like admitting that they, the enslavers, were moral reprobates. The imposition of a Black Republican regime was also a glaring example of majoritarian tyranny within a democracy. That kind of despotism was inimical to true republican liberty. The founders had feared and warned against it. Abolitionist fanaticism had corrupted the North. Only leaving the Union could save the white people of the slaveholding states. The seven Deep South cotton states began to secede, one after another.

As the crisis swelled, President-elect Lincoln was baffled by the reports of his radical and dangerous plans that were dominating political discussion in the South. How could anyone possibly believe he favored an extremist agenda when he had publicly affirmed his moderate positions on race and slavery many times? Voters need only read the text of the 1858 Lincoln-Douglas debates, which Lincoln had issued in book form as a campaign document. In the debates, Lincoln had clearly stated that he did not support abolition or equality or citizenship for African Americans. His party's platform was equally clear: Republicans did not favor such policies. Still, unwilling to risk the appearance of weakness by offering yet another public explanation, Lincoln decided, instead, to approach confidentially the one Southern leader whose friendship he was sure of.

During his single term in Congress, from 1847 to 1849, Representative Lincoln had become friendly with a fellow Whig congressman from Georgia named Alexander Stephens. The two men had bonded on their mutual admiration of the masterly use each could make of the English language for purposes of political persuasion. When Lincoln went back to Springfield in 1849, "Little Alex" Stephens stayed on in the House of Representatives; Georgia elected him to one term after another. Lincoln reckoned that his old friend must have some understanding of the Southern leaders' thinking, for Alexander Stephens had just been named "Vice President of the Confederate States of America."

On December 22, 1860, two days after South Carolina's secession, Lincoln wrote confidently to Stephens, in a letter marked "For Your Eyes Only," posing his exasperated question:

Do the people of the South really entertain fears that a Republican administration would, directly, or indirectly, interfere with their slaves, or with them, about their slaves? . . . There is no cause for such fears—The South would be in no more danger in this respect, than it was in the days of Washington—I suppose, however this does not meet the case—You think slavery is right, and ought to be extended; while we think it is wrong and ought to be restricted—That I suppose is the rub.[22]

Here Lincoln had captured the crux of the conflict precisely: "You think slavery is right, and ought to be extended; while we think it is wrong and ought to be restricted—That I suppose is the rub." The question of the moral correctness of slavery had been the wedge that fatally split the Democratic Party at its presidential nominating convention in Charleston in April 1860—the schism that had put Abraham Lincoln in the White House.

ALTERNATIVE FACTS

As the presidential election of 1860 drew near, it began to seem as though lies, distortions, and bizarre rape fantasies, bolstered by paranoia and delusional thinking, had sent half the nation rushing to embrace the greatest catastrophe in American history.

When the seven Deep South states seceded—South Carolina in December 1860, followed by Mississippi, Florida, Alabama, Georgia, Louisiana, and Texas in January and February of the new year—it was striking that the order of their departures corresponded largely with the ratio of Blacks to whites in their populations. Those with the largest Black populations went out first, having apparently the greatest stake in preserving white supremacy. Overall, the enslaved constituted nearly half—47 percent—of the populations in the first wave, the seven Deep South states that went out shortly after Lincoln's election. In contrast, in the middle and upper South slave states that remained in the Union until fighting broke out at Fort Sumter in April or that never seceded at all, enslaved people made up only 24 percent.

Those who may still wish to believe that the white South went to war in 1861 not for slavery and white supremacy but rather in defense of states' rights, or to escape economic policies that benefited only the North, or to oppose the consolidation of new powers by the federal government would do well to examine the first wave of seceded states' declarations of their reasons for renouncing the Union. Equally revealing were the arguments for separation presented by the "apostles of disunion" that those states sent out to bring on board their sister slave states in the weeks following the first round of secessions. Race and slavery were the only themes that alarmed the secessionists in 1860 and 1861. None of the insurgent statesmen nor the South's editors and clergymen emphasized states' rights, tariffs, differing economic systems, divergent cultures, or governmental consolidation as motives for breaking up the Union. It was only after the war was lost that the Southern insurgents (and their ideological heirs down to the present day) began to insist that they had not been fighting for white supremacy all along.

Within days of their secessions, most of those seven states issued declarations of independence modeled loosely on the Revolutionary example of 1776. The premise of all these documents—and, in fact, the main idea behind the secessionists' entire campaign to destroy the Union—could be summed up in a description of the Republican Party's plans that nearly all white Southerners would have accepted as accurate. That description would have gone something like this: Abraham Lincoln and the Republican Party advocate negro equality, the complete social and political equality of the Black and white races in the United States. They also favor interracial marriage. When "Old Ape" Lincoln comes to power in March 1861, he and his scheming minions will make their vaunted Negro Equality the supreme law of the land. Of course, this understanding of Republican intentions, despite being widely believed by white Southerners, was completely and demonstrably false.

Typical was Texas's contribution to the debate, its "declaration of cause" listing the Northern political crimes that had impelled the Lone Star State to leave the Union: The Republican candidate Abraham Lincoln had won the presidency with no Southern votes whatsoever. Now a tyrannical majority of Northern voters aimed to force a radical and dangerous regime on white Southerners against their will. In just four months, Texans warned, on March 4, 1861, the national government would fall into the hands of "a great sectional party . . . proclaiming the debasing doctrine of the equality of all men, irrespective of race or color—a doctrine at war with nature, in opposition to the experience of mankind, and in violation of the plainest revelations of Divine Law." Once in power, the Black Republicans would bring about "the abolition of negro slavery" and "the recognition of political equality between the white and negro races."[1] Yet neither Abraham Lincoln nor his party had ever so much as hinted at pursuing such revolutionary policies. The secessionists simply ignored the Republicans' clearly stated policy goals. That party had been founded on a defining mission that went no further than banning slavery in the western territories.

At the same time, despite the defiance inspiring these Deep South secessionists, the more thoughtful among them knew that even the greatest zeal could not counterbalance the obvious weakness of their position. Nor would such observers fail to see the hazards that could arise from their decision to leave the Union without additions to their proposed confederation. This first wave had renounced the Union and proposed uniting with other slave states to form a new sovereign Southern nation. A glance at the 1860 federal census, however, revealed that any nation they might form could only be a conspicuously weak and vulnerable one. Those seven states contained only a fraction of the fifteen slave states' overall population, wealth, and industrial capacity. Alone, they simply didn't possess the strength or numbers needed to sustain independence.

Knowing how critical it was to gain allies, they quickly dispatched "commissioners," in effect ambassadors, to the eight slave states that still remained in the Union in early 1861. Those eight states divided geographically into two tiers of four states each, running across the country from the Atlantic to the Mississippi. Immediately north of the Deep South were Virginia, North Carolina, Tennessee, and Arkansas. Just above them lay the next tier—the border slave states of Maryland, Delaware, Kentucky, and Missouri.

Mississippi moved first. Three weeks after Lincoln's election, the state's governor insisted that secession was the only way to escape a future of "Black Republican politics and free negro morals" that would plunge their happy state into "a cesspool of vice, crime and infamy."[2] The Mississippi legislature followed up the governor's call to arms by sending forth its ambassadors to convince their sister slave states to leave the Union and come together to form a new nation dedicated to the proposition that the negro is not equal to the white man. Historian Charles B. Dew's groundbreaking book *Apostles of Disunion* tells the story of these ambassadors, and the book's title itself neatly encapsulates their mission.

Alabama acted next. A week after South Carolina's secession, and with their own secession imminent, Alabamians sent Democratic stalwart Stephen F. Hale to Kentucky to plead with the leaders of that border state to follow the lower South's example. The electoral triumph of the Black Republicans, Hale told Kentucky governor Beriah Magoffin, was "nothing less than an open declaration of war, for the triumph of this new theory of government destroys the property of the South, lays waste her fields, and inaugurates all the horrors of a San Domingo [Haitian] servile insurrection, consigning her citizens to assassinations and her wives and daughters to pollution and violation to gratify the lust of half-civilized Africans."[3] In 1864, John Wilkes Booth would echo this interpretation of Lincoln's election as a declaration of war against the white South when he wrote,

"The very nomination of Abraham Lincoln four years ago, spoke plainly—war, war upon Southern rights and institutions. His election proved it."[4] Hale, who had apparently never read (or had completely dismissed) the 1860 Republican platform, made stunningly false claims about the incoming party's intentions: "They have demanded, and now demand, equality between the white and negro races, under our Constitution; equality in representation, equality in [the] right of suffrage, equality in the honors and emoluments of office, equality in the social circle, equality in the rights of matrimony."[5]

All this was pure paranoid fantasy. While the Republicans' 1860 party platform singled out the proposition that "all men are created equal" as the fountainhead of American nationhood, not a single sentence "demanded" social and political equality for Blacks. Hale's accusation that the Republicans supported "equality in the rights of matrimony" was even more preposterously untrue. Yet these blatant lies and the familiar, instinctive resort to dark sexual fears was incessantly repeated and unquestioningly accepted by most white Southerners. The enslavers' hatred and fear had translated them into a hallucinatory realm of alternative facts and political psychosis.

Directly refuting the charges of Northern Democrats and Southern secessionists alike, and widely disseminated by the press throughout every region of the land, the platform the Republican delegates had drafted at their presidential nominating convention in Chicago in May 1860 declared that "the maintenance inviolate of the rights of the states, and especially the right of each state to order and control its own domestic institutions according to its own judgment exclusively, is essential to that balance of powers on which the perfection and endurance of our political fabric depends."[6] This explicit promise never to meddle with Southern slavery apparently made no impression on those to whom it was addressed.

Their projections of their own ugly sexual fantasies onto

Black men had disordered the thinking of many Southern whites. One secessionist raged: "Submit to have our wives and daughters to choose between death and gratifying the hellish lust of the negro!! Better ten thousand deaths than submission to Black Republicanism."[7] (It hardly bears mention that the Republican platform that year contained no plank calling for the mass rape of white Southern womanhood.)

Proslavery Democrats in the North were equally mistaken about Republican intentions and equally gripped by the same unseemly sexual fears. The *New York Herald*, the nation's most important Democratic newspaper at the time, predicted that Lincoln's election would bring about an "African amalgamation with the fair daughters of the Anglo Saxon, Celtic, and Teutonic races."[8] A New York Democrat charged that Lincoln and his party had made "negrology . . . their political stock," resulting in "its natural fruit—nigger—the eternal nigger. They ate nigger—they drank nigger—they (at least the amalgamationists) slept nigger."[9]

One of the most extravagant denunciations of the Republican Party's alleged promotion of negro equality, a screed altogether remarkable for its unbridled ferocity, appeared not in the South but in the North, in a mad-dog editorial in a Democratic paper, the *Chicago Herald*. The editor seethed:

> Mr. Lincoln unequivocally places the white man and the negro on the same level. . . . The naked, greasy, bandy-shanked, blubber-lipped, monkey-headed, muskrat-scented cannibals from Congo and Guinea can come here in hoards and settle down on terms of equality with the descendants of Alfred the Great, the Von Trumps, the Russells, the Washingtons, the Lafayettes, the Emmitts! Mr. Lincoln will have no quibbling about this matter. . . . A race, which for five thousand years has fallen so low as to have almost lost the image of manhood, who eat human flesh and indulge in every horror of vice and infamy, and whose very persons offend every sense of

civilized man, are to rank at once with the races which, from their virtue and inherent strength, have, after a conflict of a thousand years, won the brilliant civilization of the nineteenth century.[10]

Saving slavery was always most critical for its contribution to the overriding aim of white supremacy: keeping the white race pure and unpolluted by the blood of the lower caste. Emancipation meant negro equality. Negro equality meant interracial marriage, amalgamation, and the end of the white race. That was what the Black Republicans wanted, claimed the Democrats. As the *Montgomery (AL) Mail*, editorialized: "If the North chooses to mullatoize itself, that is all right. Let the North be the home of the mixed race; and let the South be the home of the *white man*, proud of his race, and proud of his race's superiority!"[11] Ironically, however, the 1860 US census showed that almost all the biracial people in America (identified as "mulatto" in successive US censuses) lived in the South, the offspring of coercive encounters between white men and enslaved girls and women. So how could it be that it was the North that had chosen to "mullatoize" itself, to repeat the neologism of the Alabama editor?

The titanic irony of this obsession with Black male sexuality and the so-called pollution of the so-called white race was so pronounced as to elude easy comprehension. It was hard to see how a reality so glaringly obvious could have escaped these ardent defenders of whiteness, but they were apparently blind to the truth that they themselves were the true amalgamationists, the real race mixers. Like their slaveholding fathers, grandfathers, and great grandfathers, right down through all the generations since the first arrival of enslaved Africans, these white rapists had always been and continued to be the sires of America's population of biracial people. For two centuries, Southern white men had practiced what historian Edward Baptist called "the forced sexualization of enslaved women's bodies."[12]

That no restraint had ever held the rapists back was obvious. "Power tends to corrupt," famously pronounced Britain's Lord Acton, a man who supported the Southern white supremacists' rebellion, "and absolute power corrupts absolutely." It is hard to think of many classes of men in world history who possessed the kind of absolute power that American slaveholders held over their human property. Thomas Jefferson, one of the most eloquent advocates of human equality and, at the same time, an enslaver who impregnated a teenage girl he owned, described the malign influence of this kind of untrammeled sexual power over unwilling partners when he argued in *Notes on the State of Virginia* that "the man must be a prodigy who can retain his morals and manners undepraved under such circumstances."[13]

Sometime after the war, South Carolina's Mary Chesnut provided a bitter reflection on the sexual proclivities of the men in her elite social circle. The passage was based on a diary entry she had originally written in March 1861:

> We live surrounded by prostitutes. An abandoned woman
> is sent out of any decent house elsewhere. Who thinks any
> worse of a negro or mulatto woman for being a thing we
> can't name? God forgive us, but ours is a *monstrous* system and
> wrong and iniquity. . . . Like the patriarchs of old our men live
> all in one house with their wives and their concubines and the
> mulattos one sees in every family exactly resemble the white
> children—and every lady tells you who is the father of all the
> mulatto children in everybody's household, but those in her
> own she seems to think drop from the clouds, or pretends so
> to think."[14]

By her allusion here to "every family," Mrs. Chesnut suggested how widespread this pattern was. She also revealed the denial and willful self-deception of the white Southerners who held themselves up as stalwart defenders of racial purity.

The weight of voters in favor of the free states had been building for years as the North steadily outstripped the South in wealth and population. The 1860 election showed that the North's electoral strength now gave it a majoritarian power to dominate the political future. Southern slaveholders had finally lost the monopoly over the federal government that had been theirs since the republic's founding. The opposition had now chosen the nation's chief executive without any Southern support. Republican majorities would only continue to grow. "A party founded on the single sentiment . . . of hatred of African slavery, is now the controlling power," editorialized the *Richmond Examiner*.[15] It looked as though every future president might be a Republican or, as secessionists put it, a "Black" Republican. It took no more than their usual measure of paranoia for white Southerners to foresee the dire results that might follow.

Henry L. Benning, the disunion apostle sent by his newly seceded state of Georgia to urge separation on Virginia's deadlocked secession convention, posed a loaded question to the delegates when he addressed them in Richmond in January: "Suppose they elevated [Massachusetts abolitionist senator Charles] Sumner to the Presidency?" This horrifying prospect was eclipsed in the next sentence by the nightmare of the final degradation—an African American leading the nation as president of the United States: "Suppose they elevated Fred. Douglas[s], your escaped slave, to the Presidency?"[16]

When Lincoln wrote Alexander Stephens, the momentous year of 1860 was coming to a close. When that year had opened, the Democratic Party had been the only significant American organization that still remained truly national in scope, boasting strength in both antagonistic sections of a country bitterly divided by slavery. That controversy had by now sundered other entities like the major Protestant churches into separate Northern and Southern denominations. The old Whig Party of Lincoln and Stephens was dead, too, shattered by the turmoil brought on by the Kansas-Nebraska Act in 1854. The fight over the spread of slavery had made it impossible for Southern proslavery Whigs and Northern free labor Whigs to work toward shared goals in a single political party. In the past, though the Democracy had always been stronger, the Whigs had long remained a national party, retaining considerable strength in both the North and the South up until the moment of their dissolution.

In place of the Whig Party—though not as its successor in political principles—had arisen the Republican Party. Unlike the Whigs, however, Republicans were not a national party but rather a strictly sectional Northern one. They were strong enough to win elections but had no Southern support. Then, in 1860, the Democratic Party itself split into Northern and Southern factions.

Here it appears that we encounter a major historical enigma: if the Democratic Party, that last bastion of national unity, that had always boasted of being "the white man's party" for all Americans, if Democrats North and South spoke with one voice in support of slavery and white supremacy, why would a party in such seeming accord split in two in 1860, especially when such a division was certain to hand the presidency to the detestable Black Republicans, their opponents tainted by negro equality?

Northern and Southern white supremacists were all Democrats, but they were by no means a monolithic policy bloc. The immediate, overriding issue of 1860 was the future status of slavery in the western territories, a decision that would determine the destiny of the republic. The Republican Party had come into being a few years earlier almost entirely as an instrument to keep slavery out of the West. For their part, all Democrats, wherever they made their homes, supported slavery in the territories under certain circumstances. Any Northern Democrats opposed had by now defected to the Republicans. Yet despite all this apparent agreement, there remained the fundamental disagreement over the morality of slavery that the secessionists would use to wreck accord—and with it, their party's electoral hopes—when the Democratic delegates gathered to nominate a presidential candidate at their convention in Charleston, South Carolina, in April 1860.

It was just as President-elect Lincoln would propose six months later to Alexander Stephens—that the real issue was the morality of slavery: "You think slavery is *right*, and ought to be extended; while we think it is *wrong* and ought to be restricted— That I suppose is the rub."[17] Historian Allan Nevins told how the secessionist delegates at the Charleston convention "upbraided the Northern Democrats for treating slavery as an inherited evil; they should boldly pronounce it a positive good! If they had taken the position that slavery was right by the laws of nature and of God, they would have triumphed" over their Black Republican enemies. Nevins continued: "This Southern demand that the long-suffering Northern Democrats should avow slavery to be right, and its extension to be desirable," was angrily rejected by the Northern delegates. "Gentlemen of the South," they rebuked their Southern colleagues, "you mistake us, you mistake us! We will not do it!"[18]

The most determined secessionists wanted the convention to fail so that disunion could finally be consummated. They rejected party unity and electoral success in the coming contest. They wanted the Black Republicans to win the presidency. They would never unite around the leading contender, Lincoln's old rival Stephen A. Douglas. Douglas, though now an enslaver himself through his recent marriage to a plantation-owning Southern woman, refused to bow to Southern demands. It hardly mattered. The secessionists were not seeking to persuade. They were not looking to unite their party around one candidate, be he Douglas or one of the several other contenders whose names were put up.

These insurgent delegates aimed openly or covertly at breaking up the Union. Various compromises were within reach, but compromise would defeat their disunionist objective. They calculated that splitting the Democratic Party would assure the victory of the Republican candidate. (Abraham Lincoln would not be nominated until the following month.) Republican victory would then make Southern secession a certainty. Allan Nevins wrote that "the Southern extremists who had declared that they would never tolerate a Republican President had taken the very steps to make Republican victory certain, and had thus deliberately sealed the destruction of the national fabric."[19] In a contemporary assessment, a Virginia newspaper editor, reporting from the convention in Charleston, told his readers at home that the secessionist delegates had provoked the split "with a deliberate purpose to break up the convention if they failed to get, as they knew they would fail to get, their extreme ultimatum, and their ultimate design is to break up the Union by breaking up the Democratic party."[20] The conflict deadlocked the convention. No nominee could be chosen. Then the Southerners walked out in protest, vowing to convene a new convention themselves and pick their own Southern candidate, a man certain to be unacceptable to Northern Democrats.

And so it went. The rump Democratic convention, now composed mostly of Northern delegates, duly nominated Douglas. A little later, the secessionists reconvened to nominate John C. Breckinridge of Kentucky. Much of the wild excitement that enlivened the raucous Republican nominating convention in Chicago two weeks later sprang from the knowledge that the party's victory in the fall election was all but certain.

FILE UNDER "ASSASSINATION"

"Assassination is not an American practice or habit, and one so vicious and desperate cannot be engrafted into our political system. This conviction of mine has steadily gained strength since the civil war began. Every day's experience confirms it."[1] So wrote Abraham Lincoln's secretary of state, William H. Seward, in 1862. Three years later, one assassin killed the president, and another nearly killed Seward himself.

It is the lot of those whose pronouncements are dramatically contradicted by subsequent events to have their erring words ironically recited. Yet Seward had not been so foolish in believing assassination a practice foreign to the United States at that time. With the single exception of the deranged British house painter who tried to shoot Andrew Jackson, there had not been an attempt on the life of a leading American statesman in the republic's history. Lincoln himself agreed with Seward. "Oh, assassination of public officers is not an American crime," he once said.[2]

Maybe Lincoln would have known better had he not been so far gone in denial. His attitude toward the possibility of assassination was, in fact, a combination of denial and fatalism—the customary human response to mortality. But the White House mailbags contained all the contrary evidence needed. The election of an antislavery president had raised political passions to unprecedented levels. Southern enslavers and Northern white supremacists alike were infuriated. Moderation had been banished from the South. So the example of the past in which Seward put his faith no longer obtained.

The truth was that Abraham Lincoln had been in mortal danger from the moment he was elected president of such a violently divided nation. In the weeks following the 1860 election, death threats and gifts of poisoned fruit poured into Springfield. Carl Sandburg reported that "in the day's mail for Lincoln came letters cursing him for an ape and a baboon who had brought the country evil. He was buffoon and monster; an abortion, an idiot; they prayed he would be flogged, burned, hanged, tortured. . . . Mrs. Lincoln saw unwrapped a painting on canvas, her husband with a rope around his neck, his feet chained, his body tarred and feathered."[3]

The slave states seethed with obscene hatred for Lincoln and his party of "Black" Republicans and race-mixing "amalgamationists." With wild hyperbole, one Southern newspaper swore that the Potomac River would be "crimsoned in human gore, and Pennsylvania Avenue . . . paved ten fathoms deep in mangled bodies" before the South would "submit to such humiliation and degradation as the inauguration of Abraham Lincoln."[4] There was much talk in the South of seizing the capital before the president-elect arrived to forestall his inauguration.

Despite the threats, Abraham Lincoln would be duly sworn in as the sixteenth president of the United States on March 4, 1861, in a capital city rigid with fear and bristling with sharpshooters. More threats and warnings came to the White House after he was inaugurated. After a while, Lincoln said, it didn't much bother him: "Soon after I was nominated at Chicago, I began to receive letters threatening my life. The first one or two made me a little uncomfortable, but I came at length to look for a regular installment of this kind of correspondence in every week's mail, and up to inauguration day I was in constant receipt of such letters. It is no uncommon thing to receive them now; but they have ceased to give me any apprehension." Laughing, he continued, "there is nothing like getting *used* to things!"[5] Besides, he added, "if they kill me, I shall never die another death."[6] The erratic newspaperman Horace Greeley said Lincoln received ten thousand death threats during the war, but the editor didn't say who had kept the count.[7]

Although his secretaries tossed most death threats before he ever saw them, President Lincoln himself kept in his desk a "bulging folder in a special pigeonhole" labeled "Assassination" in his own hand.[8] Here are two examples of the kind of missives found therein:

Sir
Mr Abe Lincoln
if you don't Resign we are going to put a spider in your dumpling and play the Devil with you you god or mighty god dam sundde of a bith go to hell and buss my Ass suck my prick and call my Bolics your uncle Dick god dam a fool and goddam Abe Lincoln who would like you goddam you excuse me for using such hard words with you but you need it you are nothing but a goddam Black nigger.[9]

Old Abe Lincoln
God damn your god damned old Hellfire god damned soul to hell god damn you and your god damn family's god damned hellfired god damned soul to hell and god damnation god damn them and god damn your friends to hell god damn their god damn souls to hell and god damn their god damn families to eternal god damnation god damn souls to hell god damn them and God Almighty God damn old Hamlin [Vice Presi-

dent Hannibal] to hell God damn his God damned soul all over everywhere double damn his god damn soul to hell

Now you God damned old Abolition son of a bitch God damn you[10]

The critical word in the last letter is not, as one might suppose, the oft-repeated blasphemy but rather "Abolition." The enslavers exploded in fierce rage against any who dared question the righteousness of enslaving Africans. And, of course, abolitionists never stopped shouting about the manifest unrighteousness of slavery. So white supremacists like John Wilkes Booth hated abolitionists above all others, wanted them dead, just as the young actor had cursed in that passionate speech he wrote during the secession crisis in December 1860. They saw the moderate Abraham Lincoln as the king of the radical abolitionists.

Most of the animosity toward Lincoln and his party sprang from this kind of race hatred. The enslavers' defense of white supremacy was the explicit cause of the Southern secession and the great war that secession brought on. The enslavers had proclaimed white superiority the "corner-stone" of their new government. White supremacy was the mainspring of Booth's crime. White supremacy justified and enabled slavery. It justified holding other human beings in perpetual bondage and selling them away from their children as though they were horses or cattle.

The prospect of political murder had reared its sinister head in the "Baltimore plot" of February 1861 before Lincoln even took the oath of office.[11] As was customary in the nineteenth century, Lincoln had not campaigned for the presidency, staying home and making no public statements. He also kept quiet for more than three months after the election, even though many Americans urged him to speak out to promote reconciliation and offer compromises to placate the outraged, rebellious South.

Meanwhile, joint congressional committees and a special Peace Convention proposed new laws and constitutional amendments to resolve the crisis. Lincoln himself remained adamantly opposed to any concession that might allow slavery to spread into the West. Keeping slavery out of the territories had been the principal plank of the platform on which he'd just been elected. The angry secessionists rejected compromise in any event. They too much resented the stinging insult of trying to force on them an abolitionist president they opposed. It was the last straw.

The most important objective of all—underlying issues like labor systems, racial inferiority, or biblical justifications of slavery—was the preservation of the racial purity of the white dominant caste. Any cracks in the edifice of enslavement and white supremacy would usher in a mixed-race populace. As they pulled their own state out of the Union, South Carolina secessionists warned other white Southerners that if they remained in the Union, "abolition preachers will be on hand to consummate the marriages of your daughters to black husbands."[12]

Abraham Lincoln, of course, was no abolitionist, but he had received not one vote in ten of the eleven states that would soon decide to leave the Union. He was certainly a "sectional" candidate, just as Southerners charged. Lincoln grievously underestimated the anger and determination of Southern whites. He thought that talk of secession was mainly a bluff to wring concessions from the North. Even so, it's unlikely that anything Lincoln could have said or done at this point would have mollified the secessionists.

The threat, and soon the reality, of secession posed an unparalleled crisis. Many in the South obviously had not believed Lincoln's pledges of noninterference. Although the Republican Party platform of 1860 had promised to respect slavery in the states, and although real abolitionists didn't consider Lincoln much of an antislavery man at all, he was still considered the antislavery candidate in the presidential contest that year. In the South, he was considered to be much worse than that. Fire-eaters claimed Lincoln was a "Black Republican," a disciple of

John Brown, a bloodthirsty abolitionist fanatic with a mission to end slavery, enforce racial equality or wholesale negro superiority, and even force Black husbands on white Southern maidens. The president-elect addressed the American people for the first time almost three and a half months after the election during his roundabout, nineteen-hundred-mile, twelve-day railroad journey from his home in Springfield to his inauguration in Washington, DC. It was hardly a direct route to the capital. He left Springfield on February 11, arriving in Washington on the twenty-third. "My friends," he had said to the crowd gathered to see him off at Springfield's little train station, "I now leave, not knowing when, or whether ever, I may return, with a task before me greater than that which rested upon Washington."[13]

His three-car "Lincoln Special" made its leisurely way through Illinois, Indiana, Ohio, Pennsylvania, New York, and back into Pennsylvania before the president-elect, in response to warnings of an assassination plot, left the presidential train to make his secret 3:30 a.m. escape through Baltimore. A pilot engine went ahead of the Lincoln Special to guard against any possible sabotage to the rails. They soon found an obstruction that would have derailed the locomotive near State Line, Indiana.[14]

Biographer David Herbert Donald said the journey "combined all the elements of a traveling circus, a political campaign, and a national holiday."[15] Lincoln's purpose was "to see and be seen"—and to be heard. He succeeded in all respects, making so many speeches (at least a hundred) that he lost his voice for a time. As many as half a million Northerners got a chance to look on his odd personage. The president-elect exalted the Union and spoke of sectional reconciliation and the glorious heritage of popular government that the North and the South shared. At the same time, he vowed that he would uphold the Constitution and maintain the Union. The crowds cheered him.

His train stopped at major cities—Indianapolis, Cincinnati, Columbus, Pittsburgh, Cleveland, Buffalo, Albany, New York

City, Philadelphia, and Harrisburg—as well as at little whistle-stop villages. Everywhere, Lincoln was greeted with wild enthusiasm by a people deeply concerned about the fate of the Union. They fervently hoped he could set things right.

Midway through Lincoln's journey, on February 16, 1861, Jefferson Davis of Mississippi was inaugurated "Provisional President of the Confederate States of America" in Montgomery, Alabama. Davis was defiant. "The time for compromise has passed," he said, "and now we are determined to maintain our position, and make all who oppose us smell Southern powder, feel Southern steel."[16]

That same day, alarming reports of an assassination plot reached the presidential party, then in upstate New York.[17] Working undercover in Baltimore, Allan Pinkerton, head of the detective agency that bore his name, had learned of a conspiracy by Southern partisans to kill Lincoln on February 23 when he changed train stations in Baltimore on the final leg of his trip to Washington. Lincoln's carriage would be surrounded by a mob, and in the confusion, the conspirators would strike, shooting or stabbing him or tossing hand grenades into the carriage.[18] There were already newspaper reports, denied by Lincoln's friends, that a bomb, "an infernal machine of the most destructive character," had been discovered in a carpetbag placed on a seat in Lincoln's railroad car.[19]

Much of Baltimore—indeed, of the whole border slave state of Maryland—burned with hatred for Lincoln and the Black Republicans. Lincoln had gotten only 2.5 percent of the popular vote there.[20] Some thought that, had the federal grip on the state not been so strong, Maryland might have seceded. And Baltimore, a Democratic city known as "Mobtown," was largely pro-Southern and notorious for politically inspired riots, brawls, and murders. (Baltimore, of course, was also the hometown of John Wilkes Booth, a man whose inclinations comported well with his city's darker propensities.)

Meanwhile, in the North, the crowds that surged out to meet Lincoln at every stop provided danger enough. He was nearly crushed by hysterical mobs in several cities. In Buffalo, "a scene of the wildest confusion ensued," wrote a *New York Times* reporter. "To and fro the ruffians swayed and cries of distress were heard on all sides. The pressure was so great that it is really a wonder that many were not crushed and trampled to death. [Lincoln's] party had to struggle with might and main for their lives."[21] There were many serious injuries, including broken bones.

More warnings of an ambush in Baltimore presently arrived from such personages as Secretary of State-designate William H. Seward and General Winfield Scott, commander of the US Army. Lincoln was then in Trenton, where he had just told the New Jersey State Senate that the Americans were God's "almost chosen people."[22]

His last official duty of the trip was a flag-raising at Independence Hall in Philadelphia on February 22, Washington's birthday. After he hauled up the flag with its new thirty-fourth star for Kansas, Lincoln addressed the crowd gathered in the chill of dawn on the spot where the Declaration of Independence had been signed eighty-five years before: "I never had a feeling politically that did not spring from the sentiments embodied in the Declaration of Independence," he said, emphasizing the principle "in that Declaration giving liberty, not alone to the people of this country, but hope to the world for all future time. It was that which gave promise that in due time the weights should be lifted from the shoulders of all men, and that all should have an equal chance. This is the sentiment embodied in that Declaration of Independence." The American people must never abandon that principle. Lincoln said, "I would rather be assassinated on this spot than surrender it."[23]

Since it was public knowledge that the president-elect would arrive in Baltimore to change trains at 12:30 p.m. on February 23, the best way to avoid any ambush would be simply to go through the city at an earlier time. This is, in fact, what Lincoln did, passing through Baltimore quietly on a special train nine hours ahead of schedule.

"I did not then, nor do I now, believe I should have been assassinated had I gone through Baltimore as first contemplated; but I thought it wise to run no risk where no risk was necessary," he later said.[24] He was rather too sanguine. Would-be assassins were indeed waiting for him at the train station at the appointed hour.[25] An angry mob of fifteen thousand had gathered to meet the train on which the president-elect was supposed to be. "Come out, old Abe," they shouted to the dismay of Mary Todd Lincoln and the other passengers. "Let's have him out!" Mary Lincoln and son Tad managed to slip away unmolested.[26]

Baltimore was a powder keg ready to blow. Two months later, an enraged secessionist mob attacked with bricks, paving stones, and gunfire Massachusetts troops passing through the city on their way to Washington. The troops responded with volleys of musketry fired point blank into the faces of the rioters. Many soldiers and civilians were killed and wounded. In the words of Maryland's state song, "patriotic gore flecked the streets of Baltimore." (This song, "Maryland! My Maryland!," became one of the South's most popular battle hymns. Its verses denounced Lincoln as a "tyrant," "despot," and "Vandal" and boasted "Huzza! She spurns the northern scum!") Before long, however, batteries of Union artillery backed by a thousand men stood watch on Federal Hill overlooking the city. In any event, popular opinion in the state favored the Union. Unionist candidates would prevail in the state elections later that year.

Lincoln had feared that the sneaky feint through Baltimore might subject him to ridicule. The result was even worse than he'd anticipated. Some called him a coward. More judiciously, Manhattan diarist George Templeton Strong wrote that "this surreptitious nocturnal dodging or sneaking of the President-elect into his capital city, under cloud of night, will be used to damage

On the way to his inauguration in 1861, Lincoln made a
secret 3:00 a.m. dodge through Baltimore to evade a reported
assassination attempt. He was accused of cowardice. The
papers featured mocking cartoons of a skulking,
frightened man wearing a disguise.

Adalbert J. Volck, "Lincoln's Passage through Baltimore,"
Confederate War Etchings, 1863. Huntington Library, HM 41785.

his moral position and throw ridicule on his Administration."[27] The papers featured mocking cartoons of a skulking, frightened man wearing a disguise.

Lincoln was humiliated. Nineteenth-century American men, besotted with their cult of manliness, regarded physical cowardice as the greatest disgrace. And Abraham Lincoln, the undefeated brawler of the western frontier, was no coward. It's reasonable to suppose that some of the president's subsequent careless attitude toward his own safety came from his refusal to take again any action that might possibly be construed as cowardly.

He told a friend, "The way we skulked into this city has been a source of shame and regret to me, for it did look so cowardly."[28] Too much concern for his personal safety might seem unbecoming in a commander in chief who was asking millions of other American men to risk death, anguish, and mutilation for the Union—especially so when many believed that Abraham Lincoln bore a unique personal responsibility for the gigantic war his election had touched off. Besides, he added, it would seem undemocratic for the head of a popular government to be too closely guarded. "It would never do for a president to have guards with drawn sabers at his door, as if he fancied he were, or were trying to be, or were assuming to be, an emperor."[29] That attitude had long prevailed. Never, in the seventy-two years of American history before Lincoln's inauguration, had any thought been given to securing the president's residence or guarding the person of the chief executive. Before Lincoln, it had never been necessary.

Lincoln's protectors had also learned that there were those among the enemy who aimed not to kill the Yankee president but rather to take him prisoner. They didn't know, however, that beginning in the summer of 1864, one conspiracy to capture President Lincoln and take him south to Richmond as a hostage was being organized by a freelance secret agent named John Wilkes Booth.

14

"THE NEGRO IS NOT EQUAL
TO THE WHITE MAN"

After pouring his heart out in his never-delivered speech, the twenty-two-year-old John Wilkes Booth put aside politics and turned back to the stage. Early in 1861, he appeared in starring roles in Albany and Rochester, New York, and in Portland, Maine. For the first time, Booth was traveling alone, without an agent, arranging his own appearances with theater managers. He was now effectively managing his own career, just as he would for the next three years—right up to the moment he abruptly quit acting in May 1864 to devote himself to his conspiracy against Abraham Lincoln.

In Albany on the night of February 18, 1861, Booth, starring in *The Apostate*, found himself competing with the president-elect, who was holding a reception a few blocks away. The night of Lincoln's inauguration, Booth performed *Richard III*, already acknowledged as "his play." The *Albany Express* was effusive in its praise: "His fifth act was a prodigious piece of acting, while the last scene was truly terrible. No such fighting has ever been seen in this city. In his battle scenes the young Booth is ahead of any actor we ever saw. He throws his whole soul into his sword, giving the contest a degree of earnestness never approached, even by his father. At the end of the tragedy, three cheers were proposed. They were given with a power that almost took the roof off."[1]

The review illustrates the qualities behind the young actor's great popular appeal. The Albany audience didn't admire his elocution or his portrayal of emotional verisimilitude but rather the exciting spectacle he presented. He was already well along on the ascent that would soon make him, at so young an age, one of the most celebrated and well-paid actors in America.

When Lincoln was inaugurated on March 4, 1861, the four crucial upper South slave states—Virginia, North Carolina, Tennessee, and Arkansas—were still in the Union. When they finally did secede after the bombardment of Fort Sumter in April, these states would make up the bulk of the grand rebellion's wealth and population. Their embrace of insurrection greatly increased the white South's chances of winning independence. The white population of the four states that went out in the second wave of secession exceeded that of the seven lower South states that had gone out immediately after Lincoln's election.

Virginia, "the Mother of States," was particularly important for its wealth, resources, and the prestige of its glorious heritage of leadership in the struggle of winning American independence a lifetime earlier. (It was in recognition of this importance that the rebels immediately moved their capital city from the more readily defended Montgomery, Alabama, to Richmond, Virginia, as soon as the Old Dominion joined them.)

Though he had promised not to meddle with slavery many times before, it was Virginia and the other upper South slave states that the new president had most urgently wanted to reassure when he declared in his inaugural that "I have no purpose, directly or indirectly, to interfere with the institution of slavery in the States where it exists. I believe I have no lawful right to do so, and I have no inclination to do so."[2] But white Southerners just didn't believe him.

On April 12, as Booth was playing Prince Hamlet in Portland, Maine, the South Carolina batteries opened fire on the federal garrison at Fort Sumter, sparking the Civil War. Lincoln called out seventy-five thousand militia troops to put down an insurrection now swollen to open warfare. Outraged by this Northern coercion against their sister states, the four upper South slave states of Virginia, North Carolina, Tennessee, and Arkansas announced their secession, greatly strengthening the rebellion. John Wilkes Booth now prayed fervently for that rebellion's success.

The question naturally arises: if Booth believed so passionately in the cause of the South, why did he not join the Southern army? His sister Asia and his brother Edwin both asked him the obvious question. He told Edwin that he had promised his beloved mother he'd stay out of the fight. She was "no Roman mother." She couldn't bear the thought of sacrificing her favorite child to the god of battles. Years after the war, Edwin Booth remembered the conversation with his younger brother. "I asked him once why he did not join the Confederate army. To which he replied: 'I promised mother I would keep out of the quarrel, if possible, and am sorry that I said so.' "[3]

Wilkes gave his sister an additional explanation, one she recorded in her grieving tribute to her best-loved brother, the memoir written in 1874 and finally published in 1938, half a century after her death, as *The Unlocked Book*. Most of the Booths supported the North, but Asia, like Wilkes, had certain Southern sympathies. In the heat of an argument over the war, her brother had burst out "so help me holy God! my soul, life, and possessions are for the South," prompting Asia to ask, "Why not go fight for her, then? Every Marylander worthy of the name is fighting her battles."[4] Indeed, some Maryland men who believed that justice marched with the Southern armies had gone to join the rebellion. (More Marylanders, however, enlisted in the Union army.) Many of the Booths' childhood friends and Bel Air neighbors had taken their places in the gray-clad ranks. Not a few fell on Southern battlefields. "Many, many of our young friends had gone down in that unholy war," Asia lamented.[5]

But, as Wilkes told Asia in a conversation that probably took place in 1864, "I have only an arm to give; my brains are worth twenty men, my money worth an hundred. I have free pass everywhere, my profession, my name, is my passport."[6] He went on to tell his horrified sister how he moved as a spy throughout the Union. He mingled easily with the most distinguished society of the North, gathering intelligence. He told her how he smuggled precious quinine south. His hands were callused from nights of rowing small boats across the Potomac. He carried guns. When in Philadelphia he often stayed at his sister's house, sleeping in his clothes on a downstairs couch. Asia remembered that strange men called late at night for whispered consultations.

She knew then "that my hero was a spy, a blockade-runner, a rebel! I set the terrible words before my eyes, for I knew that each one meant death. I knew that he was today what he had been since childhood, an ardent lover of the South and her policy, an upholder of Southern principles. He was a man so single in his devotion, so unswerving in his principles, that he would yield everything for the cause he espoused."[7] In his boasting to his sister, Booth was likely exaggerating his contributions to the Southern cause.

By 1864, burgeoning Northern might threatened to overwhelm that cause. The prospect of Southern defeat was more than Booth could bear to contemplate. He was certain that Lincoln was the source of all these evil doings. Wilkes would tell his sister in the summer of 1864 that he believed Abraham Lincoln would become an American king: "*He is Bonaparte in one great move, that is, by overturning this blind Republic and making himself a king. This man's re-election which will follow his success, I tell you—will be a reign! You'll see—you'll see—that re-election means succession. . . . These false-hearted, unloyal foreigners it is, who would glory in the downfall of the Republic—and that by a* half-breed too, a man springing from the ashes of old Assanon-thime Brown, a false president yearning for kingly succession as hotly as ever did Ariston."[8]

His own father had been named for the noble slayer of such tyrants. He himself had been named for an eighteenth-century hero who had preached that rebellion to tyrants was obedience to God. The destiny of fighting this new tyrant was in his blood. The Richmond Grays at John Brown's hanging had lined up beneath the Virginia state flag. The motto of that blue banner read "Sic Semper Tyrannis"—"Thus Always to Tyrants"—beneath the image of a hero standing over a slain king. The motto also appeared on the obverse of Virginia's state seal. These were the words the assassin would shout when he sent his bullet crashing through Lincoln's skull on April 14, 1865.

For the greatest of all history's tyrants, Booth had become convinced, was the usurper Abraham Lincoln. Lincoln aimed at nothing less than crowning himself king of America in the definitive repudiation of the ideals of 1776. In the summer before Lincoln's reelection, Booth bitterly sang for his sister a popular song with the refrain, "In 1865 when Lincoln shall be King." In November 1864, Abraham Lincoln would become the first president to win a second term since Andrew Jackson's 1832 reelection—the first presidential reelection in more than a generation. King or president-for-life, Booth said, it hardly mattered which.

Asia remembered that her brother

> whispered fiercely, "That Sectional candidate should never have been President, the votes were *doubled* to seat him, he was smuggled through Maryland to the White House. Maryland is true to the core—every mother's son. Look at the cannon on the heights of Baltimore. It needed just that to keep her quiet. This man's appearance, his pedigree, his coarse low jokes and anecdotes, his vulgar similes, and his frivolity, are a disgrace to the seat he holds. Other brains rule the country.

"THE NEGRO IS NOT EQUAL TO THE WHITE MAN"

He is made the tool of the North, to crush out, or try to crush out slavery, by robbery, rapine, slaughter and bought armies. He is walking in the footprints of old John Brown, but no more fit to stand with that rugged old hero—Great God! no. John Brown was a man inspired, the grandest character of the century!"[9]

Booth was not alone. As the vast war revealed itself, scene by fiery scene, plenty of Americans, in the North as well as the South, came to believe that Lincoln had already made himself a sort of king. That Abraham Lincoln was, while living, the most hated president in the country's history will come as a surprise to those who know only the revered martyr-statesman, America's greatest secular saint. But during the Civil War, many regarded Lincoln with anything but reverence. North and South, Lincoln's foes called him tyrant, barbarian, "Abe the Widowmaker," and awarded him the title "King Abraham Africanus I."

With matchless eloquence Abraham Lincoln told the nation that the Union must be saved to keep alive for "man's vast future" the "last best, hope of earth"—the American experiment in self-government. His opponents, however, argued that the president himself was destroying America's democratic experiment by dictatorial actions, systematic violations of civil liberties, unwise policies regarding slavery, and the consolidation of immense new powers by the federal government. Lincoln was, in fact, the nation's most controversial president, and his most controversial, and most detested act was emancipation.

There is no doubt that Abraham Lincoln wielded unprecedented executive power in fighting the nation's most costly war. He began with the very act of accepting war rather than allowing the Southern states to "depart in peace." Lincoln's presidential predecessor, James Buchanan, was only one of the many who believed that, while secession itself was unconstitutional, the Constitution gave the federal government no right to "coerce" a seceded state back into the Union. Secretary of State William Seward told the painter Francis Carpenter in 1864 that the decision to preserve the Union by force of arms was the most radical and far-reaching step ever taken by the Lincoln administration, more consequential than emancipation itself.[10]

Congress was not in session when the big guns spoke in Charleston harbor. Lincoln did not wait for congressional approval to call out troops or to draw on the federal treasury in attempting to put down the rebellion, possibly skirting the Constitution by so doing. Fighting his war from a national capital surrounded by disloyal slaveholders, President Lincoln moved to suspend the writ of habeas corpus in parts of Maryland within two weeks of the bombardment of Fort Sumter. This even though the power to suspend the writ appears in article 1 of the Constitution, the section that sets forth the prerogatives of Congress. Many argued on this basis that the authority to suspend the writ belonged to the legislative branch only and that no president could lawfully exercise it. Lincoln resolutely ignored such arguments.

By the time the war ended, thousands of civilians had been arrested without warrants, held without trial, or tried by military courts. Most of those arrested, however, were not, in fact, political prisoners arrested on charges of disloyalty but rather criminals, smugglers, and merchants accused of cheating the government in contracts for war supplies. Others were deserters, spies, and Southern agents. Historian Mark E. Neely Jr., the foremost scholar of individual rights in the Civil War era, concluded that "'political prisoner' would be at best a misleading term for most of the civilians arrested by military authority."[11]

War rarely improves civil liberties. It is worth noting that suppression of dissent by the US government was more severe during WWI than during the Civil War. Nothing in the earlier war, moreover, approached the WWII internment of Japanese American citizens as an egregious violation of the Constitution.

Many of the same violations of civil liberties occurred under Jefferson Davis's government. Davis showed a greater regard for the sanctity of habeas corpus than did Lincoln. He suspended it only with the concurrence of Congress. Still, there were thousands of political prisoners in the South. Mark Neely concluded that "Abraham Lincoln and Jefferson Davis acted alike as commanders in chief when it came to the rights of the civilian population. Both showed little sincere interest in constitutional restriction on government authority in wartime. Both were obsessed with winning the war."[12]

Lincoln justified himself by invoking national survival in time of war: wasn't it better to bend parts of the Constitution a little to save the document than to lose the whole Constitution through punctilious adherence to its every provision? "Are all the laws, *but one*, to go unexecuted, and the government itself go to pieces," he argued, "lest one be violated?"[13]

Still, the unyielding power of the government was most strongly felt in Booth's native Maryland. There were more military arrests of Maryland civilians than of the citizens of any other state. Maryland arrests made up fully a third of all those detained in 1861.[14] Booth knew this from press reports and rumors traded in barrooms. It fueled his anger. Nowhere, outside the seceded territories themselves, was Lincoln more hated than in Maryland. As we have seen, Lincoln garnered only 2.5 percent of Maryland's popular vote in the 1860 presidential election. He got almost no votes at all in the five southernmost counties of the state, those on the eastern side of the Potomac.[15] One resident who had made the mistake of voting Republican was driven from his home. This was the rabidly secessionist region of Maryland the assassin would flee through in his futile attempt to escape justice in April 1865.

Four years of civil war brought down on the Southern people immense suffering. Towns were occupied, pillaged, and set ablaze. Farms and plantations went up in flames along with their crops. Private homes were looted and burned. Tens of thousands of white Southerners fled as hungry, cold, frightened refugees. Reading the signs of the times, many of the enslaved people escaped or defied their enslavers, gutting agricultural production. Those who escaped enslavement became refugees themselves, often suffering great hardships.

Meanwhile, in the North, the president's political foes condemned both his hard war policies and those policies' apparent lack of success. By the summer of 1864, as the presidential election approached, Democrats charged that although Lincoln's administration had failed to achieve victory despite enormous sacrifices of blood and treasure, he remained unwilling to talk peace or to consider any terms but the restoration of the Union and, after 1863, the abolition of slavery. Southern whites saw those terms as unconditional surrender. By 1864, many argued inaccurately that only Lincoln's intransigence about freedom for the enslaved stood in the way of a negotiated end to the killing. He was stubbornly putting the interests of Black slaves above those of white citizens.

None of this was lost on John Wilkes Booth or the millions of angry men who believed as he did. To most white Southerners, and to Northern white supremacists and Peace Democrats, Abraham Lincoln was not just the leader of a hostile polity but a man of real evil, a despot who aimed at nothing less than the destruction of free, white society and the erection in its place of some nightmare African autocracy. "What shall we call him?" asked the *Richmond Examiner* in January of 1863, responding to the Emancipation Proclamation, "coward? assassin? savage? murderer of women and babes? Shall we consider these as all embodied in the word 'fiend!' and shall we call him *that?*—Lincoln the Fiend!"[16]

"This country was formed for the *white* not for the black man," Booth insisted in a passionate denunciation of Lincoln's policies in 1864.[17] Millions of white Americans agreed with that proposition. Racial hatred lay behind much of the malice toward

Lincoln and his party. Throughout the war, the Democratic opposition in the North denounced Lincoln and the Republicans with a racist savagery never equaled in American political discourse. Some Lincoln-haters even charged that the president himself was a negro. Booth told his sister that Lincoln was a "half-breed."[18]

Lincoln's First Inaugural had deprecated war, calling instead on "the better angels of our nature."[19] His predicament had grown enormously when he took the presidential oath to protect and defend the Constitution that had long been used to protect slavery. He had now sworn to protect the institution he hated. The new president made a few attempts to reassure the South, but he refused to compromise on the extension of slavery westward or to back down on Fort Sumter. And the war came.

15

"I MUST HAVE KENTUCKY"

I'd like to have God on my side, but I must have Kentucky, Abraham Lincoln supposedly said during the first year of the Civil War.[1] Four of the fifteen slave states—the border states of Kentucky, Missouri, Maryland, and Delaware—had declined to join the eleven insurgent states in secession. If these still-loyal slave states could be persuaded to join the rebellion, the enslavers' chances of achieving independence would be greatly enhanced.

The governor of Kentucky had angrily rejected the president's call to the states for militia to put down the rebellion. His state declared its "armed neutrality" in the building crisis. "Kentucky will furnish no troops for the wicked purpose of subduing her sister Southern states," Governor Beriah Magoffin declared defiantly.[2] Kentucky could go either way, and the state remained the linchpin. "To lose Kentucky is nearly the same as losing the whole game," Lincoln calculated. "Kentucky gone, we cannot hold Missouri, nor, as I think, Maryland. These all against us, and the job on our hands is too large for us. We might as well consent to separation at once, including the surrender of this capitol."[3]

Lincoln was treading on thin political ice, listening nervously for the sound of cracking. A misstep could tip the odds against the Union. And nothing was more certain to alienate the border states and probably push them into rebellion than a move against slavery. The most radically pro-Southern of the border states was John Wilkes Booth's Maryland, though it remained firmly in the Union. Judging by the enlistments of Maryland men in the opposing armies, Unionism was apparently stronger than secessionism in the state: twice as many Maryland soldiers eventually joined the Northern rather than the Southern army.

As soon as he took office, Lincoln found himself pulled in two directions. At his left elbow, so to speak, were the radical Republicans, the abolitionists, and the antislavery clergy of many Protestant denominations, all determined to steer the president toward emancipation. The minute war broke out, the Massachusetts abolitionist senator Charles Sumner raced to the White House to tell the new president that, under his constitutional war powers, he now possessed the authority to emancipate the enslaved people in the rebellious states by executive decree. Sumner urged Lincoln to do so at once, and the senator and his allies never neglected a chance to repeat that advice in the months that followed. Their anger grew as the president failed to move decisively. Petitions demanding emancipation poured into the White House from all across the North. Committees called on Lincoln to plead freedom for the enslaved. Major newspapers came out for emancipation. There were mass prayer meetings to promote the cause.

At the same time, stationed at the president's figurative right elbow were the conservatives, moderate Republicans, many of the white people of the loyal border slave states, and the Democratic minority in Congress, all striving to keep Lincoln committed to the status quo. And despite his personal detestation of slavery, Lincoln himself had never favored immediate abolition. His own preferences were for some vaguely defined process of gradual emancipation stretched out over years or decades, with governmental compensation for enslavers, all linked to a program of colonization to rid America of its Black inhabitants by sending them overseas. As the war opened, Lincoln still considered abolition a radical expedient.

He also knew that, as pervasive as antislavery sentiment might be, there was strong opposition to emancipation in the North in 1861. Consequently—and although no one doubted that slavery was the cause of the war—the administration's war aims did not, at first, include any prospect of changes to the peculiar institution. The federal government's war remained a war for the Union—the old Union composed of states both slave and free. Had Northern victory somehow come during the first two years of the Civil War, slavery could have survived in the reunited nation.

On July 25, 1861, just four days after the disastrous Union defeat at the first battle of Bull Run, Congress passed the War Aims Resolution. It declared that the war's purpose was not "'overthrowing or interfering with the rights or established institutions [i.e., slavery] of those States,' but to 'defend and maintain the supremacy of the Constitution and to preserve the Union.'"[4] The insurgent states were in effect invited to return to the Union with slavery protected. Lincoln himself said, "In considering the policy to be adopted for suppressing the insurrection, I have been anxious and careful that the inevitable conflict for this purpose shall not degenerate into a violent and remorseless revolutionary struggle."[5] And nothing seemed more revolutionary at the time than abolition. In resisting calls for emancipation in the first year of the war, President Lincoln warned that "half the army would lay down their arms and three other states would join the rebellion."[6]

A case can be made that negrophobic racism was even more pronounced in the North than in the South. After all, white Southerners had been living with Blacks for generations. There were vast regions of the North that were completely free of Blacks and determined to stay that way. As much as 98 percent of Black people in America then lived in the slave states.[7]

After he left his native slave state of Kentucky at age seven, Abraham Lincoln himself encountered relatively few Black people before he became president and few enough then. In several midwestern states, referenda to give the vote to free Blacks were defeated by overwhelming majorities in the 1850s. African Americans were not even allowed to move into several of these states, including Lincoln's Illinois. Blacks were still denied the vote in nineteen of twenty-four Northern states in 1865.[8]

There was a small African American community in Springfield during Lincoln's residency. He lived in the Illinois capital longer than at any other place—twenty-four years in all, five as a single man and nineteen more as a husband who immediately became a father. During that time, Springfield's population increased sixfold, from about fifteen hundred to about ninety-three hundred. Of the larger number, 234 were Black, about 2.5 percent of the population. When Lincoln arrived in 1837, there were a mere twenty-six African Americans in the town, about 1.7 percent of the population. Surprisingly, six of those twenty-six Black residents were enslaved.[9] Yet Illinois was supposedly a free state carved out of the old Northwest Territory. The Northwest Ordinance of 1787, passed by Congress under the Articles of Confederation, had ruled: "There shall be neither slavery nor involuntary servitude in the said territory, otherwise than in the punishment of crimes whereof the party shall have been duly convicted."[10] (Identical wording appears in the Thirteenth Amendment to the US Constitution, which abolished slavery nationwide when it was ratified at the end of 1865.)

Nevertheless, the first two decades of the nineteenth century saw determined local resistance to the federal government's explicit prohibition on slavery in the Northwest Territory. That ban was among the terms under which the government was offering land to new settlers at attractive prices, with liberal credit for those lacking cash for lump-sum payments. Most of the pioneers who settled the lands just north of the Ohio River came from the South. (Lincoln's own parents had come from Virginia.) A good many of them hated the idea of leaving behind on the far bank of the Ohio River the system that had served them so well in their old homes. There were plenty of efforts to evade or overturn the ban, including some in Lincoln's southern Illinois. The would-be enslavers never succeeded in overturning the law, but the state legislature did contrive a system of indentured servitude that enabled whites to keep Black people in a kind of captivity resembling enslavement in many respects, though it did not allow the buying or selling of these indentured people. Some of Abraham Lincoln's in-laws and friends, as well as many of his legal clients, owned such semi-enslaved "servants" in the 1840s. These attempts to plant human bondage in free territory died away before long. Nevertheless, it is clear that Lincoln was witness to enslavement even after he left Kentucky for the nominally free territories of the Old Northwest.

Opposition to slavery did not mean sympathy or respect for African Americans. Many had joined the new Republican Party in the 1850s not to help enslaved people but to keep Blacks out of the territories and make the West white man's country. David Wilmot, the Pennsylvania Democratic congressman who proposed banning slavery from territory seized or bought from Mexico, explained that it was for "the cause and the rights of white freeman. I would preserve to free white labor a fair country, a rich inheritance, where the sons of toil, of my own race and own color, can live without the disgrace which association with negro slavery brings upon free labor."[11]

The antislavery Whig, future Radical Republican, and presumed friend of Black people Benjamin Franklin Wade of Ohio reacted venomously to the society he encountered when he first arrived in Washington, DC, as a congressman in 1851: "On the whole, this is a mean God forsaken Nigger ridden place. The Niggers are certainly the most intelligent part of the population but the Nigger smell I cannot bear, yet it is in on and about everything you see."[12] Many other white antislavery leaders voiced similar racist opinions. To counter Democratic charges that "a wild and fanatical sentimentality toward the black race" motivated the new party, Republicans were always eager to show that their policies were devised for the benefit of white Americans.[13] His party's determination to ban slavery from the western territories was "not so much in reference to the welfare of the negro," said Illinois senator Lyman Trumbull, a rival and later ally of Abraham Lincoln. It was rather "for the protection of the laboring whites, for the protection of ourselves and our liberties."[14]

During the war, most Union soldiers eventually came to accept emancipation as a means of securing victory, but many initially objected to the Emancipation Proclamation. One Ohio private declared, "We did not enlist to fight for the negro and I can tell you that *we never shall* . . . sacrafise lives for the liberty of a miserable black race of beings. . . . Abolitionism is traitorism in its darkest collar."[15] A wartime New York newspaper revealed Northern attitudes toward Blacks with the shocking observation that "filthy black niggers, greasy, sweaty, and disgusting, now jostle white people and even ladies everywhere, even at the President's levees."[16]

So it is clear that domestic politics informed Lincoln's cautious approach to slavery. It was true that the Republican Party was now suddenly ascendant. The scores of senators and congressmen who had departed Congress when their states voted for secession had almost all been Democrats. This gave Republicans in the 1860 Thirty-Seventh Congress a substantial majority of thirty-two out of forty-eight in the Senate and a smaller but still ample margin of 106 out of 176 in the House, a ratio that would be approximated when the Thirty-Eighth Congress was elected in 1862.[17]

So an upstart third party only seven years old suddenly found itself in control of both the White House and Congress—in a word, the federal government. But with eleven states now repudiating that government, the nation seemed but a shadow of its former self. And Lincoln's 39 percent of the 1860 popular vote was certainly no mandate.

Along with a hands-off approach to slavery went the limited war policy that the Lincoln administration followed during the early part of the Civil War. For too long, the president clung to the mistaken notion that most white Southerners still favored the Union—that only a minority of extremists had pushed the South into secession. Lincoln was accordingly determined to wage a limited war, a soft war to keep the loyalty of the many he believed favored national reunification. A hard war, an unlimited war, Lincoln's "remorseless revolutionary struggle," directed against the white Southern civilian population and their property, would make reconciliation difficult, maybe even impossible. The war must be limited to campaigns of armies against armies, sparing, so far as possible, civilians and their property—particularly their most important property of all—the South's four million enslaved people. When he called up the first troops in April 1861, Lincoln had promised that "the utmost care will be observed . . . to avoid any devastation, any destruction of, or interference with, property, or any disturbance of peaceful citizens."[18]

The president had the ideal leader for this kind of soft war: Major General George B. McClellan, "the Young Napoleon," the Army of the Potomac's popular thirty-five-year-old commander. The West Point alumnus was a conservative, proslavery Democrat from Pennsylvania. He was a brilliant organizer who inspired the admiration, even the worship, of the men in the ranks. To a man, the troops loved "Little Mac." In command of his regiments, brigades, divisions, and corps, McClellan had placed his acolytes, Democratic-leaning colonels and generals who thought as he did. None of these officers had any use for abolitionism or, for that matter, for Lincoln and his Republican administration. There were occasions of dark talk in the Army of the Potomac of marching on the capital to set up a military dictatorship. General McClellan blamed the administration for his lack of military success. He knew that he himself never had and never would make a mistake. He and his disciples, moreover, held Northern abolitionists and Southern fire-eaters equally guilty of provoking the war in the first place. The general said Massachusetts was just as guilty as South Carolina. McClellan lectured President Lincoln that the war "should be conducted upon the highest principles known to Christian civilization. It should not be a war looking to the subjugation of the people of any State in any event. It should not be at all a war upon population, but against armed forces and political organizations. Neither confiscation of property, political executions of persons, territorial organization of States, or forcible abolition of slavery should be contemplated for a moment."[19]

For all his charisma and administrative genius, General McClellan had a fatal flaw: he suffered from what President Lincoln called "the slows." Given command of the most powerful and best equipped army in the world, McClellan was most reluctant to commit it to battle. McClellan's egregious failure to act decisively was a combination of his procrastination and indecision, his vast overestimation of the enemy's strength, his tactical cowardice and tendency to panic, his ceaseless feuding with the War Department and the president, and a consistent discourteous refusal to accept the subordination of the military to civilian control that was so pronounced that it nearly amounted to disloyalty.

Lincoln did all he could to prod McClellan into action. Finally, early in 1862, the general unburdened himself of his closely held plans. He proposed a complicated, ponderous sea and land invasion of the Virginia peninsula formed by the York and James Rivers below Richmond. When all of the Army of the Potomac was ashore, McClellan would move against the objective from the east. Lincoln had preferred a straightforward, overland advance

*In 1862, Major General George B. McClellan, a proslavery
Democrat, commanded the most powerful army in the world—
the Union's Army of the Potomac. He nevertheless displayed a conspicuous timidity, refusing to go on the attack against Robert E. Lee. President
Lincoln soon concluded that McClellan suffered from "the slows" and
fired him after the battle of Antietam. McClellan subsequently ran a
losing campaign against his former commander in chief as the
Democratic Party's 1864 presidential candidate.*

south from Manassas against Richmond, but he didn't believe he
possessed sufficient military sagacity to overrule the general in
charge of all the Northern armies. McClellan set the campaign in
motion. Many believed the coming action would end the rebellion once and for all.

The fair prospects McClellan had of actually capturing Richmond were squandered by the general's own timidity and incompetence. A few weeks of overcautious campaigning brought the Army of the Potomac within five miles of Richmond by May 1862. But then the campaign collapsed. Pushed back from Richmond by Robert E. Lee in the bloody Seven Days' Battles, McClellan gave up the fight and retreated downriver to the protection of the big guns of the US fleet. There he remained, with no apparent intention of moving against the Southern capital again. Northern morale plummeted.

Lee presently trounced a second Union army under General John Pope at Second Manassas in August. Then, in Maryland at the savage battle of Antietam in September 1862, McClellan managed a tactical draw—although a strategic victory that turned back Lee's invasion of the North—from circumstances that would have given a bolder general a crushing victory. He refused to follow up and pursue Lee's battered army into Virginia.

Lincoln soon decided he had had enough of General McClellan, enough of limited war and the scrupulous observance of the property rights of Southern enslavers. Those approaches had failed. Public opinion shifted as military success continued to elude the North. Many now believed it was time to really hurt the secessionists. Most of all, that meant moving against slavery. Congress had already led the way by passing two Confiscation Acts permitting the freeing of slaves held by disloyal owners. One Union general, Benjamin Butler, had ignored the Fugitive Slave law by taking in thousands of Virginia escapees from enslavement, declaring them "contraband of war," or lawfully confiscated enemy property. *Contraband* soon became a synonym for Blacks escaping enslavement.

At the same time, some of the most compelling arguments for emancipation came not from the halls of government, the churches, or the editorial pages of the nation's press but from the actions of the enslaved people themselves. In Lenin's memorable formulation, they voted with their feet, escaping to the Union armies in search of freedom whenever they got the chance. Crowds of enslaved people—families, old people, and children, as well as unattached young men—ran to their masters' Yankee enemies, just as their ancestors had run to the British during the American Revolution and the War of 1812.

These African Americans understood better and earlier the true meaning of the Civil War than did most of the Northern soldiers. Most of those men had enlisted to save the Union, not to end slavery. But Blacks saw from the beginning that this was a contest between freedom and slavery. In his *Memoirs*, General William T. Sherman recounted a conversation with an aged Georgia slave: "I asked him if he understood about the war, and its progress. He said he did, that he had been looking for the 'Angel of the Lord' ever since he was knee high. And though we professed to be fighting for the Union, he supposed that Slavery was the Cause, and that our Success would be his Freedom. I asked him if all the Negro Slaves comprehended this fact, and he said they surely did."[20] The flood of runaways and their uncertain legal status put enormous pressure on Lincoln to take decisive action on the slavery question. The enslaved did much to bring about their own freedom.

President Lincoln made a final plea for gradual compensated emancipation. In July 1862, he called to the White House the congressional representatives of the loyal border slave states. He told them that if they would agree to free the enslaved in their states over an extended period, he would see to it that Congress approved millions of dollars in US bonds to pay enslavers for their human property. Lincoln said this program would bring the war to a speedy conclusion. The rebels would see that they no longer had any hope of the secession of the border states. They might even consider seeking federal compensation for their own slaves.

The president appealed to the reason and fiscal conservativism of the border states' leaders, showing them how many taxpayers' dollars could be saved by the program of compensated emancipation he wanted them to set in motion. The Civil War was now costing the nation the vast sum of $2 million a day. In the border states of Delaware, Maryland, Kentucky, Missouri, and in the District of Columbia there were 432,622 enslaved people. At a market price of $400 each, all of these people could be freed for $173,048,800 in compensation to their enslavers. The cost of waging the war for sixty-seven days came to $174,000,000. So the price of just sixty-seven days of war could permanently bind the border slave states to the Union by making them free states.[21] Lacking hope of new allies, the Southern rebellion would soon wither away, or so Lincoln predicted. Everyone could see that the war was sure to last much longer than sixty-seven more days. Despite the seemingly impeccable logic of Lincoln's presentation, the border state politicians curtly rejected his plea. They were loyal to the Union. They supported the ongoing war against the rebellion. But they had absolutely no intention of giving up slavery. It was another dead end in the limited war approach.

The president had earlier overturned two emancipation decrees announced by Union generals John C. Frémont and David Hunter in their areas of command. Abolitionists were outraged. Lincoln insisted that emancipation was the prerogative of the executive, not the military. But in overturning the generals' decrees, the president had made it clear he believed that emancipation was a legitimate measure he could use if the time was right. By July 1862, the time had come. "We must free the slaves or be ourselves subdued," Lincoln said.[22] He would proclaim emancipation. John Wilkes Booth—and millions of other white Americans, North and South—would be outraged.

Meanwhile, rumors of assassination conspiracies abounded, and more threats and warnings poured into the White House. Many of President Lincoln's advisers and friends tried to impress on him the danger he was in. The two most concerned were Secretary of War Edwin Stanton and Lincoln's Illinois lawyer friend Ward Hill Lamon. Lamon had appointed himself Lincoln's unofficial, volunteer bodyguard. Lincoln reciprocated by appointing Lamon Marshall of the District of Columbia. He was a big man, a fighter of duels, standing a burly six foot, two inches and usually burdened with a small arsenal of pistols, Bowie knives, brass knuckles, and blackjacks. He was known to sleep on the floor outside the president's White House bedroom. Lincoln dismissed Lamon's fears. "I think, for a man of accredited courage, you are the most panicky person I ever knew. You can see more dangers to me than all the other friends I have."[23]

Edwin McMasters Stanton was the tireless engine of the war effort—brilliant, impatient, irascible, and brutally rude to everyone, including the president himself. He suspected that the idea of taking out the Yankee president might suggest itself to the Southern high command as a practical military gambit as Southern prospects grew increasingly grim. In 1862, Stanton had stationed a company of infantry at the White House as guards. They camped on the grounds. The following year, Stanton also assigned a squad of cavalry to guard duty. But he remained appalled by the risks the president took. He particularly deplored Lincoln's habit of attending the theater without proper security. Lincoln politely ignored his war secretary.

The president remained resolutely fatalistic. Lincoln's abiding fatalism, his belief in something he called the "Doctrine of Necessity" that controlled all events, had begun with the sermons brimming with Calvinist predetermination he'd listened to as a boy in little Baptist churches in frontier Kentucky and Indiana. He often told law partner Billy Herndon that "what is to be will be, and no efforts nor prayers of ours can change, alter, modify, or reverse the decree."[24] Besides, he argued, he could hardly perform the duties of his office and remain perfectly safe. "I cannot be shut up in an iron cage and guarded. If I have business at the

*Edwin McMasters Stanton was the tireless engine of
the Union war effort—brilliant, impatient, irascible, and brutally
rude to everyone, including the president himself. He was deeply fearful
for Lincoln's personal safety. Stanton particularly deplored the president's habit of attending the theater without proper security.*

War Office, I must take my hat and go there, and if to kill me is
within the purposes of this rebellion, no precaution can prevent
it."[25] Lincoln believed that nothing could protect him from a determined assassin, a man willing to trade his own life for that of
the president.

On July 2, 1863, the second day of the great three-day battle
then raging at Gettysburg, Pennsylvania, Mary Todd Lincoln was
seriously injured when she was thrown from the runaway presi-

dential carriage. It was soon discovered that sabotage to the vehicle was the reason the driver had lost control of the team.[26]

Later that same year, after Lincoln delivered the Gettysburg Address in November, he was laid up for two weeks with varioloid, a mild form of smallpox. "There was some suspicion that the president had been infected by a veiled lady, who was suspected of being a Confederate Secret Service agent, who had entered the White House shortly before and managed to get close enough to Lincoln to kiss him for that purpose."[27] (It was most fortunate that the president's insanely jealous wife never learned of that encounter.)

Then, in the summer of 1864, came a warning so forcible that even Lincoln couldn't ignore it. One night at about eleven o'clock, he was nearing Soldiers' Home, his retreat in hot weather, when a shot rang out. He heard the whizz of the projectile. His hat was violently jerked from his head. His horse bolted. On examination in the morning, the hat was found to have been neatly drilled by a bullet.[28] Lincoln tried to laugh it off as an accident, but even he now saw the need for greater security. He almost never rode alone again. Stanton tried to make sure the squad of cavalry went with him when he traveled on horseback or in his carriage. Lincoln complained about the noise the clanging of the troopers' weapons and gear made. He was afraid one of the green soldiers might trigger an accidental shot. But only rarely could he escape his escort.

The poet Walt Whitman, a volunteer nurse in the capital's vast complex of military hospitals, often saw the president and his escort riding through the city: "He always has a company of twenty-five or thirty cavalry, with sabers drawn and held upright over their shoulders. They say this guard is against his personal wish, but he let his counselors have their way. The party makes no great show of uniform or horses. Mr. Lincoln on the saddle generally rides a good-sized, easy-going gray horse, is dress'd in black, somewhat rusty and dusty, wears a stiff black hat, and looks about as ordinary in attire, etc., as the commonest man."[29] Whitman's casual observation shows that any lurking conspirator could have as easily tracked the president's movements.

Beginning in November 1864, the month of the viciously contested election, the head of the Washington Metropolitan Police Force ordered, at Lamon's urging, a policeman to accompany the president at all times as a body guard. Chosen from the ranks, a cadre of four or five men served in rotation so that one was always on duty. They were armed with revolvers, but this was before any professionalization of law enforcement. Paid forty dollars a month, several of these feckless men had been disciplined in the past for taking bribes or sleeping or drinking on duty. Officer John F. Parker was not assigned to the duty until early April 1865. It was Parker who would fail to guard the presidential party at Ford's Theatre on the fatal evening of April 14.

It sometimes amused Lincoln to escape his guards, and when Stanton and Lamon weren't around, as when he visited Richmond with his son Tad on April 4, 1865, the president was free to take all the risks he wanted. To no avail, Stanton had warned him then about entering the fallen rebel capital: "Allow me respectfully to ask you to consider whether you ought to expose the nation to the consequence of any disaster to yourself in the pursuit of a treacherous and dangerous enemy like the rebel army. If it was a question concerning yourself only I should not presume to say a word. Commanding Generals are in the line of their duty in running such risks. But is the political head of a nation in the same condition[?]" Lincoln blithely wired back, "I will take care of myself."[30]

16

"A STAR OF THE FIRST MAGNITUDE"

Booth flourished during the Civil War. In his early twenties, he was already one of the most successful stage performers of his day. He had made a fortune in salaries and benefit performances, tens of thousands of dollars, and though he spent freely, he had managed to invest substantial amounts in stocks, bonds, real estate, and oil leases. The actor had earned glowing reviews, thunderous applause, and the adulation of thousands.

Not a few concluded that the young actor was possessed of authentic genius. What poor reviews he did receive didn't deter theatergoers from paying to see him. Many saw for him a brilliant future at the very pinnacle of the theatrical world. Women adored him recklessly, and he had his pick of the most beautiful—society ladies as well as actresses and prostitutes. Respected by his fellow actors, he had friends everywhere, men and women who truly admired him. He was regarded as a warmhearted gentleman, as well as a gifted actor. He was free to pick his next city, his next theater, his next play, his next salary, his next love affair. He had everything to live for. No one had more to lose from an early death. As he put it himself in November 1864, justifying his decision to throw everything over and devote himself to his plot against Lincoln:

> I know how foolish I shall be deemed, for undertaking such a step, as this, Where on the one side, I have many friends, and everything to make me happy. Where my profession *alone* has gained me an income of *more than* Twenty thousand dollars a year. And where my great personal ambition in my profession has such a great field for labor. . . . But God is my judge I love *justice*, more than I do a country, that disowns it. More than fame and wealth.[1]

He certainly understood that the course he had chosen could easily cost him his life.

Despite the money and applause and women, Booth grew desperately unhappy as the war raged. He was unhappy with history itself. His desperation became all the harder to bear each time news of renewed Northern victories or more Southern reverses reached his ears. Asia had maintained that her brother "was a man so single in his devotion, so unswerving in his principles, that he would yield everything for the cause he espoused."[2] By 1863, Union might threatened to overwhelm that cause. Fighting now what historian Allan Nevins called the "organized war," the North was finally learning how to bring its enormous advantages in wealth and population to bear. By the war's third year, the cause that Booth loved so well was going down to defeat.

Lincoln's 1864 reelection marked the last turning point, the final battle that irrevocably lost the rebellion its bid for independence. Had Lincoln's Democratic rival, the cashiered general George B. McClellan, won the presidency—as seemed highly probable in the summer of 1864—a truce followed by a negotiated peace securing Southern independence and the survival of slavery might have followed. But with the incumbent assured a second term, the only conditions for ending the war were now those on which President Lincoln himself insisted: immediate surrender and the death of slavery. White Southerners regarded such terms as unconditional surrender. Abraham Lincoln was rapidly driving the whole insurgent enterprise into what the rebels began calling the "last ditch," where the only choice lay between capitulation and death.

As the end drew nearer, John Wilkes Booth, for one, was determined to fight to the death. He would never give up. "I go to see, and share the bitter end," he said in November 1864. "It is either extermination or slavery for *themselves* (worse than death) to draw from. I would know *my* choice." He would go south, he vowed, and "will proudly beg permission to triumph or die in that same 'ditch' by her side."[3]

Other Southern whites seemed more willing to accept their approaching fate. "We are going to be wiped off the earth," mourned Dixie diarist Mary Chesnut. "The deep waters are closing over us."[4] The insurgents would lose not only the sovereign nationhood they had claimed for themselves but also their "peculiar institution," African slavery, the very thing they had gone to war to preserve. If they had swallowed their outrage at Lincoln's election and stayed in the Union, slavery might have persisted for years.

In his three and a half years as a star on national tour from November 1860 to May 1864, Booth played throughout the country—the wide expanse of the North that lay between the Atlantic and the Mississippi. Crossing the military lines was no small feat. Despite his love for the South, Booth never appeared in secessionist territory. He never left the Union or the Southern regions it had occupied. He bragged to his sister that he had a pass from General Grant to cross the military lines, but this cannot have been true. His travels did take him south to Yankee-occupied Nashville and New Orleans, where he grieved and raged to see the hard hand of the Union army bearing down on white Southern civilians. He wrote, "I have never been upon a battlefield, but, O my countrymen, could you all but see the *reality* or effects of this horrid war, as I have seen them (in *every State*, save Virginia) I know you would think like me. And would pray the Almighty to create in the Northern mind a sense of *right* and *justice* (even should it possess no seasoning of mercy)."[5]

Booth lost about half of his scheduled performances (and paydays) during his tours of late 1860 and early 1861 because of injuries. Just as the gunshot wound had shortened his first star tour in the Deep South in 1860, so the following tour in the North—in Rochester and Albany, New York, from January through April 1861, and in Portland, Maine—was marred by a series of injuries inflicted by edged weapons.

The fight to the death in the last act of *Richard III* was already famous as the young actor's most thrilling bit of stagecraft. In this, he followed the example of his famous father. Like his father, he dragged the combat out far longer than William Shakespeare had probably intended. He tumbled one hapless Richmond into the orchestra pit, breaking his shoulder, and inflicted a bloody wound on another. Sometimes his opponents begged him to hurry up and die. When the curtain finally came down, the star often found himself too exhausted to move after his supreme effort, lying on the stage panting for as much as ten minutes.

Blades menaced him offstage as well. In Albany on April 26, 1861, the amorous actor escaped an attempt on his life but sustained a slash to the face at the hands of his lover, the comely young actress Henrietta Irving. Booth's simultaneous affair with her sister had aroused her jealous rage. A newspaper reported that Miss Irving "entered the room of J. Wilkes Booth . . . and attacked him with a dirk, cutting his face badly. She did not, however, succeed in inflicting a mortal wound. Failing in this, she retired to her own room and stabbed herself, not bad enough 'to go dead.' "[6]

Though Booth's wound bled profusely, the scar near his hairline did not mar his extraordinary good looks, but he did have to take some nights off. That same month, President Lincoln proclaimed a naval blockade of the seaports of the insurgent states, while the rifles of the Sixth Massachusetts blasted a path through a Baltimore mob on the regiment's way to break the siege of Washington, further inflaming the ardently pro-Southern people of Booth's home town.

Hot weather ended the theatrical season. By October, however, the star was ready to take to the road again. His second, and altogether successful, star season spanned the fall of 1861 to midsummer of 1862. He gave 162 performances in all and hauled in the cash. This time, he appeared in larger and more important cities and for longer runs than he had during his 1860–61 tour. In February 1862, John Wilkes Booth appeared for the first time as a star in his hometown. The *Baltimore Sun* declared him "an actor that with the suddenness of a meteor now illumines the dramatic horizon in a blaze of light, attracting and entrancing in other cities thousands by that hereditary genius that made his sire so famous."[7] A few days later, the *Sun*'s friendly critic revisited his astronomical metaphor, adding that "mid the galaxy of stars that have illuminated our theatrical firmament none has shown with greater brilliancy than our young artist; admiring audiences throughout the country, comprising the learned, the discriminating, and the people at large have conferred upon him their warmest admiration, and here in his native city, crowded audiences have nightly listened to his personations with riveted attention."[8]

Earlier in the tour, a disturbing incident had taken place in Buffalo. The *Chicago Tribune* reported that the actor's Southern sympathies had gotten him in trouble during his stay in the New York city. A storefront had displayed an exhibition of war trophies—weapons and flags captured from the enemy. This instance of Yankee triumphalism angered Booth, who proceeded to smash the plate glass window and vandalize the exhibit. He was arrested and fined fifty dollars.[9]

He spent the summer with his family in Philadelphia and New York City. Booth's second star tour in 1862–63 opened in slaveholding country, in the little city of Lexington, Kentucky, on October 23. He played *Richard III* for two nights at the Opera House before moving on to a two-week engagement in Louisville.

The month before, Robert E. Lee's first invasion of the North had been blunted at the battle of Antietam, just across the Potomac in Maryland. Taking Union victory as a sign from God on behalf of the enslaved, a few days later, on September 22, 1862, President Lincoln issued the Preliminary Emancipation Proclamation. The document gave the insurgents fair warning: if they persisted in their rebellion for another one hundred days—that is until January 1, 1863—the final Emancipation Proclamation would go into effect, declaring "forever free" all the enslaved people within parts of the South then still defying United States authority. Everyone knew there was no chance of the rebels standing down.

John Wilkes Booth denounced emancipation and resorted to the old white supremacist cliché that it could only result in the extermination of the African Americans. "Yet Heaven knows *no one* would be willing to do, *more* for the negro race than I," he wrote. "Could I but see a way to still better their condition, But Lincoln's policy is only preparing the way for their total annihilation."[10]

On the momentous New Year's Day of 1863, the actor performed double roles as both brothers in *The Corsican Brothers*, a popular adaptation of a novella by Alexandre Dumas.[11] Vastly more significant were New Year's Day events in Washington, DC. That morning, the White House was thrown open for the customary reception. Any respectable white person willing to endure the line that snaked across the grounds could exchange New Year's greetings with the president himself. Abraham Lincoln worked the line for two hours, shaking hands with thousands of well-wishers and curiosity-seekers.

By the time he finished the ordeal, his huge right hand was swollen and trembling. And now he needed a steady hand. Waiting for him in his office upstairs was the engrossed parchment copy of the Emancipation Proclamation sent over from the State Department. Only his signature was required to proclaim millions of enslaved Americans free. As he dipped his pen, the president fretted that a shaky signature might make it seem he harbored doubts. "Now this signature will be closely examined," he said, "and if they find my hand trembled they will say 'he had some compunctions.'"[12] Then, with an effort of will, he firmly inscribed his name without a tremor. For Lincoln did not doubt the wisdom or the righteousness of the Emancipation Proclamation. He considered it "my greatest and most enduring contribution" and "the central act of my administration and the great event of the nineteenth century."[13] Lincoln was right, of course. Emancipation is easily the most revolutionary and far-reaching policy ever embraced by a US president.

Most white Southerners agreed that emancipation was revolutionary, seeing in Lincoln's decree a dangerous appeal to violence that threatened to bring on cycles of horror and bloodshed in an apocalyptic race war. Jefferson Davis, as we have seen, immediately condemned the proclamation as "the most execrable measure recorded in the history of guilty man."[14] The Confederate Congress called it a "gross violation of the usages of civilized warfare, an outrage on the rights of public property, and an invitation to an atrocious servile war."[15]

The final Emancipation Proclamation differed in several important ways from the Preliminary Emancipation Proclamation issued one hundred days earlier. For the first time, the president declared that formerly enslaved and other African American men would "be received into the armed forces of the United States." Significant as well, in the final document, Lincoln made no mention of colonization, the old scheme to ship Black people out of the country. The Preliminary Emancipation Proclamation had mentioned colonization as a possibility for the people freed under its provisions. Abraham Lincoln seems to have decided that if some African Americans would prove willing to give their lives

*In this rebel caricature, a brutal President Lincoln, guided by
satanic powers, treads the Constitution underfoot as he proclaims
freedom for millions of enslaved people. Liquor, John Brown, and the
horrors of the Haitian slave rebellion inspire him to compose the
document that Jefferson Davis called "the most execrable
measure recorded in the history of guilty man."*

Adalbert J. Volck, engraving, "Lincoln Drafting the Emancipation Proclamation," *Confederate War Etchings*, 1863. Huntington Library HM 41785 (8).

for their country, it *was* their true country, theirs and all their
people. He never endorsed colonization again. When the War of
the Rebellion had commenced, the Southern enslavers had been
clear about why they were leaving the Union and on what central principle they intended to found their so-called nation. That
principle was white supremacy—in practical terms the preservation of African slavery and thus the continuation of the Southern
social system. This was their reason for breaking with a federal

government now seemingly dominated by a sectional antislavery party. As Alexander Stephens declared in his "corner-stone speech," the enslavers' new republic was founded on "the great truth that the negro is not equal to the white man; that slavery, subordination to the superior race is his natural and normal condition."[16]

Yet once the gamble of rebellion had been lost, how the former enslavers and Lost Cause apologists changed their tune! Slavery, they have continued to argue ever since Appomattox, had never been a significant issue, and its defense had not been an important motive for secession. Alexander Stephens even denied having said what he was reported to have said in the "corner-stone" speech. He claimed that his meaning had been distorted, his words changed by the sloppy reporting of careless and dishonest journalists. It was Fake News.

To this day, Lincoln's detractors and neo-Confederates of all stripes, indeed all who wish to deny the centrality of white supremacy to American history and to reject the emancipationist legacy of the Civil War, delight in saying that slavery was not the cause of the war. They also love to argue that the Emancipation Proclamation was a nullity that freed no one when it was issued. "Not a single slave" and "only in those areas where the government had no powers of enforcement" are favored phrases. Wrong. While exact numbers cannot be known, the Emancipation Proclamation freed millions of enslaved Americans at the very moment that President Lincoln affixed his signature to the document.

That most of the enslaved themselves knew nothing of their suddenly changed condition did nothing to alter the reality of that change. Nor did the furious denials of the enslavers and the insurgent government at the time mean anything. Nor did it matter that most of the newly freed people would not enjoy anything resembling freedom for months or years to come, if ever. It didn't matter that some time would pass before the white people of the

South would swear through gritted teeth to uphold the Constitution and "to faithfully support all proclamations of the President made during the existing rebellion having reference to slaves."[17] It didn't even matter that not until 1865 or later would the former slave states finally ratify the Thirteenth Amendment to the US Constitution, abolishing slavery. It was true that on New Year's Day 1863, all these changes lay in the uncertain future. But it is equally true that millions gained their freedom in the same instant Abraham Lincoln lifted the nib of his pen from the parchment.

Those who remain unconvinced may find this little thought experiment helpful: We all know that in July 1776, the Continental Congress declared that "these United Colonies are, and of Right ought to be Free and Independent States . . . Absolved from all Allegiance to the British Crown." George III's government denied this assertion with indignation, adding that the patriots would be "crush'd to atoms" by British power. On the contrary, the king and his ministers insisted, the colonies were members of the British Empire and as such, subject to the rule of Parliament, which possessed absolute sovereignty within the empire. Two contradictory, indeed mutually exclusive, propositions: the patriots said that America was independent; the British king and Parliament said that America was not independent. It was a difference of opinion that would persist until Britain conceded American independence in the Treaty of Paris in 1783.

But for purposes of this experiment, let us suppose that it is now December 1776, just half a year after the Declaration of Independence. The Howe brothers' mighty army and navy, the most powerful expeditionary force the world has ever seen, remains concentrated around New York City. The Howes have inflicted a series of crushing defeats on George Washington's Continentals. In a matter of weeks, the patriot army has dissolved like a lump of sugar dropped into a cup of hot tea. More than twenty thousand strong on the Fourth of July, the Continental Army can now muster no more than twenty-five hundred dispirited, retreating soldiers, many of them barefoot in the snow, all of them hungry and freezing.

So who was right and who was wrong? Was America independent in December 1776, as the patriots insisted, despite all appearances to the contrary? Or had British military might elbowed its way onto the floor of the Continental Congress and repealed the Declaration of Independence? It seems that the answer has to be that the Americans were right. They were independent because they said so and because they meant to see the conflict through.

Just so, the Emancipation Proclamation actually freed the enslaved people held in the areas in rebellion against the authority of the United States on January 1, 1863, despite all appearances to the contrary, because that is what the document said and because the Lincoln administration meant to see it through.

Historian James McPherson has observed that "Lincoln's decision in 1862 to issue an emancipation proclamation freed himself as much as it freed the slaves—freed him from the agonizing contradiction between his antislavery convictions and his constitutional obligations."[18] Lincoln had moved slowly. He always had to remember that most of the white population of the North remained bitterly prejudiced. Whatever his personal sentiments, a president who hoped to unite the country could not disregard such widely held prejudices. Everyone knew, Lincoln had said in 1854, that "the great mass of white people will not [accept Blacks as equals]. Whether this feeling accords with justice and sound judgement, is not the sole question, if indeed, it is any part of it. A universal feeling, whether well or ill-founded, cannot be safely disregarded. We cannot, then, make them equals."[19]

If Northerners believed their president was working for abolition or racial equality, the Union war effort could founder. When he finally decided on emancipation in the summer of 1862, Lincoln understood that it had come as a war measure enacted strictly to secure Union victory, not as a humanitarian crusade.

(And when the time came, he knew better than to call the crucial document "The Abolition Proclamation.")

That same summer, Horace Greeley, the erratic editor of the influential *New-York Tribune*, urged immediate emancipation on the president in a front-page appeal. Lincoln replied in a famous, and famously misunderstood, public letter. On August 22, 1862, exactly one month before he issued the Preliminary Emancipation Proclamation, the president wrote the *New-York Herald* in a letter read by millions:

> My paramount object in this struggle *is* to save the Union, and is *not* either to save or to destroy slavery. If I could save the Union without freeing *any* slave I would do it, and if I could save it by freeing *all* the slaves I would do it; and if I could save it by freeing some and leaving others alone I would also do that. What I do about slavery, and the colored race, I do because I believe it helps to save the Union.[20]

The Preliminary Emancipation Proclamation was then resting unsigned on Lincoln's desk. He had already resolved to issue it as soon as a Union military victory could impart authority to the declaration. (Antietam would provide that victory in less than a month.) So by announcing in his public letter that all his actions regarding slavery and freedom were designed only to save the Union, Lincoln was shrewdly preparing popular acceptance of the Preliminary Emancipation Proclamation as a Union-saving measure, not as some abolitionist crusade.

Lincoln's clever ploy has been lost on his detractors past and present, who have preferred to take his words literally. Defenders of the Old South, unreconstructed rebels, and assorted neo-Confederates have eagerly seized on this letter as proof that the Yankee president cared not a whit for the enslaved Americans over whose fate the great war was raging. It didn't matter what happened to them so long as the Northern capitalism was saved. Blacks could all remain in slavery for all Lincoln cared. These detractors also have cited Lincoln's statement as proof that slavery was not the cause of the Civil War. They have been delighted to have what they believe to be conclusive evidence, an actual admission in Lincoln's own words that the so-called Great Emancipator had provoked war not to end slavery but to force the freedom-loving Southern whites to submit to the Republican Party's imperialistic ambitions to remake the United States as an all-powerful, centralized polity controlled by Northern capitalism. Talk of emancipation was only humanitarian window-dressing concealing the Republicans' remorseless grasp for tyrannical power. Or so say the angry promoters of this thoroughly ahistorical proposition, a notion that retains considerable appeal for defenders of the enslavers' insurrection, white supremacists, and the assorted congeries of antigovernment libertarians. Like all conspiracy theories, this faulty interpretation of the movement to end slavery has proven attractive to these groups. Those who are troubled by the random contingency of human affairs can take comfort in fables that provide an illusion of agency and motive in a universe devoid of meaning and purpose.

Abraham Lincoln knew that the white supremacists within the Union could be found not only among the Democratic opposition in Congress and in the slaveholding loyal border states but also in the ranks of the army and in the army's top command, in Congress and the federal departments, in the state governments, in the press, among conservative Republicans, and even in the president's own cabinet. These were the people Lincoln needed to keep on his side. A president considering emancipation didn't need to win over the radicals or the abolitionists. He already had them, whether they knew it or not. What he did need was the loyalty of Northerners opposed to Black freedom. After he finally became committed to emancipation, Lincoln continued to define it as a military tactic. He hammered away on the military importance of attacking slavery. For years, he had voiced support for colonization even though it infuriated Blacks and abolitionists.

Their anger didn't worry him. The president probably calculated that enemies like the abolitionists might win him friends among the white supremacists.

Abraham Lincoln would move toward emancipation just a step or two ahead of the Northern people. He never moved fast enough to threaten their commitment to Union victory. It was one of the most brilliantly crafted performances in American political history. Lincoln himself characterized his performance this way: "I may not have made as good a president as some other men, but I believe I have kept these discordant elements together as well as anyone could."[21] He had managed to keep the shaky coalition of Northern political factions from shattering because of its own divisions.

It seems that Lincoln may have succeeded in fooling many of the people for much of the time. He deliberately concealed the depth of his commitment to emancipation and, as the war drew to its close, his growing sympathy for equal rights. President Lincoln was not a reluctant emancipator, even though he often took pains to appear reluctant and hesitant and passive. While events sometimes controlled Lincoln, he was also in control, and his decisions were guided by his profound hatred of slavery. He was a consummate politician. His seeming reluctance, his apparent indifference to the justice of emancipation, was actually part of a highly successful strategy to hold together that fragile coalition. Indeed, one reason Lincoln's emancipationist legacy is so contested today is the very success of his efforts to obscure his goals and motives.

Frederick Douglass, once a fierce critic of Lincoln and always a man deeply suspicious of white America, concluded that "from a genuine abolition point of view, Mr. Lincoln seemed tardy, cold, dull, and indifferent, but measuring him by the sentiment of his country—a sentiment he was bound as a statesman to discuss— he was swift, zealous, radical, and determined."[22]

17

"KING ABRAHAM AFRICANUS I"

Abraham Lincoln has become the principal secular saint of our national civic religion. While living, however, Lincoln was the most controversial, the most hated, and the most threatened president in American history, and none of his policies were more controversial or more hated than emancipation. Though no such provision appears in the lines of the Emancipation Proclamation, to racists North and South, the end of enslavement itself seemed to imply racial equality as a next step—a grievous blow to the very foundation of white supremacy. And from equality, it was only one more step to amalgamation, interracial marriage. A New York publisher named Rushmore G. Horton opined that emancipation meant the end of America's greatness because it would inevitably result in the mixing of the races, and "every nation on the face of the earth where such a mixture has taken place . . . has declined in its civilization, and sunk down in ruin, as if wasted by a slow poison." The president, he continued, had sunk America in a "stinking slough of African despotism."[1] "The simple question to be decided," wrote a Kansas newspaper editor, "is whether the white man shall maintain his status of superiority or be sunk to the level of the Negro."[2]

In their opposition to emancipation, Southern enslavers

claimed to be tenderly concerned with the welfare of the enslaved people themselves. For to the enslaved, freedom was not a boon but a poison cup. The *Richmond Examiner* editorialized on November 8, 1864: "We hold that the negro is in his proper situation—that is to say, in the condition that is best for him; where he reaches his highest moral, intellectual and physical development and can enjoy the full sum of his natural happiness; in a word, that while living with the white man in the relation of slave he is in a state superior and better for him than that of freedom."[3]

Emancipation had raised the racists' rage against Lincoln. His decision to arm Black men—most of them liberated slaves—to fight and kill white men was the last straw, the ultimate betrayal of the white race. Arming Blacks, an editor asserted, was "tantamount to granting them a license to murder, rape, and pillage their former owners."[4]

Lincoln was assailed—most intensely in the summer before the 1864 presidential contest—with an obscene viciousness never equaled in American political discourse. Poisonous racial hatred was the theme of the most violent attacks. Death threats were explicit. Many Democrats insisted Lincoln no longer deserved to live. While many in the North supported Lincoln's policies, condemnations of the Emancipation Proclamation were nearly as common there as in slaveholding territory. From the border, US Senator Willard Saulsbury of Delaware predicted that the proclamation "would light [its] author to dishonor through all future generations."[5] On the floor of the House, the openly secessionist Ohio congressman Clement L. Vallandigham declared Lincoln's policy to be "an utter, disastrous, and most bloody failure."[6] On August 29, 1864, a newspaper printed far north of the Mason-Dixon Line, the *La Crosse (WI) Democrat*, editorialized that "the man who votes for Lincoln now is a traitor. . . . He who calls and allures men to certain butchery, is a murderer, and Lincoln has done all this. . . . If he is elected to misgovern for another four years, we trust some bold hand will pierce his heart with dagger point for the public good." The *Chicago Times* declared that Americans must "relieve the nation in some way of a most intolerable weight of tyranny."[7] Three weeks before the election, the *Buffalo Morning Express* predicted that "the people will soon rise, and if they cannot put Lincoln out of power by the ballot they will by the bullet."[8]

Just before election day, New York Democrats held a night-time rally for candidate George B. McClellan in Syracuse. Displayed were huge transparent banners illuminated from behind. Some read, "Free Ballots or Free Bullets. Crush the Tyrant Lincoln before He Crushes You"; "American Soil Scourged by an Unconditional Despot in Abraham Lincoln"; "Lincoln Has Murdered Three White Men to Free One Negro"; and "Resistance to a Tyrant Is Obedience to God," this last an old Booth family motto.[9] In September, the Republican-leaning *Harper's Weekly* published a catalog of epithets applied to Lincoln in the editorial pages of Northern newspapers. The list included "Filthy Story-Teller," "Despot," "Liar," "Thief," "Braggart," "Buffoon," "Usurper," "Fiend," and "Butcher."

A paper from the president's hometown, Springfield's Democratic *Illinois State Register*, remarked on "how the greatest butchers of antiquity sink into insignificance when their crimes are contrasted with those of Abraham Lincoln."[10] His enemies said he had deceitfully turned the war for the Union into an unholy crusade to end slavery. He was determined to transform the United States into a "mongrel concern of whites, negroes, mulattoes, and sambos . . . the most degraded and contemptible the world ever saw."[11]

In the South, the *Southern Illustrated News*, the insurgents' answer to the North's *Harper's Weekly* and *Frank Leslie's*, those weekly tabloids illustrated with woodcuts, ran a cartoon titled "Masks and Faces," explaining the Emancipation Proclamation. With the truncated stub of the uncompleted Washington Monument in the background, there stood a crudely rendered image of the Yankee president. By issuing his execrable proclamation, he had removed his homely Honest Abe mask to reveal the face of Satan.

So Lincoln was a tyrant, a would-be monarch, King Abraham Africanus I, bent on Africanizing America. Race-mixing was always the favored theme. One particularly ugly example, a little pamphlet printed on orange wrappers, depicted on its cover a jet-black caricature of a thick-lipped Black man embracing and kissing a white maiden. The author explained that the cover illustration showed how "the thick tufts of wool of the one lends beauty to the long, waving auburn hair of the other, and the sweet, delicate little roman nose of the one does not detract from the broad, flat nose, with expanded nostrils of the other." The pamphlet was titled *What Miscegenation Is*. Lincoln's foes had thus invented a new word for interracial marriage—*miscegenation*—a neologism that subsequently took its place in the language and the law.

Another Democratic propaganda piece, *The Lincoln Catechism*, revealed that the first of Lincoln's revised Ten Commandments was "You shall have no other God but the negro."[12] Lincoln was "crazy with 'negro on the brain.'"[13] He was the "boss nigger-lover" and was himself nothing but a "Black nigger." One Northern newspaper discussed Lincoln's negroid ancestry in some detail. The president's many flaws, an editorial suggested, are "accounted for by the idea that he is the outcrop of a remote African in his ancestry." Lincoln's appearance and manners "testify strongly of the plantation . . . of the purest Congo."

Particularly infuriating to some Northern voters was the Democratic Party's propaganda that Lincoln himself was the greatest obstacle to peace because of his obsession with African Americans. Peace and reunion, they claimed, could be readily obtained if only Lincoln would abandon his insistence on abolition. The so-called Peace Democrats argued that a cease-fire followed by negotiations would bring together the warring sections under

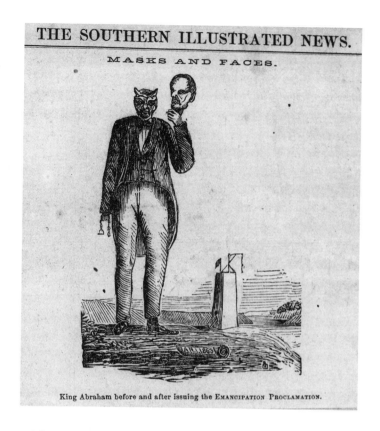

This cartoon in the Southern Illustrated News *proposed that in freeing the enslaved, the Yankee president had revealed his true, satanic character. Most white Southerners saw the Emancipation Proclamation as a merciless attempt to touch off a bloody race war in the South.*

"Masks and Faces: King Abraham after Issuing the Emancipation Proclamation," *Southern Illustrated News*, Nov. 2, 1862. Huntington Library, RB 45083.

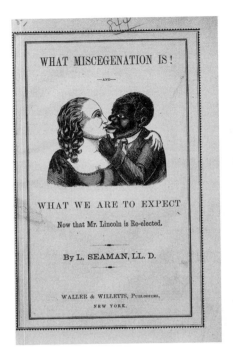

This little pamphlet is a particularly ugly example of the white supremacist propaganda Democrats used in their attempts to defeat President Lincoln's bid for reelection in 1864. Lincoln's foes even invented a new word—miscegenation—that subsequently took its place in the language and the law.

L. Seaman, *What Miscegenation Is! What We Are to Expect Now That Mr. Lincoln Is Re-elected* (New York, 1864). Huntington Library, RB 31773.

In this engraving, the insurgent caricaturist Adalbert Volck etched white supremacy's ultimate nightmare: under the veil, behind the speeches and proclamations, Abraham Lincoln was an African American.

Adalbert J. Volck, engraving, "Under the Veil," *Confederate War Etchings*, 1863. Huntington Library, HM 41785.

a single government once again if the Republican administration would simply assure the insurgents that the South could keep slavery. The notion was absurd on its face. Abraham Lincoln had promised not to move against the South's "domestic institutions" throughout his political career. Never had he been more explicit than in the pledge in his 1861 inaugural address that "I have no purpose, directly or indirectly, to interfere with the institution of slavery in the States where it exists. I believe I have no lawful right to do so, and I have no inclination to do so."[14] If such assurances could not avail in the secession winter, before a single drop of blood had been shed, what chance of reconciling the antagonists could there be in 1864, after millions of Americans had been killed, wounded, or captured, or had succumbed to disease and exposure, and after so much national treasure and private property had been lost? The truth was that Jefferson Davis's government refused to so much as consider reunion with the North, whatever the status of slavery. Davis said he'd rather form an alliance with "hyenas."

We can be sure that John Wilkes Booth absorbed all this hatred into the core of his being and there brooded over it darkly. Since childhood, he had been given to bitter, obsessive ruminations. Those who knew him during the last year of his life commented on the surprisingly personal nature of Booth's anger. It was as though he knew Lincoln intimately and had been personally hurt by him. The actor's third and final tour as a national star found him at the height of his success. This last tour opened in New York City in September 1863 and ended in Boston in May 1864. On November 2, 1863, Booth opened for the first time as a star in Washington, DC. The play was, of course, *Richard III.* The *Washington National Intelligencer* praised his performance, while the rival *Washington Morning Chronicle* panned him. But no one could argue about his popularity. A third paper reported that "every seat regular or improvised obtainable in the building was occupied, and hundreds were content" to stand.[15] These figures suggest an audience of approximately two thousand.

The venue was John T. Ford's brand-new Ford's Theatre. Ford, proprietor of Baltimore's Holliday Street Theatre, had known the Booth family for years. In 1862, Ford bought and converted to a theater the substantial building that had been home to the First Baptist Church of Washington since the 1830s. That same year, the old church was gutted by fire. Ford proceeded to rebuild and expand the building, designing it to resemble his Baltimore theater. The place accommodated an audience of fifteen hundred; additional seating could raise the number to seventeen hundred. It was ready for its grand opening when the new season commenced in the fall of 1863.

A week into Booth's run at the new theater, on November 9, President Lincoln himself came to see him there. John Hay, the president's young secretary, noted in his diary that he had "spent the evening at the theatre with the president, Mrs. Lincoln, Mrs. Hunter, Cameron and Nicolay. J. Wilkes Booth was doing *Marble Heart*. Rather tame than otherwise." Hay probably didn't mean that Booth's performance was tame, an adjective rarely if ever applied to him. The play itself just didn't include any spectacular sets or exciting scenes.[16] Lincoln may have seen Booth perform on other occasions, but we do know for certain that the next time Lincoln and Booth would be together at Ford's Theatre would be about half past ten on the evening of Good Friday, April 14, 1865.

Later in November 1863, the actor was injured again onstage at Cleveland's Academy of Music in the climactic battle that closes *Richard III*. His opponent knocked Booth's sword out of his grasp and the errant blade sliced through his eyebrow. Ever the professional, Booth battled on till the end, his face an authentic mask of blood. The audience was thrilled. The *Cleveland Herald* reported that the scene was "greatly heightened by the accident."[17]

He played three weeks in Cleveland and moved on, through unusually severe winter weather, to Leavenworth, Kansas. There he would experience much travail. Halfway through the ordeal, the actor described his adventures in a letter to a friend. He couldn't know then that his luck was about to get even worse. Booth wrote from St. Joseph, Missouri, on January 2, 1864:

> Here I am snowed in again. And God knows when I shall be able to get away. I have telegraphed St: Louis for them not to expect me. It seems to me that some of my *old luck* has returned to hunt me down. . . . I arrived at Fort [Leavenworth] with an ear frost bitten. . . . I started for a *run* and made the river (four miles) on foot. I RUN without a stop all the way. . . . I got back to the river in time to help and cut the ice that the boat might come to the shore. And after a "sea of troubles" reached this Hotel a *dead man*. Got to bed as soon as I could where I have been ever scince.[18]

Concluding his Leavenworth engagement with a performance of *Othello* on December 31, Booth had given himself four days to make it to St. Louis for his opening night at DeBar's Theatre. It would have been enough time if a historic blizzard had not frozen the plains, piled up thirty-foot snowdrifts, and brought railroad travel to a halt. The first leg of the trip, on New Year's Day 1864, took Booth from Leavenworth to Fort Leavenworth, where he visited friends. The Fort was about four miles from the Missouri River. There Booth boarded a riverboat that carried him to St. Joseph, on the Missouri side. From St. Joseph, he had hoped to continue on to St. Louis by rail. But that proved easier said than done. In the days ahead, struggling unsuccessfully to make his St. Louis opening, he would be subjected to even more extreme cold and danger. Booth was stuck in St. Joseph until January 9. Railroads were down; some trains were reported completely buried on the tracks in snowdrifts.

Booth, however, was still determined to get to St. Louis. The actor hired a four-horse sleigh to travel cross country to Breckinridge, Missouri. He had heard that trains to St. Louis were still running from there. Booth would tell a harrowing tale of making his way through deep snow and extreme cold. He even claimed he had been attacked by wolves. His difficulties didn't end when he finally boarded a train. The tracks were covered in deep snow. At one point he had to put a pistol to the conductor's head to force him to continue through the huge snowdrifts.[19] John Wilkes Booth's frigid ordeal had lasting consequences; the exposure must have been the cause of bronchial problems that impaired his speaking ability. Vocal difficulties troubled him sporadically through the rest of his acting career.

After his truncated St. Louis engagement, Booth began a two-week run at Wood's Theatre in Louisville, Kentucky. Temperatures remained unusually cold, but night after night, Louisville theatergoers braved the weather to pay homage to the young star. The unheated theater was packed, a circumstance that greatly benefited Booth's precarious financial situation. The crowds were so large that the managers turned many patrons away.

From Louisville, Booth went south to Nashville, Tennessee. It was his first foray into an insurgent region occupied by the Union military. It made him sick to see Union authority imposed on those Southerners who remained defiantly loyal to the grand rebellion. He made little effort to hide his secessionist sympathies. He played in Nashville two weeks, presenting his usual mix of Shakespearean tragedies and popular nineteenth-century dramas. George Wood's Nashville Theatre was "crowded to a perfect jam."[20]

While in Nashville, the actor met Tennessee governor Andrew Johnson.[21] Later that year, Johnson—a Democrat, rabid white supremacist, and Southern Unionist—would be elected Abraham Lincoln's vice president on the Union Party ticket and, after the assassination, would become president. Booth would attempt to see the vice president in Washington the day he killed Lincoln, leaving his calling card at his hotel. Andrew Johnson was on his list of targets.

Still fighting his cold, Booth traveled all the way south to New Orleans at the end of February 1864. New Orleans, the biggest, richest, and most important city in the South, had dropped into the US Navy's lap in April 1862, early in the war. The actor delayed for several days his opening at the old St. Charles Theatre until March 14, probably because he was still too sick to perform. (Booth probably remembered that the St. Charles was the theater where his father had made his last stage appearance just days before his 1852 death.)

"My dear boy," John Wilkes wrote a friend, "you have no idea how sick I have been."[22] Still he managed to play eighteen nights in New Orleans, one of his longer star engagements. He presented his usual battery of plays.[23] On the evenings that he did go onstage, his acting was marred by hoarseness and an indistinctness of speech on which both audiences and critics remarked. When he concluded his run on April 3 with *Richard III*, the *New Orleans Picayune* declared, "It is a matter of regret that a physical disability, we trust temporary, prevented his engagement from being so gratifying to himself or his friends as was desirable, and we look for his return here next season under more favorable auspices."[24] But Booth never returned. His acting career was nearing its end. He made only one more star engagement, his last, in Boston in April and May 1864.

Northern occupiers had imposed a harshly repressive regime on the old Crescent City's white citizens. Authorities banned rebel songs and slogans. All expressions of sympathy for the rebellion were subject to severe punishment. One unrepentant insurgent was hanged for pulling down an American flag. An official decree ruled that women who insulted Northern soldiers would be treated as prostitutes. This flagrant disrespect of Southern womanhood profoundly offended the patriarchal enslavers, men who were so proud of their chivalrous treatment of the weaker sex. (Their solicitous condescension did not, of course, extend to women of color.)

Everything he witnessed in New Orleans fanned Booth's rage. This far south, he didn't bother to disguise his feelings. Out on a night on the town with a band of friends, no doubt liquored up, Booth let out a cheer for "Jeff Davis and the Southern Confederacy," a daring act. A companion dared him to go one better and sing a few verses of the "Bonnie Blue Flag," a popular rebel anthem banned by the military authorities who ruled the occupied city. ("Hurrah! Hurrah! For Southern Rights Hurrah!" went the chorus.) Quickly surrounded by angry soldiers in blue uniforms, the glib and charming actor just as quickly talked his way out of trouble.[25] Presently, he set out on the long journey to Boston, a trip he completed in just four days.

"WE WORKED TO CAPTURE"

Sam Arnold and Mike O'Laughlen were most impressed. Both men had been childhood friends of John Wilkes Booth but hadn't seen him in years. They had read the papers and heard the talk; they already knew their old friend Johnny was one of the most popular stage performers of the day. Still, they couldn't help but be amazed that the trifling, good-natured, slow-to-learn schoolboy they'd known a dozen and more years earlier had become this strikingly handsome, sophisticated, wealthy person.

"Instead of gazing upon the countenance of the mild and timid schoolmate," Arnold said, "I now beheld a deep thinking man of the world before me, with highly distinguishing marks of beauty, intelligence, and gentlemanly refinement."[1] Suddenly, seemingly out of the blue, Booth had reappeared in their lives, inviting them to meet him at Barnum's City Hotel in Baltimore. The date was around August 8, 1864.[2] Arnold and O'Laughlen didn't know each other; they met for the first time that day at Barnum's.

Samuel Bland Arnold had first encountered Booth in 1848, when he was fourteen and the mad tragedian's favorite son was twelve. The two became friends at St. Timothy's Hall, the military boarding school both attended for several years. The two hadn't seen each other since 1852. Michael O'Laughlen had met Booth at an even younger age. In 1845, Junius Brutus Booth had bought for his family's city home a three-story brick townhouse at 62 North Exeter Street in Baltimore's Oldtown neighborhood. Directly across the street lived the O'Laughlens. The two boys quickly became fast friends. Johnny was seven then, Mike just five.[3] O'Laughlen, too, had been long out of touch with his old friend.

Arnold, the college-educated son of a prosperous Baltimore baker, was a square-built, handsome six-footer with dark hair, a mustache, and light beard. He could handle himself in a fistfight. He was fond of liquor and women, often checking into a hotel with a woman he claimed to be his wife. (He actually never married, but many years later, when he was a traumatized, misanthropic old hermit surrounded by dogs and pet chickens, Arnold would remember that as "a youth I was wild only to enjoy the pleasures of life, which I must say was bountiful. . . . No wish of my heart but was gratified and life during that period was 'one vast sea of pleasure.'")[4]

O'Laughlen, Booth's boyhood neighbor, was a somewhat smaller man, standing, like the actor himself, around five eight. He, too, was dark and good-looking, a hawk-faced man sporting a black mustache and imperial goatee. He enjoyed getting tanked up on alcohol as much as Booth and Arnold. Testimony later revealed that O'Laughlen was a member of the secret brotherhood known as the Knights of the Golden Circle.[5] Theirs was a conspiratorial, imperialistic fantasy of a new empire for slavery comprising the US cotton states enlarged by the seizure of Mexico and Central America, along with Spanish Cuba and the rest of the Caribbean islands. The so-called Golden Circle was the Gulf Coast itself, circling round from the tip of Florida to the shores of Nicaragua.

The Knights envisioned a new white supremacist slaveholding

nation, independent of the Yankee North. In 1864, the Knights would play an important part in the Northwest conspiracy, working to prevent President Lincoln's reelection. George Wren, an actor who knew Booth, said the young man himself had joined the sinister secret brotherhood when he was making his way as an apprentice actor at the Marshall Theatre in Richmond in 1859. "There is no question in my mind," Wren testified, "that [Booth] is a Knight of the Golden Circle and a very prominent man in it."[6]

It wasn't just nostalgia that had drawn John Wilkes Booth to these two. He could be certain where their loyalties lay: both had served in the insurgent army. Indeed, although they never encountered one another, Arnold and O'Laughlen had marched in different companies in the same regiment—the First Maryland, CSA. Arnold had served until shortly after the first battle of Bull Run, when he was discharged for illness. He made his way to Georgia, where he worked for the war effort, manufacturing gunpowder.

In 1864, when he learned his mother was dying, he returned to Baltimore. Arnold was dismayed to find that political sentiments in his native state had shifted so dramatically. Most people seemed to have transferred their allegiance to the Union. In November 1864, Maryland voters even adopted a new constitution that abolished slavery within the state, a step unthinkable just a short time before. It seemed to Arnold another step in the Black Republican program to "Africanize" America and impoverish the South.

Lincoln, who had gotten just 2.5 percent of the Maryland popular vote for president in November 1860, carried the state with 55 percent four years later. The rising tide of victory had buoyed the president's stature in the eyes of the people. Arnold found himself ostracized in his native state for having worn a rebel uniform. He was completely adrift now, a college graduate without a job, occasionally helping out on his brother's farm as a day laborer.

O'Laughlen had also served two years in the First Maryland

before being discharged. He returned home, took the Oath of Allegiance to the United States he had no intention of honoring, and began working in his brother's feed store.[7] Both men were adrift and ripe for some new enterprise. Both were short of funds. Both were rebels and veteran soldiers.

Booth was charming, the perfect host in his luxurious suite at Barnum's. He offered his friends wine and cigars and entertained them with stories of his travels and successes. Inevitably, talk turned to the war. The three Southern sympathizers lamented the South's grim prospects. Outnumbered, outgunned, outproduced, and blockaded, their people hungry and their treasury bare, the white Southerners seemed to be hanging on by their fingernails. It was true that they had so far stymied the two grand Union offensives launched against them that spring—Grant against Richmond and Sherman against Atlanta—but in the long run, defeat seemed all too probable.

The white South's greatest disadvantage lay in manpower. From 1861 to 1865, more than three million men marched in the Civil War armies. More than two million fought for the North, while just half that number served the South. Eight million Southern whites amounted to less than half of the North's twenty million. The remaining four million enslaved Southerners were anything but supporters of the rebellion. Southern soldiers, moreover, had been deserting at catastrophic rates. They sensed the approach of defeat, and their people at home were desperate for their help. Wives and parents appealed to soldiers to flee the ranks and come home to help their hungry, frightened families. Many tens of thousands were absent from their regiments without leave. By the third year of the war, the South probably had more skulking deserters than active troops still in the field. By the summer of 1864, Southern armies were outnumbered two to one in most theaters.

That fall, Jefferson Davis toured the South, pleading for the deserters to return to their commands. "What though misfortune has befallen our arms," he insisted in September in Macon, Georgia, "our cause is not lost." However, he continued, "two-thirds of our men are absent—some sick, some wounded, but most of them absent without leave." And the South had "not many men between 18 and 45 left."[8] Without a major influx of new fighting men, the rebellion might well be doomed.

John Wilkes Booth had a plan for replenishing Southern ranks. There was a pool of fresh soldiers available. While it is difficult to establish exact numbers, some claimed that as many as seventy-eight thousand captured veterans were being held in Yankee prisoner of war camps by 1865.[9] These prisoners constituted a mighty army in themselves, a host larger than Lee's Army of Northern Virginia. Their numbers had swollen dramatically since the exchange of prisoners had ended.

Exchange of prisoners of war by belligerent powers was a common practice in the nineteenth century. It had obtained in the American Civil War for more than a year. Race was the ever-present issue on which the prisoner exchange had foundered. When the United States began fielding regiments of colored troops, the Southern high command was presented with a new set of problems. Most pressing was what to do with Black prisoners of war. Often the Southern soldiers themselves settled this question right there on the battlefield, slaughtering colored troops when they tried to surrender. Some official responses were equally harsh. Certain Southern generals ordered that all Blacks taken in the uniform of the United States Colored Troops, along with their white officers, be summarily executed. Jefferson Davis had earlier threatened to turn white officers commanding Black regiments over to state authorities for trial as insurrectionaries inciting slave revolts. The punishment for that crime, of course, was death.

Most notorious of the Southern atrocities was the mass murder of more than two hundred Black soldiers and their white officers after their surrender at Fort Pillow, Tennessee, in April 1864. This was almost a year after the US Colored Troops had

*When the Union sent Black men into battle as the US Colored
Troops, the insurgents were outraged. They often took no prisoners.
Most notorious was the mass murder of more than two hundred Black
soldiers and their white officers after their surrender at Fort Pillow,
Tennessee. Commanding the massacre was General Nathan Bedford
Forrest. Before the war, Forrest had been a slave dealer. After
the war, he helped found the Ku Klux Klan.*

"The War in Tennessee—Rebel Massacre of the Union Troops after
the Surrender at Fort Pillow, April 12," *Frank Leslie's Illustrated
Newspaper*, April 24, 1864. Huntington Library, RB 762274.

first proved their courage in battle, impressing many Northerners, including President Lincoln, who had doubted their valor
and willingness to sacrifice themselves. Watching a regiment US
Colored Troops charging a rebel line under heavy fire, a Union
officer declared, "The problem is solved. The negro is a man, a
soldier, a hero."[10]

Before the war, Forrest had been a slave dealer. After the war, he helped found the Ku Klux Klan. General Forrest's overwhelming numbers quickly forced the surrender of the smaller Union garrison dug in on the banks of the Mississippi south of Memphis.

When the Black soldiers threw down their rifles and raised their arms, the rebels didn't hesitate. "No quarter! No quarter!" they shouted. "Kill the damned niggers; shoot them down!" "The slaughter was awful—words cannot describe the scene," said a Southern sergeant. "The poor deluded Negroes would run up to our men, fall upon their knees, and with uplifted hands scream for mercy, but they were ordered to their feet and then shot down." (It is hardly surprising that Black veterans soon began treating surrendering Southerners the same way, shouting "Fort Pillow and revenge!" as they lynched, bayonetted, and gunned them down.)[11]

But there was a major problem: about 135,000 of the 180,000 Black men who served in the Union army had formerly been enslaved and had only recently escaped from their enslavers. They were private property. The government had no legal justification for depriving owners of their property by putting that property to death. It was ruled that these men must be returned to slavery.

Whether execution or enslavement, these approaches clearly did not provide for their exchange for Southern prisoners held by the North. Lincoln and the Union high command insisted that the Black soldiers be treated no differently from whites and be traded man for man for rebel soldiers. They threatened to retaliate in like manner if Southerners started executing prisoners. They countered the threat of reenslavement with the promise that for every Black fighter returned to slavery, one captured Southern soldier would be put to hard labor. Stalemate. Neither side would back down or compromise.[12] Man-for-man exchange implied racial equality, foremost among the propositions Southern white supremacists had gone to war to deny.

A Virginia newspaper, the *Lynchburg Republican*, raged against the mere suggestion that Black and white prisoners be traded on an equal basis:

> When Lincoln first armed negroes against us, we all remember what just indignation it excited throughout the world, and how revolting it appeared to the minds of our people; and when insult was added to injury, by requiring us to exchange negroes for white men, the base proposition was indignantly rejected as worthy only of such a brutal nature. . . . To this day, thousands of our soldiers are languishing in Northern prisons, because neither they nor we are willing to acknowledge Lincoln's negroes as their equals.[13]

The prisoners themselves might actually have been willing to concede the point to gain release. In any event, prisoner exchange ended in 1863. The outcome favored the North, with its ample sources of new troops, and disadvantaged the South, so short of soldiers. For this reason, General-in-Chief Grant wanted the prohibition to stay in place, whatever the status of Black prisoners. (Exchanges were finally resumed in January of 1865.)

The plan Booth unfolded to Arnold and O'Laughlen that afternoon was simple but stunning in its audacity. He proposed capturing President Lincoln and carrying him south to Richmond as a hostage to negotiate the release of the men held in Northern prisoner of war camps. Booth explained. "In Northern prison camps are many thousands of our men the United States Government refuses to exchange. . . . Aside from then great suffering they are compelled to undergo, we are sadly in want of them as soldiers. We cannot spare one man, whereas the United States Government is willing to let their own soldiers remain in our prisons because she has no need of the men."[14] (Booth was obviously ignoring the racial dimensions of the controversy.)

That August afternoon in Booth's hotel suite, the three young men smoked and drank and talked for hours. The actor's performance was persuasive. Arnold characterized Booth as "one possessing an uninterrupted flow of conversational power."[15] He appealed to their patriotism and ambition, promising lasting glory. He offered to support them financially. He had given them the impression that he had limitless wealth. (Booth would continue to use money—more often the promise than the actual payment—to recruit new coconspirators.) Arnold and O'Laughlen both signed on, swearing themselves to secrecy. Booth's conspiracy had gained its first two recruits. (Both, however, would back out before the fatal moment.)

In recalling his recruitment, Arnold did not neglect a nod to the influence of drink, the heady stimulation of alcohol that permeated Booth's world and elevated all his hopes: "When the brain was to a great extent clouded by drink and reason, in a measure, had lost its power of concentrating thought, O'Laughlen and myself entered into the enterprise with Booth, after taking an oath to secrecy and good faith."[16] Increasingly, Booth was navigating his way through a sea of liquor. He drank every day, and he drank all day long—from morning to the moment he fell asleep. It is notable that not once, not at this first meeting nor at any time thereafter, is Booth known to have told Arnold and O'Laughlen that he was working under orders from or in consort with Jefferson Davis's government.

Booth did tell them how he planned to pull it off. The presidential family customarily spent many summer nights in a cottage at Soldiers' Home, a military retirement home in the District of Columbia. Sited on high ground three miles north of the government district, Soldiers' Home was considerably cooler in hot weather than the White House, seated as it was on the Potomac's malarial mudflats. Late at night, often after a last visit to the War Department's telegraph office, the president would ride there on horseback, usually alone, to join his family. He also traveled by carriage to and from Soldiers' Home and other destinations around the city, particularly military hospitals. The actor proposed seizing the president on the road with a well-rehearsed team of conspirators. The driver could be disposed of and the presidential carriage itself converted into a getaway vehicle. If Lincoln was captured on horseback, a buggy would be used to carry him south. (Booth later bought a buggy and team.) Then he told Arnold and O'Laughlen to sit tight and wait for him to contact them again. After the August meeting, they wouldn't see him again until the following January.

Arnold and O'Laughlen would spend most of their time waiting for the start of the conspiracy by drinking on Booth's tab every night in Washington saloons. They passed themselves off as salesmen of oil stocks. A spy later testified that "Booth had to provide the money to keep this band together, and they were all drinking, expensive people."[17] In the meantime, Booth himself would refine his plans, buy weapons and supplies, and travel to Canada to consult with the rebel underground in Montreal.

The capture idea was neither new nor original to Booth. Lincoln's enemies had always included those who plotted not to kill him but to take him prisoner.[18] The idea of seizing the Yankee president suggested itself to secessionists even before the war began. Rumors had convinced General Winfield Scott in 1861 that a plot existed to forestall Lincoln's inauguration by grabbing him before he could be sworn in. By the fall of that year, an influential New Orleans magazine, De Bow's Review, could report that "were it not that Lincoln is so securely guarded, I have reason to know that he would have been brought a captive to Richmond ere this."[19] Newspapers in the North as well as the South continued to mention the possibility as the war went on. For example, a full description of one imagined presidential abduction, complete with a detailed escape route, appeared on the front page of the New York Daily Tribune on March 19, 1864, a few months before Booth set his own conspiracy in motion.[20] The actor may have seen one of these articles.

The other possibility, of course, is that Booth was receiving information and instructions from the Secret Service Bureau in Richmond.[21] His plan closely resembled the two plots undertaken by the Southern military and Secret Service. When he met with Arnold and O'Laughlen, Booth hadn't been in Washington, DC, for a long time. How was he so well informed about Lincoln's habit of sleeping at Soldiers' Home, not to mention his movements and means of travel? The actor had done no scouting himself, and before he brought Arnold and O'Laughlen on board, he had no known accomplices. A clandestine source of intelligence is certainly a possibility.

Of course, journalism does not represent government policy, but those articles about abduction do show that the capture of a head of state was considered a justifiable act of war. Indeed, United States General Order No. 100—known as the "Code of War"—put forward at the administration's request by Columbia University legal expert Francis Lieber in April 1863, stated that military necessity "allows the capturing of every armed enemy, and every enemy of importance to the hostile government."[22] (The Code of War did declare assassination unlawful.)

At first, Jefferson Davis vetoed taking any action against his Yankee counterpart. His reasoning was simple: he still opposed outright assassination, and any attempt to capture Lincoln could easily result in his death. The first man known to have proposed such a scheme to Davis was a cousin by marriage, a young Southern officer named Joseph Walker Taylor. Wounded when U. S. Grant overwhelmed the rebels at Fort Donelson in Tennessee in February 1862, Taylor recovered before boldly crossing the lines in civilian clothes. He made his way to Washington. There he observed Lincoln's habits, even exchanging a few words with the president at a White House reception.

He noted that Lincoln often rode from the White House to Soldiers' Home alone and at night. When he got back to the South, he told Jeff Davis in a personal meeting that he could snatch Lincoln and bring him to Richmond "just as easily as I could walk over your doorstep." Davis said no. He knew Lincoln was a "Western" man. "I suppose Lincoln is a man of courage," he said; "he would undoubtedly resist being captured. . . . I could not stand the imputation of having let Mr. Lincoln be assassinated."[23]

There was certainly that danger. Even if the team succeeded in subduing the prodigiously strong Lincoln without hurting him, they would still have to extract him from a capital city garrisoned by tens of thousands of soldiers and bring him through one hundred miles of occupied territory. Any attempt at rescue might result in a confused firefight that killed the hostage himself. Lincoln could be hit by a stray bullet. Overwhelmed and surrounded, facing certain death or capture themselves, the kidnappers might decide that their only option was to kill him on the spot. Davis didn't want that. In 1862, he had not yet become angry enough to countenance the enemy leader's assassination. But many other rebels and Southern sympathizers entertained no such scruples.

The next official proposal to capture Lincoln came from Colonel Bradley T. Johnson two years after Taylor's offer, in the summer of 1864, the same period Booth was setting his own plot in motion. Johnson proposed capturing Lincoln at night at Soldiers' Home with a force of two hundred elite cavalry. His idea went up the chain of command and received approval for further consideration. Colonel Johnson intended to work with his commander, General Wade Hampton, and Hampton's commander, General Jubal Early.

That summer, Davis and Lee had ordered General Early's army to drive the Yankees out of the Shenandoah Valley and then proceed north to threaten Washington, DC. Lee hoped that the need to send reinforcements from the Army of the Potomac to relieve Washington would weaken Grant's ongoing siege of Richmond. Though plans were never finalized, the presumption was probably that Colonel Johnson, carrying with him the captive President Lincoln, would find his way to Jubal Early's army near Washington.

Early's soldiers did get close enough to Washington to see the dome of the Capitol and to fire a few shots in the direction of Abraham Lincoln, who was then imprudently exposing himself on the parapet of Fort Stevens. ("Get down, you damned fool, before you get shot!" Captain Oliver Wendell Holmes Jr. is said to have shouted at the president.)[24] Nevertheless, the ambitious offensive ended in Early's defeat and retreat back into the Shenandoah Valley. In the meantime, Bradley Johnson had been promoted to general commanding a brigade in Early's army. He was effectively out of the abduction business. His mission against Lincoln was aborted.[25]

Significantly, however, Jefferson Davis had changed his thinking since he had turned down Taylor's proposal two years earlier. The authors of *Come Retribution: The Confederate Secret Service and the Assassination of Lincoln* assert that Bradley Johnson's plan "could not have been seriously considered without the sanction of top Confederate authorities. General Wade Hampton would never have given his approval to Johnson without clearing the idea with Secretary of War Seddon and probably with General Robert E. Lee and President Davis. The political and military consequences of abducting Lincoln would have been enormous. The Confederate government, it seems, had undergone a change of heart. . . . Direct action against Lincoln himself was no longer unthinkable."[26]

A third abduction plot, put forward by Captain Thomas Nelson Conrad, was also approved by Jefferson Davis. Conrad, a clergyman turned secret agent, had no trouble slipping into Washington and passing as a loyal civilian. In mid-September 1864, two months after Bradley Johnson's plan fell through, Conrad got his orders. The orders came from Jefferson Davis himself through his secretary of state, Judah Benjamin, and his secretary of war, James A. Seddon. The authors of *Come Retribution* state that "it is inconceivable that Seddon would have approved and supported Conrad's mission without first clearing it with Davis."[27] The secretary of war also ordered special cavalry brigades to support Conrad in his mission.

The Army of Northern Virginia transferred Conrad himself from his regimental chaplaincy to the "Secret Service Department."[28] He received $400 in gold. (Only Davis could authorize disbursements for Secret Service activities in gold coin.) Conrad began by "reconnoitering the White House . . . to ascertain Mr. Lincoln's customary movements."[29] Like the others, he quickly determined that the president's nighttime rides to Soldiers' Home offered the best chance for a successful capture. Like Booth, Conrad planned to take his captive across the eastern branch of the Potomac into Southern Maryland, following the Secret Service Bureau's clandestine mail route south and back across the big river into Virginia.

In 1863, Secretary of War Stanton had ordered cavalry to begin escorting the president on his outings. The next time Conrad went to spy on Lincoln, the president was accompanied by twenty-five or thirty heavily armed horsemen. Conrad had planned to strike with a team of four. His plan was obviously no longer feasible. It was, however, clearly authorized by Jefferson Davis.

Just what was it that had so drastically changed Davis's thinking about capturing (and possibly killing) his Northern counterpart? The prospect of defeat and absolute subjugation by the hated Yankees was the most important reason, but the Dahlgren Raid on Richmond in March 1864 stands out as one defining event. The episode takes its name from its leader, the Army of the Potomac's Colonel Ulric Dahlgren, the one-legged war hero who was the son of the great naval ordnance innovator Admiral John A. Dahlgren. The twenty-one-year-old colonel was also a personal friend of Abraham Lincoln's.

Colonel Dahlgren's main purpose was freeing the Union prisoners of war held under dreadful conditions in Richmond's two prisons. The president was particularly concerned about these twelve thousand sick, freezing, starving men. The freed prisoners would be armed and, fighting alongside the raiders, would lay the enemy's capital to waste. It presently turned out that Dahlgren may have had some other objectives. Baffled by poor planning and a rain-swollen, unfordable James River, the mission ended in catastrophe. In the confused and rainy midnight retreat that followed, Colonel Dahlgren was blown out of his saddle by four bullets and killed instantly.

When dawn came the morning of March 3, 1864, soldiers searching his body found papers that soon electrified the entire South. One was an address to his command, outlining their mission: "We hope to release the prisoners from Belle Island first, and having seen them fairly started, we will cross the James River into Richmond, destroying the bridges after us and exhorting the released prisoners to destroy and burn the hateful city; and do not allow the rebel leader Davis and his traitorous crew to escape." An enclosed memorandum read "Jeff. Davis and his cabinet must be killed on the spot."[30]

The Southern high command hastened to make the most of the "Dahlgren Papers," publishing photographic facsimiles of the documents. The Union's military and political high command disavowed any knowledge of Colonel Dahlgren's resort to "black flag" warfare. Admiral Dahlgren denounced the papers as forgeries. But no one in the South doubted their authenticity.

The insurgents were likely correct. While the Dahlgren Papers themselves may have been forged, the raid, if not its specific objectives, was almost certainly approved by President Lincoln and Secretary of War Stanton. About a year earlier, his May 8, 1863, letter to General Joseph Hooker, then commander of the Army of the Potomac, revealed that Lincoln had no qualms about striking at the rebel leader. Conveying information provided by a just-exchanged prisoner of war, Lincoln told Hooker that a recent Union cavalry raid near Richmond had missed an opportunity: The man had said that "there was not a sound pair [of] legs in Richmond, and that our men, had they known it, could have safely gone in and burnt everything & brought us Jeff. Davis."[31]

The Dahlgren Raid united the South in outrage. Added to such previous crimes as emancipating slaves and putting guns into the hands of Black savages, the Yankees had now definitively revealed the Satanic nature of their national character. Demonic themes dominated condemnations of Lincoln's policies in the Southern press. The *Richmond Daily Dispatch* ran an editorial headlined "The Last Raid of the Infernals." Readers were urged to resist "a foe who has proved himself to be the most unscrupulous as he is the most brutal and fiendlike that ever made war on a people." Virginians were asked if the raiders were "warriors? Are they soldiers, taken in the performance of duties recognized by the loosest construction in the code of civilized warfare? Or are they assassins, barbarians, thugs? . . . Are they not barbarians redolent with more hellish purposes than were the Goth, the Hun or the Saracen?"

Colonel Dahlgren became "Ulric the Hun." His corpse was mutilated and publicly displayed in Richmond before being tumbled into an unmarked grave. On March 7, the *Richmond Enquirer* pondered: "What would have been the condition of Richmond . . . had Dahlgren succeeded? Imagine ten to twelve thousand brutal soldiers released from captivity, inflamed with liquor and burning with lust, turned loose with arms in their hands. . . . Picture the smoking ruins, the dishonored women and the murdered men of Richmond."[32]

General Robert E. Lee said Dahlgren's plans were "unchristian and atrocious," adding that "the blood boils with indignation in the veins of every officer and man as they read the account of the barbarous and inhuman plot."[33] Secretary of State Judah Benjamin registered his astonishment that, having stooped to such atrocities, the Yankees could still "profess a desire that we should live with them as brethren under one Government."[34] If the Yankees are going to fight this way, everyone said, so should we. No one was more infuriated than John Wilkes Booth, who raged against "the vile and savage acts committed on my countrymen their wives & helpless children."[35]

"COME RETRIBUTION"

White Southerners burned for revenge, and Jefferson Davis was determined to give it to them. Fresh anger flared late in 1864 over the widespread destruction of homes and property by invading Yankee armies—particularly the depredations of General Sherman in Georgia and the Carolinas and General Sheridan in the Shenandoah Valley. This fierce appetite for revenge, combined with the South's ever more desperate military situation, would point the insurgents to all the stratagems of irregular, "black flag" warfare they could imagine. These included massive propaganda efforts to influence the 1864 presidential election, the fomenting of armed revolt by dissidents in the North, mass breakouts of prisoners of war, bank robbery, arson attacks on shipping and supply depots, plans to recruit an army to attack from Canada, attempts to burn down New York City and poison its water supply, the assassination of military officers and local officials, phony peace initiatives, the hijacking of ships and trains, germ warfare with smallpox and yellow fever, and finally the decapitation of the United States government by killing its president and other top leaders. In the end, assassination became the South's last, best hope for independence. One can lump all these activities together under the rubric of terrorism.

The author of the only book-length study of the Dahlgren Raid argues that the incident merely provided Southerners with an excuse to pursue the irregular warfare they would have resorted to in any case, given their diminishing chances of military success.[1] And military success still meant, above all, the preservation of slavery and white supremacy. At the late hour of January 6, 1865, the *Macon (GA) Telegraph* reminded its readers what the war had always been about: "It should be constantly kept in view, through all the bloody phases of this relentless war, that slavery was the *casus belli*—that the principle of State Sovereignty, and its sequence, the right of secession, were important to the South principally, or solely, as the armor that encased her peculiar institution—and that every life that has been lost in this struggle was an offering upon the altar of African Slavery."[2]

It has been argued that John Wilkes Booth never had the slightest intention of capturing Lincoln, that his plan from the beginning was to murder the president. The kidnapping plot was merely a ploy to recruit accomplices who would have balked at murder.[3] It is true that by the beginning of 1865, Jefferson Davis did want Abraham Lincoln dead. He sent a team of commandos from the Torpedo Bureau to blow up the White House in April 1865. So when Booth finally struck that month, his actions comported with the wishes of the insurgent leader, even if the assassin was not acting under Davis's direct orders.

Booth's extensive preparations for the abduction and escape probably mean that the capture plot was at least for a time more than a mere ploy. There is no doubt, however, that after the Dahlgren Raid the Southern high command committed itself to a hard war policy—irregular warfare, terrorism, black flag warfare. It was now a war not just against Northern armies but against the Northern civilian population and its political leadership. One

*Jefferson Davis of Mississippi was the first and
only president of the great rebellion, which its authors
had styled the "Confederate States of America."*

Library of Congress, Prints and Photographs
Division, LC-USZ62–129742.

Southern general said simply, "In my opinion all means of destroying our brutal enemies are lawful and proper."[4] The Union
had been waging a hard war on the Southern people ever since
General McClellan had fallen by the wayside.

Jefferson Davis—working closely with the brilliant Judah Benjamin, who was both his secretary of state and the chief of the

Secret Service Bureau—set in motion in 1864 a vast and interlocking set of initiatives known collectively as the Northwest conspiracy. The conspiracy was directed from Richmond, run out of Canada, and funded by an immense allocation of $1 million in gold from the depleted Southern treasury. The conspirators held a misplaced confidence in their presumed alliance with hundreds of thousands of disloyal Northern civilians in the Midwest. This enormous commitment of wealth from the South's moribund economy indicates the importance of the hopes the Richmond government held for irregular operations to destabilize the North and prevent President Lincoln's reelection. Despite the predominant role he would later assume, in 1864 John Wilkes Booth was still but a minor player in the great conspiracy.

After his August meeting with Arnold and O'Laughlen in Baltimore, Booth moved on to New York City. There, staying at Edwin's house, where his mother lived, the young actor was laid low for three weeks by a severe case of erysipelas on his right arm. Erysipelas is a brilliantly red, rapidly spreading streptococcus infection of the skin. In the nineteenth century, the disease, accompanied by fever, chills, delirium, and intense pain, was debilitating, even life-threatening.[5]

Asia Booth Clarke remembered an episode of this illness that later seemed to take on a dreamlike prophetic quality, revealing her brother in all his vulnerable beauty. She said that Wilkes

> was once stopping at Edwin's New York house, and, suffering from a diseased arm, he fainted from the acute pain, and Junius carried him and laid him upon his bed. As he lay there in his shirt-sleeves so pale and death-like, we all felt how wondrously beautiful he was. It was a picture that took hold deeply in all our hearts, for soon he was to lie dead among his foes, and not one of us should gaze upon his face. As we saw it then, pallid and death-like on his bed, we were to ponder it all our lives.[6]

Booth's signature appears in Boston's Parker House hotel register under the date July 26. So do the names of four other men, three giving their residences as Canada and one as Baltimore. Assassination scholars have identified these four as probable secret agents, registered under aliases. They were likely in Boston to meet with Booth. That meeting "has all the earmarks of a conference with an agenda."[7] That agenda could only have been the conspiracy against Lincoln. It was less than two weeks after the meeting at the Parker House that Booth—now somehow so well informed about the president's movements—summoned Arnold and O'Laughlen to see him in Baltimore.

Then in September, he traveled to the Pennsylvania oil country, where he spent about three weeks closing out his money-losing operations there. He transferred his remaining holdings to his brother Junius and his sister Rosalie. He knew that an 1862 law authorized government seizure of all the property of a traitor. He wanted to divest himself of everything he owned to prevent that possibility. In any event, he was planning to quit the North for good. The actor intended to ship his large and valuable theatrical wardrobe to Montreal. The trunks full of costumes, props, and playbooks would be sent from Canada into the South through the Union blockade on a fast ship out of Nassau. Booth intended to start over as an actor in the South. He meant to "commence the world anew" he said.[8] And he had a plan that, if successful, would undoubtedly make him the biggest star on the Southern stage, not to mention the South's most popular hero. Booth had also vowed to link arms with the rebels and die fighting with them in their "last ditch." But if he was prepared to accept death, he wasn't obliged to seek it—not if there was another, better way to retrieve Southern fortunes.

His next stop was Montreal, the city then known as "Little Richmond." On October 18, 1864, he checked into the St. Lawrence Hall. There the Southerners' "Canadian cabinet" was in full session. Montreal was nest to an unsavory collection of spies and secret operatives, escaped prisoners of war, blockade runners and arms smugglers, Union deserters and draft dodgers, grifters and imposters seeking rebel gold, refugees, double agents, couriers on their way to Richmond or London, would-be assassins, foreign soldiers of fortune, government officials in exile, and plenty of veteran Southern officers. These subversives enjoyed the covert cooperation of Canadian authorities, suddenly grown apprehensive of the prodigious new military strength of the United States, a nation that now boasted the largest army and navy in the world. A small brigade of Union detectives and undercover officers sent to Canada by Stanton watched the subversives' every move.

There was also a goodly contingent of Northern traitors in the United States who claimed to be eager to work with the Southerners to bring an end to the war. The Knights of the Golden Circle had evolved into the "Order of American Knights," which subsequently became the "Sons of Liberty." With Copperheads and Peace Democrats added to these secret brotherhoods, the disloyal elements in the Northwest were said to have amounted to half a million men. They were presumably united in their determination to overthrow the Lincoln administration. They also aimed to end the fighting with a truce followed by negotiations to seek the reunification of North and South.

Such an outcome could only have resulted in Southern independence. Whatever hopes of sectional reconciliation these disloyal midwesterners may have entertained, the Southern insurgents themselves were adamant in their refusal ever again to live with Yankees under a common government. If compromise and reconciliation had been out of reach in 1860–61, it was delusional to imagine that it might be possible in 1864, after three years of savage killing. "There is no nation on the earth which is so heartily detested and execrated in the Confederacy as the butcher nation of the North," the *Richmond Inquirer* editorialized. "Voluntary reunion with them! A union of hyenas, vampyres, and thugs would be about as probable and practicable."[9]

The prospect of a pro-Southern army, tens of thousands strong, rising up in Indiana, Illinois, Kentucky, Ohio, Missouri, and the upper Midwest, must have greatly exceeded the most wildly optimistic dreams of the conspirators. An anti-Lincoln rebellion in the Northwest would mean peace and Southern independence. "The government designated the United States has no sovereignty," went the oath sworn by members of the Sons of Liberty; "resistance by force of arms is not revolution but assertion of right."[10]

Canadian agents fed the traitors gold coin and greenbacks and shipped them crates of revolvers labeled as Sunday school books. Major revolts were planned. A massive uprising to seize Kentucky for the South would coincide with an invasion of the state by a Southern army. Another rebellion would take over Chicago during the Democratic Party's convention in that city in August. Cadres of veterans would come from Canada to lead the armies of Northern volunteers. The brotherhood of traitors had its hierarchy of rank, state and local officers, a solemn loyalty oath, secret passwords and recognition signs, plenty of weapons, and highly ambitious plans to carry the whole Northwest into secession and alliance with the South. All they lacked was courage and determination. Union spies, moreover, had completely infiltrated their organizations.

Unfortunately for the Southern rebellion, the Sons of Liberty and their sympathizers turned out to be just another dream. However great their numbers, however violent their speeches and proclamations, when it came to risking their lives, when there was a chance of actually getting shot, almost none of the volunteers kept their promises to turn out. Despite their brave talk, these civilians simply had no stomach to die fighting in the streets of Chicago or Indianapolis. They disappointed their

Southern masters again and again. Start the revolution without us, they seemed to be saying. The planned uprisings were all stillborn. Indeed, every plot fostered by the conspirators' Canadian cabinet ended in failure.

Three "commissioners," politicians appointed personally by and answering directly to Jefferson Davis, were supposedly in charge of Canadian operations and the entire Northwest conspiracy. They were charged with coordinating plans, determining priorities, gathering intelligence, assigning troops to specific operations, providing funding from their vast gold reserve, and communicating with Richmond. The rebel commissioners were largely incompetent, but they spoke with the considerable authority of $1 million in gold. After the war, some of the Secret Service gold seems to have ended up in the pockets of members of the Canadian cabinet.

Booth plotted with insurgent officials in Montreal for ten days that October. He talked for hours with the burly, heavily bearded George N. Sanders of Kentucky, a former Pierce administration diplomat. A devotee of "tyrannicide," Sanders had joined in a plot to assassinate French emperor Napoleon III during his time as a diplomat in London. Mingling with European revolutionaries, he had become an adherent of "the theory of the dagger," which maintained that assassination was the surest road to political success. His motto was "death to tyrants!" Booth and Sanders shared a fanatical commitment to Southern victory and fanatical hatred for Abraham Lincoln.[11] Sanders's son, a Southern major, had just died as a prisoner of war, a circumstance that no doubt sharpened the father's resolve. Booth and Sanders were observed drinking together and talking privately for hours. While no one managed to overhear their conversations, it's not hard to imagine what advice Sanders might have given Booth.

Before leaving Montreal, Booth secured letters of introduction from Southern spymaster Patrick C. Martin to several agents in southern Maryland. The headquarters of the Canadian con-

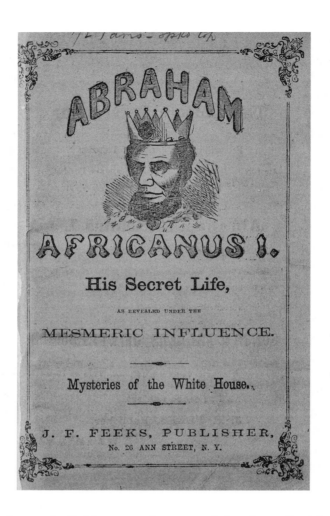

An example of white supremacist propaganda from the presidential
election of 1864. Lincoln's enemies charged him with usurping kingly
powers by defying the Constitution and disregarding civil liberties,
all in favor of Black Americans at the expense of whites.

Abraham Africanus I. His Secret Life [. . .] (New York, 1864).
Huntington Library, RB 35996.

spirators was in Toronto. Patrick Martin was head of operations in Montreal. The introductions to the agents in southern Maryland that Martin provided would prove invaluable in planning the abduction route, in enlisting new recruits for the conspiracy, and in Booth's escape across the Potomac after he killed Lincoln. Martin was a former Baltimore whiskey merchant and sea captain turned blockade runner and rebel operative. He was a huge man, so massive across the shoulders that his head looked undersized.

Patrick Martin was also the blockade runner to whom Booth entrusted his theatrical wardrobe. Captaining his own ship, the one-hundred-foot schooner *Marie Victoria*, Martin left Montreal in November, bound for Nassau. There, the cargo would be turned over to a swift blockade runner to slip it into Wilmington, North Carolina, by then the only port remaining open to the insurgency. But the *Marie Victoria* foundered in a violent storm on the St. Lawrence River. Martin and all on board perished. Though it was later salvaged, Booth's wardrobe was ruined.[12]

Although he did not set it in motion, Jefferson Davis did approve of one plot that aimed at killing Abraham Lincoln. Many Northern civilians were expected to die as well. In fact, the plan was "directed against the masses of Northern people solely to create death."[13] This conspiracy relied on what we would call a weapon of mass destruction—specifically, biological warfare.

Yellow fever was one of the most dreaded diseases in the world until the twentieth century. African in origin, brought to the Americas by the slave trade in the seventeenth century, it was a tropical disease that could strike populations as far north as New York and Philadelphia. Also known as black vomit, yellow jack, and bronze john, it took its name from the yellow tone that jaundice, caused by liver damage, gave to sufferers' complexions. In its severe form, yellow fever killed about half of those afflicted, a higher mortality rate than smallpox. It is hardly surprising that it was so greatly feared.

During George Washington's presidency, in the summer of 1793, Philadelphia, then the nation's capital, was ravaged by a yellow fever epidemic that killed a tenth of the population and completely shut down the federal government. President Washington and other officials fled to the countryside for safety. As usual, cold weather ended that epidemic. Epidemics also took place in New York, Baltimore, New Orleans, Memphis, Savannah, and many smaller port cities. Universally thought to be a contagious disease, easily transmissible between people, yellow fever is actually spread only by the bite of an infected *Aedis aegypti* mosquito. Dr. Walter Reed finally discovered the true etiology of the disease in about 1900.

In the Civil War era, one of the foremost American authorities on yellow fever was Dr. Luke Blackburn. A Kentuckian, Dr. Blackburn was a passionate supporter of the South and a sworn enemy of Abraham Lincoln. He had gained his medical reputation by bravely coming forward to deal with several yellow fever epidemics before the war. He had also published a treatise on the disease. Like most other authorities, he firmly believed it to be contagious.

As the South declined inexorably toward defeat, it occurred to Blackburn that yellow fever could be weaponized as a deadly bludgeon for striking back at the hated Yankees. He would gather infected clothing and bedding contaminated by the bodily emissions of patients who had died of yellow fever and send that material into selected Northern cities. Blackburn also planned a special gift for President Lincoln himself.[14]

Dr. Blackburn was in Canada in April 1864, when a severe yellow fever epidemic hit Bermuda, then a center for Southern blockade runners. He hastened to the island, where he helped treat the sick in the hospitals while packing eight large trunks with clothing and bedding he believed infected with yellow fever. He also prepared a small suitcase with several elegant shirts, similarly contaminated, that he intended to send to the White House as an admirer's gift to the president.

The good doctor also managed to obtain a supply of clothing he believed contaminated with smallpox. The yellow fever material was for use in warm climates, smallpox for cooler, more northerly regions. He shipped all of it back to Canada to arrange for its diffusion into Yankeedom. It may be worth noting that John Wilkes Booth played cards and drank with Dr. Blackburn in Montreal in October 1864.[15]

In Halifax, Blackburn engaged a shifty operative, one Godfrey Joseph Hyams, formerly of Helena, Arkansas, to handle his filthy cargo. He promised Hyams the immense sum of $100,000, of which the man received exactly $100. Hyams succeeded in shipping the trunks to Boston, New York City, and Washington, DC, as well as to New Bern, North Carolina, and Norfolk, Virginia, two Southern cities occupied by the US Army. In those places, the contents were sold at auction and ended up in used clothing stores, a common practice at the time. Had yellow fever actually been contagious, this campaign might have spread the disease far and wide. Blackburn boasted that the trunk sent to Washington was so contaminated that it would "kill them at sixty yards distance."[16] The doctor himself made sure that the "fine leather valise with some very elegant dress shirts" was duly sent to President Lincoln.

Dr. Blackburn had ordered his agent "to kill and destroy as many of the Northern army, or people of the place you go to." The physician was sure that "an epidemic of the deadly disease would prove devastating to Northern war efforts."[17] In the end, no one was sickened or killed, but the bioterror operation still aroused a great deal of concern—some of it among the insurgents themselves.

Most alarmed was a certain Reverend Kensey Johns Stewart of Virginia. Rev. Stewart was another Southern man of the cloth who had found his way into the employ of the Secret Service Bureau. Stationed in Canada, he soon learned of Dr. Blackburn's germ warfare project. Stewart was appalled. The reverend was an acquaintance of Jefferson Davis. In December 1864, he wrote directly to the president, imploring him to put a halt to Blackburn's nefarious plot. He told Davis that "I cannot regard you as being capable of expecting the blessing of God upon, or being personally associated with the instruments & plans [of Blackburn's bioterrorism]. As our country has been and is entirely dependent upon God, we cannot afford to displease him. Therefore, it cannot be our policy to employ wicked men to destroy the persons & property of private citizens, by inhumane & cruel acts."[18]

Jefferson Davis boasted of personally reading every letter addressed to him. He certainly wouldn't have neglected a letter from a man he knew. So he doubtless knew of the yellow fever plot. Yet he did not order Blackburn to stand down. The plot proceeded unhindered. Davis was clearly willing to sanction initiatives that aimed at killing Abraham Lincoln and untold numbers of Northern noncombatants.

"RIGHT OR WRONG, GOD JUDGE ME"

Booth was back in Washington from Montreal on November 9, the day after President Lincoln's reelection. He checked into the National Hotel, his usual home when in the capital. He was now romancing another resident of the National, the amiable Lucy Lambert Hale, daughter to the abolitionist New Hampshire senator John Parker Hale.

Hale had campaigned as the antislavery candidate for president on the Free-Soil Party ticket in 1852. His daughter was the Washington belle whose charms had attracted the attention of such eligible bachelors as John Hay and Oliver Wendell Holmes Jr. She was even rumored to be romantically involved with Robert Todd Lincoln, though that young man later angrily denied it.[1] Her father's senatorial term would end on inauguration day, March 4, 1865. He'd failed to win reelection in November. President Lincoln would soften the blow by making Hale the new US minister to Spain. The post came with a handsome $12,000 salary.

The plump, bright-eyed Lucy also had the distinction of being secretly engaged to marry J. Wilkes Booth, the only woman he ever honored with such a commitment. She had told him her only objection to him was that he was an actor. He countered that his only objection to her was that she was an abolitionist.[2] The two traveled together and checked into hotels as man and wife. The young couple had agreed that she would accompany her family to Spain for one year and then come home and marry Booth, with or without her father's consent.[3] It is highly unlikely that the ambassador-designate knew of his youngest daughter's involvement with the star.

Booth told a friend that Lucy was worth more to him than all the wealth of the oil fields. Cynics might suspect that he valued her most for the access he hoped she could provide to high Republican circles, but the family and friends of both believed their mutual love was completely sincere. After the catastrophe, Asia said that her brother "was engaged to Miss Hale. They were devoted lovers and she has written broken-hearted letters to Edwin about it. Their marriage was to have been in a year. . . . That was the decision only a few days before the fearful calamity. Some terrible oath hurried him to this wretched end."[4]

John Wilkes's actor friend John Mathews, who knew about the conspiracy, recalled a conversation in which Booth had asked him, "Were you ever in love?" When Mathews said no, his friend replied, "I wish I could say as much. I am a captive. You cannot understand how I feel." Booth continued, "If it were not for that girl, how clear the future would be to me! How easily could I grasp the ambition closest to my heart—the release of the Confederate prisoners. If it were not for her, I could feel easy. Think of it, John, that at this time in my life—just starting as it were, I should be in love. I am. I am in love."[5] In one of the often-remarked ironies of the assassination, Booth spoke these words while sprawled out on the bed in Mathews's rented room in the Petersen house across the street from Ford's Theatre. This was the very bed Abraham Lincoln would die on in a few weeks' time.

Despite his attachment to Miss Hale, the actor continued his old ways. While spending his evenings with Lucy in Washington restaurants, theaters, and drawing rooms, he often bedded down for the night with a pretty young prostitute named Ella Starr. He'd brought her down from Baltimore and set her up in a brothel. (Authorities cataloged more than 450 such establishments in the District of Columbia at the time.) Ella wasn't sure if she was nineteen or twenty—one or the other, she said. Another of Ella's clients was said to be Vice President Andrew Johnson, but the girl loved John Wilkes Booth with all her heart. People said she was as "fierce as a tigress in her devotion" to him. Booth and Ella may have spent the night of April 13 together, the night before the fatal performance at Ford's Theatre. When Ella heard that her beloved had shot the president, she tried to kill herself with chloroform. Doctors revived her.[6]

A week after his return to the capital, Booth opened an account with the Washington office of Jay Cooke & Co., Bankers. He deposited $1,500. He later deposited an additional $250. While in Montreal he had already deposited $400 in gold in the Ontario Bank, also buying a bill of exchange for another $300 in gold dollars. A banker in Canada testified that some of the money Booth deposited came from a man identified only as "Davis," known to be a financial agent in the Southern underground in Canada.[7]

The actor now had money to finance his conspiracy and, if need be, to escape abroad, into the South, or within the United States itself. The source of Booth's substantial deposits was likely Jeff Davis's Secret Service Bureau. He had not been acting. His oil investments had only lost money. The spies in Montreal probably gave him the cash, some of it in United States gold coin. As it turned out, it wasn't enough for his purposes. By February, he was broke again.

The signal event of 1864 was the reelection of President Lincoln on November 8. He became the first American president to win a second term since Andrew Jackson's 1832 reelection, more than a generation earlier. In the four-way race in 1860, Lincoln had garnered only 39 percent of the popular vote. In 1864, he got 55 percent and won a landslide victory of 212 to 21 in the Electoral College.

Lincoln's electoral victory had been by no means a sure thing. That summer, widespread discouragement with the military situation had darkened the North's hopes for a speedy end to the war. Most calamitous was the stagnation of the two massive offensives hurled against the South in the spring—Grant's campaign against Richmond and Sherman's drive on Atlanta.

All summer Grant's Army of the Potomac had slugged it out with Lee's Army of Northern Virginia in a series of brutal battles. The war's most sustained and carnivorous fighting saw sixty-five thousand Union soldiers killed, captured, or wounded. These horrific casualties seemed to have gained Grant nothing but costly stalemate—a trench warfare siege of Lee's army outside Richmond. He seemed no closer to taking the Southern capital than McClellan had been in 1862.

Fewer men died in Sherman's campaign, but his western Army of the Tennessee had also been stymied in a drawn-out war of maneuver. Atlanta remained out of reach. The nation longed for peace. If the Peace Democrats and the propagandists of the Secret Service Bureau could convince Northern voters that Lincoln himself was the main obstacle to peace, he couldn't possibly win reelection. And peace in 1864 might have meant Southern independence and the preservation of slavery.

Lincoln himself despaired. "I am going to be beaten," he reckoned, "and unless some great change takes place *badly* beaten."[8] The Republican Party started calling itself the "Union" Party. In June the Union convention in Baltimore nominated Abraham Lincoln for a second term. The party platform called for the unconditional surrender of the enemy armies and passage of a Thirteenth Amendment to the Constitution, outlawing slavery: the platform called for its "utter and complete extirpation from the soil of the Republic."[9]

At the Democrats' August convention in Chicago, the party's peace faction composed a platform that declared that the war had been "four years of failure" and advocated a negotiated peace. Slavery would be preserved. The platform seemed to imply a willingness to accept Southern independence. Peace came first, Union a distant second. The Democratic nominee was General George B. McClellan.

In one of the most bitter presidential campaigns in American history—charged throughout with obscene appeals to racial hatred—the Democrats accused Lincoln of stubbornly fighting an unwinnable war and sacrificing the lives of hundreds of thousands of white men to gain the freedom of Black slaves. Of course, they continued, emancipation would inevitably result in racial equality and interracial marriage. When the Democrats staged a McClellan rally in Peoria, Illinois, one of their giant banners read, "Ours is a White Man's Government, Defile it not with Miscegenation."[10] The Democrats' satirical "Black Republican Prayer" asked that

> the blessings of Emancipation may extend throughout our unhappy land, and the illustrious, sweet-scented Sambo nestle in the bosom of every Abolition woman, that she may be quickened by the pure blood of the majestic African, and the spirit of amalgamation shine forth in all its splendor and glory, that we may become a regenerated nation of half-breeds, and mongrels, and the distinction of color be forever consigned to oblivion, and that we may live in bonds of fraternal love, union, and equality with the Almighty Nigger, henceforth, now and forever. Amen.[11]

Leaders in Richmond and Canada sensed their great opportunity. They embarked on a sophisticated propaganda campaign aimed at convincing Northern voters that the main obstacle to peace and reunion was Lincoln himself. The Niagara Falls "peace conference" of July 1864 was one battle in this campaign. The

Maryland voters approved a new state constitution in November of 1864 outlawing slavery, an outcome unthinkable only a short time before.

"Celebrating the Abolition of Negro Slavery in Maryland," *Frank Leslie's Illustrated Newspaper*, Nov. 19, 1864. Huntington Library, RB 762274.

Secret Service Bureau had found an unwitting ally in the person of Horace Greeley, the mercurial editor of the *New York Tribune*. In early July, Greeley told the president that "two Ambassadors of Davis & Co" had arrived in Canada "with full & complete powers for a peace."[12] In fact, these men, members of the Canadian cabinet, had no authority whatsoever to negotiate in the name of Jefferson Davis's government. Greeley urged Lincoln to bring the Southerners to Washington for talks.

Lincoln responded by declaring that he remained ready to consider a proposal, from those in authority in Richmond, that encompassed his "indispensable terms": the surrender of all hostile armies, the restoration of the Union, and the abolition of slavery. The president sent his private secretary, John Hay, to meet with Greeley and the Southern agents at Niagara Falls, Canada. At this meeting on July 18, Hay gave them Lincoln's letter, addressed "To Whom it may concern," setting out his terms.

The Davis government and Lincoln's opponents in the North were quick to use the exchange to make it appear that only Lincoln and his stubborn insistence on emancipation stood in the way of ending the war and reuniting the two warring sections. Southern men like John Wilkes Booth were enraged by Lincoln's refusal to negotiate with the emissaries. Particularly galling to Southern gentlemen was the refusal of the churlish Yankee president even to address them in terms of respect, rudely directing his letter "To Whom it may concern."[13] A Democratic newspaper raged that "tens of thousands of white men must bite the dust to allay the negro mania of the President."[14] By now, all observers agreed that Lincoln would lose in November.

Then, on September 3, the political landscape was utterly transformed by General William Tecumseh Sherman's triumphant telegram: "Atlanta is ours and fairly won." Many contended that the capture of Atlanta amounted to the greatest Union victory of the war, particularly coming when it did.[15] Northern mo-

Major General William Tecumseh Sherman's capture of Atlanta on Sept. 3, 1864, transformed the political landscape and clinched President Lincoln's reelection in November.

Library of Congress, Prints and Photographs Division, LC-DIG-cwpb-07136.

rale soared while the insurgents' hearts sank to new depths of despair.

Northern optimism got a further boost two weeks later when General Philip Sheridan won the series of crushing victories that destroyed Jubal Early's army in the Shenandoah Valley. Then Sheridan proceeded to lay the valley waste, depriving the Army of Northern Virginia of one of its most important sources of provisions. Farms and crops in the fields were put to the torch. Locals called it the "burning time." So comprehensive was the destruction, Grant joked, that a crow flying over the Shenandoah Valley would have to carry his own rations. Lee's hungry soldiers grew hungrier still. And even before the fall of Atlanta, the Union had won a great naval victory when Admiral David Farragut had "damn[ed] the torpedoes" to seize Mobile, Alabama, the South's last port on the Gulf of Mexico.

No longer did the Democrats' characterization of the war as "four years of failure" seem quite so apt. Lincoln's reelection suddenly looked much more likely. John G. Nicolay, the president's principal secretary, predicted that the "Atlanta victory alone ought to win the Presidential contest for us." He observed: "There is a perfect revolution in feeling. Three weeks ago, our friends everywhere were despondent, almost to the point of giving up the contest in despair. Now they are hopeful, jubilant, hard at work and confident of success."[16]

The Civil War had seen several major turning points when the morale of the opposing sides rose or fell in proportion to success. These included Grant's victories on the western rivers, the failure of McClellan's offensive against Richmond in 1862, Antietam and the Emancipation Proclamation later that year, the twin Union triumphs at Vicksburg and Gettysburg in July 1863, and Sherman's capture of Atlanta and his March to the Sea in 1864.

But the war's most important turning point was Lincoln's reelection. Lincoln won on a platform of fighting the war through to victory and ending slavery forever. These terms encompassed the utter extinguishment of the so-called Confederate States of America. It is tempting to look back on Lincoln's election on November 8, 1864, as the day the South actually lost the Civil War. The last chance of snatching victory from the jaws of defeat by a change in presidential administrations had vanished. But to the Southern high command, and to a defiant partisan named John Wilkes Booth, the cause seemed far from lost. These men believed that the South could still prevail in its gigantic struggle for independent nationhood and white supremacy. All that was required for victory was that iron defiance Jefferson Davis called the South's "unquenchable resolve."

Junius Brutus Booth Jr. returned from a ten-year sojourn in California in May 1864. He met his younger brother for the first time in a decade. The last time he'd seen him, Johnny had been a boy of sixteen. Now, Junius "found his brother Wilkes strongly in sympathy with the Southern cause, and endeavored with frequent and earnest arguments to dissuade him."[17] But it was like talking to a wall. Junius presently concluded that on the question of the justice of the war, his brother was "a monomaniac on the subject & not worthwhile arguing with."[18]

Junius did persuade Wilkes to appear onstage with him and Edwin in a special benefit performance. The younger brother had hesitated to go along because he was so estranged from Edwin, a strong Union man, over politics. Edwin told his friend Adam Badeau, an aide to U. S. Grant, that "he had long and violent discussions with his brother at this time. Wilkes declared his wish for the success of the Rebellion so decidedly that Edwin finally told him he should go elsewhere to make such sentiments known; that he was not at liberty to express them in the house of a Union man."[19]

And so, on November 25, John Wilkes Booth was back in New York City to perform *Julius Caesar* in the grand "Shakespeare Benefit" with his brothers. He played Marc Anthony, Edwin the heroic assassin Brutus, while Junius Brutus Booth played Cassius. Proceeds from the benefit went to erect the statue of William Shakespeare that still stands in Central Park. (The year 1864 was the three hundredth anniversary of the birth of the Elizabethan playwright.) Though a second Shakespeare statue benefit was planned for April 1865, the November performance would be the only time the three brothers appeared onstage together. The benefit netted $3,500 toward the Shakespeare statue.[20] The youngest of the brothers must have been struck by the timeliness of this particular tragedy, a drama centered on conspiracy and assassination under the shadow of civil war. It almost seems a shame he couldn't have played the noble Brutus, one of his greatest heroes. In one of the final entries the despairing fugitive assassin scribbled in his little pocket diary, he compared himself again to Shakespeare's Roman hero.

The night of the performance, a gang of arsonists sent from Canada tried to burn down New York City by setting fire to nineteen Manhattan hotels simultaneously, along with Barnum's Museum. They were armed with bottles of "Greek Fire," the ancient fire accelerant based on phosphorous. They checked into their rooms, piled up furniture and bedding, and soaked it with the flammable liquid. The phosphorous spontaneously burst into flame. To conceal the crime, the arsonists locked the doors and windows of their rooms when they fled. This was a blunder—it deprived the fires of the oxygen needed to burn fiercely. The performance of the Greek Fire, mixed by a Montreal pharmacist, was also disappointing. None of the hotels went up in flames. The fires were all put out before doing much damage.

But news of the operation sent the city into an uproar the next day. The *New York Times* ran a screaming, all-caps headline: "THE REBEL PLOT. ATTEMPT TO BURN THE CITY. ALL THE PRINCIPAL HOTELS SET ON FIRE."[21] The Booth brothers didn't need to read about it in the papers. They had firsthand knowledge of the arson attack. They had presented *Julius Caesar* the night of the fires at the Winter Garden Theatre on Broadway. Next door to the Winter Garden was the Lafarge House, one of the arsonists' targets.

The theater was crowded to "suffocation" with two thousand people. Despite the placement of many extra seats, it was standing room only. Scalpers were getting twenty dollars for a seat, one hundred for a box. All of New York, it seemed, wanted to see the celebrated Booth brothers together on one stage. About midway through the play there was a commotion in the rear of the audience. The fire in the hotel next door had already been put out, but the smell of smoke in the theater was palpable. Then the fire trucks pulled up outside with clanging bells and shouting crews. "Fire! Fire!" someone cried out, and the huge audience panicked. The crowd was far too large to permit an orderly evacuation. Fortunately, Edwin Booth and others succeeded in calming the crowd before a fatal stampede could occur.

The play resumed after about half an hour. It was a resounding success. "The three brothers stood side by side, again and again, before the curtain, to receive the lavish applause mingled with waving of handkerchiefs and every mark of enthusiasm." Critics thought that J. Wilkes Booth "carried off the honors of the occasion" and got the most applause.[22]

The next morning, at Edwin's house, the three brothers quarreled bitterly about the war. Junius said the fire-setters should be tracked down and lynched. He declared Southern defeat certain. Edwin told his younger brother that he had voted for Lincoln and that he prayed daily for Union victory. John Wilkes, who had met the leader of the arsonists in Montreal the month before, argued that the destruction of New York City would have been a legitimate act of war and fitting retribution for the many acts of Northern barbarism in the South. He insisted that Lincoln meant to crown himself king of the United States. Tempers rose; no minds were changed.

It was probably shortly after Lincoln's reelection that Booth wrote the two most significant of his letters to survive, the "to whom it may concern" letter and the letter to his "Dearest beloved Mother."[23] These two documents provide the most forceful statements of his passionate love for the South, his support for slavery and white supremacy, his hatred for Lincoln, and his despair as inexorable defeat overtook the cause. It was apparent that his abilities as a prose stylist had improved since he composed his semicoherent "allow me a few words" speech during the secession crisis in December 1860. He gave the two letters to Asia to lock up in her safe in her big house in Philadelphia.

Booth's "Dearest beloved Mother" letter to Mary Ann Holmes Booth was both a farewell and an apology for breaking the promise he had made her not to take up arms for the South. He tried to justify his decision:

> Dearest Mother, though, I owe you all, *there* is another duty. A noble duty for the sake of liberty and humanity due to my Country—For, four years I have lived (I may say) A *slave* in the north (A favored slave its true, but no less hateful to me on that account.) Not daring to express my thoughts or sentiments, even in my own home Constantly hearing every principle, dear to my heart, denounced as treasonable, And knowing the vile and savage acts committed on my countrymen their wives & helpless children, that I have cursed my wilful idleness, And begun to deem myself a coward and to despise my own existence. . . . For four years I have borne it mostly for your dear sake, And for you alone, have I also struggled to fight off this desire to begone, but it seems that uncontrollable fate, moving me for its ends, takes me from you, dear Mother, to do what work I can for a poor oppressed downtrodden people. . . . I cannot longer resist the inclination, to go and share the sufferings of my brave countrymen, holding an unequal strife (for every right human & divine) against the most ruthless enemy, the world has ever known. You can answer for me dearest Mother (although none of you think with me) that I have not a *single selfish motive* to spur me on to this, nothing save the sacred duty, I feel I *owe the cause I love.* the cause of the South.

It had been agony for him to live as "a hidden lie among my country's foes. . . . I feel that I am right in the justness of my cause." He swore to her that he was willing to give his life for that cause, as indeed he soon would.

He opened his "to whom it may concern" letter with an angry challenge: "Right, or wrong, God, judge me, not man," and his words still quiver with barely controlled fury:

All hope for peace is dead, my prayers have proved as idle as my hopes. God's will be done. I go to see, and share the bitter end. I have ever held the South were right. The very nomination of Abraham Lincoln four years ago, spoke plainly—war, war upon Southern rights and institutions. His election proved it. . . . This country was formed for the *white* not for the black man. And looking upon *African slavery* from the same standpoint, held by those noble framers of our Constitution. I for one, have ever considered *it*, one of the greatest blessings (both for themselves and us,) that God even bestowed upon a favored nation. . . . I aided in the capture and execution of John Brown, Who was a murderer on our Western Border, and who was fairly *tried* and *convicted*,—before an impartial judge & jury—of treason. . . . But what was a crime in poor John Brown is now considered (by themselves) as the greatest and only virtue, of the whole Republican party. Strange transmigration, *vice* to become a *virtue*. Simply because *more* indulge in it. I thought then, *as now*, that the abolitionists, *were the only traitors* in the land, And that the entire party, deserved the fate of poor old Brown. . . . But God is my judge I love *justice*, more than I do a country, that disowns it. More than fame and wealth. More (Heaven pardon me if wrong) more than a happy home. I have never been upon a battlefield, but, O my countrymen, could you all but see the *reality* or effects of this horrid war, as I have seen them (in *every State*, save Virginia) I know you would think like me. And would pray the Almighty to create in the northern mind a sense of *right* and *justice* (even should it possess no seasoning of mercy.)

He ended with the stark promise that he would keep less than half a year later when he vowed "to triumph or die":

It is either extermination or slavery for *themselves* (worse than death) to draw from. I would know *my* choice. My love (as things stand today) is for the South alone. Nor, do I deem it a dishonor in attempting to make for her a prisoner of this man, to whom she owes so much of misery. If success attends me, I go penniless to her side. They say she has found *that* "last ditch" which the north have so long derided, and been endeavoring to force her in, forgetting they are our brothers, and that its impolitic to goad an enemy to madness. Should I reach her in safety and find it true, I will proudly beg permission to triumph or die in that same "ditch" by her side.

He signed himself "*A Confederate*, At present, doing duty *upon his own responsibility*." On some later date, probably January of 1865, Booth retrieved the letter from Asia's safe and amended it by striking out, in a different ink and with a different pen, the words "At present." Here he had seemed to declare that he was not at that time (November 1864) working under the orders of the insurgent government. By crossing out "At present," he seems to have been renouncing the option that he might at some future time begin working for the insurgents. Was he telling the truth?

COUNTDOWN

As the year ended, Booth made several trips into southern Maryland. His reputation as a wealthy actor made it easy to pass off his rides along the backroads of the secret mail line as an investor's search for property. He made his first foray on November 11, 1864, two days after he got back from Canada. He was scouting the route to Richmond and recruiting local Secret Service agents to aid his planned escape with the captive Yankee president or his flight as a fugitive assassin. If he had already decided to kill rather than capture, he didn't enlighten his collaborators.

The five southernmost counties of Maryland, cut off from Virginia by the miles-wide Potomac River, never had a chance to quit the Union and formally join the rebellion. Yet most of the whites there were as fervent secessionists as the inhabitants of South Carolina or Mississippi. Loosely occupied by federal troops, they supported the Southern cause in every way they could—as spies, couriers, postmen, slave catchers, arms smugglers, and operators of safe houses and signal stations. Mail went both north and south along the secret line.

In the 1860 presidential election, Lincoln had gotten only twelve votes in all five of the southernmost Maryland counties. (And one of those Republican voters was driven from his home.) Booth would flee through two of these counties after the murder—Prince George's County, where Lincoln got exactly one vote, and Charles County, where he got all of six.[1] Most whites were united in their hatred for King Abraham Africanus. The enslavers among them were further enraged when the new Maryland state constitution suddenly freed their slaves without compensation in November 1864.

Booth traveled from Washington by stagecoach to the Charles County village of Bryantown, where he checked into a tavern for the night. He was looking for Dr. William Queen, a seventy-six-year-old country doctor. Booth carried the letter of introduction to Dr. Queen he'd gotten from Patrick C. Martin in Montreal the month before. Despite his advanced age, Dr. Queen was an ardent supporter of the cause and a member of the local underground. Booth's letter of introduction came from one member of the Secret Service Bureau to another. John Wilkes Booth may not have been acting under direct orders from the Bureau, but there's no doubt he was working closely with its agents. Martin's letters also meant the actor was properly vouched for, essential in an environment swarming with spies, double agents, and federal detectives. All strangers were regarded with suspicion.

The next morning, Booth was taken to Dr. Queen's house, where he spent the night. Like many other members of the conspiracy, Queen was a Roman Catholic. The next day was Sunday, and Booth accompanied Dr. Queen to services at St. Mary's Catholic Church. There he was introduced to Dr. Samuel Alexander Mudd. Dr. Mudd, a thirty-two-year-old tobacco planter, was a much younger country doctor, only six years older than Booth. The actor had an introduction from Martin to Mudd, as well. Though also a Catholic, Mudd did not attend St. Mary's parish. He was there by special arrangement to meet Booth.

Dr. Mudd was a leading member of the underground and would become one of Booth's most valuable accomplices. On

John Wilkes Booth was recognized as one of the best-dressed men in the country.

the night of April 14–15, the doctor would set the fractured small bone in the assassin's left leg, broken in his leap from the presidential box to the stage of Ford's Theatre. Throughout the war, Dr. Mudd's profession had given him cover to ride the roads at night on rebel business. His farm was a safe house for fugitives and escaped prisoners of war, an occasional arms depot, and a station on the clandestine mail route that ran from Richmond to Montreal.

The mild-looking father of four, his premature baldness balanced by his luxuriant reddish moustache and chin whiskers, Mudd was a prosperous man whose father had given him a small tobacco plantation. He had owned eleven slaves. But he had just seen his net worth plunge dramatically when the new Maryland Constitution freed his slaves. He lost thousands of dollars. At the same time, without slave labor, the value of local tobacco land had plummeted. Mudd's farm was suddenly worth much less.

Dr. Mudd had long been active as a catcher of fugitive Blacks. He had a reputation as a harsh master, who had once shot one of his own slaves in the leg. He hated Lincoln and the Black Republicans.[2] His friendship with Booth would come within inches of putting the doctor's head in a noose. As it was, Mudd got a sentence of life imprisonment, of which he served only four years. He actually deserved hanging as much as the four hapless conspirators who did fall from the gallows. Booth spent Sunday night at Dr. Queen's house and returned to Washington on Monday.

It was through Dr. Mudd that Booth met the one who would become his right-hand man. John Harrison Surratt, alias John Harrison, alias John Watson, alias John Agostini, etcetera, was just twenty years old in 1864, six years younger than Booth. But he was already an experienced courier and spy. Surratt would recruit most of the other conspirators for Booth. He had been an agent of the Secret Service Bureau since May 1863.[3] He took some of his clandestine assignments directly from Jefferson Davis and Judah Benjamin, meeting frequently with the top leaders themselves. They considered young Surratt brave, trustworthy, and absolutely loyal to the cause.

Before the war, Surratt had studied in a Catholic seminary, intending to become a priest. He found his true calling, however, as a secret warrior for the white South. A tall, intelligent-looking man bronzed by days on horseback, he shuttled back and forth between Richmond and Canada by horse, wagon, railroad, and steamboat, evading the Union military and the ubiquitous detectives. Surratt described those detectives as surpassingly stupid men. He hid his dispatches in hollowed-out boot heels or under the boards of wagon beds. Once he hid secret papers in a laudatory biography of John Brown, no doubt reckoning such an abolitionist book as effective camouflage. Dipping into the volume on the long railroad journey, Surratt was astonished to learn that the man white Southerners considered a murderous terrorist had been canonized as a new Yankee saint.

The courier had shot his way out of trouble, he claimed, in a "score" of wild firefights. On at least two occasions, he murdered in cold blood unarmed Yankees—escaped prisoners of war—he encountered on his missions.[4] Dr. Mudd introduced Surratt to Booth in December. No one knows if Surratt was acting under orders from Richmond when he joined Booth's plot.

John Surratt's contacts with the Davis government suggest but do not prove that his superiors knew about Booth. Moreover, supportive of the notion that Booth may have been in direct touch with the Secret Service Bureau was an intriguing item found in the search of his room at the National Hotel on April 15, the day Abraham Lincoln died. It was an alphabetical cyphering chart, used for encoding and decoding secret documents. A rudimentary enciphering system by today's standards, the device did allow for a letter-for-letter substitution that made the encoded document completely unreadable to the uninitiated. To work the system, the spy needed the secret fifteen-letter key phrase. For some time, that key phrase had been "Complete Victory." As defeat drew near in 1865 and the desire for revenge grew, the Bureau changed the key to "Come Retribution." A matching enciphering chart, identical to Booth's, had been found in spymaster Judah Benjamin's office after the capture of Richmond.

Like the other conspirators, Surratt hated African Americans. After the assassination, he bragged, "We have killed Lincoln, the niggers' friend."[5] Before the crime, he had indiscreetly declared that "he and Booth had some bloody work to do; they were going to kill Abe Lincoln, the dammed old scoundrel; that he had ruined Maryland and the country." Notably, this admission of intent to kill was made in January 1865, when the mission was still ostensibly limited to seizing the president.[6]

Surratt worked out of his family's Surratt House, a tavern, hostelry, and post office in the little village of Surrattsville, Maryland. Only thirteen miles south of Washington, DC, Surrattsville was nevertheless described by one journalist as "a suburb of Richmond, ignorant and rebel to the brim."[7] Surratt's mother, Mary Elizabeth Surratt, and his sister Anna made the tavern their home during the early years of the Civil War. An older brother was serving in the Southern army.

Almost as soon as the war broke out, the Surratt tavern became a stop on the secret mail line and a safe house and meeting place for spies.[8] John's father had been the postmaster of Surrattsville. The senior John Surratt was "an impetuous Southerner, full of prejudice and hate toward the Yankees—as was almost everyone in southern Maryland—outspoken in his convictions and proud of every Southern victory."[9] When the older man drank himself to death, his son became postmaster, a position he held until the government fired him in 1863 for "disloyalty." The authorities apparently had some idea what he was up to. His mother then rented the tavern for $500 a year to an inebriate named John M. Lloyd, a former DC policeman. In 1864, Mrs. Surratt moved her family into the other property she had inherited from her late husband—a four-story brick townhouse that still stands on Washington's H Street. She began taking in boarders and soon had several paying tenants. Rent was $35 a month. John Surratt lived there when he wasn't on the road. Several of the conspirators would make the Surratt boardinghouse their temporary home. The place quickly became a rebel safe house in the national capital.

John Surratt was the luckiest of the conspirators, the only one who escaped punishment almost entirely. After the assassination, he fled to Canada and from there to Europe. Extradited from Egypt in 1867, his civil trial by a Maryland jury of Southern sympathizers ended in a hung jury. He went free. He lived until 1916, haunted by the knowledge that his association with Booth had sent his wretched mother to the gallows.

Dr. Mudd had also introduced Booth to Thomas Harbin, one of the most important agents in southern Maryland. He was active on both sides of the Potomac but worked out of a signal station in Virginia's King George County directly across the river from Charles County, Maryland. Harbin also reported personally to Davis and Benjamin. Harbin thought Booth sounded like "a crazy fellow" but agreed to help. He would play an important role in Booth's futile escape attempt.

Surratt and Harbin knew a likely river-runner, George Andrew Atzerodt, alias Andrew Atwood. Surratt enlisted him in January. Atzerodt, born in the Kingdom of Prussia in 1835, was three years older than Booth. A slight curvature of the spine gave him a hunched look and his apelike profile was heightened by his massive arms and shoulders, bulked up by many nights of oaring across the tidewater Potomac. His hair was long and oily. He had a receding chin and forehead and a sparse beard. He was illiterate and spoke broken English. Atzerodt wore the same greasy coat every day. Exasperated, Booth finally bought him a new jacket.

Atzerodt and his brother ran a haphazard carriage business in the little Potomac River town of Port Tobacco, Maryland. George spent more time in the village taverns than in his shop. He drank so much that even the champion boozer John Wilkes Booth told him to sober up. When drunk, he was wont to hint of his involvement in an important secret undertaking that would make him rich. In Port Tobacco, Atzerodt had a reputation as a coward who once jumped out of a tavern window to avoid a fight.

Atzerodt's real profession was smuggling passengers and cargo across the heavily patrolled Potomac in the dead of night. His knowledge of the big river's intricate inlets and tributaries and the timing of its tides, as well as his familiarity with the patrols of the federal gunboats, would be invaluable in any attempt to get the captive Lincoln or the fugitive assassins across the Potomac into Virginia. The impoverished German was promised the fantastic sum of $20,000 for his participation. The immigrant was preoccupied with money since he had so little of it. Later, he was seen flashing wads of greenbacks. Atzerodt had been borrowing the boats of others for his midnight crossings. Presently Booth paid $250 for a boat of his own to avoid relying on outsiders. The boat was hidden away in the mouth of a creek but in the end was never used.

Atzerodt's role in the conspiracy was greatly enlarged on the fatal Friday April 14, when Booth suddenly ordered him to murder Vice President Andrew Johnson. Though Booth bullied him into agreeing, there was little chance the cowardly German would carry out the assignment. He preferred to pawn his revolver, get drunk on the proceeds, and make a run for it. He was arrested a few days later. Well aware of the boatman's unreliability, Booth gave primary responsibility for killing Johnson to David Herold.[10]

The Prussian oaf and the suave actor could hardly have been more different. Yet Atzerodt and Booth thought alike when it came to race. Not a native-born American himself, Atzerodt contemptuously dismissed millions of real Americans on the basis of their color. Asked about Atzerodt's political beliefs, one acquaintance simply replied, "He always hated the niggers."[11] In talks with his religious adviser before his hanging, he explained how much he detested Blacks and how much he admired the institution of slavery as a system for holding them down. Atzerodt·wanted African Americans kept in ignorance. He had been much impressed, he said, by a sermon he'd once heard in which the minister had explained that their black skin meant the entire negro race was cursed by God. He had joined the conspiracy, he asserted, because of his support of slavery.[12] After his arrest, Atzerodt sang like a bird, offering many confessions to many interrogators. He was mostly truthful. But all his talking couldn't save him from death on the gallows with the three other condemned conspirators.

David Edgar Herold had known Booth, Surratt, and Atzerodt for years before he joined the conspiracy. In 1865 Herold's defense attorney made a valiant but unsuccessful attempt to save him from the hangman by presenting him as a candidate for clemency by reason of his "trifling," feeble-minded, childish nature. He was just a pathetic dupe, his attorney argued, easily misled by the wily assassin. The reputation stuck. Historians of the assassination have often portrayed him as a near-idiot with the mind of an eleven-year-old.

The truth was rather different. Despite his squint-faced, disheveled look, little Davey Herold was a well-educated middle-class youth who had studied pharmacology at Georgetown College. He earned a degree in 1860. He held a respectable position as a pharmacist's clerk. Twenty-three years old in 1865, he was arguably immature and irresponsible but no simpleton. Indeed, the transcript of Herold's verbal sparring with his interrogators after his arrest reveals an agile mind capable of conceding minor truths to conceal larger ones. He did talk too much; everyone agreed he was a "blab." Davey lived in the large Herold family home near the Navy Yard with his widowed mother and seven sisters, all of whom spoiled him. The gregarious Herold and the witty, alcoholic Atzerodt became fast friends, clowning around together in the streets and taverns of Washington City.

The popular star actor made friends everywhere he went. Booth had become friendly with Herold back in 1863 during his run at the brand-new Ford's Theatre. Booth's interest in the young man can be explained by Herold's obsessive indulgence in his favorite pastime—hunting and riding through the backcountry of southern Maryland. No one knew the baffling byways and people of Charles County better than Herold. He was an ideal guide. He was also expert with gun and horse. Herold quit his drugstore job in September 1864, when he became involved with the conspiracy. He didn't need the salary now that Booth was supporting him. One witness said he saw Herold, in a saloon, paying for drinks with "a large roll of bills, several thousand dollars."[13] (This seems unlikely, given the financial problems Booth was facing at the time.)

The one quality Davey Herold possessed in abundance was loyalty. He idolized Booth. He selflessly accompanied and cared for the badly injured assassin during the entire twelve days of their flight through Maryland and Virginia. He could easily have deserted Booth and melted away into the populace, perhaps escaping justice altogether. Instead, he stayed the course, was captured with the assassin, tried, convicted, and hanged with the other three on July 7, 1865.

John Surratt was instrumental in bringing on board the conspiracy's most enigmatic and sinister recruit, Lewis Thornton Powell, alias Lewis Payne or Paine, alias the Reverend Wood, alias Jim Moore, alias Mr. Kincheloe, etcetera. Six feet, two inches and 180 pounds, the handsome, dark-haired, blue-eyed soldier was the brute strength of the gang, often portrayed as Booth's brutal, dim-witted puppet. The real Lewis Thornton Powell, however, was a preacher's son who played chess and was fond of reading medical books. He dressed well and was perfectly capable of projecting an air of good breeding. When he went on trial for his assassination attempt on Secretary of State William Seward, the *Washington Star* described him as "very tall with an athletic, gladiatorial frame" and the "massive robustness of animal manhood in the most stalwart type."[14]

Twenty years old in 1864, the hulking Powell had been only seventeen in 1861, when he had enlisted in the Second Florida Infantry, CSA. One of Powell's brothers died fighting for the South. Another was badly wounded. He himself was the survivor of three years of the most savage fighting the Army of Northern Virginia had experienced. He fought in the bloody battles of the Seven Days' campaign that blunted McClellan's drive on Richmond in 1862. A hospital stay spared him the carnage of Second Manassas and Antietam. He played his part in the dreadful slaughter of Yankees at Fredericksburg at year's end. He came through all this preternatural violence unhurt, but his luck ran out at Gettysburg in July 1863. There he was shot in the wrist and captured. He was working as a volunteer nurse in a military hospital in Baltimore when he escaped and headed south to rejoin his Florida regiment. He got no farther than northern Virginia, where he joined up with Colonel John Singleton Mosby's legendary corps of irregular cavalry, Mosby's Rangers.

Powell rode with Mosby from late 1863 until January 1865. Mosby's elite cavalry fought more as guerrillas than regulars. Most of them lived in private homes among the people of this Yankee-occupied region of northern Virginia. They could vanish into the neighborhood in a few moments. Avoiding pitched battles, Mosby had perfected the art of the surprise attack, striking fast and hard, then disappearing before counterattack could be brought to bear. People called him the "Gray Ghost." Colonel Mosby worked closely with the Secret Service Bureau in undercover work behind the lines.

Powell soon distinguished himself among Mosby's daring, fiercely independent horsemen. He was the "terrible Lewis

Powell, the boldest of the bold and the rashest of the reckless." "Powell had the reputation for having killed a great many men, and when any desperate matter was to be undertaken, he was selected."[15] The big horse soldier spoke casually of "scattering the brains" of Yankee prisoners. Traumatized by the years of killing, Powell was dangerously unbalanced, ready to strike out violently at the slightest provocation. His defense attorney tried to get him off on a plea of insanity, arguing, "We know that slavery made him immoral, that war made him a murderer, and that necessity, revenge, and delusion made him an assassin."[16] The insanity defense was by then well established in American law, but the Union officers who sat in judgment unhesitatingly condemned Powell to death. Photographs of the rebel horseman reveal his exceptionally thick, muscular neck. It is hardly surprising that the drop from the gallows failed to break that neck at his hanging on July 7, 1865. Powell strangled painfully for several minutes before expiring. The three other condemned who dangled alongside him had all died swiftly of severed spinal cords.

While riding with Mosby's Rangers, Powell was also carrying out missions for the Secret Service Bureau. Witnesses later reported seeing him in Richmond, Washington, Baltimore, New York, Niagara Falls, and Montreal, all when he was supposedly a private soldier stationed in northern Virginia.[17] Before his hanging, Powell admitted that "for months previous, while in the Secret Service of the Confederacy, he had journeyed back and forth from Richmond to Washington and Baltimore in conference with prominent men of the latter city. These men kept him in funds and encouraged him with dreams of glory and the everlasting gratitude of the Southern people. . . . He had been their honored guest in palatial homes and with means they supplied, had come and gone at their bidding."[18]

On January 13, 1865, Powell abruptly left Mosby's Rangers, riding into Union lines at Fairfax Courthouse. He sold his horse and was given a parole as a civilian refugee. His devotion to the cause of the South makes his desertion of that cause seem quite implausible. His so-called desertion was actually a detachment from Mosby's corps to serve undercover behind the lines. Powell was most likely acting under Secret Service Bureau orders when he rode into the federal camp to surrender.

He immediately made his way to a safe house in Baltimore. On January 21, 1865, a week after Powell's desertion, John Surratt traveled to Baltimore to deliver $300 from Booth. The money was for Powell's living expenses. A connection through the Secret Service Bureau would seem to be the only satisfactory explanation for Booth's assistance to Powell. Then, when Surratt telegraphed him, Powell came on to Washington to join the gang on March 14, exactly one month before the assassination.

It is most significant that, as assassination authority Edward Steers Jr. has pointed out, except for his two boyhood friends, Arnold and O'Laughlen, Booth found all of the recruits for his conspiracy through the Secret Service Bureau.[19] Canadian spymaster Patrick C. Martin's letter had introduced him to Dr. Samuel Mudd. Dr. Mudd, in turn, put him in touch with spies John Surratt and Thomas Harbin. Surratt and Harbin recruited Atzerodt. Booth already knew Herold, but Surratt vouched for him. Surratt also was instrumental in bringing in Lewis Powell, though the Bureau itself may have sent Powell to join the conspiracy. Thomas Harbin, for his part, introduced Booth to several agents along the route to Richmond who would prove most useful in the actor's hopeless attempt to escape justice.

J. Wilkes Booth played the lead in *Romeo and Juliet* in the penultimate performance of his acting career at Grover's Theatre in Washington on January 20, 1865. The play was a benefit for his dear friend the actress Avonia Stanhope Jones. Romeo had to go on in a borrowed costume since his $25,000 theatrical wardrobe was now at the bottom of the St. Lawrence River. The *National Intelligencer* gushed: "No such *Romeo* ever trod the boards. What perfect acting! We have never seen a *Romeo* bearing any near comparison with the acting of Booth. His death scene was the most remarkable and fearfully natural that we have seen for years upon the stage. His elocution was faultless."[20]

By this time, however, John Wilkes Booth no longer cared what the critics wrote of him. He had other things on his mind.

"EVERY DROP OF BLOOD"

General-in-Chief Grant ordered the resumption of the prisoner exchange cartel on January 25, 1865. Three thousand men a week were soon being traded. The justification for Booth's supposed abduction plot had thus become moot. There was no longer an objective to bargain for with a captive Lincoln. Nevertheless, the actor forged ahead. He must have been intent on murder, not kidnapping. Perhaps he had meant to kill all along.

At the beginning of the second week in January, Booth met in Baltimore with Arnold and O'Laughlen. It was the first time they'd seen each other since their initial meeting in Barnum's Hotel back in August. Booth wanted to turn over to them the heavy trunk of weapons, gear, and provisions he'd bought in New York City the month before. It was so weighty the actor feared that shipping it might result in suspicion and investigation. Packed inside was a modest arsenal of small arms, including two state-of-the-art Spencer Carbines. One of the first effective repeating rifles, the lever-action Spencer fired seven times without reloading. It fed new .56-caliber rounds into the firing chamber from a tubular magazine in the butt. It could be reloaded with seven fresh rounds in a single movement. President Lincoln had tried and approved the rifle himself, cranking off seven fast rounds at a target set up on the White House grounds.

Many Northern soldiers, particularly cavalry units, were armed with these repeating rifles during the latter years of the war. The gun was first used in combat at Gettysburg in July 1863. The Spencer provided vastly superior firepower over single-shot, muzzle-loading rifle muskets. Supplies were supposedly restricted to the military, but Booth seems to have had no trouble obtaining two in New York City at $300 apiece. His trunk also held four Colt revolvers with holsters and belts; three fine "Rio Grande Camp Knives," foot-long Bowie knives made of English Sheffield steel; ammunition; two sets of handcuffs and a set of leg irons; a forty-foot length of rope to trip up the horses of pursuing cavalry; a big wrench for removing the wheels of the presidential carriage to load it on to a boat; as well as canteens and canned food. Booth bought a buggy and horse for his men to drive some of the gear to Washington. They took enough on the buggy to lighten the trunk sufficiently to ship. Then they made their way to the capital and met the actor at Ford's Theatre. They stabled the horse and buggy in the alley behind the theater and stashed the weapons and gear. At the same time, Booth sent other provisions for his escape, to the farm of the helpful Dr. Samuel A. Mudd.

Another abortive peace initiative—the Hampton Roads Conference—took place on February 3, 1865. President Lincoln and Secretary of State William H. Seward met with three commissioners appointed by Jefferson Davis aboard the US steamboat *River Queen* anchored at Hampton Roads, the great harbor at the mouth of Chesapeake Bay. The negotiators had little chance of reaching agreement. The terms demanded by Lincoln and Davis were diametrically opposed. Davis's objective was peace between "our two countries." Lincoln spoke only of "our one common country." Lincoln remained unbending: he insisted on the surrender of the insurgent armies, reunion under the government of the United States, and the abolition of slavery.

Jefferson Davis was equally determined: he insisted on independent, sovereign nationhood for the confederation of slave states that claimed to have left the Union. "We are fighting for INDEPENDENCE and that, or extermination, we will have," he declared. "You may 'emancipate' every negro in the Confederacy, but *we will be free*. We will govern ourselves . . . if we have to see every Southern plantation sacked, and every Southern city in flames."[1]

Davis's three commissioners were prominent peace advocates within his government. Knowing their cause lost, they were sincere and eager to compromise, but they were hampered by their chief's preconditions. Nevertheless, they tried valiantly, though without success, to come up with a solution that might satisfy both sides. President Lincoln made their hopeless task no easier by insisting that the United States would never accept that the white Southerners' so-called nation, their "Confederate States of America," possessed the slightest measure of legitimacy. There had never been a Southern nation, only a gigantic rebellion. The leaders of that rebellion could not expect to make treaties. The insurgents could only lay down their arms and surrender by accepting Lincoln's indispensable terms. Or they could choose to fight on until irrevocable defeat swiftly brought them to utter ruin.

The Southerners played the only card they had: the Mexican invasion gambit. They tried to persuade President Lincoln to order a cease-fire between the opposing armies and launch a joint North-South invasion of Mexico to overthrow the French puppet, Emperor Maximillian. Fighting side by side against a foreign enemy to uphold the Monroe Doctrine, Jeff Davis's commissioners said, would work to reconcile North and South. The ultimate question of reunification or Southern independence could be postponed until after victory. President Lincoln definitively, categorically, and conclusively rejected this proposal. He wanted a surrender, not a truce or a treaty or a cease-fire.

It was true that there was considerable concern in the North over French emperor Louis Napoleon's audacious bid to create a new empire in Mexico. Taking advantage of the American Civil War and justifying the action by Mexico's vast indebtedness to European lenders, the French had invaded in June 1863, overthrowing the legitimate, republican government and installing a usurper, the Hapsburg archduke Ferdinand Maximilian, as "Emperor of Mexico." The coup was not just a blow against the Monroe Doctrine and the Mexican people; it was also an antidemocratic, monarchical movement in a hemisphere in which most governments were at least ostensibly republican.

"One war at a time," Lincoln had said in 1862, when war with Britain had threatened. That rule still obtained. Now was not the time for going to war over Mexico. Lincoln and Seward were wise enough to see that the problem would solve itself when the Civil War ended. They also understood that if it did come to war with France, the US would need no help from the South. The United States of America now possessed sufficient military might to crush every other power in the Western Hemisphere. The apprehensive British sent reinforcements to Canada, but Queen Victoria herself admitted that Britain could not hold Canada against a US invasion.[2] The French were equally desirous of avoiding any conflict with the powerful Americans. They would abandon Emperor Maximilian after the Union finally destroyed the rebellion. He would be overthrown and shot dead by the Mexican people.

The commissioners at Hampton Roads stubbornly continued to push the Mexican scheme. It was their only hope for an outcome short of unconditional surrender or more futile warfare. Fruitlessly, they proposed the plan again several times in different language. As often as they did, Lincoln told them no again, in different language. At last, the Southerners had to accept that Lincoln wasn't buying.

Since all three of them—unlike Jefferson Davis himself—recognized the utter hopelessness of their cause, they probed Lincoln on the status of the South after its surrender—that is, on conditions for the reconstruction of the Union. Their principal concern, of course, was the future of slavery. Was there any way for the South to return to the Union with slavery intact? In answer, Secretary Seward then informed the Southern statesmen that Congress had just days before approved and sent to the states for ratification a Thirteenth Amendment to the Constitution, abolishing slavery.

The Thirteenth, the first amendment in more than sixty years and one of the most concise, reads simply "Neither slavery nor involuntary servitude, except as a punishment for a crime whereof the party shall have been duly convicted, shall exist within the United States, or any place subject to their jurisdiction." (That wording came from the old Confederation Congress's Northwest Ordinance of 1787.) Three states had already ratified the amendment, Seward added. And by this time, two of the four loyal slave states—Missouri and Maryland—had abolished slavery within their borders by legislative means. Only Kentucky and Delaware remained as slave states within the Union. If we do rejoin the Union, the Southerners asked, could our states vote against ratification of the Thirteenth Amendment? It was a moot point. Lincoln held out little hope for any compromise that would save slavery in the long term. He told them that the institution was effectively dead already.

He did dangle the possibility of compensation by the federal government to enslavers for their human property. The sum he named was $400 million, a small fraction of the peculiar institution's prewar value. Lincoln had always been an advocate of compensation for the enslavers. His conciliatory proposal at the conference that day was an instance of wishful thinking overriding good judgment. Lincoln should have recognized that, given the ongoing four-year storm of rage and hatred, almost no one in the North would have been willing to pay reparations to the despicable traitors who had killed so many of their sons and husbands, brothers and fathers. A politician as savvy as Abraham Lincoln should have known that almost no one agreed with him on compensation, not among the Northern people, not among the editors and preachers, not in the army, not in Congress, and not in his own cabinet. He may have been intoxicated by the spirit of malice toward none and charity toward all that he would evoke a month later in his Second Inaugural Address. When Lincoln proposed compensated emancipation to his cabinet on February 6, so unanimous and so definitive was the secretaries' repudiation that the president dropped the idea altogether. "You are all against me," he sighed.[3]

Desperate to stave off emancipation, the Southerners aboard the *River Queen* pulled out all the old white supremacist claims that enslavement was the ideal condition for African Americans. They revealed at the same time the delusional thinking that had for so long distorted the worldview of white Southerners. Slavery was beneficial to whites and Blacks alike, they told Lincoln and Seward. The enslaved people were happy in bondage; freedom would be a disaster for them. They seemed really to believe this.

One of the strongest arguments against emancipation, the enslavers believed, was their conviction that these people would perish by starvation if set free. Blacks were simply too lazy, improvident, and irresponsible to work to support themselves without white overseers to drive them. Commissioner Robert M. T. Hunter, former US senator from Virginia and now president pro tempore of the Southern Senate, tried to convince President Lincoln of this irredeemable Black fecklessness. Hunter told Lincoln that he simply didn't understand racial realities. In fact, only Southern enslavers truly understood the character and propensities of Black people. After all, the two races had lived side by side in the South for centuries. Every white Southerner knew that it was virtually impossible to get a decent day's work out of the enslaved. They had to be constantly monitored, threatened with, and not infrequently subjected to, painful physical punishment to get them to do anything. (It apparently didn't occur to the enslavers that withholding labor might be a tactic the people employed to resist their enslavement.)

Hunter had insisted that the result of emancipation would be that "no work would be done, nothing would be cultivated, and both blacks and whites would *starve!*"[4] (The whites would presumably perish along with the Blacks because whites could hardly be expected to work for their own support.) Such talk was just the old white supremacist cliché that African Americans were childlike innocents who needed the regulation and protection provided by the South's benign institution.

As he so often did, Abraham Lincoln didn't directly contradict Hunter but responded instead with a story:

> Mr. Hunter, you ought to know a great deal better about this argument than I, for you have always lived under a slave system. I can only reply that it reminds me of a man out of Illinois by the name of Case, who undertook a few years ago to raise a very large herd of hogs. It was great trouble to *feed* them, and how to get around this was a puzzle to him. At length he hit on the plan of planting an immense field of potatoes, and when they were sufficiently grown, he turned the whole herd out into the field, and let them have full swing, thus saving not only the labor of feeding the hogs, but also that of digging the potatoes.[5]

Case was pleased with himself, Lincoln continued. But then a neighbor raised a point that the farmer hadn't considered. " 'Mr. Case, this is all very fine,' he said. 'Your hogs are doing very well just now, but you know out here in Illinois the frost comes early and the ground freezes a foot deep. Then what are you going to do?' " Case thought about it. " 'Well,' he eventually answered, 'it may come pretty hard on their *snouts*, but in the end it will be root hog, or die.' "[6]

Lincoln went on to tell Hunter that "in the dire contingency that you name, whites and blacks alike will have to look out for themselves; and I have an abiding faith that they will go about it in a fashion that will undeceive you in a very agreeable way."[7] (The president was chagrined later when the story leaked, fearing it might make him appear callous or frivolous.) The conference broke up without reaching any agreement.

Meanwhile, Booth was shuttling back and forth between Washington and New York with side trips to Philadelphia and Baltimore. Sam Arnold later wrote that "Booth, through riotous living and dissipation, was compelled to visit the city of New York for the purpose of replenishing his squandered means. His absence continued for most of the first three weeks of February."[8]

Booth had withdrawn a final $600 from his account with Jay Cooke and Company, reducing his available balance to a mere $25. He went to New York to get more money, presumably from Southern agents or sympathizers. The city had long been the center of Secret Service Bureau activities in the North. At first, he stayed at his brother Edwin's house, where his mother also lived. Presently, the brothers' political disagreements reached the breaking point. Edwin finally threw him out on the sidewalk, saying he couldn't express his traitorous sentiments in "the house of a Union man." Thereafter the embittered younger man found other lodgings.

Throughout the war, New York City had been a hotbed of disloyalty, site of the horrific antiadministration draft riots in the summer of 1863. When the war first broke out, New York's mayor had proposed that his city leave the Union to become a sovereign city-state, independent of both North and South. There was in the city a cabal of wealthy, pro-Southern Democrats. Booth spoke of being entertained in their Manhattan mansions. They may have been slipping him cash.

John Surratt and Samuel Arnold lived into the twentieth century. Both insisted till the end of their lives that the Davis government had played no part in Booth's conspiracy. But if he wasn't being directly supported by the Southern government, he was aided by sympathizers in the North with identical objectives. (And, of course, Arnold and Surratt were hardly privy to all of Booth's secrets.)

At the end of January, probably in a gambling den on Baltimore's Monument Square, Booth met with Lewis Powell for the first time, no doubt briefing the big soldier on his plans.[9] Then Powell got himself in a bind. A virulent racist himself, he became enraged when he received some sass from a Black serving woman in his boardinghouse. He beat her badly, knocking her down and kicking her. He was arrested and charged with spying, the reasons for this charge not appearing in the record.

Powell took the Oath of Allegiance on March 13 and was released on parole with the condition that he remain well away from the front, specifically north of Philadelphia, for the duration of the war. Ignoring his parole, Powell went to Washington to meet with Booth and the other conspirators the very next day. The others began calling him "Mosby." He claimed to be a Baptist preacher when he first checked in at the Surratt boardinghouse. Given his fearsome demeanor, some of his fellow boarders were skeptical about his ability to win souls for the Lord.

Six months had now passed since Booth's first meeting with Arnold and O'Laughlen at Barnum's Hotel in Baltimore in early August 1864. The conspirators had been idle all that time, hanging out and drinking while waiting for orders from Booth. Some of them began to grow restive. Booth's continuing financial embarrassment meant that he could no longer support his gang as generously as he had in the past. Arnold, for one, was dissatisfied.

He complained that "Booth was absent from the city of Washington the best part of the month of February. . . . During the Entire Month of February the project was at a standstill and seeming apathy, seldom meeting with Booth."[10]

February slipped into March. The great event of March 1865 was Abraham Lincoln's inauguration for a second presidential term. Despite the relentless rain that day, many tens of thousands, the largest crowd ever to attend an inauguration, witnessed the outdoor event. Among them was the famous young actor. The next month, drunk and belligerent in a Manhattan saloon called the House of Lords, on Friday, April 7, exactly one week before the deadly rendezvous at Ford's, Booth had slammed his fist down on the bar and burst out, "What a splendid chance I had to kill the President on the 4th of March!" He said that "he could live in history if he committed it."[11] It wasn't just the brandy talking; he had indeed been there on March 4.

Booth had not gone to the Capitol that day to listen to speeches. Nevertheless, Abraham Lincoln gave a speech—his Second Inaugural Address—the extraordinary meditation on history that the president considered his most enduring literary creation. The actor didn't hear much of it. By the time Lincoln began speaking, Booth, his heart pounding, was racing down a corridor, looking for a way out onto the East Front of the Capitol, where the ceremony was taking place. It had to be a way that took him away from the squad of Capitol police he'd just tussled with. The officers had forcibly prevented him from getting close to President Lincoln. Had Booth really meant to kill Lincoln that day?

He'd come provided with an official admission ticket, the gift of Lucy Hale. Miss Hale had gotten it from her father, abolitionist senator John Parker Hale of New Hampshire. His senatorial term would end that very day. He'd been defeated for reelection in November. The ticket entitled the bearer to admission to the Senate Chamber, where the new senators and the new vice president, Unionist Democrat Andrew Johnson of Tennessee, would be sworn in, as well as to a place outside on the platform erected on the East Front, where President Lincoln would deliver his inaugural address and take the oath.

Tickets had been handed out promiscuously. There were more bearers than could be accommodated. So Booth had to fight his way into the Senate Chamber to hear a drunken Andrew Johnson disgrace himself with a rambling, incoherent, overlong, defiant speech. When the malevolent white supremacist who would serve almost all of the second term Abraham Lincoln had been elected to was finally pulled away from the podium and the new senators sworn in, marshals escorted the president and the rest of the dignitaries from the Senate Chamber. The crowd surged forward, eager to follow the presidential party out onto the East Front.

Down a corridor of double rows of policemen holding back the crowd, the procession passed through the Rotunda and out the big doors. Leading the way was Lincoln's volunteer bodyguard, Ward Hill Lamon, the Illinois friend the president had appointed Marshal of the District of Columbia. Lamon customarily went armed with a couple of pistols, a Bowie knife, and a sap or two. As Lincoln passed, Booth shoved his way through the police line and pushed himself into the procession a few feet behind the president. Lamon didn't see him.

The lieutenant of the Capitol police grabbed Booth by the arm and called for help. "He was very strong," the officer said. "His resistance was so determined that he succeeded in dragging me out of the line and at one time broke loose from my grasp." Booth seemed like "a lunatic or out of his right mind. He looked so wild and was so unnecessarily excited."[12] A federal official, the commissioner of DC public buildings, stepped in front of Booth and pushed him back. "He gave me a fiendish stare and looked very fierce and angry that we would not let him go on," that man would later testify.[13]

Alarmed, a policeman slammed the great doors shut, deadening the roar of the crowd outside greeting the president's appearance. His way blocked, Booth stopped struggling and let the police push him back into the crowd. He eventually ended up in the audience outside, standing behind and above the president.

Had Booth really intended to make his move on inauguration day? He was by no means committed to the kidnapping scheme, despite the assurances he gave his gullible coconspirators. Assassination may have always been his preference. The best guess would seem to be that he was toying with the notion of striking on March 4. Maybe he was leaving it up to fate. If he could get close enough in the first place, that would be the time to decide whether or not to attack. He didn't know what he might do if the chance came. He was a most impulsive man. At the same time, he knew that if he killed Lincoln in the crowded Capitol, his chances of escape, to say nothing of survival, were nil. He still wanted to get away. He still wanted to live.

In his Second Inaugural Address, Abraham Lincoln gave America the most explicitly religious of the nation's great state papers. For Lincoln had experienced a religious awakening. During the war, he had come to believe, for the first time, in a personal God. From his earliest years, Lincoln had been a skeptic in matters of faith. As a young man, he had been obsessed with mortality, dismayed that the awful sovereignty of death had cast its shadow of crushing futility over all human endeavor. Deeply wounded by the death of his mother when he was only nine, crushed with grief again by the death of his older sister Sarah in childbirth, and then hurt once more by the passing of his teenaged sweetheart Ann Rutledge, young Lincoln felt abandoned in an indifferent universe. A fatalist, he often told his longtime law partner Billy Herndon that "what is to be will be, and no efforts nor prayers of ours can change, alter, modify, or reverse the decree."[14] In 1854, Lincoln took Herndon to task for invoking God in a speech. Herndon recalled that Lincoln "insisted that no such personality ever existed."[15] Lincoln's first law partner, John T. Stuart, flatly declared the man "an avowed and open Infidel—Sometimes bordered on atheism. . . . Lincoln went further against Christian beliefs—& doctrines & principles than any man I ever heard: he shocked me."[16]

Presently, as he began to rise in the political world, this supremely ambitious man prudently tried to bury all talk of his unorthodoxy. His friends and supporters helped him in this revisionism, sometimes going further than Lincoln himself was willing to go, as when a friend seized and tossed into a flaming stove the "little Book of Infidelity" Lincoln had written, knowing that the sentiments it contained would blast his political prospects if they ever became public. Though Lincoln thereafter guarded his religious skepticism behind a scrupulous silence, there's no evidence that he abandoned it before becoming president.

But as the astounding Civil War unfurled itself, coil by bloody coil, the president became haunted by the armies of the slain, killed in a war his election had touched off. Then, a conversion followed when the 1862 death of his favorite child, Willy, wounded him so profoundly. Abraham Lincoln discovered that he had become, after all, a believer in God. Lincoln's conversion brought him little in the way of spiritual peace, however. For his was a bleak bowing to the implacable will of a remote, mysterious being, one who intervened in history but who seemed to value justice more than forgiveness or mercy.

"The will of God prevails," Lincoln had mused in the gloomy summer of 1864, when Grant and Sherman remained stalemated in the East and the West and his own prospects for reelection were blighted:

> In great contests each party claims to act in accordance with the will of God. Both may be, and one must be, wrong. God cannot be for and against the same thing at the same time. In the present civil war it is quite possible that God's purpose is

*Abraham Lincoln, midwar. The president in November
of 1863, the month of the Gettysburg Address.*

Library of Congress, Prints and Photographs Division,
Meserve no. 85 LC-DIG-ppmsca-19305.

something different from the purpose of either party. . . . I am almost ready to say that this is probably true; that God wills this contest, and wills that it shall not end yet. By his mere great power on the minds of the now contestants, he could have either saved or destroyed the Union without a human contest. Yet the contest began. And, having begun, he could give the final victory to either side any day. Yet the contest proceeds.[17]

So Lincoln's was a God who could end the war's immense human suffering with a shrug but who chose instead to let the suffering continue, a God who heard the prayers of Northern Christians and Southern white Christians yet refused to take either side. By March 4, 1865, about seven hundred thousand Americans had died, and Abraham Lincoln had come to some conclusions regarding the divine purpose he had speculated about a few months earlier. He knew now that God's purpose was to chastise America. The war was God's punishment for the sin of American slavery.

This was hardly a novel idea. Lincoln himself had proposed it as early as his 1852 eulogy for Henry Clay. Clergymen had been sermonizing about it ever since the war began. Slavery had long been regarded as the Great Republic's Original Sin. No less a figure than James Madison had lamented "the dreadful fruitfulness of the original sin of the African trade."[18] On the floor of the Constitutional Convention in the summer of 1787, slaveholding delegate George Mason had prophetically warned that "slavery brings the judgment of heaven on a Country. As nations cannot be rewarded or punished in the next world they must be in this. By an inevitable chain of causes & effects providence punishes national sins, by national calamities."[19] But Abraham Lincoln had his own inimitable way of framing the grim proposition.

It had rained all night before inauguration day, and Washington City with its unpaved streets was one vast sea of mud.

Carriages mired in it up to their axles. People struggled to walk through it. Shoes and boots and the hems of women's long skirts were caked with it. It rained hard again later in the morning, drenching the tens of thousands standing along the route of the inaugural parade and gathered around the Capitol. Rain continued as the hour for the ceremony approached. If rain didn't let up, the proceedings would move indoors and the thousands of waiting spectators would miss the president's speech.

But as Lincoln picked up his printed one-page address to begin, the clouds suddenly parted, and the city was illuminated with brilliant sunlight, the first in days—an omen, believers concluded. One African American observer in the crowd that day recorded in his diary that

> on the fourth of March 1865 on Saturday the hon Abraham
> Lincoln taken his seat. Before he came out on the porch the
> wind blew and it rained without intermission and as soon
> as Mr. Lincoln came out the wind ceas blowing and the rain
> ceased raining and the Sun came out and wear as clar as could
> be and calm and at the mean time there was a Star made
> its apperence west rite over the Capitol and it shined just as
> bright as it could be.[20]

Walt Whitman also observed this rare and curious astronomical phenomenon of stars visible in bright daylight when he described the noon time sky "so bathed with flooding splendor from heaven's most excellent sun, with an atmosphere of sweetness, so clear it showed the stars, long, long before they were due."[21]

And so, as Booth made his escape from the police, Lincoln began to speak, his shrill, penetrating voice carrying clearly out across the immense crowd of onlookers stretching down the east steps and out across the Capitol's muddy grounds. At least half of this immense crowd were Black people, eager to see and hear the man many of them had come to regard as their savior.

This was a momentous day for people of color. The first

avowedly antislavery president in American history was starting a second term. The inaugural parade that morning had included African Americans for the first time. Members of a Black Masonic order took their place in the procession. Four companies of the Forty-Fifth Colored Infantry marched behind the cavalry—Black warriors, hundreds of strong men armed with .58-caliber rifles.

As the president neared his soaring peroration, invoking charity and healing, he revealed his visionary grasp of divine intention:

> If we shall suppose that American Slavery is one of those offences which . . . [God] now wills to remove, and that He gives to both North and South, this terrible war, as the woe due to those by whom the offence came, shall we discern therein any departure from those divine attributes which the believers in a Living God always ascribe to Him? Fondly do we hope— fervently do we pray—that this mighty scourge of war may speedily pass away. Yet, if God wills that it continue, until all the wealth piled by the bond-man's two hundred and fifty years of unrequited toil shall be sunk, and until every drop of blood drawn with the lash, shall be paid by another drawn with the sword, as was said three thousand years ago, so still it must be said "the judgments of the Lord, are true and righteous altogether."[22]

Accept the ancient formula of retribution for wrongdoing and everything falls into place: an enormous penalty exacted for an enormous wrong. An American wrong—Lincoln had been careful to say "American Slavery" not "Southern slavery." The Civil War's final death toll came to a staggering three-quarters of a million out of a population of a little over thirty million. That 750,000 souls exceeds the combined total killed in every other war the United States has ever fought. An equivalent butcher's bill in early twenty-first-century America, with a population ten times that of the Civil War nation, would be seven to eight million dead.

Frederick Douglass told the president later at the White House reception that his address was "a sacred effort." Many called it a sermon. Army of the Potomac cavalry colonel Charles Francis Adams Jr., commander of a Black regiment, wrote his father, the US minister to Great Britain: "That rail-splitting lawyer is one of the wonders of the day. . . . This inaugural strikes me in its grand simplicity and directness as being for all time the historic keynote of this war." Ralph Waldo Emerson thought "it was likely to outlive anything now in print in the English language."[23]

If John Wilkes Booth had an opinion of Lincoln's masterpiece, he never shared it with anyone. He walked from the Capitol back to the National Hotel with the hotel's night clerk. That evening, as President Lincoln shook hands with six thousand at the reception, a witness saw Booth at the Lichau House saloon on Louisiana Avenue, "drinking and talking privately" with Mike O'Laughlen.[24] It was said that the actor was even bold enough to attend the inaugural ball two nights later, squiring his fiancée, Lucy Hale.[25]

UNHAPPY WITH HISTORY

Booth treated his wavering accomplices to a theater outing and an all-night dinner party at a fancy restaurant on March 15. The evening began in high spirits only to end at dawn with an exchange of drunken death threats. First, Lewis Powell and John Surratt escorted two young women who boarded at Mary Surratt's to Ford's Theatre to take in a play. Booth had gone all out; he had reserved for his friends the theater's state box, the scene of the crime that was now only a month away. The box was available to anyone willing to pay the ten-dollar price, so long as the president himself was not in attendance. And that night President and Mrs. Lincoln were across town at Grover's Theatre taking in *The Magic Flute*.

Most of all, Booth wanted his two most reliable and experienced henchmen to get a good look at the layout of Ford's. He dropped in on them during the play to brief them on the theater's concealed hallways, rear exit, and passageway beneath the stage. They could talk freely in the privacy of the vestibule outside the state box. Booth had a new plan for capturing Lincoln. Rather than overtaking the president's carriage on the open road, the gang would grab him in Ford's Theatre. He promised to explain everything at the party.

The actor had reserved a private dining room on the second floor of Gautier's fashionable "eating saloon" on Pennsylvania Avenue. All of the gang was there. It would be the first and only time that all the major conspirators who are known to history would be together in one place. Some of them were meeting for the first time. The first recruits, Arnold and O'Laughlen, had never met Powell, Herold, or Atzerodt. Before tonight, they'd encountered Surratt only once and that briefly. Powell was introduced as "Mosby," Atzerodt as "Port Tobacco." Circumstances prevented the attendance of two other members of the conspiracy—Dr. Samuel A. Mudd and Mrs. Mary Surratt. It is quite possible there were other conspirators. Just before he was hanged, Powell had asserted that "you haven't got one half of them." Nevertheless, the five who attended this meeting—Powell, Herold, Atzerodt, Arnold, and O'Laughlen—were at this point the most important of the plotters, for it was to them that Booth gave the most important assignments.

Booth's private room came with its own waiter. He served them oysters, whiskey, wine, champagne, and cigars. They played a few hands of poker. It was long after midnight before the waiter cleared away the last of the dinner things and withdrew. Booth tipped him a dollar. Then the actor got down to business, bulling ahead with his plan to snatch Lincoln out of Ford's as though they had all agreed to it. He gave his men their assignments. Booth, along with Arnold and Atzerodt, would seize Lincoln in the box. They'd handcuff him and lower him to the stage, where Powell would be waiting to take him in hand. The others would join Powell and together they'd all manhandle their prisoner back across the stage and out the rear door into the alley, where a carriage would be waiting. As they made their move, Herold and O'Laughlen would throw the master switch to the theater's

BOOTH AND HIS ASSOCIATES.

The public was fascinated by every aspect of the assassination and avidly bought up prints like this group portrait of Booth and his gang. Omitted is John Surratt. It was rather awkward that he had succeeded in making his escape. Mary Surratt (also not pictured), Lewis Powell, David Herold, and George Atzerodt were hanged on July 7, 1865.

"Booth and His Associates," Library of Congress, Prints and Photographs Division, LC-DIG-ppmsca-41678.

gas lighting, plunging the audience into darkness and confusion. They'd race across the bridge into Maryland before pursuit could be organized.   Arnold was the first to object. Booth already knew he was dissatisfied and ready to absent himself. More than seven months had now passed since Booth had recruited the first two conspirators. They'd grown sick of waiting around. Arnold insisted that the actor's new plan was "impracticable" and dangerous. It would never work, and he wanted no part of it. He told Booth, "I wanted a chance for my life and I intended to have it— that he could be the leader of the party, but not my executioner. I wanted a shadow of a chance for my life."[1]

Booth angrily accused Arnold of breaking the oath he had taken. It was insubordination to a superior officer in time of war, punishable by death. "Don't you know you are liable to be shot?" he threatened. Two can play at that game, Arnold countered, opening his coat to reveal the revolver at his waist. "If you feel inclined to shoot me, you have no further to go. I shall defend myself."[2] The two men glared across the table.

O'Laughlen was also opposed. Arnold cogently pointed out that the exchange of prisoners had already resumed. What was the point of taking Lincoln now? Powell and Atzerodt said nothing. Booth slammed his fist on the table and burst out, "Well, gentlemen, if the worst comes to the worst, I shall know what to do." The others immediately understood that the actor meant he would kill Lincoln. They wanted no part of that. All the men stood up from the table and reached for their hats, ready to walk out on Booth. He did what he could to calm them down, offering an apology of sorts. "Too much champagne," he said sheepishly. Booth had been sobered by the ultimatum Arnold had just presented him with. Booth's boyhood friend now declared that if an abduction attempt was not made within a week, he would drop out of the conspiracy.

The other man at the table, John Surratt, Booth's right-hand man, later claimed that he also objected to the new plan. He testified that he had told the others that he suspected that government detectives had learned what the gang was up to. Surratt further claimed that he, like Arnold, had argued for abandoning the scheme altogether. There is reason, however, to question his veracity. By the time John Surratt recounted his version of events, he and Sam Arnold were the only survivors of the all-night party at Gautier's. The party's host and his other guests—Booth, Powell, Herold, and Atzerodt—were all dead. Surratt, who lived until 1916, told his story over the years in sworn testimony, in a public lecture, and in several newspaper interviews. He naturally tried to fashion a narrative that distanced him as much as possible from Booth. He had ample cause to lie and little chance of getting caught. So his account of the meeting at Gautier's Restaurant may be the reverse of what actually took place. Rather than objecting to the new plan, Surratt may have thrown his weight behind Booth. He certainly remained loyal to the conspiracy. The problem, from Booth's point of view, was that the courier was never in Washington except briefly during this period. He only passed through the city, going north or south on his missions.

Booth's threat to kill Lincoln was telling. Indeed, the whole capture-in-the-theater scenario, before an audience of more than a thousand, was so far-fetched, so laughably complicated, and so unlikely to succeed that it's reasonable to assume that Booth proposed it merely as a blind to assassinate Lincoln—his true intent. But it was now obvious he could never get his gang to go along.

Given that Arnold had threatened to drop out if no attempt was made within a week, it was rather remarkable that a chance for grabbing Lincoln on the road seemingly did appear just two days after Arnold voiced his deadline. A theater company was planning to stage a matinee performance of the popular comedy *Still Waters Run Deep* at the Campbell military hospital out of the city on the Seventh Street Road. President Lincoln, who had visited the patients at Campbell hospital recently, supposedly planned to attend the play on March 17, 1865. They could ambush his carriage on the Seventh Street Road. It was a return to the original plan.

The gang swung into action early that afternoon. Herold got the weapons and gear back from Arnold and O'Laughlen's hiding place and took them in the buggy out of the city into Maryland to meet up with others after they snatched Lincoln. Booth, Surratt, Powell, Atzerodt, Arnold, and O'Laughlen armed themselves, mounted up, and rode out separately on the Seventh Street Road. The riders left the city, passing into farming country and rendezvoused at an outdoor beer garden and restaurant where they could watch the road. It was a mile or so from the hospital where the play would take place.

After a few obligatory drinks, Booth rode alone to the hospital to check on the president. When he got back, he told his men that the operation was off—Lincoln hadn't shown up. The others panicked. They were sure the president's cancellation meant the government was on to them. They feared immediate arrest. Leaving separately, they hurried back to the city.

Booth, however, had known all along that the president wouldn't be there. The morning papers had announced that that afternoon, Lincoln would be at the National Hotel—Booth's own hotel—where he would accept the presentation of a captured battle flag from an Indiana regiment. Booth even managed to get back to the National in time to attend the event. He made himself conspicuous there with his exaggerated glaring and scowling at the president. As he had on Inauguration Day, Booth tried to push close to Lincoln during the ceremony. The dense crowd kept him back.[3] It seems unlikely that he was trying to close in on the president to kidnap him. Nor had he struggled to approach Lincoln in the Capitol on Inauguration Day to accomplish a capture. Alone, without his men, all Booth could hope to do was kill.

So why had Booth mobilized his whole gang to engage in this charade of an aborted kidnapping? In *American Brutus*, Michael Kauffman contends that Booth planned the exercise to renew his men's commitment and to implicate them legally in a criminal conspiracy. He could then use their complicity to threaten them if they ever tried to abandon him.[4] His gang had been highly skeptical of the success of the proposed capture on the Seventh Street Road. Arnold characterized it as "the most quixotic and visionary undertaking that ever entered a sane man's brain. I looked upon him as demented, but made no objection. . . . We looked upon him as a madman, yet could offer no objection, from the fact that we had given our word to assist him."[5]

Arnold's statement is a measure of the authority the actor exercised over his gang of conspirators. John Wilkes Booth was a hard man to say no to. His domineering personality, magnified by the manic energy he was displaying then, combined with his cunning and his verbal skills, gave him the power to command obedience from his unwilling accomplices.

A little later, Booth learned that the president had gone to visit Grant's army and would not be attending any operas at Ford's as had been reported. The actor's last stage performance took place the day after the aborted capture attempt. It was a benefit at Ford's for his actor friend John McCullough.[6] Booth would appear next on that stage on Black Friday, April 14.

In the audience at McCullough's benefit were Surratt, Powell, Atzerodt, Herold, and a certain Louis J. Weichmann. This last-named member of the impromptu theater party was impressed, even frightened, by J. Wilkes Booth's acting the part of an evil villain. "Never in my life did I witness a man play with so much intensity and passion as Booth did on that occasion," Weichmann said. "The hideous, malevolent expression of his distorted countenance, the fierce glare and ugly roll of his eyes, which seemed ready to burst from their sockets . . . are yet present with me."[7] (To play the part of an evil villain consumed with hatred, all the actor had to do was think of Abraham Lincoln.)

This Louis Weichmann was an old Catholic seminary friend

of John Surratt's. He was now boarding at Mrs. Surratt's H Street townhouse. Like his friend John, Weichmann had decided he didn't have a true calling to the life of a Catholic priest. He, too, dropped out of the seminary. Friend to both John Surratt and his mother, Weichmann was almost a member of the family at the boardinghouse. Since the H Street house was one of the conspirators' meeting places, Weichmann met the others. He hung around the edges of the conspiracy, trying to learn what was going on, eavesdropping when he could, working to uncover secrets. The tubby, good-looking young man of twenty-three seemed at times willing to take some part, despite his position as a US Army clerk who wore a blue uniform to work.

The others rejected him as a comrade, however, for the simple reason that he couldn't handle a gun or a horse. Yet Weichmann was of no little interest to Booth. He worked for the US Army's commissioner of prisoners of war. The clerk spied on his own government for Booth, providing numbers and locations of prisoners held in the North. He also let the actor use his government office for after-hours meetings. At the same time, recognizing his possible legal exposure as an accomplice, Weichmann was warning his superior officers about the suspicious crew that congregated at the Surratt boardinghouse. His commanders didn't take him seriously. Weichmann was the personification of ambivalence, playing for both sides. He would be the government's star witness at the trial of the conspirators.

Louis Weichmann died in 1902. His indispensable eyewitness narrative, *A True History of the Assassination of Abraham Lincoln and of the Conspiracy of 1865*, although not published until 1975, made him also one of history's star witnesses. Many of the episodes and details of the conspiracy are known only through him. Like Arnold and Surratt—two other young participants who survived to see the twentieth century—the rest of Weichmann's life would be embittered by his brief association with John Wilkes

Booth. His role as government witness and the death of Mary Surratt that resulted from his testimony earned him many enemies.

After the calamity on the Seventh Street Road, the conspirators believed that the whole mission had been abandoned or at least postponed indefinitely. Booth led them to think he thought so, too. He told Arnold and O'Laughlen just that when they met for the last time on March 30. He also told them to sell the buggy and horses they'd been keeping at the ready to transport their captive. When Arnold asked him about the gang's substantial arsenal, Booth told them to keep the weapons for themselves or simply sell them, just as they wished. Booth had no further use for them. The actor said he was going to return to the stage. He said he was through with conspiracies. That evening he went to Ford's with Lucy Hale and her sister.

The gang scattered. On the orders of the Secret Service Bureau, Surratt headed for Richmond, escorting a notorious Southern spy named Sarah Slater, who was carrying dispatches from Canada. When he got there, he met with Judah Benjamin, who sent him back north to Montreal with messages for the Canadian cabinet. O'Laughlen moved back to Baltimore. Atzerodt went to ground. Sam Arnold moved to his brother's farm outside Baltimore on March 20. Then he actually got himself a job working in an army sutler's store at Old Fort Comfort, Virginia, near the huge army base at City Point. While actively conspiring against the government, Arnold had written Secretary of War Edwin Stanton, humbly asking for consideration for any position the government might consider him qualified to fill. Stanton himself doubtless never saw Arnold's letter, but, through a family friend, the young man was offered a clerkship in the government-licensed store at the base that sold goods to soldiers. He started work there on April 2. Powell, who had probably divined his leader's true intentions, hung on in Baltimore and New York, ready for murderous action.

Booth himself hurried to New York on March 21. There his fiancée, Miss Lucy Hale, was staying with friends in a Fifth Avenue mansion. She was taking Spanish lessons to prepare for her sojourn abroad. She was definitely going to Spain with her family in May. Some have taken Lucy's imminent departure as a sign that the couple had abandoned their wedding plans. Stronger evidence, however, suggests that they had merely delayed their marriage.[8] Since Powell was in New York at the time, he went drinking with Booth.[9]

At the Winter Garden Theatre on March 22, Wilkes shared Edwin's triumph when he watched his brother give the final performance of his renowned one-hundred-night run in the role of Hamlet. The unprecedented achievement and the preternatural genius of his acting "gained for him the position by which . . . all other actors were judged. He became the standard to which all aspired and none reached." The hundred nights would live on in theatrical history. Statues of Edwin Booth as Hamlet soon appeared. He was acknowledged "the Prince of Players," the greatest Hamlet of all time. John Wilkes himself declared: "There's but one Hamlet to my mind, that of my brother Edwin. You see, between ourselves, he is Hamlet, melancholy and all."[10]

As we have seen, Booth had long before armed himself with a derringer as his weapon of choice. This was the gun he used to murder Abraham Lincoln. It was a small, easily concealed, single-shot .44-caliber pocket pistol often loaded with a .41-caliber ball. The low-velocity, heavy-caliber weapon was deadly at close range. He'd been carrying it at least since his days as a twenty-year-old apprentice actor at Richmond's Marshall Theatre.[11] He was still packing it five years later. Shortly before the assassination, he had threatened fellow actor Samuel Knapp Chester: "I carry a derringer loaded to shoot every one that betrays me."[12]

Booth's gun was a genuine Deringer, manufactured by the Henry Deringer Company of Philadelphia, but like all such small pistols, it went by the generic name *derringer*. Firearms

The derringer that killed Abraham Lincoln.

Shutterstock Photography; courtesy of Ford's Theatre
National Historic Site, National Park Service.

have never been entirely utilitarian. Booth's little gun bespoke craftsmanship, even elegance. The derringer sported a handsome walnut stock neatly checkered to give purchase to the grip and curving into a butt just long enough for the shooter to get his second and third fingers around. Booth's was the deluxe model of a gun often sold in sets of two for about twenty-five dollars for the pair. On the deluxe model, the barrel, lock, and hammer were finished in gleaming German silver and engraved with floral tracings. The lock bore the cartouche "DERINGER PHILADEL." A little bead front sight sat atop the muzzle, hardly necessary at the point-blank ranges the gun was meant to be used. Loaded with its quarter-ounce ball and twenty grains of black powder, the derringer weighed just nine ounces, half a pound, and was no bigger than a man's hand.

Booth seems to have carried this nasty little belly gun most of the time. In January 1865, according to the spy Thomas Harbin, Booth killed an aggressive dog with his derringer while visiting Port Tobacco, Maryland. He'd gone to the river town to inspect a boat he'd just bought to carry the captive president across the Potomac.[13] The two days before the assassination, he pulled his derringer on another fellow actor, George W. Wren, who had told Booth that if he were such a strong secessionist, he should have joined the Southern army. "At this he got very angry," Wren recalled. " 'You call me a coward, do you' said he, and drew his pistol at once." When Wren protested that he was unarmed, Booth relented.[14]

Witnesses described other occasions when the actor, enraged by an insult to his beloved Confederacy or backtalk from an African American, reached for his hip pocket, vowing to shoot, before his friends restrained him. He could have hidden nothing bigger than a derringer in his well-tailored trousers. Like any knowledgeable shootist, Booth preferred the more accurate and powerful revolver, a six-shooter. He favored Colt revolvers. He performed his shooting gallery stunts with revolvers. He occasionally carried a revolver and, while on the run after the murder, two of them. But such bulky handguns were hard to conceal, best carried in a holster slung from a belt.

Threatening displays of the little derringer took place in late 1864, when Booth was inspecting one of his investment properties—the oil well operated by his Dramatic Oil Company—in Franklin, Pennsylvania, then the heart of the great petroleum boom of the 1860s. Speculators were making and losing fortunes overnight leasing and selling promising drilling sites. Some even drilled for oil. Like so many others, Booth ended up losing quite a substantial sum—$6,000—when his well came in dry. That loss, combined with the thousands he had sunk into financing his conspiracy and his neglect of his lucrative stage career, was the reason he was so short of funds in the winter and spring of 1865. It is also reason to believe he was not then getting much help from the Secret Service Bureau.

As the tension mounted with approaching Northern victory, Booth's hair-trigger temper grew ever more dangerous. He seemed close to repeating his father's pattern of irrational homicidal fury. Crossing the Allegheny River on a ferry, the actor got into an argument with a passenger named Titus Ridgway. When Booth denounced Lincoln, Ridgway angrily snarled that his remark was "a damned lie!" Booth shouted, "I will never allow a man to call me a liar!" He brandished the derringer. Ridgway tried to run him through with a boat pole tipped with an iron spike. The crew of the ferry pulled the two men apart before any damage was done.[15]

Witnesses recalled another altercation, this one with racial overtones. Booth was waiting for a shave in a barbershop in Franklin when an African American, one Cale Marshall, came in and began rejoicing in a Northern battlefield victory. This was more than the actor could stomach. He rebuked the man: "Is that the way you talk among gentlemen and with your hat on too?" (Southern gentlemen like Booth expected Blacks to doff their hats in the presence of white men.) Marshall was having none of it. "When I go into a parlor among ladies, I take my hat off," he boldly retorted, "but when I go into a bar-room or a barber shop or any other public place, I keep my hat on."[16] Booth turned white with rage at the man's disrespect and impertinence. For a Black to contradict a white man in public was intolerable. Booth reached into his hip pocket for the derringer. Two friends grabbed him, pinioned his arms, and hustled him out of the place.

The derringer wasn't even that important. For years, Booth had worked out in gymnasia to strengthen his formidable musculature. He knew he could kill another man with his bare hands if he had to. Once he almost did. The victim was his brother-in-law, John Sleeper Clarke, sister Asia's husband. Clarke, a boyhood chum of Edwin's, would become one of England's most popular comedians of the late nineteenth century. Wilkes had no use for Clarke. He resented him for marrying his sister, exploiting her, Booth thought, to gain a close association with the Booth name, powerful as it was in the theatrical world. Booth also believed that Asia's love for her brother was meant to be paramount, not to be usurped by any husband. (The couple's marriage did turn out to be a most unhappy one for Asia.) Besides, Clarke, like Edwin, favored the North.

In 1909, a veteran actor who had known both men told what happened when, one time early in the war, the two were traveling together in a railroad carriage. Clarke began talking about the war, recounting Union victories. Wilkes said nothing, glowering across the cabin. Then his brother-in-law happened to insult Jefferson Davis:

> As the words were uttered Booth sprang up and hurled himself upon Clarke in a wild tempest of fury, catching him by the throat. Other passengers tried to interfere, but Booth held his hold, to all appearances bent upon strangling his brother-in-law. He swung Clarke side to side while his grip tightened. His face was drawn and twisted with rage. Slowly his anger left him and his hold relaxed, none too soon for Clarke. Clarke hardly knew what had happened and looked at his assailant in amazement, gasping for breath. Booth stood over him with a dramatic gesture. "Never, if you value your life," he said tersely, "never speak in that way to me of a man and a cause I hold sacred."[17]

Feeling so strongly, think of the humiliation and rage the man had to swallow when Yankee victory finally came!

The *Washington Evening Star* reported that President Lincoln would take in an opera at Ford's Theatre on March 29. The journal had been misinformed, however. At General Grant's urging, the president had left Washington on March 23 to visit the Army of the Potomac. Grant wanted the president to observe the siege of the insurgents' capital that had been going on since the previous summer. Lincoln and Grant may have suspected that the capture of Richmond was near at hand. Lincoln wouldn't return to Washington until Sunday, April 9.

Booth, however, believed the newspaper report about the night at the opera. It turned out he had not turned his back on conspiracy after all. He saw another chance. He frantically tried to mobilize his gang for a new strike against the president at the opera. They must have been surprised to hear from him. All of them had understood that the conspiracy was over. He ordered Powell back from New York.

Booth had no way to contact Arnold, so he wired O'Laughlen in Baltimore: "Get word to Sam. Come on, with or without him. Wednesday morning. We sell that day sure. Don't fail. J. Wilkes Booth."[18] O'Laughlen managed to get word to Arnold, who hurried into Baltimore. The two men's actions were more evidence of the powerful influence Booth exercised over his crew. Both of them had told the actor they were finished, yet here they were, hastening to obey his summons. They seemed unable to refuse him.

When he got to Baltimore, Arnold learned that Booth and O'Laughlen had left for Washington without him.[19] So he wrote Booth a letter dated "March 27, 1865," and signed "SAM":

Dear John:
Was the business so important that you could not remain in Balto. till I saw you? I came as soon as I could, but found that you had gone to W[ashingto]n. . . . You know full well that the G[overnmen]t suspicions something is going on there; therefore the undertaking is becoming more complicated. Why not, for the present, desist? . . . None, no not one, were more in favor of the enterprise than myself, and to-day would be there, had you not done as you have—by this I mean, manner of proceeding. . . . Time more propitious will arrive yet.

Do not act rashly or in haste. I would prefer your first query, "go and see how it will be taken in R[ichmon]d, and ere long I shall be better prepared to again be with you."[20]

Arnold was reluctant to mail the letter to Booth. He knew it could be used against him as conclusive proof that he had been part of Booth's conspiracy. After debating for three days, he finally put it in the mail. Though Arnold later begged Booth to destroy the incriminating letter, the actor left it in a hotel room for the detectives to find, a deliberate and successful attempt to implicate Arnold. In about three months' time, Samuel Bland Arnold, Johnny Booth's boyhood friend, would be sentenced by the government of the United States to life imprisonment for his part in the conspiracy.

All through April, the newspapers' extra editions carried full accounts of new Yankee triumphs under screaming headlines. Not a detail could have escaped John Wilkes Booth. The stories hurt him deeply. Richmond was his beloved city. Asia said that "this idealized city of his love had a deeper hold upon his heart than any feminine beauty."[21] Now the dearest place was conquered, burned, and occupied by the detested Yankees. Worse still, Richmond, and with it the entire South, had been basely dishonored by the North's barbaric resort to Black soldiers. Did Booth cringe with new anguish when he heard the shameful news that the first Union troops to enter the flaming capital of rebeldom had been regiments of the United States Colored Troops?[22]

News of these Northern triumphs fell like hammer blows on Booth. Furious, ashamed, and filled with desperate self-loathing, he was drinking hard, pouring the stuff down. "Brandy, brandy, brandy!" he cried as he strode into a saloon or billiards hall.[23] One barkeep remembered "the amazing quantity of liquor Booth drank. . . . It was more than a spree, I could see that." The man decided that "Booth was crazy, but he didn't show it."[24]

It was true that Booth had been unhinged since the fall of

Richmond. He talked recklessly of riding through the streets of Washington waving a rebel flag. Looking south across the Potomac, he sobbed, "Virginia! Virginia!" His sister said his lament for his adopted state was "like a wail from the heart of a Roman father for his slaughtered child."[25]

The soldiers of the Southern armies accepted defeat a good deal more readily than did Booth, who insisted that Lee should never have surrendered. It wasn't just the brandy. "If Wilkes Booth was mad, his mind lost its balance between the fall of Richmond and the terrific end," wrote Asia. But she never really believed he was mad.[26] Booth was rather supremely unhappy with history itself. He could not abide the outcome of the nineteenth century's greatest war. Most bitter of all was the thought that, while hundreds of thousands had laid down their lives for the South and for white America, he—John Booth—had done so little. There was a kind of desperate pain in him that only death could mend. He told his mother he had begun to hate himself: "to deem myself a coward and to despise my own existence."[27]

Despite what he told his family and friends, John Wilkes Booth hadn't given up on the cause of the South. Had he not vowed to die first? In Booth's disordered mind, hope and despair became two sides of a single coin. Some remnant of hope often seems to accompany even that measure of despair that might appear to preclude all such notions. For all his sorrow and anger, Booth had bursts of manic optimism. He still hoped for the redemption of his beloved cause. He refused to believe that the South was really defeated. It must have allayed his pain to imagine an outcome different from the one that history had presented. Perhaps it was not too late. Besides, if he accepted that the war was over, he would be giving up his last chance to prove his courage and redeem himself for having avoided battle. If he gave up, he'd be also obliged to renounce his lifelong ambition to change history and win immortal fame. It was unacceptable.

On Monday, April 10, the day Washington learned of Lee's

surrender, the young actor showed that even that final catastrophe could not kill his hope. On that day, Louis Weichmann "jested Booth about the fall of Richmond and told him [he] thought the Confederacy had gone up. 'No, it is not gone up yet,' [Booth] answered excitedly and, pulling out a Perrine's war map out of his pocket, began to show the different routes which [General Joseph E.] Johnston would take to the mountains, where, [Booth] thought, he could make a stubborn resistance."[28] "For six months we had worked to capture," Booth would write after he killed Lincoln. "But our cause being almost lost, something decisive & great must be done."[29] He had known for a long time what that "something decisive & great" must be.

Speaking of Lincoln's April 4 visit to Richmond, presidential secretaries Nicolay and Hay reflected that "never in the history of the world did the head of a mighty nation and the conqueror of a great rebellion enter the chief city of the insurgents in such humbleness and simplicity."[30] Booth didn't see anything humble about it. "Ned, did you hear what that old scoundrel did the other day?" he asked an actor friend. "Why, that old scoundrel Lincoln went into Jeff Davis's house in Richmond, sat down and threw his long legs over the arm of the chair and squirted tobacco juice all over the place. Somebody ought to kill him."[31] (Lincoln didn't use tobacco.) Booth's last sentence was spoken so loudly in a crowded place that he thoroughly frightened the man he was talking to. One could get arrested for less.

Though she claimed to be "of the North," Booth's sister Asia had her own Southern sympathies. She agreed with her brother that Lincoln's visit to Richmond had been a graceless, arrogant provocation, the one thing that finally pushed Wilkes over the edge. "The fall of Richmond," Asia wrote, "rang in with a maddening, exasperating clang of joy, and [Lincoln's] triumphant entry into the fallen city (which was not magnanimous) breathed air afresh upon the fire that consumed him."[32]

24

"MIGHT MAKES RIGHT"

People today greet momentous events through glowing screens. In Lincoln's day, they took to the streets, where news traveled swiftly by word of mouth. All through the first half of April, beginning with the surrender of Richmond on the third, the streets of Washington City had seen a perpetual carnival and a frenzy of participatory democracy. There had been the first "Grand Illumination" for Richmond's fall. Another, for Lee's surrender, blazed on Thursday, April 13. One more took place the night of the assassination, Friday, April 14, for the four-year anniversary of the surrender of Fort Sumter. All the other nights also saw some kind of celebration. The days were almost as wild as the nights. Government workers were released from their desks. Businesses closed, while the saloons and taverns did land office business. A joke circulating that week claimed that a new government ordinance called for the immediate arrest of any man found to be sober. By now, the celebrations had continued for more than a week.

The crowds surged back and forth through the streets and squares, looking for excitement. There were concerts, ringing church bells, the universal shaking of hands and passing of bottles, fireworks, and speeches. Sailors from the Navy Yard dragged artillery through the streets, pausing now and then to blast the cannon off, breaking nearby windows when they did. Wild men ran about, howling as they beat on kettles and pots. Guns shot at the sky. Anything to make a racket.

Serenading was a popular custom. Crowds would gather before the home of some distinguished figure to serenade him with patriotic anthems. Then the statesman would appear, rewarding them with a rousing speech. Seward and Stanton were frequently called on. Huge crowds serenaded the White House the night of Monday, April 10, the day news of Lee's surrender electrified the capital. Lincoln appeared briefly but declined to make a speech. He promised a major address the following evening but said, "I shall have nothing to say then if it is all dribbled out of me now."[1] He told the band to play "Dixie" and disappeared back into the White House. So the thousands gathered again to hear him on Tuesday, April 11.

It had been a wet spring, and that night it rained on and off. On the foggy eastern horizon, the dome of the Capitol shone like a full moon. Across the Potomac, high on the Virginia hills, stood old Arlington mansion, all its windows ablaze. Once the grand home of Robert E. Lee, Arlington was now a shantytown encampment for thousands of newly freed people, as well as a burgeoning military cemetery. A happy mob there was waving torches and singing "The Year of Jubilee."

As soon as the war had gotten going in earnest, the US Army had found itself sadly in need of ample and sufficient burial grounds. Perched on the Virginia heights just across the Potomac from the District of Columbia, Robert E. Lee's Arlington plantation clearly formed a strategic position, high ground from which artillery could dominate the nation's capital. Union troops occupied the place after the Lees fled. Colonel Lee's wife, Mary Custis, a great-granddaughter of Martha Washington, actually held the property title. At first, the troops stationed there refrained from entering the house and respected the Lees' private property. That didn't last long. Soon, soldiers were bedded down throughout the mansion, and the family's things were looted or destroyed. A more serious and lasting insult came when the military command ruled that the property would henceforth be a last resting place for the Union dead, that immense legion of the fallen that grew larger day by day. The gravediggers were ordered to plant the corpses right up to the garden wall of Arlington house so that no one would ever want to live there again. Robert E. Lee's betrayal in siding with the rebellion had provoked great bitterness in the Union. Lee had been educated at government expense at West Point, had drawn an officer's salary his entire adult life, had lived in army housing, had been supplied with horses and rations, and had enjoyed the confidence and esteem of the US military establishment. As a commissioned officer, Colonel Lee had sworn to preserve and protect the Constitution; instead, the apostate tried to destroy it. Turning his home into one vast graveyard had seemed a fitting rebuke.

When Lincoln appeared that night at the White House's second-story window facing Lafayette Park, a reporter wrote: "There was something terrible in the enthusiasm with which the beloved Chief Magistrate was received. Cheers upon cheers, wave after wave of applause, rolled up, the President modestly standing quiet until it was all over."[2]

Seen from out in the crowd, the light from the White House window diffused in the misty air, seeming to embrace Abraham Lincoln in a luminous halo. Looking the other way, out from the White House, Mary Lincoln's friend, the former slave Elizabeth Keckley, thought the crowd resembled "a black, gently swelling sea. The swaying motion of the crowd, in the dim uncertain light, was like the rising and falling of billows. . . . Close to the house the faces were plainly discernable, but they faded into mere ghostly outlines on the outskirts of the assembly; and what added to the weird, spectral beauty of the scene was the confused hum of voices that rose above the sea of forms."[3]

The audience was charged up for a powerful dose of patriotic triumphalism—a red-white-and-blue, spread-eagled celebration of victory, the invincible might of Union arms, the indomitable courage of the soldiers and sailors, and the humiliation of the hated traitors—all of it as exuberant and unrestrained as their own alcohol-fueled happiness. They were disappointed. Lincoln did acknowledge the occasion's joy. "We meet not in sorrow, but in gladness of heart," he began.[4] He praised General Grant and the Army of the Potomac. For the most part, however, he gave his excited audience a dry, almost legalistic, analysis of his plans for the reconstruction of the state of Louisiana. Instead of speaking without a text as he often did, the president carefully read his speech from a closely written, eleven-page manuscript. He'd spent most of the day writing it. As he finished each page, he dropped the leaf to the floor where it was immediately snatched up by twelve-year-old Tad. "Another! Another!" urged the irrepressible boy.

At the front of the thousands gathered there that night were three angry men who had nothing at all to celebrate—John Wilkes Booth, Lewis Powell, and David Herold. Booth got right down to business. He ordered Powell to shoot Lincoln. Powell, though he regarded Booth as his superior officer, refused to obey. "No, I will not do it," he said. It was too risky. Besides, it was by no means a sure thing, a difficult shot with a handgun. Powell walked off, leaving Booth and Herold there to listen to Lincoln.

The president was endorsing the reconstructed government of Louisiana as the state prepared to petition Congress for readmission to the Union. Many white men who had taken the Oath of Allegiance were permitted to vote in Louisiana elections. Those voters had approved a new state constitution abolishing slavery, a requirement for readmission. Then Lincoln made an altogether extraordinary suggestion: "It is also unsatisfactory to some that the elective franchise is not given to the colored man. I would myself prefer that it were now conferred on the very intelligent, and on those who serve our cause as soldiers."[5] This was the first time any American president had publicly advocated giving the vote to some Black men. Lincoln had already privately urged the governor of Louisiana he had appointed to do so.

Some in the crowd had grown restless. Some had already wandered off, looking for more excitement or more liquor. But John Wilkes Booth had been listening carefully. "That means nig- ger citizenship!" he growled. "Now, by God, I'll put him through! That is the last speech he will ever make."[6] Seventy-two hours later, he would make good on that promise. That speech from the White House window on Tuesday, April 11 turned out to be the last public address of the statesman whose astonishing ascent owed so much to his consummate skill as an orator.

So there it is, in the words of Booth's angry reaction, as ex- plicit as it could possibly be: Lincoln died because he proposed giving the vote to some African American men. He died for Black civil rights. As Lincoln biographer Michael Burlingame has writ- ten: "Thus Lincoln was a martyr to black civil rights, as much as Martin Luther King and other activists who fell victim to racist violence a century later."[7]

As one April day slid into the next, Booth couldn't seem to put away enough liquor or put in enough time at the shooting galleries. He didn't spend quite as much time in the shooting par- lors as he did in the saloons, but he went shooting almost every other day during the week before the assassination. A few weeks earlier, in a New York City shooting gallery at 600 Broadway, Booth had used a photograph of President Lincoln for his target.[8] The actor, who had started blasting away as soon as he was big enough to hold a gun, certainly didn't need the practice. As a boy in the Maryland woods, he had honed his skill on quick squirrels

The White House in 1865.

Library of Congress, Prints and Photographs
Division, LC-DIG-ppmsca-33275.

and rabbits and flitting birds on the wing, all much harder targets than big, lumbering humans.

Thursday, April 6 found Booth blowing off some of his rage by showing off at a Boston pistol range near his hotel. He was a prodigy with weapons, as good with a real pistol as he was with a stage sword. Apparently no amount of alcohol could blunt his deadly aim. The range grew quieter that day as the other shooters turned from their targets to watch Booth's feats. He fired backward, over his shoulder, from under his arm, and between his legs, the bullet striking home each time. Magnified in the low-ceilinged gallery, gunshots punished the ears, and smoke stung the eyes. The summer before, on dozens of smoky Virginia battlefields a few hundred miles to the south, the rifle fire had roared on in continuous rolls of musketry. The deep booming of the artillery carried farther, but the musketry, the musketry. Hearing the ripping roll of tens of thousands of rifles from the sunny steps of Richmond's Capitol some ten miles distant, John Reagan, Jeff Davis's postmaster general, had remarked, "It is that that kills men."[9]

On Saturday, April 8, less than a week before his fateful meeting with Lincoln, Booth returned to Washington from his sojourn in Boston and New York. He wouldn't leave the capital again until he escaped Ford's Theatre late on the night of Friday, April 14. On Monday, April 10, he went shooting at a pistol range at Ninth and Pennsylvania Avenue, not far from Ford's.

That morning, Booth had been jolted awake—if he'd slept at all—by the explosion of nine hundred cannon ranged across the city. As Secretary of the Navy Gideon Welles recorded in his diary, "At day dawn a salute of several guns was fired. The first discharge proclaimed, as plain as words, the capture of Lee and his army, which the papers detailed. The tidings were spread over the country during the night, and the nation seems delirious with joy. Guns are firing—bells ringing, flags flying, men laughing, children cheering—all, all jubilant. This surrender of the great rebel Captain and the most formidable and reliable army of the secessionists virtually terminates the rebellion."[10] The next day, Tuesday, April 11, the day of Lincoln's last speech, an agitated Booth was banging away again at the same pistol range. A drunken veteran with a paralyzed arm saw him there.[11]

Except for Baltimore, no city in the Union was more disloyal or more proslavery than the national capital itself. The District of Columbia had, after all, been originally carved out of the slave states of Maryland and Virginia. Until 1850, Washington City had been a major emporium with traders in human beings profitably selling Chesapeake people south to the cotton states. Enslavement was not abolished in the District of Columbia until the second year of the Civil War. Throughout the war, the city's many "secesh" residents—those who favored the great rebellion—had longed to see a conquering Southern army marching through the streets, an eventuality that had seemed possible on more than one occasion.

By early 1865, Washington was indeed full of rebel soldiers. But it was hardly the secesh dream come true. These men were deserters and prisoners of war. As the siege of Petersburg and the war itself neared inevitable conclusion, Lee's Army of Northern Virginia was shedding soldiers at an appalling rate. His cold, starving men called the flooded trenches they left behind "Fort Hell" and "Fort Damnation." Companies of deserters, hundreds of them, made the no-man's-land crossing every night to surrender to the Yankees. "Hundreds are deserting nightly," agonized Robert E. Lee, arguing with his government for increased authority to kill more of his own soldiers for desertion.[12]

Lee was as determined to punish his deserters in 1865 as he had been in 1859, when he punished three runaways who had fled his Arlington estate. After they were recaptured, Lee paid the local constable to whip the two men and one woman on their bare backs. The men each got fifty lashes, the woman twenty. After the flogging, their raw backs were scrubbed with salty brine. The master of Arlington personally directed the entire procedure.[13]

Thousands of deserters trudged into Washington in February and March. Attached to bands of their countrymen already taken in battle, they passed along city streets in long gray columns— emaciated, ragged, barefoot, and disheartened. As Terry Alford has pointed out, the blundering guards who mistakenly inserted some prisoners into Lincoln's inaugural parade seemed to mimic the ancient Roman practice of displaying defeated enemies in victorious generals' triumphs.[14]

On the afternoon of the assassination, about six hours before he pulled the trigger, Booth was on Pennsylvania Avenue with his friend and fellow actor John Mathews. They were watching in amazement the passage of a long column of high-ranking war prisoners. They were witnessing what amounted to the funeral parade of the Southern insurgency. Marching wearily past were more than four hundred officers from the Army of Northern Virginia. Most had been captured at the battle of Sayler's Creek, three days before Lee's surrender. Among them were eight captured generals. As officers, these prisoners were better uniformed than private soldiers. Some still wore tarnished gold braid or their old insignia of rank. But there was no disguising the ordeal they'd endured. Their uniforms were tattered and faded. Some of the men appeared malnourished. A deep sadness kept pace with the prisoners. These men were the forlorn wreckage of one of the finest armies the world had ever seen.

In the past, the loyal citizens of Washington had been wont to greet Southern prisoners with jeers and curses, if not with volleys of stones and garbage. In contrast, the crowds on the sidewalks that Good Friday were silent, as though subdued by the historic grandeur of the momentous times they were living through. They may have felt a measure of sympathy, even admiration, for the proud men who had kept the faith until the end. John Wilkes Booth was certainly moved. Slapping his hand to his forehead, he burst out: "Great God! I no longer have a country!"[15] The paradox was that he was still willing to kill and die for that vanished country.

Booth thought all the celebrations obscene. "I can't see why there should be such rejoicing," he exclaimed.[16] The whole American people had suffered a great tragedy: a noble civilization had gone under. Southerners had suffered more than any previous generation of Americans. The South lay in ruins. A quarter of its military-age men lay in their graves. Even Union men should see that this was no time for songs and laughter.

Emancipation by executive decree had wiped out billions of dollars of wealth. That disastrously unwise presidential usurpation, white Southerners believed, had also set loose on the South millions of ignorant, slow-witted innocents doomed to die out by their own feckless improvidence. These people were meant to be slaves. Booth's last letter to his mother, written just twenty hours before the assassination, was informed by a kind of despairing resignation:

> April 14,
> 2 A.M.
> Dearest Mother:
> I know you expect a letter from me, and am sure you will hardly forgive me. But indeed I have nothing to write about. Everything is dull; that is, has been till last night. (The illumination.) Everything was bright and splendid. More so in my eyes if it had been a display in a nobler cause. But so goes the world. Might makes right.[17]

Mary Ann Booth received this letter just moments after news of her son's crime had devastated her. Mother Booth had intuitively feared for the safety of her favorite boy in the final weeks of the Civil War. She sensed that his desperation and rage were pushing him to strike out. On March 28, 1865, she had written him:

> My dear Boy: . . . I did part with you sadly—& I still feel sad, very much so. . . . I feel miserable enough. I never yet doubted your love & devotion to me—in fact I always gave praise for being the fondest of all my boys, but since you leave me to grief I must doubt it. I am no Roman Mother. I love my dear ones before Country or anything else. Heaven guard you is my Constant Prayer.[18]

God did not hear Mother's prayers: Booth grew only more desperate. Some thought he seemed crazed. Asked where he was going at one point during the final week, he answered, "I am going to Hell."[19] The parade of victories, the triumphalist mocking of the South, the endless drunken rejoicing, the Black soldiers, the salutes and songs and fireworks—all of it built to a crescendo of fury and despair in Booth's unstable head. The heavy drinking and lack of sleep only accelerated his descent.

Underlying his anger was racial hatred. Nothing about Northern victory disturbed Booth more than the prospect of the white supremacist edifice being turned on its head. Visiting Ford's Theatre on Wednesday, April 12, with just two days to go, Booth snarled, "We are all slaves now. If a man were to go out and insult a nigger now he would be knocked down by the nigger and nothing would be done to the nigger." Better not insult one then, said the ticket taker. Henry Clay Ford, brother of the owner of the theater that bore the family name, continued that Booth "just went on talking about niggers, and we would not argue with him any more. . . . He talked about prisoners coming in with a colored guard over them. He said it was a shame thus to hurt the feelings of the Southern people."[20]

Ford also testified that Booth "asked me repeatedly if the President was not coming [to Ford's Theatre] with such language as this, Why don't the old bugger come there sometimes. . . . He had said down in Mr. Potentine's saloon . . . that something would happen in two weeks that would astonish the world. Mr. Brady remarked What are you going to do, kill Jeff Davis, take Richmond or play Hamlet a hundred nights?" But John Wilkes Booth did not say what he was going to do.[21]

The once-invincible Army of Northern Virginia had not only surrendered—it was disbanded, scattered. General Grant had given all the soldiers paroles, as Lee himself had requested. The men would not be marched into prisoner of war camps. Instead, they were free to return to their homes in peace so long as they refrained from any further rebellion against the United States. Every soldier in the army had personally signed his parole, giving his word to abide by the settlement. Even now, Lee's veterans were making their ways home. General Grant had given them free pass to travel on the US Army military railroads.[22]

A handful of remnant insurgent armies were still in the field, it was true, but their dissolution was inevitable. At the beginning of 1865, Union troops had outnumbered the Southern survivors four to one. By mid-April, with Lee's army gone up, the disparity was even greater than that. Most of the exhausted soldiers in those few remaining armies did not wait for the formal surrender ceremonies. They left the ranks in droves—deserting by regiments, officers, and all. The war was over.

White Southerners presently discovered that they greeted defeat not only with sorrow and anger but also with a measure of relief. It had been a long and agonizing war. The odds against them had been long from the start. So long as enough of the Northern people remained united in a determination to impose the preservation of the Union by force of arms, the white South was almost certain to lose. In 1861, the rebelling states had commanded only 12 percent of the manufacturing capacity of the North.[23] The Union had lavished immense wealth on the pursuit of victory, staggering sums the South could not hope to match. The population of the North was almost twice that of the South. And about a third of the population of the so-called Confederacy were enslaved African Americans, the very people who hoped most ardently for Union victory.

Yankee soldiers had also fought much better than the Southrons had expected. The Southrons' vaunted invincibility had proved a myth. The defiant men who had once vowed to die in the "last ditch" before deserting the cause now understood that with the cause irretrievably lost, as it was, there was little further point in dying. Better to remain aboveground to help rebuild the shattered South.

For the former insurgents, the foremost item in this work of Southern restoration would be reestablishing the whites' dominion over the millions of suddenly free African Americans and assuring that that dominion would prevail far into the future. The one element the conquered white Southerners were determined to salvage from the ruins of their society was white supremacy.

But the South was finished as a military power. White Southerners had lost the war, and they knew they'd have to find a way to live with that defeat.

At this juncture, it took not hope but a species of delusion to imagine that the South could somehow yet prevail. But John Wilkes Booth still found hope in the cold ashes of irrevocable defeat. Booth was not clinically psychotic, but he was so angry, distraught, agitated, alcohol-addled, and depressed that his resemblance to an actual madman was more than just approximate. If he could have destroyed the entire Yankee nation with a single blow, he would have struck. He couldn't bear the thought of letting his last chance for historical immortality slip away. Ever since he was a boy, Booth had spoken of his great ambition to win a thousand years of fame by some spectacular act of destruction—some deed like overthrowing a world-famous monument or burning down civilization's greatest library. Not so long ago, he had declared that the man who killed Lincoln would make himself more famous than George Washington.[24]

Here is evident the striking difference in the life-motives of the assassin and his victim. The young Abraham Lincoln had dreamed of winning fame by helping to better the human condition. John Wilkes Booth—still young himself at twenty-six—wanted instead to win fame by destroying something great. Now he thought the destruction of the whole Yankee government would suit his purposes nicely.

So Booth's plans shifted again in the face of altered circumstances. If he had ever seriously considered capturing Lincoln, he had abandoned that approach in favor of murder. With the end now at hand, he moved from merely killing the Yankee president to decapitating the United States government itself by wiping out a whole cadre of top leaders. At its most expansive, his list of victims included not only Abraham Lincoln but also Vice President Johnson, Secretary of State Seward, Lieutenant General U. S. Grant, and probably Secretary of War Stanton and others. The shock and confusion of so great a bloodletting could give the South time to pull itself together, or so Booth hoped.

It's possible this new tactic of mass assassination was proposed to Booth by officials in Richmond or Montreal. They had their own mischief afoot. At the same time Booth was planning his new offensive, Jefferson Davis sent a team of saboteurs to Washington. Their mission was to blow up the White House with Lincoln and his cabinet inside.

It is doubtful that John Wilkes Booth knew much about the Constitution or the 1792 federal statute regarding presidential succession. Yet if he was assuming that the simultaneous elimination of the president, vice president, and secretary of state would bring about governmental chaos, the law bears him out. Weichmann recorded a conversation between Booth and his friend John F. Coyle, a newspaperman. Booth asked Coyle, " 'Suppose Lincoln was killed, what would be the result?' Mr. Coyle replied 'Johnson would succeed.' Then [Booth] said, 'But if he was killed?' 'Then Seward,' answered Mr. Coyle, and Booth continued 'But suppose he was killed, then what?' 'Then anarchy or whatever the Constitution provides,' and, laughing, Mr. Coyle said. 'But what nonsense: they don't make Brutuses nowadays.' Booth shook his head and said, 'No—no, they do not.' "[25] (That order has changed: the 1947 Presidential Succession Act made the Speaker of the House third in line after the vice president.)

With the president, vice president, and secretary of state dead, the office of the presidency in the Civil War era would have devolved temporarily on the president pro tempore of the Senate. That acting president would have served until an election is held to pick a new president. But the officer the Constitution designated to initiate the new election process is the secretary of state. If Booth's plan succeeded, therefore, before the work of finding a new president could even begin, the acting president would have to nominate and the Senate confirm a new secretary of state. It was not likely such matters would have proceeded smoothly on

Capitol Hill in the contentious year 1865. One might speculate that it could have taken months to inaugurate a new president under the circumstances that John Wilkes Booth and Jefferson Davis aimed to bring about.

For it was apparent that Jefferson Davis and the Secret Service Bureau in Richmond agreed with John Wilkes Booth that the mass assassination of the leading members of the Lincoln administration was a last gambit now worth a try. Like Booth, Davis could evidently sustain hope in an environment that dictated hopelessness. His attitude to the last was one of intransigence. His final state paper, "Message to the People of the Confederate States of America," fairly bristled with defiance. Writing on Tuesday, April 4, the day Lincoln walked the streets of Richmond, Davis contended that the loss of his capital was a blessing in disguise: victory was now more certain than ever: "We have now entered upon a new phase of a struggle, the memory of which is to endure for all ages. . . . Relieved from the necessity of guarding cities . . . with our army free to move from point to point . . . nothing is now needed to render our triumph certain, but the exhibition of our own unquenchable resolve. Let us but will it, and we are free."[26]

Just before the evacuation of Richmond, the Secret Service Bureau, acting on Davis's orders, had dispatched an action team to infiltrate Washington. The team included one of the clandestine Torpedo Bureau's top operatives, a veteran demolition man named Thomas Harney. It was said that "wherever Harney went, the Yankees suffered casualties and loss of equipment from explosive devices."[27] Sergeant Harney carried a small arsenal of explosive ordinance. The target was the White House.

As underdogs, the rebels had been obliged to seek tactical advantages through military innovation. They were well ahead of the North in the "wizard war" of explosive weaponry. The Torpedo Bureau, headquartered in Richmond, pushed this secret work forward. Torpedo Bureau operatives worked closely with agents of the Secret Service Bureau, devising missions and the weapons to carry them out.

The technicians who built the bombs called their principal weapons "torpedoes." We call them mines. Designed for use on land ("subterra torpedoes") or in the water, these devices could be command-detonated by electrical impulse, could set themselves off when disturbed or stepped on, or be detonated by a timer. The naval models, packed with hundreds of pounds of gunpowder, were greatly feared by the US Navy. The weapons' destructive powers were displayed when Admiral David Farragut "damn[ed] the torpedoes," ran his fleet past the forts, and captured Mobile Bay on August 5, 1864. While the navy gained a great victory that day, the lead ship in Farragut's column, the new ironclad monitor *Tecumseh*, one of the most advanced warships afloat, ran over a powerful mine. The ironclad heeled over and went down like a stone. Only 21 of the crew of 114 managed to get clear before the final plunge.

The Southern military had employed land mines as early as the Peninsular Campaign in 1862 and continued to plant them throughout the war. Usually on the attack, the Northern military saw no need to match the South's use of these fixed, defensive weapons. The Torpedo Bureau fabricated time bombs detonated by clock mechanisms ("horological torpedoes") for sabotage and hand grenades for combat. One of their time bombs devastated Grant's main supply depot at City Point, Virginia, on August 9, 1864. An initial explosion in an ammunition barge set off a chain, soon a crescendo, of secondary explosions as the many ordnance dumps on the base blew up. Most of the base and some of the shipping in the river were destroyed. Fifty-four troops were killed, more than one hundred wounded. Vast stockpiles of supplies— ammunition, weapons, gear, horses and wagons, uniforms, and rations—went up.

Particularly cunning were the Torpedo Bureau's little bombs disguised as lumps of coal. With proper emplacement, these would be shoveled into the fireboxes of the steam engines of enemy locomotives and steamboats, with predictable results. Apparently delighted by the clever ruse, Jefferson Davis kept one of these devilish lumps of coal on his desk as a memento of Southern ingenuity. It was sitting there the day Lincoln made his famous visit to the "White House of the Confederacy." (President Lincoln himself "expressed great contempt for cowardly assaults of such nature.")[28]

Thomas Harney and his cargo of explosives left Richmond on March 31, just two days before the city fell. The high command had ordered Colonel Mosby to insert Harney's team into the capital and help them escape after the deed was done. Recognizing the importance of the operation, Mosby gave them a strong escort of 150 of his hard-riding rangers. On Monday, April 10, however, the unit was attacked by Union cavalry and forced to make a run for it. Sergeant Harney and his bomb-making supplies were captured. The White House would stand another day.

There may have been another plot to bomb the White House. After Booth made his last return from New York to Washington on Saturday, April 8, he told George Atzerodt an interesting tale. Atzerodt testified that

> Booth said he had met a party in New York who would get the prest. certain. They were going to mine pres[ident's] House near the War Dept. They knew an entrance to accomplish it through. Spoke about getting friends of the prest. to get up an entertainment & they would mix in it, have a serenade & thus get at the prest. & party. These were understood to be projects. Booth said if he did not get him quick the New York crowd would. Booth knew the New York party apparently by a sign. [Atzerodt] saw Booth give some kind of a sign to two parties on the Avenue who he said were from New York.[29]

There is no other evidence that this new plot really existed, whether it was actually the Harney operation, whether it was run out of Richmond or Canada, or was planned by Northern traitors or freelance agents like Booth.

Nevertheless, if Booth knew of the Secret Service Bureau's plan to kill President Lincoln and his cabinet by blowing up the White House, that knowledge would certainly have encouraged the actor's formulation of his own scheme of governmental decapitation. The Harney mission may have inspired Booth's scheme in the first place. He had known for months that the high command wanted Abraham Lincoln dead. Now he knew that they also wanted to wipe out as much of the administration as possible. While probably not operating under orders from Davis's government, Booth could be sure that the attack he was planning comported with the current strategy of that government.

25

GOOD FRIDAY, 1865

April 14, 1865, was the happiest day of Abraham Lincoln's life. It was the first day he had allowed himself to believe the Civil War was really over. Mary Lincoln was surprised by her husband's unaccustomed happiness during the long, carefree carriage ride to the Navy Yard the couple took that afternoon. "I never saw him so supremely cheerful—his manner was even playful," she recalled. "'Dear husband, you almost startle me, by your great cheerfulness.'" He replied, "'Well I may feel so, Mary, I consider *this day*, the war had come to a close. We must *both*, be more cheerful in the future. Between the war & the loss of our darling Willie—we have both been very miserable.'"[1]

Often the couple had company on their outings, but today Lincoln said he wanted to be alone with Mary—alone, that is, except for the squad of troopers who rode, as always, alongside them. The Lincolns spoke of the future. They could hope that it might be a happier time. First thing that morning, just as Lincoln was finishing his usual breakfast of a single egg and coffee, two congressmen about to leave for California had dropped by the White House to say goodbye. Lincoln had exclaimed to his visitors, "How I would rejoice to make that trip! But public duties chain me down here, and I can only envy you its pleasures."[2]

As they drove through Washington City that balmy afternoon, he told his wife how much he wanted to see California. They might even move there after the presidency, he said. He thought their two sons would find greater opportunities on the Pacific coast. He intended to "go to California over the Rocky Mountains and see the prospects of the soldiers &c. &c digging gold to pay the National debt." (The National Debt had reached a prodigious $2,366,055,000.)[3] Besides the trip to California, Lincoln mentioned the possibility of practicing law again in Springfield or Chicago, a tour of Europe, and perhaps even a visit to Jerusalem.

The Lincolns did not speak of the past, the four hellish years that had taught them how truly wretched people can be. The growing legions of dead and wounded, the opposition's attacks combined with his own party's incessant political in-fighting, and the storm of violence that consumed America had all tortured the president. Just as disturbing was his wife's mental disorder, which had led to her embezzlement of government funds and the huge debts run up by her maniacal spending on jewelry, clothes, furniture, and silver. For a time, Mary herself had been so crazed by grief over the death of Willie that her husband warned her she was headed for a stay in St. Elizabeth's, the government lunatic asylum across the river. They hoped that now they could put much of that misery behind them.

The cruel ordeal had been as punishing to Abraham Lincoln's body as it had been to his soul. Many observers were amazed by how much the president had aged. Four years of war had left him looking a decade older. Fifty-two at his first inauguration, Lincoln had been one of the youngest US presidents. As the years of war passed, remembered his brilliant young secretary John Hay, "his demeanor and disposition changed . . . he was in mind, body, and nerves a very different man. . . . He continued always the same kindly, genial, and cordial spirit he had been at first; but the boisterous laughter became less frequent year by year; the eye grew veiled by constant mediation on momentous subjects; the air of reserve and detachment from his surroundings increased. He aged with great rapidity."[4]

At the Navy Yard, the presidential couple toured the ironclad monitor *Montauk*. The warship was undergoing repairs. It had been battered in the capture of Fort Fisher, the recent naval victory that had deprived the South of its last open seaport, Wilmington, North Carolina. The warship's surgeon recalled that the Lincolns "seemed very happy."[5] He would see them again at Ford's Theatre that night.

In the midst of a rainy month, Good Friday had arrived a warm, sunny spring day. With the mercury headed for sixty-eight, the weather seemed to match the president's jubilant spirits. Flowers bloomed on the White House grounds. Flowering trees and shrubs—dogwoods, redbuds, azaleas, and lilacs—blossomed throughout the capital. By the time the Lincolns left for Ford's Theatre that night, however, it had turned cool and drizzly, with occasional rain and fog.

When they had come together that morning for what turned out to be the last cabinet meeting of the Lincoln presidency, his secretaries had also remarked on the joyful demeanor of their usually preoccupied boss. "He was more cheerful and happy than I had ever seen him," declared Edwin Stanton. "Didn't the chief look grand this morning?" he exclaimed.[6] Iowa senator James Harlan, whose daughter was to marry Lincoln's son Robert, visited the White House later that day. Harlan was convinced the president "was, in fact, transformed. That indescribable sadness had been suddenly changed for an equally indescribable expression of serene joy, as if conscious that the great purpose of his life had been achieved."[7]

Further buoying Lincoln's mood that morning was recurrence of a familiar dream that he believed promised more good news. Lincoln's ascent from the Indiana frontier to the White House had been a remarkable one, but he still clung to some of the folk superstitions of his Hoosier boyhood. He believed that dreams could presage future events. This particular dream had come to him in the past, just before several important turning points in the war.

On that Friday morning, Lincoln and his cabinet—indeed, the entire nation—were waiting for the final piece of victory to fall into place. They expected word from North Carolina of the surrender of the last major insurgent army. General Joseph E. Johnston commanded a remnant of the once-powerful Army of Tennessee, the South's principal western army throughout the war. That army had been nearly destroyed in two Southern bloodbaths at the battles of Franklin and Nashville in Tennessee at the end of 1864 under the command of the calamitous John Bell Hood. Johnston had replaced Hood after the crushing defeats. Jefferson Davis subsequently transferred the Army of Tennessee to the Carolinas since there was essentially no insurgent country remaining to defend in the West.

The much larger Army of the Tennessee, commanded by General William T. Sherman, was now menacing Johnston's despairing survivors. Sherman's army had also come from the West to the East—by way of the March to the Sea and the follow-up thrust north into the Carolinas. Lincoln was sure his dream foretold Johnston's capitulation. (Lincoln and his cabinet couldn't know that even as they spoke, the surrender of the Army of Tennessee was being debated by Jefferson Davis and his fugitive cabinet.)

All through the winter and spring of 1864–65, Sherman's sixty thousand tough western veterans had rampaged almost unopposed through the Southern heartland. Turning their backs on the burnt-out ruins of Atlanta in November, they had driven south and east through Georgia, leaving behind a swath of destruction sixty miles wide and three hundred miles long. Savannah gave up without a fight at year's end when the Yankees reached the sea.

Sherman's vengeful and even more destructive "Smoky March" through the arch-secessionist state of South Carolina followed hard on the heels of Georgia's ordeal. Before long a wind-driven firestorm leveled half of Columbia, the state capital. Sherman said he didn't order it, but he didn't appear to regret it much either. Proud Charleston, the fire-eaters' original cradle of secession, a city that had withstood Union siege for years, now surrendered at the mere rumor of Sherman's approach. The massive destruction ceased as soon as Sherman's army crossed into North Carolina, a state the Yankees considered far less responsible for bringing on the war than its southern neighbor. His ranks swollen with reinforcements to ninety thousand to oppose Johnston's twenty thousand survivors, the red-headed Yankee general was maneuvering against the enemy near Goldsboro. The outcome seemed certain, but official Washington was anxiously awaiting news.

The cabinet met at eleven. General Grant, who came a little late, said he was "hourly" expecting word from Sherman. At the president's request, Grant briefly and modestly described the surrender of Robert E. Lee's Army of Northern Virginia five days earlier. "What terms did you make for the common soldiers?" Lincoln asked. "I told them," Grant replied, "to go back to their homes and families, and they would not be molested, if they did nothing more."[8] Lincoln nodded his approval. These were the terms he had implicitly suggested to his general-in-chief.

Lincoln spoke of the dream the night before that he expected might foretell some momentous event. Navy Secretary Gideon Welles asked about "this remarkable dream" and recorded Lincoln's reply in the long diary entry he composed three days after the assassination. Regarding news from Sherman, the President remarked it would, he had no doubt come soon, and come favorable, for he had last night the usual dream which he had preceding nearly every great and important event of the war. Generally the news had been favorable which succeeded this dream, and the dream itself was always the same. I inquired what this remarkable dream could be. He said it related to the water—that he seemed to be in some singular, indescribable vessel, and that he was moving with great rapidity. That he had this dream preceding Sumter, Bull Run, Antietam, Gettysburg, Stones River, Vicksburg, Wilmington, etc. . . . I had, the President remarked, this strange dream again last night, and we shall, judging from the past, have great news very soon. I think it must be from Sherman.[9]

Word from Sherman never came that day. Delayed by blunders on Sherman's part, the surrender of Johnston's army was not concluded until April 26. If the president's dream had indeed been prophetic, it was seemingly the glimmer of some other great event that had been proffered the dreamer the night before Good Friday.

Frederick W. Seward attended the meeting as acting secretary of state, filling in for his bedbound father. Very much the junior member of the table, the thirty-five-year-old Seward spoke up in the discussion of the president's recurring dream. Some of the cabinet secretaries had dismissed it as coincidence. Seward sensibly suggested that the dreams had recurred whenever "there were possibilities of great change or disaster, and the vague feeling of uncertainty may have led to the dim vision in sleep." "Perhaps," said Lincoln thoughtfully. "Perhaps that is the explanation."[10]

The secretary of state's son was sitting in for his father because the older man had been gravely injured in a carriage accident on Wednesday, April 5. For a time, his life was despaired of. When the driver stepped down from the carriage to fix a door, the horses panicked and bolted. The carriage sped along the street at dangerous speeds, trailing the horses' reins and carrying the secretary, his young daughter, and a friend. Seward poised himself at the open door, preparing to leap down and seize the reins when a violent lurch toppled him from his perch and threw him, face first, onto the pavement. He broke his jaw in two places and his right arm above the elbow. Unconscious and bleeding heavily, he had also sustained a severe concussion. A passing soldier halted the runaway team. The US surgeon general pronounced Seward's concussion a more serious injury than the broken bones or lacerations. Brain trauma put Seward into a delirium that persisted for days, though he did have moments of clarity.

Bystanders had him carried back to his big house on Lafayette Square, cattycorner to the White House, where doctors wired his broken jaw and set his arm. When he came to, he was delirious, but within a few days, it was clear that he would survive. Doctors called several times a day. A family team of his wife, daughter, and two sons settled in to watch over his recovery. They were helped by a wounded soldier assigned as a nurse from the Invalid Corps—one George Foster Robinson. Sergeant Robinson had taken a bullet to the leg in the fighting outside Richmond and was sent to the Invalid Corps to recover. By Friday, April 14, Seward was considerably improved. But he still suffered occasional spells of delirium and was confined to his bed.

That Friday morning, an overwrought John Wilkes Booth was burning for revenge against Abraham Lincoln for the many grievous wrongs he had so unjustly inflicted on the South. The object of Booth's hatred, in contrast, had put aside all thought of retribution. He was content to leave that with God. "Let us judge not, that we be not judged," he said more than once.

On the day of his remarkable visit to Richmond, Lincoln had suggested to his commanders there how they might treat the defeated people: "If I was in your place I'd let 'em up easy, let 'em up easy."[11] In his Second Inaugural, he had memorably invoked malice toward none with charity for all and warned against judging others. In this, his last cabinet meeting, he insisted again that "there would be no persecutions, no bloody work. . . . None need expect he would take any part in hanging or killing those men, even the worst of them. Frighten them out of the country, open the gates, let down the bars, scare them off."[12] (Some of the Southern leaders were, indeed, fleeing into foreign exile at that moment.) Stanton said that Lincoln displayed "in marked degree the kindness and humanity of his disposition, and the tender and forgiving spirit that so eminently distinguished him."[13]

The day before, the news that General Grant was coming to Washington had reawakened the frustrated and distraught John Wilkes Booth and set into motion his last and only successful attack. He was brimming with new energy. As long as Grant stayed with his Army of the Potomac, he was out of reach. On the streets of Washington City, however, he was in danger. It was easy for Booth to imagine some public event at which Lincoln and Grant might appear together, perhaps vulnerable to attack. The general was usually accompanied by aides and staff officers, but no one was assigned to protect him.

The general-in-chief arrived in the capital Friday morning and headed straight to the White House for the cabinet meeting. He didn't know that he had succeeded in inserting his name into Booth's list of targets. That list now included Lincoln, Johnson, Grant, and Seward, with Stanton as a tantalizing possibility. Someone scouted the Stanton home on Thursday, and a figure was seen lurking about there the night of the assassination.

We don't know if Booth had learned that the federal authorities had intercepted and captured Sergeant Harney's Torpedo Bureau demolition team sent to blow up the White House. In fact, it is not certain that he knew of Harney's mission at all. In any event, he drove forward his own scheme of mass assassination with all the manic determination he could muster.

Booth ignored the long odds against the success of his new plan. Taking out so many important figures would not be easy.

*Booth hoped that Lieutenant General U. S. Grant
and President Lincoln would be sitting side by side in the
state box like a pair of shooting-gallery targets. But Grant
declined the president's invitation to attend because of
his wife's distaste for Mary Todd Lincoln.*

Library of Congress, Prints and Photographs
Division, LC-DIG-cwpb-05204.

Twice in the past month—at the inauguration and at the presentation of the captured rebel flag at the National Hotel on March 17—Booth had struggled mightily, but unsuccessfully, to push himself close to President Lincoln. We cannot know if he would have struck on one of those occasions if the chance had come. Booth did not know when or if another chance to close on the president might occur. Expanding the list of targets had greatly magnified the difficulty of planning a coordinated attack on all of them. With Richmond evacuated and Jeff Davis a fugitive, he could expect no help from the South. Booth was, in fact, poorly equipped to meet such a challenge. He lacked funds, allies and accomplices, as well as sound intelligence about his intended targets. The only target he could confidently locate was the bedridden Seward. For his own part, Booth lacked prudence, sobriety, and the ability to think clearly and plan wisely.

Most important, he was woefully short of man power. Arnold was lost to him, working in the soldiers' store near Fortress Monroe. Mike O'Laughlen had declared himself out of the enterprise. John Surratt was away on a mission given him by the spymasters in Canada. He was gathering intelligence on the prisoner of war camp in Elmira, New York. The Canadian cabinet was considering a raid on the camp to free the thousands of Southern veterans imprisoned there. Surratt was also reluctant to return to Washington because he believed, quite correctly, that the ubiquitous government detectives intended to arrest him on sight. They had already been to his mother's H Street boardinghouse looking for him. Surratt would be the only member of the gang to escape the intensive manhunt that followed the assassination.

On the plus side, Lewis Powell was as solid as a stone wall. He regarded Booth as his superior officer in a highly irregular military unit. Powell called him "Captain." David Herold was also irreproachably loyal, taking Booth's orders with cheerful obedience. George Andrew Atzerodt had reappeared from beneath whatever rock he'd been hiding under. He was still hoping to get rich and stuck by Booth. Atzerodt was compromised by alcoholism and cowardice, but Booth thought he could intimidate the German into following orders. In any event, Atzerodt was valuable as a midnight river pilot who had crossed the broad Potomac many times. Booth also knew he could count on the local spies and stationmasters on the secret mail line through southern Maryland and into Virginia. These men, all of them agents of the Secret Service Bureau, had agreed to help him move the captive

Lincoln. Surely they'd be just as eager to protect Lincoln's killer.

On Thursday, April 13, Booth had sent Herold and Atzerodt to gather intelligence on Vice President Andrew Johnson, who was living in the Kirkwood House. Johnson was pointed out to them in the hotel dining room. Now they could recognize him on sight. The next morning, the day of the assassination, Atzerodt rented a room at the Kirkwood House. It was on the second floor, Johnson's on the first, but the hotel room could still serve as a base for actions aimed at the vice president.

That afternoon, Booth and Lewis Powell had made an open reconnaissance of Secretary of State Seward's house. Booth flirted with and quizzed the pretty housekeeper. Speaking through an open window, Powell solicitously asked George Robinson, the invalid soldier-nurse, about Seward's condition. Sergeant Robinson thought the polite, well-dressed young man was merely a concerned citizen. Indeed, so concerned was this citizen that he returned to the Seward home the next day, when he asked again about the secretary while no doubt considering his tactics for the attack he would make a few hours later.

Meanwhile, John Wilkes Booth had taken the Thursday morning train to Baltimore. He meant to find Mike O'Laughlen and bring him back to Washington. He was desperately short of accomplices. This again suggests that Booth was operating independently of the Southern government. If he was acting under orders of the Secret Service Bureau, it surely would have provided him with all the fighters he needed.

Booth succeeded in persuading O'Laughlen. Though he did not travel with Booth, O'Laughlen presently took the 3:30 train down to the capital with three friends, ostensibly to see another grand illumination for the raising of the national flag over Fort Sumter in South Carolina. The four men also intended to do some serious drinking. Thousands were crowding into the city for the festivities.

That evening, a suspicious man behaving strangely appeared

at Secretary of War Stanton's home. He wanted to see Stanton. He said he had important information for him. When he learned that he could not see Stanton, he asked to speak with General Grant. This, too, was denied him. He had identified himself, unconvincingly, as a friend of Stanton's. "I am a lawyer in town," he said. "I know him very well." The Stantons and the Grants were out on the front steps, looking up at the fireworks blossoming in the night sky. The stranger stood quite near Stanton for a few moments but made no attempt to speak with him. Then he entered the Stanton home uninvited but disappeared promptly when told to leave. Several witnesses, including Secretary Stanton's son, positively identified the intruder as Michael O'Laughlen. If he had indeed abandoned the conspiracy, what was he doing scouting Stanton's home?

In *American Brutus*, Michael Kauffman speculates that O'Laughlen was there to warn Stanton about the danger but couldn't summon up the courage to speak to the secretary. O'Laughlen had met with Booth at the National Hotel that morning. Kauffman believes that O'Laughlen had come to Washington that day to persuade Booth to hold off.[14]

In *Decapitating the Union*, however, John Fazio concluded that O'Laughlen was there on Booth's orders, to reconnoiter the place for the assassination of the secretary of war. A meeting at the National Hotel on Thursday was likely where Booth gave O'Laughlen his mission. The two met at the hotel again the morning of the assassination, when O'Laughlen no doubt gave his chief a report on the Stanton place.

That evening, about half past ten, as Booth and Powell were attacking Lincoln and Seward, various witnesses told of a man lurking around Stanton's home, standing on the porch and hiding behind a tree box. But there were too many witnesses—soldiers and civilians in the streets then. An attacker would be unlikely to get away. The suspicious stranger made off without trying to enter the house.[15] Was it O'Laughlen? We will never know.

If Booth slept at all the night before the assassination, it wasn't at his hotel. Chambermaids found the bed in room 228 at the National unslept in. Maybe he spent the night with his sweet little prostitute, Ella Starr. Always a night person, his usual hour for rising was ten. He took breakfast in the National's dining room about that time. Reports vary: the actor may have eaten alone, or he may have breakfasted with one, or perhaps two, young women who have never been identified.

Then he hit the streets. Booth hardly stopped moving that day. He hurried on foot and on horseback through the streets of Washington City, ducking into hotels, boardinghouses, theaters, and saloons. Frequently during his peregrinations, he stopped into barrooms for quick shots with acquaintances he encountered. He kept himself well lubricated.

After a shave in a barbershop, his first stop was the Surratt boardinghouse, on H Street. He had matters to settle with the lady of the house. It was the first of his three visits to the place on Friday, a circumstance not helpful to Mrs. Surratt's attorney's efforts to save her life when the government put her on trial for her part in the conspiracy. On March 17, the day of the gang's clownish attempt at overtaking the president's carriage on the Seventh Street Road, Davey Herold had loaded the weapons and gear into Booth's buggy and driven over the river into Maryland. He was to meet up with the others when they came along with the captive Lincoln. When that failed to come to pass, Herold had dumped the weapons at the Surratt tavern. Barkeep John Lloyd, Mary Surratt's tenant, objected strongly. He said he was "uneasy," fearful of being implicated. Lloyd wasn't privy to the conspirators' plans, but he knew they were up to no good. All of them knew that the authorities were watching the Surrattsville tavern intently. Indeed, ten days later, federal detectives would arrest Augustus Howell, a Southern spy and courier, at the Surratt tavern.

John Surratt calmed Lloyd's anxiety about the two Spencer carbines by hiding them behind an unfinished wall above the kitchen. It was a good hiding place. The police who arrested Augustus Howell no doubt searched the tavern. They didn't find the guns. Those repeating rifles could be of vital importance to the conspirators' escape, whether in an abduction or after an assassination. If the fugitives had to shoot it out with pursuers, they'd need more firepower than their Colt revolvers provided.

Booth needed to be sure that he could get his hands on the weapons at a moment's notice—without delay or confusion. Because of his own poor planning, he now had to pick up the weapons and other supplies on his escape run from Ford's, when every moment would be precious. To get hung up in Surrattsville for even a short time might prove fatal. Booth wanted to be absolutely certain that Lloyd would have the weapons ready that night. He may have been apprehensive that the tavern keeper would let him down. Lloyd was, after all, a hopeless drunk who was often comatose at that time of night.

Booth had planned to visit Lloyd himself that morning to make sure. He also wanted to drop off some field glasses he meant to take with him on his run. When he dropped in on her, Mrs. Surratt told him she was planning to go to Surrattsville herself to collect a debt. Her friend Louis Weichmann had agreed to drive her down. She could give Lloyd Booth's instructions and leave the field glasses, saving the actor a trip. When she asked Booth for the use of his buggy, he told her he'd sold it but gave her ten dollars to rent one. Booth came by again about 2:30 that afternoon, his second visit to the boardinghouse, when he dropped off the field glasses in a brown paper package tied with string. He would see Mary Surratt again shortly before the murder.

It was hardly surprising that Mary Surratt and Lou Weichmann found John Lloyd "staggering drunk" when they arrived in Surrattsville about 5:00. He was, in fact, "more drunk than she had ever seen him before."[16] Lloyd himself later testified that "I was right smart in liquor that afternoon, and after night I got more so."[17] He passed out on a couch about eight. Herold had to pound on the door to get him up when he and Booth showed up about midnight.

Mary Surratt had told her inebriated tenant "to get those shooting-irons and two bottles of whiskey ready, as some persons would call for them that night." Lloyd said that "I could not divine what they wanted of these carbines, and I was very anxious to have them taken away. . . . I went to work and got them out of their hiding place and put them in my room."[18] By giving Lloyd those simple instructions, Mary Surratt had stuck her tender neck into the hangman's noose. The testimony of Lloyd and Weichmann, confirmed by a statement of Atzerodt, would convict her. Drunk as he may have been, Lloyd later insisted under oath that he remembered everything that took place that night.

John Wilkes Booth strode into Ford's Theatre about noon. He would be in and out of the theater all day and throughout the evening, before and after the performance began. This was not unusual. The place was the closest thing to a home Booth had, especially since he'd been banished from Edwin's Manhattan home, where his mother and sister lived. His mail came to him at Ford's, not at his hotel, and anyone trying to find him would look there first. Henry Clay Ford, brother of owner John T. Ford, was managing the enterprise at the time. As Booth arrived, Harry Ford called out, "Here comes the handsomest man in the United States!" Someone handed him his mail. Booth tore open a letter and sat on the steps reading it. Once he laughed and muttered, "That damned woman!"[19]

Shortly before Booth arrived at Ford's, welcome news had come from the White House. The Lincolns had accepted Harry Ford's invitation—President and Mrs. Lincoln would attend the performance of *Our American Cousin* that evening. And they were bringing General Grant and his wife, Julia. Ford had been worried about poor attendance. Ticket sales tended to drop off on religious holidays. Many solid citizens might be reluctant to be found in such morally dubious precincts as a theater on Good

Ford's Theatre draped in mourning a few days after the tragedy.
The government seized the building, and more than a century
would pass before another play would be staged there.

Friday. Now the presence of President Lincoln, and particularly that of the illustrious general-in-chief of the armies of the United States, would assure a full house. People would come just to get a glimpse of these distinguished figures. Grant, the shining champion of Union victory, was at that moment, just five days after Appomattox, a more celebrated and popular hero than Abraham Lincoln himself.

Ford hurried to get word of his famous guests to the newspapers. They duly announced it in their afternoon editions. Booth showed little reaction to the news that two of his principal targets would be sitting side by side like a pair of shooting gallery targets in the state box, but his heart no doubt commenced to pound with excitement. Witnesses did say he seemed to become "abstracted." Booth slipped away. No one saw him leave. He was headed to a nearby stable to rent a horse for his escape.

Harry Ford and his staff got to work preparing for the presidential visit. The partition between boxes 7 and 8 was removed to expand the space to make the state box. The box was the farthest to the right looking toward the stage. A janitor lugged up the big red-velvet rocking chair in which the president customarily sat. Two red-velvet armchairs, a red-velvet sofa, and six cane chairs completed the furnishings. The president's rocking chair was placed in the far left of the box. Most of the audience would be unable to see him there. The box was already framed with heavy drapery. Ford proceeded to hang over the balustrade two American flags and between them a small blue treasury department regimental flag. Centering and completing the arrangement was a gilt-framed engraving of Gilbert Stuart's iconic portrait of George Washington.

Luckily for Ulysses and Julia Grant, the Lincolns' planned theater party fell through. The Grants decided they'd rather go to New Jersey to see their children. More pressing than the parental motive for declining the president's invitation was Julia Grant's determination to avoid the company of Mary Lincoln at all costs. She feared the president's mentally unbalanced wife. The two women had shared a series of highly unpleasant encounters when the Lincolns had visited the Army of the Potomac three weeks earlier. The first time the two met, Julia Grant made the mistake of sitting down next to the First Lady. "How dare you be seated until I invite you?" Mary Lincoln had angrily demanded.[20]

The next day at City Point, Lincoln reviewed the soldiers of General E. O. C. Ord's Army of the James. The president and his generals rode past the troops on horseback. Mrs. Lincoln and Mrs. Grant followed in an ambulance. Riding with the review-

The state box at Ford's Theatre several days after the murder.
Missing is the small Treasury Department flag that snagged Booth's
spur and caused him to fall awkwardly, breaking his leg.

ing party was General Ord's pretty young wife. As "soon as Mrs. Lincoln discovered this her rage was beyond all bounds," Grant's aide Adam Badeau reported. "'What does that woman mean,' Mary Lincoln exclaimed, 'by riding by the side of the President? and ahead of me? . . .' She was in a frenzy of excitement, and language and action both became more extravagant every moment." When Julia Grant tried to calm the First Lady, Mary Lincoln turned, raging, on her: "I suppose you think you'll get to the White House yourself don't you? Oh! You had better take it if you can get it. 'Tis very nice."[21]

Mary Lincoln then attacked Mrs. Ord with obscenities when the two were introduced following the review, reducing the poor woman to tears. Badeau recalled that Mary Lincoln continued to attack her husband in public over the episode during the rest of their visit. The aide called this behavior an "inexpressible public mortification" that Lincoln endured with "an expression of pain and sadness that cut one to the heart, but also with calmness and dignity."[22] Little wonder that Julia Grant didn't relish the idea of spending two hours with the First Lady within the confines of a private theater box. General Grant had had his own experience with Mrs. Lincoln's explosive temper just the night before. He concurred with his wife's decision that they absent themselves.

Booth and his men watched the Grants closely all day to make sure that they would be at Ford's that evening. They eventually made the disappointing discovery that the couple was headed out of town. Later that afternoon, Booth, mounted on his rented horse, was talking to his actor friend, John Mathews, who was standing near him on the sidewalk. It was just after they had witnessed the sorrowful parade of captured officers.

Mathews suddenly burst out, "John! There goes General Grant! I understand he is coming to the theater tonight with the president." Booth hurriedly said goodbye to his friend and, spurring his horse, raced after the carriage. He saw that it was piled high with luggage as though the Grants were driving to the train station. He swept past the vehicle, wheeled about and galloped back to approach so close that he practically stuck his head in the window. He glared at Grant "in a disagreeable manner." "General," said a friend who was riding with him, "everyone wants to see you." "Yes," replied Grant, "but I do not care for such glances. They are not friendly."[23]

Julia Grant recognized the raven-haired, pale-faced horseman. At lunch in the Willard Hotel's dining room a few hours earlier, Booth and some other men had come in and sat down near her table. They had brazenly followed her into the place. She was alarmed that they stared at her so intently. She was certain they were trying to overhear her conversation. Now she was sure it was "this same dark, pale man" who had just approached their carriage so aggressively.[24]

With the Grants out of the picture, the Lincolns invited a young couple they were friendly with to go to the play with them. Clara Harris, daughter of New York senator Ira Harris, and combat veteran Major Henry Rathbone were not only engaged to marry but were also step-siblings, having been raised in the same household after their widowed parents married. The two young people had accompanied the presidential couple on some of their afternoon carriage rides.

Booth appeared that afternoon at the desk of the Kirkwood House. He was trying to establish where Vice President Johnson would be that night. Told the man was not in, Booth penned a note to leave in his box: "Don't wish to disturb you; are you at home? J. Wilkes Booth."[25] Booth had met Johnson in Nashville during his two-week engagement at Wood's Theatre in February 1864. The message was later to arouse suspicion that the man who by the crime ascended to the presidential chair had been involved in Lincoln's murder. The accusation was raised during the 1867 Johnson impeachment proceedings in the House. Mary Lincoln needed no congressional testimony to convince her of Johnson's guilt. She had written a friend:

GOOD FRIDAY, 1865

335

That, miserable inebriate Johnson, had cognizance of my husband's death—*Why*, was *that card* of Booth's, found in his box, some acquaintance certainly existed—I have been deeply impressed, with the harrowing thought, that *he*, had an understanding with the conspirators & *they*, knew *their man*. Did not Booth, say, "There is one thing, he would not tell." There is said, to be honor, among thieves. No one ever heard, of Johnson, regretting my sainted husband's death, he never wrote me a line of condolence, and behaved in the most brutal way.[26]

But there is no evidence whatsoever that Johnson was involved with Booth.

That night, about eight o'clock, Booth met with his remaining henchmen, Atzerodt, Herold, and Powell, in the latter's room at the Herndon House. Powell, a wanted man, had been staying inside and taking his meals in his room. He was afraid of being recognized and arrested on the streets. Herold had gone to fetch Atzerodt to the meeting. Earlier that day, Atzerodt had rented room 126 in the Kirkwood House, on Booth's orders, providing a base for the strike against Johnson. Before leaving the Kirkwood House, Herold went up to Atzerodt's room with him, where he produced from one boot a Colt revolver and a Bowie knife from the other. Investigators noted later that all six chambers of the revolver were "loaded and capped."

The accompanying edged weapon was a "Rio Grande Camp knife" forged for the American export market by the renowned English Sheffield steel foundry. On the blade was engraved the motto "America, Land of the Free." Booth and Powell both had nearly identical Bowie knives that they would soon wield with bloody effect. The foot-long weapons had nine-inch, razor-sharp blades. Herold's knife never hurt anyone. He left the weapons, along with a coat, in Atzerodt's room, providing important evidence for the investigators. Herold never retrieved his weapons for the planned attack on Johnson because Atzerodt refused to give him the key to the room. (Atzerodt had his own Rio Grande Camp Bowie knife. He tossed his in a gutter outside the vice president's hotel, where it was picked up and turned over to the police.)

As the four men talked in Powell's room 6 at the Herndon House, the streets outside belonged to the noisy revelers. The inexhaustible victory party was still ongoing. The men in room 6 meant to put a stop to all rejoicing. Booth now gave his men their new assignments, self-assuredly laying out his plan as though they were all in agreement.

Booth would kill Lincoln. He knew by then that Grant would not be present. (Later, however, a would-be assassin tried to breach General Grant's security and get into his train car in Delaware during his railroad trip. This additional member of the conspiracy has never been identified.)[27] Powell would kill the bedridden secretary of state. Booth then ordered Atzerodt and Herold to murder Vice President Johnson at the Kirkwood House. This was the first George Atzerodt had heard of any killing. "I did not come for that and [am] not willing to murder a person," he objected.[28] Booth was not prepared to take no for an answer. "Boy, boy," he said, closing in on Atzerodt. "What is to become of you?" He punched the German in the face. Atzerodt fell to the floor. "You *must* kill Johnson," Booth shouted, threatening to blow his brains out. He continued to cajole, bully, and threaten the hapless boatman until he most reluctantly acquiesced. Still, Booth knew there was little chance Atzerodt would really follow through. He had already decided that Herold would have to kill Johnson. Herold had agreed. That was the reason he had stashed his revolver and Bowie knife in Atzerodt's room at the Kirkwood. But Booth insisted that Atzerodt had to go along to help Davey. To this much, the unhappy man had to agree.[29]

Most historians of the assassination have presented the traditional narrative that David Herold backed up Lewis Powell in his attempt to assassinate Secretary of State William H. Seward at his house on Lafayette Square. In this iteration, Herold waited outside, holding their horses, as Powell entered the Seward home on his deadly mission. Powell was unfamiliar with Washington City. Herold was along to guide the escape. On hearing the screams from the Seward house, the story goes, Herold panicked and fled, leaving Powell to lose his way and eventually fall into the hands of law enforcement.

It is more likely, however, that Herold was actually with Atzerodt at the Kirkwood House at that time for the strike against Vice President Johnson.[30] A witness did confirm that Atzerodt was at the hotel at the time of the attacks against Lincoln and Seward. It is possible that Herold did guide Powell to the Seward house before hurrying back to Johnson's hotel to join Atzerodt. Witnesses described seeing Powell's horse tied to the iron fence around Lafayette Square when the Southern veteran was slashing and stabbing the five men in the secretary's house. No one, however, saw a second horse or a man holding the horses. At the same time, Atzerodt may have aborted the attempt on Johnson by refusing to let Herold retrieve his pistol and knife from the locked hotel room.

BLACK FRIDAY, 1865

Two busy saloons flanked Ford's Theatre on Tenth Street. To the south of the theater was the Star Saloon. To the north was the barroom and restaurant of James Ferguson. Ferguson and Booth were on friendly terms. The actor was in his place almost every day. Indeed, he was a regular at both bars, where his liberality in buying drinks for the house had made him a welcome patron. It was in the Star Saloon that the assassin would down a last, fortifying shot of whiskey just minutes before the murder.

Barkeep James Ferguson was one of the only eyewitnesses who actually saw Booth enter the box and shoot Lincoln. He watched the whole thing through opera glasses. Ferguson was a strong Union man. Any drinker who expressed rebel sympathies in Ferguson's barroom could expect to meet with immediate violence at the hands of the proprietor. Ferguson called one secesh a "damned hungry son of a bitch" and pitched him out onto the sidewalk. He told the man if he ever came back, "I will break your neck or have you arrested."[1]

John Wilkes Booth was capable of discretion when it suited his purposes. It was only when he was sure he was speaking to another of Southern sympathies that he cut loose with his rants and rages against Lincoln. He had never said a disloyal word in the hearing of this particular friend. He knew Ferguson idolized Lincoln and Grant. At this point in history, so soon after Appomattox, the three-star lieutenant general ranked higher in Ferguson's hierarchy of heroes than did the president. He said that Grant "was a great favorite of mine." The afternoon of April 14, Harry Ford told him, "Jim, your favorite is going to be in our theater tonight, and if you want to see him you must secure a good seat."[2]

So when the curtain went up on *Our American Cousin* at eight o'clock, Jim Ferguson was seated in the front row of the dress circle, stage right, directly across from the state box. He could look straight into it, and with his opera glasses, he was sure to get a good view of the occupants. Like much of the theater's audience of as many as fifteen hundred that night, Ferguson was far more interested in observing the two most famous men in America than in watching the threadbare old comedy.

As a performer in good standing and an old family friend, Booth had unlimited access to Ford's Theatre. Early that evening, on his second visit of the day to Ford's, he found opportunity to make some alterations to the state box. No one remembered seeing him. The state box had three doors, one outer and two inner doors with a dark, eight-foot-long passage between. Since box numbers 7 and 8 were usually set up as two separate boxes, each had its own door from the passage. Both doors had broken locks. The box 8 door was used as the entrance when 7 and 8 were combined to make the state box. It was directly behind the rocking chair that had been placed there for the president.

Booth was concerned only with the box 8 door. Probably using a gimlet and a pen knife, he drilled and cut a small peephole that allowed him to spy on the occupants without opening the door. Taking a small plank from a nearby music stand, he chiseled a notch in the plaster baseboard near the outer door. That door opened inward. With the plank wedged between the door and the notch he'd cut in the wall, it would be jammed, nearly impossible to push open from the outside.

By the time the last Lincoln cabinet meeting broke up at about 2 p.m., news had already spread that the president and the lieutenant general would be together that evening at Ford's Theatre. Before he left the White House, War Secretary Stanton voiced his strong opposition to the excursion. "He had for some months," Stanton said, "been aware that threats of assassination were being made by certain evil-minded persons against the leaders of the Federal government and army. . . . The presence of the President of the nation and the Lieutenant-General of the armies at any public function at such a critical hour was simply courting disaster."[3] With the defeat of the South, rage against Lincoln had only swollen in some quarters. Warnings of impending assassination came from as far away as Paris. Stanton also worried that the whole capital city had worked itself into a state of joyous frenzy approaching anarchy.

The president himself was apparently more apprehensive for his safety than usual that night. He told his friend Noah Brooks, the newspaperman, that he was reluctant—perhaps even fearful—to go to the theater.[4] He may still have been troubled by his strange recurrent dream of the swift, mysterious vessel. If the dream did, indeed, mean that something important was soon to happen, that event was yet to come. But since his attendance had been announced in the papers, he felt obliged to go so as not to disappoint the people.

The president's fanatically dedicated volunteer protector, his old Illinois friend Ward Hill Lamon, would probably have accompanied the Lincolns had he been in town. Like Stanton, he abhorred the president's theater outings. He might have stopped Booth. But the president had just sent Lamon to Richmond on a political errand. Lamon spent the rest of his life explaining his absence. He would carry with him at all times Lincoln's written orders dispatching him to Richmond as proof that he had not abandoned his friend. So Abraham Lincoln had to trust to luck and to his police bodyguard, John F. Parker.

In considering Lincoln's protection that fatal Friday night, there is even the remarkable possibility, impossible to verify, that the president himself was carrying a loaded derringer in the pocket of his custom-made Brooks Brothers overcoat with the image of an American eagle bearing in its beak a banner with the motto "One Country, One Destiny" skillfully embroidered into its silk lining. There are no living descendants of Abraham and Mary Lincoln. The last Lincoln was a great-grandson, the late Robert Todd Lincoln Beckwith. For whatever measure of immortality Abraham Lincoln has attained, it was not on the biological model of mindless but perpetual genetic replication. When Bob Beckwith died without issue in 1985, the Lincoln line winked out forever.

Beckwith had been custodian of a treasure house of relics and memorabilia and the last source of family tradition. He asserted categorically that Abraham Lincoln had provided himself with a firearm the night of his assassination. Moreover, Beckwith stated, it was a .44-caliber derringer manufactured by the Henry Deringer Company, a pistol identical to Booth's. Beckwith had inherited Lincoln's derringer along with its history, but the gun had been stolen from his home.[5] If the story could be confirmed, would it change our understanding of the assassination in any way?[6]

Another friend of Booth's, John Deery, ran a billiards saloon the actor frequented. Deery remembered that that spring Booth seemed anxious and distracted and that he was drinking more heavily than usual: "For a period of about ten days before the assassination, he visited my place every day, sometime[s] in the afternoon, sometimes in the evenings. . . . During that last week at Washington he sometimes drank at my bar as much as a quart of brandy in the space of less than two hours. . . . I believe Booth was as much crazed by the liquor he drank that week as by any motive when he shot Lincoln."[7]

But the alcohol was merely a tranquilizer and a fount of liquid courage. Booth was motivated to kill by his hatred for Lincoln and by the ideology of white supremacy. He made his usual appearance at Deery's place about four o'clock the afternoon of the murder. He put away his customary quart of brandy. This went on top of the various shots he'd already tossed down that day and the others he would swallow in the remaining few hours. No one could argue that he was sober.

By the time he left Deery's place, the countdown had begun in earnest. Mounted on his rented mare, he stopped to watch the sorrowful procession of Southern prisoners with his actor friend John Mathews. Two years later, Mathews recounted his conversation with Booth at that time when he testified under oath in the House Judiciary Committee's impeachment investigation of President Andrew Johnson. "'Johnny,' Booth had said. 'I wish to ask you a favor; will you do it for me?' I said, 'Of course.' Said he, 'I have a letter which I wish you to deliver to the publishers of the National Intelligencer [an influential Washington triweekly] to-morrow morning, unless I see you in the meantime.'"[8] Booth handed him the letter, stamped and sealed in a National Hotel envelope. Mathews slipped it into the inside breast pocket of his suit jacket and promptly forgot about it.

Mathews had a major role in *Our American Cousin* that evening. When he learned that his friend was the assassin, he ripped the letter open and read it with mounting terror. It was another declaration of Booth's political beliefs and, more importantly, his justification of his impending killing of the malign author of all America's woes. Booth was defending the murder he had already committed by the time Mathews read his letter.

The actor was terrified. Booth's letter was evidence enough to hang him a dozen times over. The president of the United States had been murdered. Hours before that event, John Mathews had possessed a document that told of the forthcoming assassination in the handwriting of the assassin himself. That information would have saved Abraham Lincoln's life. Yet Mathews had withheld it. He had no way to prove that he hadn't read the letter until after the deed was done. It didn't require much rumination on Mathews's part to decide on a course of action. He saw no need to consult an attorney. He quickly burned the letter and didn't speak of it for two years, when he was sure his legal jeopardy had passed. Even later, in 1881, at the urging of a journalist, Mathews tried to reconstruct Booth's letter from memory. He couldn't do it. It had been too long, even for an actor who had memorized countless lines of drama and comedy. All he could summon up with certainty was the assassin's closing paragraph:

> For a long time I have devoted my energies, my time and money, to the accomplishment of a certain end. I have been disappointed. The moment has arrived when I must change my plans. Many will blame me for what I am about to do, but posterity, I am sure, will justify me. Men who love their country better than gold and life.
>
> John W. Booth, Payne [Powell's alias], Herold, Atzerodt[9]

Booth had thus made sure to implicate his accomplices.

The Lincolns and their guests arrived about half an hour after the play started. They tried to approach the box unobtrusively along the outside of the dress circle, behind and to the right of the audience. Nevertheless, the president was spotted immediately. The people rose from their seats, cheered and applauded, waved hats and handkerchiefs, and stamped their feet. The orchestra burst into a rousing rendition of "Hail to the Chief." For here was a chief indeed—the chief magistrate of a mighty nation in its hour of triumph. Lincoln responded with bows, smiles, and a wave. He looked exhausted. Delighted by the reception, a radiantly happy Mary Lincoln curtsied her thanks.

The state box on the right of the theater looked out diagonally across the stage. Most of the audience was seated to the left of the box. So when Lincoln sat down in the big red-velvet rocking chair, behind the drapes and flags, he was not visible to most of the theatergoers. Only a lucky few, like Jim Ferguson, had a view into the box. Lincoln, however, frequently revealed himself by leaning forward on the balustrade to study the audience below. Mary sat at her husband's right. To Mary's right sat Clara Harris with her fiancé, the red-headed, mutton-chopped combat veteran Major Henry Rathbone. The audience below sat on wicker-bottomed wooden chairs.

Many noted that General Grant had not come in with the president. Jim Ferguson, for one, was not yet entirely disappointed. He suspected that Grant, known to dislike fanfare and applause, would try to sneak into the theater later. So rather than attending to *Our American Cousin*, Ferguson kept his opera glasses trained on the dress circle approach to the box and the box itself, determined not to miss his hero's arrival.

The president's messenger Charles Forbes had seated himself in a chair near the entrance to the passageway outside of the box. Policeman John Parker vanished, either taking a seat somewhere to watch the play or, more likely, ducking into one of the taverns to wet his whistle. He'd been reprimanded more than once for drinking on duty, one of the long list of disciplinary offenses on his unenviable service record. Parker wasn't worried. Before he left the White House that evening, he and the doorkeeper had agreed that no harm would come to the president.

Meanwhile, Booth made his way to Ford's Theatre for the fourth and last time that day. He walked his getaway horse up the alley to the rear door of the building. He enlisted a boy to hold the skittish mare ready for a quick escape. Booth was dressed in black—a black sack suit, a black slouch hat, and a pair of custom, thigh-length riding boots with a pistol holster sewn inside one leg. Spurs were on his heels. His plan required him to enter the front of the theater.

As soon as he stepped inside, he saw that the arrangement of the scenery prevented his passing across the stage without being seen by the audience. He needed to get across and out onto Tenth Street so that he could enter the theater from the front. The actor knew his way around. He lifted a trapdoor in the floor and climbed down into the dark, dirt-floored basement beneath the stage. From above came the muffled voices of the actors. Booth made his way through the darkness to a stairway he ascended. He was now across the stage. He ducked out a door on the south side of the building and strolled down the walkway that ran between Ford's and the Star Saloon. When he hit Tenth Street, he turned right and stepped into the barroom. Booth gulped down a whiskey and called for water to wash it down. He left the saloon and walked north a few feet to enter the front door of Ford's.

Booth climbed the curving flight of stairs to the dress circle. He was now on the same level, but opposite, the state box. The dress circle was crowded. He paused for a few minutes to let the play proceed. He was waiting for a certain scene onstage, the moment he had chosen to strike. When he started for the box again, Booth had to push his way through, much to the annoyance of patrons watching from along the back wall. One irritated army officer decided that the rude man was drunk.

Booth had attracted notice. People were now watching him closely. He took from his pocket a little bundle of calling cards. He picked one and handed the card to Forbes. The two men exchanged words that no one overheard and that Forbes never revealed. Several witnesses thought they were arguing. Then, with Forbes's apparent consent, Booth opened the door and stepped inside.

Nothing has ever been learned of the card that gained Booth admission. John Fazio speculates that it might have been a Se-

cret Service Bureau forgery of the president's handwritten instructions to admit the actor.[10] He makes a good case. Lucy Hale
thought it had been her senator father's card. But to what purpose? Forbes knew Senator Hale. He would never have mistaken
Booth for the older man. Of course, Booth's own status as a famous actor might have been enough to admit him into the presence of the stagestruck president.

It was now nearly 10:30. The Lincolns were enjoying the play,
laughing at the puns and silly jokes. Most of all, they were enjoying each other's company, happy in the renewed love they felt and
in the hopes they shared for happier times to come. Mary rested
her head against Abraham's shoulder and held his hand. "What
will Miss Harris think of me hanging on you so," she asked play-
fully. "She won't think anything about it," her husband replied in
the last words he ever spoke.[11]

The actor timed his moves carefully. He knew *Our American
Cousin* by heart from the nine back-to-back performances he had
appeared in as an extra during his days as an apprentice actor in
Richmond.[12] He had chosen a moment in act 3, scene 2, when the
only actor on the stage would deliver a crack that always brought
loud laughter. He calculated that the noise might disguise the
sound of the shot. The moment would come when the comedy's
crude but endearing protagonist, Asa Trenchard, a folksy New
England Yankee, demolished a pretentious, aristocratic English
snob with a devastating retort as she swept angrily from the stage.

Once inside the passage, Booth moved quickly. He used the
plank to bar the door. He probably looked through his little peephole before pushing in. The derringer was in his right hand, the
Bowie knife in his left. Estimates of the time that passed between
the moment he stepped into the box and his escape down the alley on his speeding horse range from a mere ten seconds to a full
minute.

The murder itself was instantaneous. Walt Whitman would
call it "one brief flash of lightning-illumination—one simple,

THE ASSASSINATION OF PRESIDENT LINCOLN,
AT FORD'S THEATRE WASHINGTON. D.C. APRIL 14TH 1865.

This Currier & Ives print provided a reasonably accurate depiction of the fatal moment.

"The Assassination of President Lincoln," Currier and Ives, lithograph, 1865. Huntington Library, pri675 (36).

fierce deed."[13] Naturally, the attentive Jim Ferguson, still waiting for U. S. Grant, saw it all through his opera glasses. He testified that Booth fired as soon as he stepped into the box: "Upon the door opening, I saw the flash of a pistol."[14] Booth had moved on Lincoln with the derringer already leveled and no doubt freshly loaded and capped. Booth poised the gun a few inches behind Lincoln's head. When the audience exploded in laughter, he squeezed the trigger. The president was looking down at the audience to his left. Or he may have been turning his head to the left because he suddenly sensed something behind him. The quarter-ounce ball punched a neat hole through his skull behind the left ear. The slug's trajectory coursed diagonally through the brain to end up somewhere behind the right eye.

The president raised his right arm convulsively from the arm rest when the bullet struck. Then his head slumped to his chest as though he were peacefully sleeping. Booth dropped the empty pistol and shifted the blade to his right hand. Immediately before firing, Booth had shouted, "Sic semper tyrannis!" The audience didn't hear him then, but they did when he shouted the same words seconds later from the front of the box. He had a few more final lines to deliver when he reached the stage.

Complete silence followed the shot—in the box, on the stage, among the audience. The laughter had not concealed the report, but no one knew what it meant. Then Henry Rathbone saw a white-faced, black-clad figure rush out of the gun smoke to his left. Though startled and confused, he threw himself on the intruder. He grappled with Booth. "Let me go or I will kill you!" shouted the assassin. "No, I will not!" Rathbone countered, grasping for the other's throat. Then he saw, raised arm's length above him, a big blade about to drive down through the top of his shoulder into his heart. Like Booth, Rathbone was a fencer. He adroitly parried the fatal thrust with an uplifted left arm. Shocking pain told him he had not escaped injury. The Bowie knife had cut deep to the bone the inside of his arm from armpit to elbow. Rathbone fell back.

Booth began to climb over the balustrade. He shouted, "Sic semper" again. Rathbone said he shouted "Freedom!" before he jumped. Others thought they heard "The South shall be free!"[15] Rather than leaping directly to the stage, Booth meant to lower himself down, reducing the fall by the length of his own height. Before he got over, Rathbone was at him again, grabbing him around the body and retaining a grip on his coat as he fell away. Booth dropped free. Rathbone ended up with only a pulled-away button in his hand. But he had thrown off the assassin's acrobatic leap.

One of Booth's spurs caught in the small blue treasury department flag. A ripping sound came as he pulled the flag down onto the stage with him. He landed off-balance, his right foot on the stage but his left leg under him, the foot folded backward. Whether he felt the pain then or only later, Booth had broken the smaller bone in his left leg—the tibia—two inches above the ankle joint. The tibia is not the leg's major weight-bearing bone. It can be just possible to walk—though with pain and difficulty— on a broken tibia.

Booth sprang readily enough to his feet. Some witnesses would say that he moved like a man with an injured leg; others thought he appeared perfectly sound. Facing the audience now, the big knife he held aloft glittered in the footlights as the actor delivered his favorite line for a third time: "Sic semper tyrannis!" He followed it with "the South is avenged!"

When the derringer's explosion rang through the theater and a dark figure suddenly shouted and tumbled over the balustrade onto the stage, many in the audience assumed it was some impromptu addition to the comedy. There was an interval of confused silence. Then Mary Lincoln began to shriek incoherently, loudly voicing sounds that were not language. The distracted woman was on her feet waving her arms over her head. "Stop that man!" Rathbone shouted as Booth began to escape downstage. Understanding finally came to the theatergoers when Clara Harris cried out, "He has shot the president!" Pandemonium replaced the confused silence. There were groans and curses, yells and screams and shouts of rage. The uproar was heard up and down the block outside. The whole audience was on its feet at once. Panicked, many made for the exits. More surged forward toward the stage. There was the sound of wooden chairs breaking. One combat veteran said, "The crowd went mad. A wilder sight I never saw in battle, even."[16] Rathbone shouted again from the box above. Mary, still shrieking loudly, put an arm around her husband's neck to keep him from sliding out of the chair.

As Booth made his way downstage toward the rear door and his waiting horse, he locked eyes with Jim Ferguson in his front-row seat. "I-I-I have done it!" the assassin told him. It was almost as though Booth was surprised that after all the anxious months of waiting and scheming, he had finally achieved his great purpose. Probably anaesthetized by the adrenaline of fear and excitement, the assassin moved swiftly for a man with a broken leg. He pushed aside actors, bowled over the conductor of the orchestra, leaped out of the back door, knocked down the boy holding his horse, mounted up, and went galloping down the alley at top speed, his steed's flying hooves throwing back gravel behind him.

As the assassin made his escape, the crowd's rage rose to a deafening roar. "Kill him! Shoot him! Lynch him! Burn the theater!" shouted men "white faced with wrath." "Strong men wept, and cursed, and tore the seats in the impotence of their anger," said one who was there.[17] Walt Whitman, who was not there, nevertheless wrote that "people burst through chairs and railings and break them up—there is inextricable terror and confusion—women faint—quiet, feeble persons fall and are trampled on—many cries of agony are heard—the broad stage fills to suffocation with a dense and motley crowd like some horrible carnival."[18]

Other voices called for calm. The mayor of Washington urged the mob to leave the building. That happened soon enough when a company of fierce soldiers burst in, with bayonets fixed to their rifles and orders to clear the theater. They were enraged by the attack on their president. "Clear out! clear out, you sons of bitches!" was among the milder commands they shouted.[19] The crowd fled.

At about the same moment Booth was sneaking up on Lin-

*Manacled after his capture, Lewis Thornton Powell was
John Wilkes Booth's muscular warrior. Powell was by no means
the dim-witted brute the newspapers made him out to be, but he
was a prolific killer of men, schooled in the ways of death by
three years of the most savage combat of the Civil War.*

coln, Lewis Powell, clean-shaven and spruced up, rang the bell of Secretary of State Seward's spacious three-story house on Lafayette Square near the White House. In his hand he held a small package wrapped in brown paper tied with string. He was wearing a spiffy tan duster, a fine pair of new boots, and black cassimere pants. The brim of his slouch hat was pulled down almost to his eyes. Concealed on his person were a .36-caliber Whitney six-shooter and another one of Booth's four "Rio Grande Camp" Bowie knives.

Nineteen-year-old William Bell, the Sewards' Black house servant, opened the door. Powell, speaking politely in a soft voice, told Bell he had come on orders from the family's physician with medicine for the badly injured man upstairs. (The ploy of passing himself off as a pharmacy clerk had been suggested by former pharmacy clerk David Herold.) Moreover, Powell told Bell, he had been strictly instructed to give the package to no one but Secretary Seward himself, in person. He had instructions about the medicine to convey.

Bell told the man in the doorway that his request could not possibly be accommodated. The recuperating patient was sleeping and couldn't be disturbed. Repeating that he must see Seward, the formidable Powell pushed past the small-framed Bell. He started up the stairs, his new boots clumping loudly on the steps. Walking backward, Bell preceded him up, telling Powell to stop and pleading with him to walk more quietly.

The thudding of the big man's boots brought Frederick Seward, dressed in his underwear, out of his second-floor bedroom at the top of the stairs. He blocked Powell's way and began arguing with him about entering his father's room. For a moment, the hulking soldier seemed to acquiesce, turning and descending a couple of steps. Then he spun around, pulled his big revolver, leveled it at the other man's head, thumbed back the hammer, and pulled the trigger. There was a loud metallic click but no explosion. Misfire—the hammer had fallen on a defective percussion cap. Rather than cocking the gun again to fire the load in the next chamber—he had five more shots—Powell used it as a bludgeon. He struck Frederick powerful blows on the top of the head, opening two gaping fractures in his skull. The victim would lie in a coma for days, his life despaired of. So forceful were the blows that the revolver broke apart. Powell pulled his Bowie knife. William Bell ran out into the street shouting, "Murder!"

Hearing the tumult, Seward's sensitive, twenty-year-old daughter, Fanny, stuck her head out of the recovery room and called for quiet. Now Powell knew where his target was. He pushed into the sick room and immediately attacked the nurse, Sergeant George Robinson, cutting him on the forehead and beating him to the floor with the pommel of the knife. Then he knocked down Fanny and set to work on the secretary of state. Raising the blade high over his head, he stabbed straight down powerfully several times but punctured only the bed. Then he slashed Seward's head. The wire and bandage contraption that held the broken jaw in place may have protected the great blood vessels in the throat. Powell then inflicted two large and ugly, but not fatal, wounds to the man's face. On Seward's left cheek, he opened a cut several inches long. The right side was completely laid open, from the eyebrow down to the jawline. Seward's whole cheek fell away from his head. His bloody tongue and his broken jaw bone were visible through the gash. The victim managed to roll off the bed, luckily ending up between the bed and the wall.

By then, the injured Sergeant Robinson was up and at the assailant. He was rewarded with several deep stab wounds to his neck and shoulder, but he continued to grapple with Powell, dragging him to the floor. The two men somehow rolled out into the hallway. Here Major Augustus Seward, the older son, joined the fight. He got cut on the forehead and hand. But Powell had had enough. He probably assumed he'd killed Seward. He broke away from the fight and went pounding down the stairs. Com-

Secretary of State William H. Seward was Lincoln's closest friend in the cabinet. After Lewis Powell carved him up with a Bowie knife, Seward never allowed photographs of the mutilated right side of his face.

ing up was a state department courier on duty in the secretary's home. Powell stabbed him in the back and then ran out into the street, shouting, "I'm mad! I'm mad!" He leaped into his saddle and trotted away, tossing the big knife in the gutter. The warrior was now unarmed and that by choice.

The would-be assassin had left behind in the blood-splattered house five wounded men but no corpses. They untangled Seward from the bloody sheets to see if he was still alive. He looked hideous, bleeding heavily from his laid-open face. But he opened his

The Bowie knife wielded by Lewis Powell in his bloody attack on Secretary of State William H. Seward and the four other men he encountered in Seward's home. Powell's assault took place at the same moment Booth was shooting the president across town at Ford's Theatre. The assassin had acquired four of these weapons with their razor-sharp blades.

Rio Grande Camp Knife. Wm. Jackson & Co., Sheaf Island Works, Sheffield, UK, steel blade, bone handle, leather sheath; 12½ inches, blade 8¼ inches. Huntington Library, George Foster Robinson Papers.

eyes and said clearly, "I am not dead, send for a surgeon, send for the police, close the house."

When physicians examined him, they agreed that the wounds were not mortal. But Seward was scarred for life. After the attack, he rarely allowed photographers to shoot the mutilated right side of his face. William Seward would serve as secretary of state under President Johnson until the second term to which Abraham Lincoln had been elected ended, in 1869. He and Gideon Welles were the only two cabinet members to serve the entirety of Lincoln's two terms.

Sergeant George Foster Robinson was naturally the hero of the hour. The government rewarded him with $5,000 cash, a hefty medal of pure gold struck by order of Congress bearing a bust portrait of Robinson on one side and a depiction of the fight in the sick room on the obverse. He was guaranteed government employment for the rest of his life. There was one more thing Robinson wanted. He asked if he could have as a memento the Bowie knife Powell had wielded in the attack on his five victims. Stanton was happy to oblige him. Like many veterans, Robinson moved to California. Many years later, when his descendants donated his papers to the Huntington Library, the fearsome weapon, still razor sharp, came with the collection. The gold medal was long gone.

For years, Powell's Bowie knife—quite out of place among autograph letters, journals, memoranda, letter books, diaries, and other paper artifacts—reposed in obscurity in the manuscript stacks of the Huntington Library. The weapon was in no way lost among that repository's incomparable holdings of many millions of documents, merely overlooked; its significance as the knife used in the Seward assassination attempt had been forgotten. Compounding the problem were the claims of a prominent assassination collector that he owned the Powell knife. About thirty years ago, during my tenure as the Huntington Library's Norris Foundation curator of American manuscripts, I stumbled on the Bowie knife and recognized it for what it was.

Powell later admitted that he actually felt remorse—an emotion unfamiliar to true psychopaths—while riding away. He hadn't intended to hurt anyone but the secretary of state himself, and now he had put down four other men, maybe killed them. He was suddenly afraid he had committed a crime rather than an act of war. His escape from that crime was no more successful than his attempt to carry it out. His horse came up lame, and he abandoned it. His duster was covered with blood. He threw it away. The next day, a citizen turned it in to the police, who immediately recognized its significance. He had lost his hat in the struggle. So universal was the wearing of hats by men in that era that the authorities simply told the public to be on the lookout for a man without a hat.

Powell set off on foot through the unfamiliar city. He was soon lost. He spent one uncomfortable night in the branches of a tree and slept another night within the spooky confines of Congressional Cemetery. Cold and hungry, he finally found his way to Mary Surratt's boardinghouse. That turned out to be the worst place in the world he could have chosen.

A LONG, UGLY NIGHT

As the audience rioted below, calls for a doctor, for water, for stimulants came from the state box. Booth's door brace worked perfectly. The harder those outside pushed against the door, the more jammed it became. Rathbone finally spotted the plank and kicked it away. The first physician to reach the stricken man was Dr. Charles Augustus Leale, a twenty-three-year-old army surgeon on duty in one of Washington's many military hospitals. He'd graduated from medical school just six weeks before. He'd come to Ford's Theatre that night just to see President Lincoln. Seated in the dress circle forty feet from the state box, he'd observed Booth enter seconds before the sound of the shot. He'd seen him go over the balustrade, hit the stage with a loud thud, and brandish his gleaming blade.

Dr. Leale found Lincoln slumped in the rocking chair, held there by his wife. The president was to all appearances a dead man. Mary Lincoln grasped Dr. Leale's hand as soon as he identified himself as a surgeon. "Oh, doctor, is he dead?" she sobbed. "Can he recover? Will you take charge of him? Do what you can for him. Oh, my dear husband!" They laid the wounded man flat on his back on the floor of the box. He was not breathing, and Dr. Leale could find no pulse.

"Remembering the flashing dagger in the hand of the assassin, and the severely bleeding wound of Major Rathbone, I assumed the President had been stabbed," Dr. Leale recalled.[1] The entire box—floor, walls, and furniture—was covered with blood, nearly all of it Rathbone's. Clara Harris herself was "saturated" with blood from head to foot. They stripped Lincoln to the waist to find the knife wound, cutting and tearing away his jacket and his white shirt. Those in the box were only the first that night to be struck by the contrast between Lincoln's lined and aged face and his athlete's body—the impressive muscles of his arms and chest hidden under his loose-fitting suits. With such strength, it's possible Lincoln really could have fought off a kidnapping attempt.

They found no wound on his body. Checking his patient's pupils, Dr. Leale saw evidence of brain injury. Lincoln's hair was matted with blood. Running his fingers over the president's head, Dr. Leale's heart sank when he found the entry wound blown through the skull by Booth's bullet. A gruesome fluid of half-clotted blood mingled with fragments of brain tissue had oozed steadily from the perfectly round hole in the back of Lincoln's head. The flow would continue until his heart stopped beating nine hours later, though it was often cut off when clots formed. At this point, Dr. Leale pried a blood clot out of the wound with his finger, relieving pressure on the brain, so that Lincoln's breathing and heartbeat resumed.

"The wound is mortal," Dr. Leale said. "It is impossible for him to recover."[2] Other physicians who had reached the box by that time concurred with the obvious diagnosis. Mary Lincoln was already hysterical with shock and grief. The little group crowded into the box agreed that it would not be proper for the president of the United States to die in a theater. The medical men, however, were sure that the dying man could never survive a bumpy carriage ride to the White House over Washington's unpaved streets. They had to find somewhere nearby.

Several men lifted him from the floor and carried him out of the theater. Dr. Leale held his head. A young lieutenant unsheathed his sword to clear a path through the crowd. The sorrowful procession left behind a trail of blood and brains. Bystanders moved aside, keeping a perfect silence. Mary Lincoln, left behind, shrieked in her anguish, "Where is my husband? Where is my husband?"

The streets of Washington, DC, had already been crowded when the soldiers drove the audience out of the theater. That day, April 14, 1865, was the four-year anniversary of the surrender of Fort Sumter. To commemorate the beginning and the victorious end of the Civil War, thousands of loyal citizens had gathered at the old fort in Charleston harbor, now battered to rubble by Union gunboats, to raise again the original American flag that had been hauled down in defeat in 1861. The crowds at the fort celebrated victory with songs, speeches, and prayers of thanks to God. Flag-bedecked warships in the harbor fired salutes. The rejoicing multitudes were all visiting Northerners or local African Americans. The white citizens of Charleston, the original secessionists, stayed in their homes, bitter and despairing.

To the people of Washington City, the Fort Sumter anniversary was a good excuse for another joyful, drunken illumination of the national capital. Celebrations ended abruptly when the crowds collided with the audience fleeing from Ford's and shouting the shocking news. "The President is shot!" This brought people out of their homes. It seemed that the whole population of Washington was surging through the city in wild excitement. "The President is killed!" they hollered.

They soon ran into a mob coming from the opposite direction shouting, "Secretary Seward is murdered in his bed."[3] The wildest rumors sped through the crowds: The entire cabinet and all their families had been slaughtered. The vice president and

General Grant were dead. Robert E. Lee was marching on the city with a reconstituted army. Assassins and conspirators lurked everywhere.

So people were packed tightly on that whole block of Tenth Street when the party carrying the president came out of the theater. They stopped in the middle of the crowd, not sure where to go. Then a man holding a candle called out from the steps of the Petersen boardinghouse across the street, "Bring him in here. Bring him in here."

They carried Lincoln up an outside staircase to a second-story doorway and down a hall to a back bedroom. They laid him on the room's single bed. In a bizarre coincidence, Booth's friend John Mathews had recently rented that very room in the boardinghouse. On March 16, Booth had paid him a visit. While they talked, the assassin had lounged across the bed on which they had just laid Abraham Lincoln.[4] Meanwhile, Mary Lincoln, collapsed on a sofa in the front parlor, had lost all semblance of control. Her screams could be heard by the crowds outside in the street. "Oh! Why didn't he kill me?" she repeated; "why didn't he kill me?"

The bed was too short for the dying man's six-foot-four frame. They laid him across it diagonally, his head and upper body propped up with pillows. After clearing the room, the doctors stripped him naked but found no other injuries. They covered him with a sheet. More physicians and dignitaries began to arrive. Dr. Leale relinquished his patient to the care of more senior medical men, including US Surgeon General Joseph K. Barnes. But the young man stayed on all through the long, ugly night's deathwatch, holding Lincoln's hand much of the time, so the dying man would know in his darkness that "he was in touch with humanity and had a friend."[5]

War Secretary Edwin Stanton and Navy Secretary Gideon Welles arrived together. Hurrying from the White House came the president's son Robert and his secretary, John Hay. Other cabinet members, congressmen, senators, government officials, and military officers made their way to the Petersen house, crowding into the little nine-by-seventeen-foot bedroom. Most stayed only a short time. Vice President Johnson stopped in briefly. Someone who knew how much Mary Lincoln detested him suggested he leave. Soldiers went away with him as bodyguards.

Gideon Welles described Lincoln's appearance when he and Stanton arrived:

> The giant sufferer lay extended diagonally across the bed which was not long enough for him. He had been stripped of his clothes. His large arms, which were occasionally exposed were of a size which one would scarce have expected from his spare appearance. His slow, full respiration lifted the clothes. His features were calm and striking. I had never seen them appear to better advantage for the first hour, perhaps, that I was there. After that his right eye began to swell and became discolored.[6]

Stanton immediately took charge, not only of the chaotic scene in the Petersen house but also of the entire United States. He made himself acting president. Taking over a room adjacent to the death chamber, surrounded by aides and couriers, the war secretary interviewed witnesses and dictated bulletins and orders that runners rushed to the nearest telegraph office. He seemed made of iron, the only man calm and decisive in the great crisis. Below the surface, however, he was deeply distraught, keeping back his tears by an effort of will. Before the night was over, he would be weeping like a child.

Stanton quickly established the identity of the assassin. His orders went out forbidding any persons from entering or leaving the city. He dispatched soldiers and detectives to hunt for Booth and his accomplices. Stanton sent news of the murder to military commanders and civil authorities throughout the nation. He mobilized the tens of thousands of men in the system of defensive forts ringing Washington, DC. He informed the press. By early morning, newspapers across the country would be turning out black-bordered extras announcing the terrible news. The papers stated that Seward and his son Frederick, as well as Lincoln, were dead.

While Stanton labored to steady the nation, Gideon Welles stayed with his president. "The room was small and over-crowded," he wrote in his diary. "The surgeons and members of the Cabinet were as many as should have been in the room, but there were many more. . . . About once an hour Mrs. Lincoln would repair to the bedside of her dying husband and remain until overcome by emotion." Welles had stood on his feet for hours. Then, just when the old man thought he would collapse from fatigue, came a reprieve: "there being a vacant chair at the foot of the bed, I occupied it for nearly two hours, listening to the heavy groans, and witnessing the wasting life of the good and great man who was expiring before me."[7]

Adding horror to the nightmare were Robert Lincoln's sobs, his mother's shrieks and wails, and her dying husband's loud, hoarse, and irregular breathing. The raw tragedy and the stifling air in the little room got to the navy secretary. He took a short walk to clear his head. "Large groups of people were gathered every few rods," Welles wrote, "all anxious and solicitous. Some-one stepped forward as I passed, to enquire into the condition of the President, and to ask if there was no hope. Intense grief exhibited itself on every countenance when I replied that the President could survive but a short time. The colored people es-pecially—and there were at this time more of them perhaps than of whites—were painfully affected."[8]

Later that day, after Lincoln had died, Gideon Welles expe-rienced a sense of unreality: "For myself, wearied, shocked, ex-hausted but not inclined to sleep, the day passed off strangely." He walked over to the White House, where Lincoln's autopsy was taking place. "There was a cheerless cold rain and everything seemed gloomy. On the Avenue in front of the White House were several hundred colored people, mostly women and children, weeping and wailing their loss. . . . They seemed not to know what was to be their fate since their great benefactor was dead, and their hopeless grief affected me more than anything else, though strong and brave men wept when I met them."⁹

The government would issue a number of reward posters for the capture of the assassins in the days that followed. A special one was boldly titled "APPEAL TO THE COLORED PEOPLE!" The accompanying text placed the blame squarely on slavery and white supremacy:

> Your President has been murdered! He has fallen by the assassin and without a moment's warning, simply and solely because he was your friend and the friend of the country. Had he been unfaithful to you and the great cause of human freedom, he might have lived. The pistol from which he met his death, though held by Booth, was fired by the hands of treason and slavery. . . . Large rewards have been offered by the Government. . . . But I feel that you need no such stimulus as this. You will hunt down this cowardly assassin of your best friend, as you would the murderer of your own father.¹⁰

The doctors were amazed that Abraham Lincoln had been strong enough to survive as long as he had, but as dawn showed gray at the windows, it was clear that the end was near. Whenever a clot formed, pressure in the brain built up, suppressing respiration and heartbeat. Lincoln approached death. When one of the surgeons removed the clot from the bullet hole, Lincoln's vital signs improved. Others described the disturbing changes Lincoln's face underwent as time passed. The right side of his face turned dark with bruising and both his eyes bulged out, the right eye with the bullet behind it more conspicuously than the left.

There were other distressing sights and sounds. "His face looked ghastly," said one who looked into the death room. "He lay with head on pillow, and his eyes, all bloodshot almost protruding from their sockets. . . . His jaw had fallen down upon his breast, showing his teeth." His breathing came as "one of the most dismal, mournful, moaning noises ever heard." "His breathing was deep," said another witness, Secretary of the Interior John Usher, "almost a snore . . . almost a moan."[11]

They continued to switch out the blood-soaked pillows under his head. When they knew that Mary Lincoln was about to enter the death room, they put a clean white towel under her husband's head to spare her the sight of the copious gore. "Kill me! Kill me! Kill me, too!" the distracted woman cried. "Shoot me, too!"[12] On her final visit, her husband's breathing stopped for a time and then suddenly started up again with a jerk and a loud, harsh snort. Shocked, Mary jumped to her feet, screamed, fainted away. Stanton stormed into the room and commanded: "Take that woman out and do not let her in again."[13]

Surgeon General Barnes sat at the head of the bed, taking Lincoln's pulse. From time to time, he put his ear down on the dying man's chest to listen to his heart. Lincoln's breathing stopped repeatedly but always started up again. Finally, it didn't. His heart "fluttered" for a few seconds and stopped forever. "He is gone," Dr. Barnes said simply. He folded Lincoln's arms across his chest. There was a complete silence of several minutes in the little room. Death had come at 7:22 on the morning of Saturday, April 15, 1865.

The minister of the Presbyterian church the Lincolns sometimes attended prayed aloud. Edwin Stanton was weeping openly. The indomitable war secretary, tears streaming down his face, spoke a few memorable words that seemed to be chiseled in stone the moment they came out of his mouth: "Now he belongs to the ages." Another witness, Stanton's stenographer, would later claim that the secretary had actually said "Now he belongs to the angels." This is unlikely. Edwin Stanton no more believed in angels than had Abraham Lincoln. He did believe in ages, though, the ages of history, for he himself had lived through an age of war.

They placed silver half dollars on Lincoln's eyes and tied up his gaping jaw. A few hours later, Andrew Johnson swore to protect and defend the Constitution and became the seventeenth president of the United States of America.

"HUNTED LIKE A DOG"

At the moment of Abraham Lincoln's death, his assassin was sleeping in the house of an accomplice in southern Maryland some thirty miles southeast of Washington. The exhausted young man would sleep away most of that morning.

All through the night before, as his victim's life was slipping away, the assassin was making his escape. Leaving the alley behind the theater, Booth pushed his little mare hard, galloping east on F Street. On his right, to the south, loomed the Capitol, its bright dome throwing the rider's shadow across the massive façade of the Patent Office. He bore south and east, headed for the Navy Yard Bridge over the Potomac's eastern branch. Maryland waited on the far shore. News of the assassination was flying out swiftly from Ford's Theatre, but Booth was outrunning it. Before he got to the bridge, he slowed to a sedate pace as though he was in no hurry at all. Still, the soldiers guarding the Washington end could see that the sweating horse had been ridden hard.

When the sergeant commanding the squad asked his name, he calmly replied "Booth." The soldier told him the bridge was closed to all traffic after 9 p.m. It was now pushing 11:00. Booth pleaded ignorance of the regulation. He added that he'd been waiting for the moon to light his way before leaving the city. The well-spoken young horseman appeared to be a gentleman. Besides, the war was over. The sergeant let Booth pass. Minutes later, the cavalier guard allowed Davey Herold to cross over, as well. On the Maryland side, Booth spurred his horse on, his way lighted by a big moon two days past full.

He left behind him a capital city, and soon an entire nation, convulsed by fear and fury. As the news flew across the country, the North was suddenly plunged into mourning. The stunningly abrupt reversal from joyous celebration to profound grief sent the popular mind reeling. With great sorrow came great anger. Anger swelled to homicidal madness. Enraged mobs, savage for revenge, were attacking anyone suspected of disloyalty. One resident of Washington foolish enough to voice approval for Lincoln's murder was shot dead on the spot. The killer walked free, a hero.

The dead man was hardly alone. Acts of vengeful vigilante violence took place throughout the country in the days that followed. Scores, perhaps hundreds, of Copperheads, Peace Democrats, supposed traitors, and other suspected insurgent sympathizers died at the hands of their infuriated fellow citizens.[1] Others barely survived beatings, mock hangings, and tar-and-featherings. Rarely did police intervene. The offices of many antiadministration newspapers were sacked. Homes of suspected secessionists were looted and burned. Soldiers surrounded Washington's Old Capitol Prison to keep the mobs from breaking in to lynch the hundreds of insurgent prisoners of war confined there.

Whole cities were draped in black. Bricks and bullets flew through the windows of houses that failed to display emblems of mourning. Stores quickly sold out of black crepe and black ribbon. There were more than a few suicides by devastated admirers of the slain president. One of Dr. Leale's hospital patients, an officer recovering from an amputation, died of shock at the news.[2]

War Secretary Edwin Stanton and his minions were not as

homicidal as the mobs of rioters, but their treatment of both suspects and potential witnesses was exceedingly harsh. Hundreds of innocent people were thrown into vile prisons on no charges, denied court appearances, and held for weeks or months. The slightest association with Booth or the events of April 14 was all it took. Authorities imprisoned the entire cast of *Our American Cousin*, everyone who worked at Ford's Theatre, and all the male members of the Ford family. Witnesses were treated as severely as suspects. Anyone whose testimony might prove valuable later was thrown in jail. The assassin's devastated family was not spared. Junius Brutus Booth was locked up for weeks. Asia Booth Clarke, heavily pregnant with twins, was spared confinement, but her house was ransacked, and a detective was assigned to watch her twenty-four hours a day, following her from room to room. "I can give you no idea of the desolation which has fallen upon us," Asia wrote a friend.[3] Imprisoned, as well, was her husband, John Sleeper Clarke, who had given the assassin's "To whom it may concern" and "Dearest Beloved Mother" letters to the press. Edwin Booth, protected by powerful friends and by his reputation as a great actor, was not molested. He went into hiding and announced to the public that he would never appear on a stage again. Even the stableman who had rented Booth his horse was jailed without charges.

The response in the South was naturally entirely different. White Southerners were almost universally delighted by the demise of the Yankee ogre. Caroline Jones, wife of a Georgia Presbyterian minister, spoke for multitudes when she hailed "the righteous retribution against Lincoln. One sweet drop among so much that is painful is that he at least cannot raise his howl of diabolical triumph over us."[4] Another Southern woman accorded "all honor to J. Wilkes Booth, who has rid the world of a tyrant and made himself famous for generations," a sentiment that neatly mirrored Booth's own.[5] He was still the boy who had once cried out, "Fame, fame! I must have fame!"[6]

If they lived under the occupation of the Union army, however, the unrepentant insurgents were exceedingly punctilious in eschewing in public even the slightest hint of celebratory words or actions. They well understood the consequences. All their discretion, however, did not always preserve them from the vengeance of the furious Northern soldiery. Some Southrons were attacked and murdered in the lawlessness that continued for weeks. At bayonet point, white Southerners were forced to decorate their homes with black emblems and enact rituals of mourning for the man they hated.[7] In contrast, the grief of Black Southerners was altogether heartfelt. They feared that their newly gained freedom would be taken from them.

Jefferson Davis, the fugitive chief of a defunct government, was in Charlotte, North Carolina, when a telegram came telling him of the assassination. The owner of the house he was staying in there reported that Davis said, "If it is to be done at all, it would be better if it were well done; and if the same had been done to Andy Johnson, the beast, and to Secretary Stanton, the job would then be complete."[8]

Later, Davis carefully crafted a sort of official statement on the death of Abraham Lincoln. He adopted a sober, statesmanlike tone in hopes of deceiving history and the political heirs of Lincoln in the administration that would decide his fate: "I certainly have no special regard for Mr. Lincoln," he said, "but there are a great many men whose end I would much rather have heard than his. I fear it will be disastrous for our people and I regret it deeply."[9] Nevertheless, there may be some who will find it difficult to believe that Jefferson Davis deeply regretted an outcome that the government he headed had worked so hard to achieve.

At their rendezvous spot some miles south of the river, Booth met up with Davey Herold, in whose company he would spend the rest of his life, all twelve days of it. They set out for Surrattsville, riding hard on the deserted country roads—riding as hard as Booth could tolerate, that is. When the adrenaline and excitement had drained away, his broken leg had become acutely painful. It hurt too much to put his foot in the stirrup, making him unsteady in the saddle, reduced to hanging on with one hand like a novice rider.

With proper treatment and time to recuperate, the fractured ankle would have been more an inconvenience than a serious injury. But for a man on the run, pursued by furies, it was an impediment of the worst sort. When Booth finally dismounted a few hours later, he found he couldn't walk unassisted. Had he not been forced to deviate so far off his escape route to seek medical care, the assassin might well have made it across the Potomac to Virginia the night of the murder as he had planned, rather than a full nine days later. That might have given him time to disappear into the Deep South. He could have hidden indefinitely among sympathetic insurgents or made his way out of the country. Mexico and Spain were the destinations he favored.

As it was, he had lost his head start on his pursuers. By the time he was fit enough to start running again, southern Maryland was swarming with US cavalry and detectives. Navy patrol boats crisscrossed the Potomac. Booth and Herold were forced to hunker down. They lost days hiding out in the woods before they could even make their first attempt to get across the river.

When the two men reached the Surratt Tavern about midnight, Herold pounded on the door to rouse the sodden John Lloyd. The first thing Davey did when he stepped inside was grab a bottle of whiskey, take a healthy slug, and hand it up to Booth, who nearly drained it. The barkeep brought out the two Spencers, the field glasses, and a box of cartridges. Herold seized one of the carbines. Booth refused the second—he couldn't carry the heavy weapon while riding with a broken leg. Then the assassin asked Lloyd if he wanted to hear some news. The man expressed indifference, but Booth could not resist boasting that "we have killed President Lincoln and Secretary Seward."[10] Lloyd said nothing. Soon Booth and Herold were headed south again. Lloyd went back inside and passed out.

Desperate for some relief from the agony of his leg, Booth could count himself lucky to know a nearby physician certain to be both helpful and discreet. One of his accomplices in the abduction scheme, the Secret Service Bureau agent Dr. Samuel A. Mudd, lived a few hours south. Booth knew the way. He'd spent a night at Mudd's house not so long ago. They got to the Mudd farm about 4:00 a.m. Herold pounded on the door while Booth waited astride his horse. Dr. Mudd came out, got Booth off his horse, and helped him stumble into the house. As soon as he put a match to the oil lamp in the front parlor, the doctor recognized his visitor, who hadn't identified himself. He would later tell interrogators that he had no idea that his patient had been John Wilkes Booth and no idea that Booth had killed the president. He was lying, and the detectives knew it.

The injured leg was so swollen, Dr. Mudd couldn't pull off the boot. He cut it away with a scalpel. He left the boot under a bed, its owner's name inked on the inside, more evidence toward the doctor's eventual conviction. Mudd considered Booth's injury a minor one. He fashioned a crude splint from pieces of a hat box. The doctor and one of his assistants made an equally crude pair of crutches from scrap wood. An old shoe was found to replace the cutaway boot. Booth borrowed a razor and shaved off his distinctive mustache.

The sun would be up before long. Booth knew it was too dangerous to travel in daylight. News of the assassination would be reaching southern Maryland just about now. Awake for nearly twenty-four hectic hours, he craved sleep. Mudd helped him up the stairs to a spare bedroom. Utterly exhausted, Booth collapsed as though clubbed from behind, unconscious when he hit the bed.

While his patient slept, Dr. Mudd rode to town on an errand

and soon learned of Lincoln's murder and the identity of the killer. He was justifiably terrified. Already involved in the underground, he had sheltered and aided the assassins, a hanging offense. Furious with Booth for putting him in such grave jeopardy, he threw the two fugitives out of his house. What he did not do was to notify any of the federal authorities—military or law enforcement—who were coursing through the area by the time he confronted Booth. Furthermore, he promised he would continue to keep quiet about their visit. That promise he would not keep.

Booth could just manage to sit a horse and hobble about on his homemade crutches after the obliging doctor splinted his leg, but he was significantly crippled. In the days to come, the pain would only grow worse as his left leg swelled and blackened. The injury had become infected. Meanwhile, cavalry patrols, federal detectives, and bounty hunters ranged throughout the Maryland countryside, their eagerness to find the fugitives sharpened by a fierce appetite for revenge and the offer of a spectacular $100,000 reward. The reward swelled as states and cities contributed more.

Dr. Mudd did render the fugitives a further service by sending them on to a reliable secret operative, one Captain Samuel Cox. Captain Cox was a wealthy planter who had owned thirty-seven slaves before freedom came. He was a firm believer in the subordination of Blacks to white supremacy and committed to enforcing it. In 1862, Cox and his overseer had dragged a rebellious enslaved man named Scroggins behind a horse. Then they subjected him to a marathon whipping session that lasted from

OPPOSITE: *"$100,000 REWARD!" The pursuers' fierce appetite for revenge against Lincoln's killer was sharpened by the huge rewards offered for him. Original photographs of Booth, Herold, and John Surratt were pasted to the top of the poster.*

Huntington Library, RB 132715.

SURRAT.   **BOOTH.**   **HAROLD.**

War Department, Washington, April 20, 1865,

 # $100,000 REWARD!

THE MURDERER

Of our late beloved President, Abraham Lincoln,

IS STILL AT LARGE.

$50,000 REWARD

Will be paid by this Department for his apprehension, in addition to any reward offered by Municipal Authorities or State Executives.

$25,000 REWARD

Will be paid for the apprehension of JOHN H. SURRATT, one of Booth's Accomplices.

$25,000 REWARD

Will be paid for the apprehension of David C. Harold, another of Booth's accomplices.

LIBERAL REWARDS will be paid for any information that shall conduce to the arrest of either of the above-named criminals, or their accomplices.

All persons harboring or secreting the said persons, or either of them, or aiding or assisting their concealment or escape, will be treated as accomplices in the murder of the President and the attempted assassination of the Secretary of State, and shall be subject to trial before a Military Commission and the punishment of DEATH.

Let the stain of innocent blood be removed from the land by the arrest and punishment of the murderers.

All good citizens are exhorted to aid public justice on this occasion. Every man should consider his own conscience charged with this solemn duty, and rest neither night nor day until it be accomplished.

EDWIN M. STANTON, Secretary of War.

DESCRIPTIONS.—BOOTH is Five Feet 7 or 8 inches high, slender build, high forehead, black hair, black eyes, and wears a heavy black moustache.

JOHN H. SURRAT is about 5 feet, 9 inches. Hair rather thin and dark; eyes rather light; no beard. Would weigh 145 or 150 pounds. Complexion rather pale and clear, with color in his cheeks. Wore light clothes of fine quality. Shoulders square; cheek bones rather prominent; chin narrow; ears projecting at the top; forehead rather low and square, but broad. Parts his hair on the right side; neck rather long. His lips are firmly set. A slim man.

DAVID C. HAROLD is five feet six inches high, hair dark, eyes dark, eyebrows rather heavy, full face, nose short, hand short and fleshy, feet small, instep high, round bodied, naturally quick and active, slightly closes his eyes when looking at a person.

NOTICE.—In addition to the above, State and other authorities have offered rewards amounting to almost one hundred thousand dollars, making an aggregate of about TWO HUNDRED THOUSAND DOLLARS.

afternoon until three in the morning. Left to die, Scroggins lived fifteen hours before perishing from his injuries.[11]

Booth and Herold left the Mudd farm in the early evening to arrive at Cox's plantation, Rich Hill, near midnight on Saturday, April 15. One full day had now passed since the assassination. On Sunday morning, America would awaken to the "Black Easter" of 1865. Hundreds of sermons preached that Easter Sunday from Northern pulpits would liken the sacrifice of the martyred president to that of the resurrected savior. It wasn't hard to figure what that made John Wilkes Booth himself: he had become the "American Judas."

An ardent secessionist, Captain Cox considered his surprise guests heroes of the expiring cause. The three men talked for hours. Their host fed them and let them rest for a time. By dawn, it was time to move on. Northern cavalry were searching the area, and the nearby Potomac was full of navy warships. Booth and Herold had to be well hidden. As much as he may have welcomed the murder of the Yankee president, Cox definitely didn't want the fugitives discovered anywhere on his nine-hundred-acre plantation. He had his overseer lead them to an obscure little clearing in the woods over his property line. The place was hidden among the thickets of a pine forest. Booth was most disgruntled at being turned out of the house. "I thought he was a man of Southern feelings," he muttered angrily. Cox did promise, however, to send another agent who would get them across the Potomac.

Booth and Herold settled down to wait in the wet and gloomy clearing. The place was most disheartening. At noon they were immured in shadowed twilight. They would have been horrified if they had known they'd be stuck there for five miserable days. Their two nervous, hungry, and noisy horses could give away the hiding place. The overseer helped Herold lead the horses down to a marsh that bordered the Potomac. They shot each in the head. The bodies, still saddled, sunk out of sight in the swamp.

Now they were without transportation. Booth obviously couldn't walk. If they succeeded in reaching the Virginia shore, they'd have to find new horses or a wagon or a buggy before they could resume their escape. At least they were well armed. Buckled around Booth's waist were two revolvers and the big Bowie knife. In his pocket he carried a five-inch switchblade. Herold had the formidable Spencer carbine slung over his shoulder on cotton cord. He had unavoidably left his revolver and Bowie knife in Atzerodt's room at the Kirkwood Hotel.

Before long, the man Samuel Cox had promised made his appearance. Thomas A. Jones was head of the Confederate Signal Service in southern Maryland, responsible for the clandestine traffic going both ways across the Potomac. "Scarcely a night passed," Jones said, "that I did not take or send someone to Virginia."[12] He had made hundreds of nighttime crossings of the big river in little boats, carrying mail, passengers, and valuable cargo like medicine and bundles of Northern newspapers. Both Jefferson Davis and Robert E. Lee studied Northern newspapers avidly, often picking up valuable intelligence. Soon Jones would be providing newspapers to John Wilkes Booth, who was desperately anxious to learn what the world thought of his deed.

Thomas Jones was friendly and reassuring. He promised he would give his life, if necessary, to protect the pair of bedraggled fugitives. He meant it. The next day, when a suspicious federal captain told him of the vast reward offered for the assassin, Jones, a poor man, remarked, "That is a great deal of money, and ought to get him, if money can do it."[13] Jones came to see them every day. He couldn't ease their misery, however. The waiting made Booth frantic. He had to get across the river. Jones told him to be patient. There were just too many searchers around the usual river crossing places to make an attempt now.

The two men suffered severely. The fear of death was ever-present. They could hardly sleep on the hard ground, wrapped in only a single blanket, through the long cold nights. Sometimes it rained on them. Booth's infected leg tormented him constantly. They were grateful for plain rations Jones brought to them, but they were always hungry. Their only drink came from a little spring nearby. As heavily as he had been drinking over the past several weeks, it is a clinical certainty that Booth experienced the miseries of withdrawal after a few days without alcohol.

The first thing the assassin had asked his new friend for was newspapers. He was horrified and astonished when Jones brought an assortment on his next visit. Worse than the cold and hunger in the wet thickets, worse even than the pain of his swollen leg, were these reports of his deed. He was stunned to read that the world, apparently even much of the South, condemned him as one of the most diabolical criminals who had ever lived. Booth could hardly believe it. He had expected to be hailed as a hero in the North and the South—America's noble Brutus. Not only was he a vicious killer, they were saying, but he was also a base coward who had shot an unarmed man from behind. (Of course, the assassin would have been comforted had he known with what wild rejoicing Lincoln's murder was privately greeted throughout the slave states.)

Booth carried a little leather-bound pocket almanac and memorandum book for the year 1864 with dated blank pages. Roiling with anguish at what he had read, he found a pencil stub and tried to vindicate himself on the blank pages:

> Until today nothing was ever thought of sacrificing to our country's wrongs. For six months we had worked to capture. But our cause being almost lost, something decisive & great must be done. . . . I struck boldly and not as the papers say. I walked with a firm step through a thousand of his friends, was stopped, but pushed on. A Col[onel] was at his side. I shouted Sic semper *before* I fired. In jumping broke my leg. I passed all his pickets, rode sixty miles that night, with the bones of

my leg tearing the flesh at every jump. I can never repent it, though we hated to kill: Our country owed all her troubles to him, and God simply made me the instrument of his punishment.[14]

Booth had actually ridden thirty miles that night, not sixty. Moreover, since the injury was a simple fracture in which the ends of the broken bone were not separated, the bone couldn't have been "tearing at the flesh at every jump." No doubt it felt like it, though. He sounded like old John Brown when he called himself an instrument of God.

They had been hiding in the woods since Easter Sunday, April 16. Not until Thursday, April 20 did Thomas Jones judge it safe to attempt a midnight crossing. It was already dark by the time Jones reached Booth and Herold. "The coast seems to be clear and the darkness favors us," he told them. "Let us make the attempt."[15] With Booth astride his horse, Jones took them to his fourteen-foot-long fishing skiff hidden among the reeds of a little creek that emptied into the Potomac. He produced a pocket compass in a little wooden box. Lighting a candle, Jones showed him how to steer the 190-degree course that would take them across to Virginia. As Jones shoved the little craft out into the stream, Booth thanked him fervently, with trembling voice: "God bless you, my dear friend, for all you have done for me. Good-bye, old fellow."[16]

It was a foggy night—good for concealment, bad for navigation. Despite the fog, Booth made a tent of his coat to hide the candle light from any searching eyes. Head beneath the folds, he tried to keep the jiggling compass needle pointed true, steering with a tiller in the stern while faithful Davey Herold did the rowing. They were fighting rough water, wind, and strong tidal currents. A southerly course of about nine miles would have taken them to their desired Virginia landfall. Yet despite the compass, they traveled mostly west.

Then, after hours on the water, Herold suddenly froze at the oars as the lights of a ship pierced the fog to their right. It could only be a Yankee patrol boat, and it was moving rapidly ahead. They sat still, hearts pounding, as the ship passed right in front of them. It came so close the men in the skiff could plainly hear the crew talking. But it was all an illusion, a lesson in relativity. The gunboat, the eighty-foot USS *Juniper*, was anchored motionless in the river. It was their little skiff that was actually moving, pushed steadily to their right and up river by wind and floodtide.

Once past the threat, now disoriented, they continued north. They made landfall in the dark, they knew not where. When dawn broke, Herold recognized the landscape. After an entire night spent crossing the Potomac to reach Virginia, they were back in Maryland and closer to Washington than before. One week had now passed since the murder. Booth proceeded to make a second and final entry in his little memo book-diary dated "Friday 21."

Booth's self-pity and self-deception stood out starkly in the lines he scribbled. He declared that if Southerners really did condemn him, it could only be because they had become "a degenerate people." When he wrote that "[a] country groaned beneath this tyranny and prayed for this end," he was saying that he had expected that most of the North would also rejoice in Lincoln's death. He had been sure that the letter he had left to be published in the *National Intelligencer* would justify him and clear him of all reproach, but apparently the government had suppressed it. (It never occurred to him that John Mathews had destroyed it.) If the world only understood his motives, Booth was certain, he would stand vindicated and be applauded by all. He considered returning to Washington to explain himself to what he believed would be a receptive audience. Such are the delusions of a fanatic. He obviously would have been lynched before he could have opened his mouth. He wrote in his little book:

> After being hunted like a dog through swamps, woods, and
> last night being chased by gun boats till I was forced to return

wet cold and starving, with every mans hand against me, I am here in despair. And why; For doing what Brutus was honored for, what made [William] Tell a Hero. And yet I for striking down a greater tyrant than they ever knew am looked upon as a common cutthroat. My action was purer than either of theirs. One, hoped to be great himself. The other had not only his countrys but his own wrongs to avenge. I hoped for no gain. I knew no private wrong. I struck for my country and that alone. A country groaned beneath this tyranny and prayed for this end. Yet now behold the cold hand they extend to me. . . . Yet I cannot see any wrong except in serving a degenerate people. The little, the very little I left behind to clear my name, the Govmt will not allow to be printed. So ends all. For my country I have given up all that makes life sweet and Holy, brought misery on my family, and am sure there is no pardon in Heaven for me since man condemns me so. . . . To night I will once more try the river with the intent to cross, though I have a greater desire to return to Washington and in a measure clear my name which I feel I can do. I do not repent the blow I struck. I may before God but not to man. I think I have done well, though I am abandoned, with the curse of Cain upon me. When if the world knew my heart, *that one* blow would have made me great, though I did desire no greatness. . . . To night I try to escape these blood hounds once more. Who who can read his fate. God's will be done. I have too great a soul to die like a criminal. Oh may he, may he spare me that and let me die bravely.[17]

They had pulled the boat into a little inlet. There they hid out for two days and a night. For some reason, they did not make another try on the night of the morning they landed on the Maryland shore, Friday, April 21. Perhaps they were too exhausted. Perhaps too many gunboats were plying the river. They ventured out the following night. This time they made it. When they stepped ashore on Sunday, April 23, they were at last in Virginia. Booth's spirits rose. The Old Dominion, he was sure, would accord him a hero's welcome—medical care, food, clean clothes, rest, and protection, as well as a generous measure of gratitude and adulation. He was in for more disappointment.

THE LAST ACT

Booth and Herold had been fortunate to land on the Virginia shore not far from the home of the next contact Thomas Jones had given them. Mrs. Elizabeth Quesenberry was a well-born widow whose place was a stop on the clandestine mail route. Herold made his way to her house and asked for help for his brother, a soldier with a wounded leg. By now, Booth and Herold naturally looked like a couple of bums, unshaven, their hands and faces filthy, hair standing on end, clothes tattered and besmirched with mud.

Mrs. Quesenberry was inclined at first to send the smelly stranger on his way. Then, moved by sympathy for a soldier hurt in Dixie's holy crusade, she thought better of it. She sent for her friend Thomas Harbin, the Secret Service Bureau's principal operative in the area. He was camping nearby, so he appeared almost immediately. John Wilkes Booth and Thomas Harbin had met several times in late 1864 and early 1865 to discuss the planned abduction.

Harbin knew David Herold as well, knew him to be a follower of Booth. So the spy was stricken with fear the moment he recognized the grubby young man. Herold's presence could only mean that the assassin himself was nearby. And J. Wilkes Booth was nothing but a walking death sentence. He could send anyone suspected of helping him straight to the gallows. Nevertheless, Harbin was still loyal to the lost cause. He followed Herold back to Booth's hiding place.

Thomas Harbin enlisted a poor farmer, one of his underground helpers named William Bryant, to provide a couple of horses to carry Booth and Herold to their next destination. Bryant rode with them to bring his horses back. Harbin went along part way on his own horse. On the ride, Booth told him that "he had no regret. He was not remorseful, rather took a rude joy in his act."[1] Booth said he aimed to reach the last major rebel army in the field, General Joseph E. Johnston's Army of Tennessee in North Carolina. From there, he would make his way to Mexico. Spain might be the next stop. He knew Spain had no extradition treaty with the United States. And, of course, Lucy Hale was there.

The spymaster pitied the doomed young man. He told Booth he would never get away. "The Government is hunting you on all sides," he warned. "They will capture you or shoot you." "They will never capture me," Booth countered. He would kill himself first, he vowed, patting a revolver.[2] Thomas Harbin then left the others, turning off for home.

Their destination was the home of the genteel Dr. Richard H. Stuart, an ardent secessionist and enslaver who had done all he could to further the cause. Now, however, like his cousin Robert E. Lee, he was satisfied that the war was definitively lost and over. He had no more help to give. When he learned who his unexpected visitors were, he became mightily alarmed by the grim consequences of harboring Lincoln's killer. He ordered them off his place peremptorily. William Bryant had brought them, and Dr. Stuart commanded Bryant to take them away again. Booth was outraged and baffled by Stuart's reception. It hardly comported with the solicitude and admiration he had expected to receive from Virginians. Dr. Stuart did condescend to suggest that William Lucas, a free-born Black who lived nearby, might be able to put them up for the night.

As it turned out, the hapless Will Lucas had no choice in the matter. Booth pushed his way into the man's one-room shack, announced that he was sleeping there, and threatened him with his Bowie knife when he objected. "Old man, how do you like that?" he asked, brandishing the big, shiny blade. Lucas admitted that he didn't like it at all. The blade was still stained with Henry Rathbone's blood. Booth also announced that he was taking Lucas's wagon and team in the morning to continue his flight south. Terrified of the intruders, Lucas and his sick wife spent a sleepless night outside on their porch.[3] It was just as well. Booth wouldn't have slept in the same room with Black people anyway.

In the morning the parties came to a more satisfactory arrangement. Booth paid William Lucas a generous twenty-five dollars for the one-night rental of his house. Then, for an additional twenty dollars, his twenty-year-old son, Charlie, would hitch the team to the wagon and drive them ten miles down to Port Conway. There they would cross the Rappahannock River and continue their flight south. They set out early on the morning of Monday, April 24. Charlie Lucas left them at Port Conway. There they found themselves stymied again. The man who could take them across the Rappahannock was in the middle of the river setting out his fishing nets. He didn't intend to miss the bountiful spring shad run. It came only once a year. He wouldn't ferry them over until he was finished.

Then the arrival of three horsemen changed everything. Booth and Herold must have been overjoyed to see that the riders wore rebel cavalry uniforms. The garrulous Herold was first to approach them. He spoke to a trooper named Willie Jett, introducing himself as David E. Boyd, late of the Army of Northern Virginia. The man on crutches was his brother, John William

Boyd (J. W. B.), wounded at the siege of Petersburg. For some reason, Herold assumed that the three cavalrymen, all of whom were younger than he, were determined to continue fighting. He asked if they were headed south to join Johnston's army. Were they on their way to Mexico? He and his brother wanted to join them. Like almost all their comrades, however, these veterans were done fighting. General Robert E. Lee and their own commander, Colonel John S. Mosby, had settled the matter to their satisfaction by surrendering and accepting Yankee paroles. It was all over. They themselves were on their way to turn themselves in and be paroled.

Willie Jett distrusted the two strangers. They didn't seem like soldiers. The man on crutches was wearing a beat-up business suit. Rebels didn't carry Spencer carbines like Herold's; they couldn't get ammunition for them. This eagerness to fight on made no sense. "I cannot go with any man that I do not know anything about," Jett said. "Who *are* you?" There was nothing for it, Herold decided. "We are the assassinators of the President," he replied nervously. "Yonder is J. Wilkes Booth, the man who killed Lincoln."[4] Astonished, Jett called over the only officer in his little party, Lieutenant Mortimer Ruggles, the twenty-year-old son of a Southern general. Booth crutched his way over to join them.

"I suppose you have been told who I am?" Booth asked. He straightened up, put a hand on the butt of one of his revolvers and defiantly declared, "Yes, I am John Wilkes Booth, the slayer of Abraham Lincoln, and I am worth just $175,000 to the man who captures me."[5] Like Thomas Jones, the young cavalrymen valued their honor more than the enormous award, millions in today's money. They assured the assassin they would never take "blood money." Booth was a hero to them. Their commander, Colonel Mosby, a man they revered, had said when he heard of the assassination, "By God I could take that man in my arms."[6] "We will help you," Lieutenant Ruggles said. "We will take you across the river." Jett promised, "I want to do the best I can for you." "God bless you," breathed John Wilkes Booth.[7] This was the kind of response he had longed for ever since he fled Washington.

It was obvious to Mosby's rangers that Booth was suffering intense pain from his leg and powerful fear from the great danger he was in. The courage with which he bore his suffering impressed them. Lieutenant Ruggles recalled that "the coolness of the man won our admiration, for we saw that he was wounded, desperate, and at bay. His face was haggard, pinched with suffering, his dark eyes sunken, but strangely bright."[8]

They set Booth up on a horse, and they all ferried across the Rappahannock River to the little colonial town of Port Royal, on the south bank opposite Port Conway. Willie Jett, a local boy, took charge of finding a refuge for the fugitives. After asking around in Port Royal, he decided to try at Richard Garrett's farm, about three miles south of town. Two of Garrett's sons had served in the Southern army and recently came home safe. He should be glad to take in a wounded survivor. All agreed it would be best for Booth to maintain his identity as John W. Boyd, late of the Army of Northern Virginia.

They rode south, five men on three horses. When they arrived that afternoon about three o'clock, Richard Garrett gladly welcomed the injured soldier to stay and rest a day or two. Mosby's cavalrymen rode off. They had promised to get Booth and Herold across the Rappahannock. That done, they considered their obligation fulfilled. The fugitives were now Richard Garrett's problem. Of course, the unfortunate farmer had no idea how big a problem they were. He hadn't even heard of Lincoln's assassination yet.

Despite his anxiety and pain and his unwashed condition, Booth proved to be a delightful houseguest at first. He had always loved little girls. Among his nine children, Richard Garrett had three of them, aged three to ten. Booth played happily with the girls in the front yard. He showed them his JWB tattoo and told them he had inked it himself. He delighted in amazing them with his magic powers as he made the magnetic needle of his compass swing by bringing the steel blade of a pocket knife near it. The girls were smitten by the handsome stranger. Young as they were, they would remember the encounter the rest of their lives, long into the twentieth century.

Despite all the setbacks and the huge manhunt, Booth apparently still thought he had a chance to get clean away. Over his mantle, Garrett had hung a giant school map of the United States. Booth asked that it be taken down so he could study it. He made notes on a piece of paper and traced a line in pencil from his location in Virginia all the way across the continent to Mexico. Years later, one of Garrett's sons sold the map with Booth's itinerary to a collector.

Booth ate with the family that evening. News of the assassination had just reached them, and the Garretts were talking excitedly about it. When Annie, an older Garrett daughter, speculated that the assassin had been paid a big price to kill Lincoln, Booth spoke up for the first time. "No, Miss, it is my opinion he was not paid," he said. "He did it for notoriety's sake." When someone mentioned the gigantic fortune offered as a reward, now up to $140,000, Booth said he was surprised it wasn't $500,000.[9]

He spent the night in the bedroom of Jack and Will Garrett, the two older sons who had just returned from the war. The brothers shared a bed and gave the injured man the other for himself. Davy Herold had gone into the nearby town of Bowling Green with the Mosby men. He desperately needed a new pair of shoes. It was the only night during the twelve-day escape that Booth and Herold did not sleep in the same place. History does not reveal whether suitable footwear was acquired, but it is known that Herold and the three Mosby troopers found time to visit a local brothel kept by an accommodating woman and her four adult daughters.[10]

Events the next day soon convinced the Garretts that taking

in the wounded soldier may not have been such a good idea after all. Booth himself was most content. Rising late, he was refreshed by his first good night's sleep in weeks, the first night in a bed since Dr. Mudd's house nine days before. He would have been happy to stay with the Garretts forever. He reclined indolently on a bench on the porch of the farmhouse, drowsing and smoking a pipe he had borrowed. Jack and Will Garrett stopped by to chat with him as they went about their chores.

Then came the sound of approaching horses. Booth struggled to his feet, clearly alarmed. He told Jack to get his weapons from the bedroom upstairs. When young Garrett didn't move fast enough, Booth shouted, "You go and get my pistols!" As the man buckled on the heavy gun belt, Jack Garrett could only think that John W. Boyd was behaving like a guilty man. The riders on the road were only the Mosby men bringing back David Herold. Davey appeared, walking up the lane to the farmhouse with the carbine still slung over his shoulder.

He had enjoyed yesterday's visit to the whorehouse so much that he had gone back again that morning. The whores would soon be telling the federal detectives all about it. Booth and Herold were happy to be reunited. Herold asked Jack Garrett if he could also spend that night in the farmhouse with Booth. Jack didn't want either one of them to stay now. He put them off by saying the decision belonged to his absent father.

Then came the sound of approaching horses once more. This time they were coming at a gallop. It was the two Mosby rangers again. Lieutenant Ruggles shouted out a warning that forty Yankee cavalrymen were headed their way. The rangers fled. Booth and Herold hastened to hide themselves in a thicket behind the house. The Yankees pounded south, passing in plain sight and a cloud of dust on the road about a quarter mile from the Garrett home.

Now Jack understood. The strangers were wanted men, and judging from the size of the squad pursuing them, the Yankees considered their capture important. When Booth and Herold emerged from hiding, Jack ordered them to leave at once. He knew the Yankees had an unpleasant habit of burning down houses that concealed fugitives.

There remained the practical problem: Booth couldn't walk. They couldn't leave the Garrett place without transportation. Jack realized reluctantly that he was going to have to take them himself. Now it was getting dark, but Jack agreed to take them south to Orange, the county seat, in a farm wagon first thing in the morning. He refused to let them sleep in the house, however. They'd have to bunk in the nearby tobacco barn. Booth was offended and angry, as usual.

Richard Garrett had returned home. By now the father and his two older sons had become thoroughly frightened by the presence of these heavily armed intruders. They were sure the men would try to steal their horses while the family slept. Herold had asked earlier about buying horses. So when Booth and Herold bedded down in the tobacco barn, Will quietly locked the door from the outside with a big iron padlock. Still fearful for their horses, Jack and Will wrapped themselves in blankets and settled down for the night to keep watch in a corncrib next to the barn.

If the four men got any sleep in their uncomfortable berths, neither they nor anyone else at the Garrett place slept after thirty horsemen from the Sixteenth New York Cavalry Regiment came charging down the lane. It was about 2:30 in morning. The family dogs barked wildly. The galloping troopers hallooed and shouted back and forth exultantly. Their sabers and gear clattered as they came. The men in the tobacco barn and the corncrib heard them surround the house. The detectives dismounted, stomped over the porch, and began pounding on the door as though they meant to break it down. Booth and Herold tried to make a break for it but found that they were locked in.

For some time now, Stanton's searchers had been concentrating on southern Maryland. They still had no reason to think

Booth had made it across the Potomac to Virginia. Yet the assassin's trail had gone cold after the last reported stop at Samuel Cox's house. Tracking that trail hadn't been hard at first. Lincoln's avengers in uniform were angry and violent, lacking any concern for the legal rights of those they interrogated. Their investigatory technique relied heavily on the death threats they seemed perfectly willing to carry out.

A few such threats persuaded tavern keeper John Lloyd to talk freely about Booth and Herold's midnight visit. The authorities had the choice of treating Lloyd as a witness or putting him on trial for his life as an accomplice. Either way, he'd be locked up. They saved his neck when they decided he'd make a valuable witness.

Dr. Samuel A. Mudd was not so lucky. After lying, prevaricating, changing his story, repeatedly contradicting himself, and then being caught out cold when his wife told an entirely different story, he finally confessed to setting Booth's leg. He continued to insist he hadn't recognized his patient. No one believed him. They put him on trial for his life. Mudd was convicted. He was fortunate enough to be sentenced to life at hard labor rather than to the hanging his complicity actually merited.

Subjected to the same harsh treatment, the two tough spies who had given Booth the most help—Samuel Cox and Thomas Jones—uttered not a helpful word. Of course, they were thrown into prison. The government had no hard evidence against them, however. The authorities reluctantly let them go after two months in filthy, vermin-infested little cells. The federals never caught Thomas Harbin. He fled into foreign exile for years.

Back in Washington, Colonel Lafayette C. Baker commanded the National Detective Police, the predecessor of the US Secret Service. He reported directly to War Secretary Stanton, who had put him in charge of the search for John Wilkes Booth. On Monday, April 24, a report came to the War Department that two men had been seen crossing on the Potomac on Easter Sunday,

April 16. (That was the day Booth and Herold had gone into hiding in the woods.) The men seen crossing the river were, in fact, Thomas Harbin and one of his agents.

Misleading as it may have been, the reported sighting galvanized Colonel Baker. He was sure the two men had been Booth and Herold. All his men were still on the hunt in southern Maryland. He quickly organized a new ad hoc unit and sent it by steamship down the Potomac to the Northern Neck of Virginia, the broad peninsula formed by the Potomac and Rappahannock Rivers that the two fugitives had just crossed.

Colonel Baker and his detectives—indeed, everyone else pursuing the assassin—were spurred on by more than just the purest patriotism. None of them had lost sight of the enormous monetary reward. They had no desire to share the prize with competitors. This naturally hampered cooperation. The hunters were all inclined to hoard and hide any leads they got. Colonel Lafayette Baker, who had seen the telegram by accident, did not share with anyone the report of the men sighted crossing the Potomac. Though he never left Washington, Baker managed to secure for himself a substantial portion of the reward.

The new search party was under the overall command of the chief of Baker's detectives, Everton Conger, a wounded veteran who held the rank of lieutenant colonel. Lieutenant Edward Doherty commanded the troopers from the Sixteenth New York Cavalry Regiment. Colonel Baker also sent along his cousin Luther Byron Baker, another of the National Detective Police officers. The senior noncommissioned officer was Sergeant Boston Corbett, a fearless fighter and a very strange character indeed.

The pursuers knew that the fugitives had to cross the Rappahannock River. The best place to do that was Port Conway. So when the men and their horses came ashore from the army transport ship, that's where they headed. Witnesses that the federals encountered in Virginia proved more willing to talk to the Yankees than had their counterparts across the river. Without being unduly threatened or abused, William Rollins, the Port Conway fisherman, and his wife, Bettie, gave the searchers all the information they needed to find Booth. Shown a photograph of the assassin, the couple confirmed he had crossed the Rappahannock the day before. They added that he shaved off his mustache, confirming Dr. Mudd's report.

Most valuable of all, Bettie Rollins told them that one of the cavalrymen the fugitives had left with was a local man named Willie Jett. Furthermore, she told them that Jett was likely staying in a hotel in nearby Bowling Green. The eighteen-year-old trooper was courting the sixteen-year-old daughter of the hotel's owner.[11]

It was about midnight by the time Conger's men surrounded the Star Hotel in Bowling Green. An employee took them to the room where Willie Jett was sound asleep. Screwing the muzzle of his Colt .44 firmly into the boy's ear, Colonel Conger inquired as to whether he might presume to solicit Private Jett's gracious assistance in a matter of some little importance. The young man replied that he was quite ready to take them straight to Booth. He asked only that he be placed under arrest so that his neighbors wouldn't think he was willingly helping the Yankees. Willie Jett rode at the head of the party with the detectives on the way to the Garrett farm.

The pounding on his front door had brought out old man Garrett. He opened up dressed in his nightshirt and holding a candle. The detectives demanded Booth and Herold. Confused, half-asleep, and frightened, Garrett stammered evasively that he thought the fugitives might be hiding in the woods. The detectives were having none of that. They dragged him into the front yard, bound his arms, threw a noosed rope over a tree limb, and prepared to give him a half-lynching. A few moments of strangling at the end of a rope often won the cooperation of reluctant witnesses after they were finally lowered to the ground.

Jack Garrett appeared out of the darkness. "Don't injure father," he begged. "I will tell you about these men. They are in the barn."[12] Will appeared, too. Guns were immediately shoved into both brothers' faces. The barn was quickly surrounded. Though Booth urged him to freeze, Herold continued to stumble around inside, still looking for a way out and making plenty of noise in the process. There was no point in pretending he wasn't there. Booth answered when Luther Baker yelled at him to come out. Thus began a shouted conversation that would go on for some time.

Booth refused to come out. Baker then ordered Jack Garrett to go into the barn and get the wanted man to surrender. The padlocked door was opened. Jack refused to enter. Booth would surely shoot him, he objected. Baker countered that he'd shoot him himself and burn down the whole farm if he didn't obey. Jack fearfully entered the pitch-dark barn. He could see nothing. A form dimly appeared before him—Booth. He cursed the young man for betraying him. Jack tried to persuade the wanted man to give up. The barn was surrounded, he said, and escape was impossible. Furious with a host he considered treacherous, Booth leveled a revolver. As much as Jack may have feared the detectives, at that point he feared Booth a good deal more. He ran out of the barn and refused to go back in.

Then Baker shouted that if the men inside didn't come out, he'd set fire to the barn. Booth asked for time to consider, and Baker agreed. After time had passed, Baker renewed his threat. "This is hard," Booth shouted back. "We are guilty of no crime. If I have done anything, I did for the good of my country. At least I fancied so." Then the cornered assassin made a fantastic proposal. "I am a cripple and alone. Give me a chance for my life. Be fair and give me a show. Draw off your men fifty yards, and I will come out and fight you."[13] Booth had no intention of dying with a noose around his neck like old John Brown. He wanted the Yankees to consummate the suicide he had vowed to commit.

But the detectives meant to take him alive.

David Herold wanted to give himself up. Booth wouldn't let him. By now, Everton Conger had run out of patience with his subordinate's negotiations. As Luther Baker continued to argue with the assassin through the barn's front door, Conger went around back and, reaching through a gap in the wall, set fire to a pile of hay inside. When he saw the flames, Herold panicked. "I am going," he said; "I don't intend to be burnt alive." Booth cursed him. "Get away from me, you damned coward."[14] Imploring the besiegers to hold their fire, Herold came to the door, sticking his hands out first to show he was unarmed. He was seized roughly, dragged across the barnyard, and tied to a tree.

By now the fire was blazing. The dried-out planks and timbers of the old building went up almost as fast as the straw. Tobacco barns were designed for drying the freshly harvested leaves before the product was crammed into hogsheads for shipment. Wide gaps were left between the planks of the walls for ample air flow. So when the fire lit up the interior, the cavalrymen could clearly see Booth through the gaps in the walls. The flames at his feet illuminated the star actor like the footlights of the last act.

Sergeant Boston Corbett saw him clearly. He had been turned down twice when he had volunteered to go in alone to get Booth. "It was time the man was shot," he had told his lieutenant.[15] That time was now. Corbett rested his left forearm against the wall. He steadied his revolver on the arm and took careful aim. Booth was moving awkwardly toward the door, away from the fire behind him. Leaning against one of the crutches, he gripped the Spencer carbine in one hand and a revolver in the other. Then Boston Corbett fired.

The .44-caliber conical bullet plowed through Booth's neck from right to left and exited to hit the barn's opposite wall with a thud. The slug partially severed Booth's spinal cord and shattered two of his cervical vertebrae. In that instant, he was para-

*The burning straw at his feet flared like the footlights of the last
act, and, so lighted, the star actor was an easy target when a veteran
sergeant fired a .44-caliber bullet through his neck, severing his
spinal column. He died two hours later.*

lyzed from the neck down. He dropped like a puppet with its
strings cut. The two detectives rushed into the burning barn and
grabbed Booth as soon as he hit the floor. "Why did you shoot
him?" Baker asked Conger. "I didn't shoot him," Conger said.
"He shot himself." But Baker had been watching Booth intently
at the moment he was hit. He insisted the man hadn't shot himself. They dragged him out of the flaming barn.

Sergeant Corbett eventually came forward to report that he
was the one who had shot Booth. When Lieutenant Doherty an-

grily demanded why he had fired without orders, the sergeant replied, "God Almighty told me to." He was telling the truth. God often spoke to him. Everyone knew he was crazy. Before the war, troubled by unchaste thoughts, Corbett had castrated himself with a pair of scissors. Comrades tolerated him, however, since he was such a deadly fighter. He had saved the day on more than one occasion. During his battlefield heroics, he was wont to shout "Glory to God! Amen!" each time he killed an enemy soldier.

Detectives Conger and Baker were surprised to discover that Booth was still alive. He was trying to talk but able to bring forth only the faintest whisper. Conger leaned over and put his ear to the dying man's mouth. Booth's lips moved. The detective repeated back the words to make sure he had heard correctly. "Tell mother I die for my country." The old tobacco barn had become a tower of flame reaching above the treetops. The heat was so intense they had to move Booth up to the porch of the Garrett house.

Booth lived about two more hours in intense agony. "Kill, kill me," he begged repeatedly. "We don't want to kill you," said Everton Conger. "We want to get you well." That would never happen. Unable to breathe properly, Booth was slowly suffocating, drowning in open air. His lips turned blue. The Garrett women did all they could for him. Even the detectives were kind. Very near the end, just as the first rays of the sun were touching the treetops, the dying man whispered that he wanted to see his paralyzed hands. Baker held them up. "Useless, unless—" was the actor's final line. Booth soon stiffened, threw back his head, and expired with a final gasp.

It was Wednesday, April 26, 1865. Twelve days of flight had brought the assassin less than one hundred miles from Ford's Theatre. Silence prevailed among the men standing around the corpse. Suddenly, they realized how tired they were. They'd been going for two days without rest. Now they were swaying on their feet from fatigue. Still, there was more to be done. The men at Garrett's farm had the news all America had been waiting to hear.

The troopers rolled up the body in a rough wool army blanket. One of the Garrett women stitched it closed. Booth's feet stuck out the end. The cavalrymen conveyed their precious cargo by wagon to the steamboat that would carry it on to Washington, DC. The dead man's blood dripped down from the wagon bed, forming dark lozenges in the dust of the road. Chief Detective Everton Conger had gotten to Washington some hours before the party conveying the corpse. He had left before Booth died. Conger naturally wanted to be the first to report to Secretary of War Stanton. As proof, or as trophies, he brought the war secretary Booth's revolvers and knives, his little diary, and his compass. Little carte de visite photographs of five young women were stuck in the diary. Four were actress friends. The fifth was Lucy Hale. Before long, former senator John P. Hale would ask for a private, confidential meeting with President Johnson. Not a word of his daughter's involvement with the assassin subsequently appeared in the press.

Colonel Conger had also brought along Sergeant Boston Corbett so that the war secretary himself could pass judgment on the overhasty killing that had taken place early that morning. Corbett was a small man of five four who wore his hair long and parted down the middle in the manner of Christ in a medieval altarpiece. With the little trooper standing rigidly at attention before him, Stanton intoned: "The traitor is dead. The patriot lives; he has spared the country expense, continued excitement and trouble. Release the patriot."[16] Corbett walked free to serve his God.

RECKONINGS

Though inventive minds would spin fantastic conspiratorial mythologies predicated on the fallacy that the man killed in the burning barn had not actually been John Wilkes Booth, the assassin was as dead as his victim. The government of the United States, personified by the iron-willed Edwin Stanton, was absolutely determined to bring to justice the murderer of President Lincoln, and the government made absolutely certain that the dead man in the army blanket was really Booth.

Back in Washington, on a warship anchored in the river, the assassin's body was autopsied and identified beyond doubt by witnesses who had known the man. Probably few were moved to pity by the autopsy's concluding sentence: "Paralysis of the entire body was immediate, and all the horrors of consciousness of suffering and death must have been present to the assassin during the two hours he lingered."[1]

Then, to assure that the assassin's grave would not become a rebel shrine, Stanton ordered the corpse secretly buried beneath the floor of a locked room in the Washington Arsenal. He pocketed the only key. In 1869, President Andrew Johnson finally agreed to release the body to the Booth family. At a Baltimore undertaking parlor, the decomposed cadaver in the old ammunition crate was identified again, this time by his brother Joseph, theater friends, and a dentist who had filled one of Booth's teeth. His old mother and his sister Rosalie sat by, weeping. The assassin's head, severed in the 1865 autopsy, was passed from hand to hand, and everyone agreed that this was all that remained of John Wilkes Booth. They bundled the wreckage into a fancy coffin and buried it in an unmarked grave in the Booth family plot in Baltimore's Greenmount Cemetery. There he remains to this day. His resting place was never a secret, however. For years after the war, his grave was piled high with flowers on Confederate Memorial Day.

Though the capture of the assassin himself had consumed twelve days of intense effort by hundreds of searchers, his accomplices fell into the government's hands in no time. Only the lucky John Surratt escaped. Detectives had called at Mary Surratt's boardinghouse shortly after the assassination. She admitted to having seen Booth three times that day. Certain of her guilt, they held off arresting her, watching her house on the off chance that Booth might come by again. Two days after Lincoln died, the detectives returned to arrest everyone in the house. The unhappy woman said she'd been expecting them. Her daughter wept and wailed. The devotedly Catholic Mary Surratt asked only that she be allowed to kneel on the floor to pray before they took her away. It would be the last moment of freedom she ever experienced.

As she prayed, there was a knock at the door. Who could it be but Lewis Powell? He'd found his way to the one place in Washington where he was sure he'd find help and shelter. The detectives drew their guns. Powell's clumsy lies got him nowhere. He was quickly recognized as the bloodthirsty brute who had knifed five men at the secretary of state's home.

Atzerodt had fled north. He was supposed to go south, instead, to meet up with Booth and Herold in Maryland and ferry them across the Potomac. Terrified when he learned of Lincoln's death, all he wanted to do was get as far away as he could. Earlier that night, Atzerodt had aroused the suspicion of a stableman from whom he had rented a horse. Fearful that the scruffy character meant to steal the mount, the man followed him. Atzerodt, as ordered by Booth, made his way to Vice President Johnson's hotel, the Kirkwood House, arriving at ten o'clock, just before Booth and Powell were both about to spring their attacks. He tethered the horse and went into the hotel. He had that morning rented room 126, and it was there that Davey Herold had stashed his revolver and Bowie knife. The stableman waited outside. After half an hour, Atzerodt came out of the hotel and rode away.[2]

We may speculate that Atzerodt met Herold at the Kirkwood House. (As we have seen, in this iteration, Herold was not with Powell at Seward's house as the traditional narrative has it.) Booth had ordered the two men to kill the vice president. Atzerodt had refused when Booth had assigned the murder to him just hours before. Only reluctantly had he agreed to back up Herold in the attempt. It seems reasonable to suppose that Atzerodt aborted the whole scheme by preventing Herold from retrieving his pistol and knife from the locked hotel room. He claimed he didn't have the key with him. Unarmed, Herold was stymied and perhaps even relieved. Herold went over the bridge to rendezvous with Booth.

For his part, Atzerodt turned in his rented horse. Then he rode a streetcar aimlessly through the city. An acquaintance who encountered him in the vehicle testified that the German was so frightened he was actually trembling. Atzerodt subsequently checked into the Pennsylvania House, slept a few hours, and left early enough to dodge paying the bill. In Georgetown, he pawned the Colt revolver Booth had given him for ten dollars. He was now unarmed, since he had already thrown his Bowie knife into the street, where it was found and turned over to the police. But at least he now had money for drink, so essential to his well-being.

He was headed for Montgomery County, Maryland, north of the capital, where he had family. All roads out of the city were barricaded by soldiers and detectives. Stanton had ordered that no one be allowed to leave the capital without being interrogated. There was a long line of backed up vehicles when Atzerodt got to the checkpoint he needed to pass. As he waited, he bought liquor for the soldiers manning the barricade. Despite the early hour, they were glad to accept. He also treated a teamster, who returned the favor by giving Atzerodt a lift. When they got to the checkpoint, the guards questioned the teamster but not his passenger. The next day was Easter. He was welcomed at the home of a family friend in Germantown. There Atzerodt enjoyed an Easter Sunday dinner with other guests. He foolishly tried to impress them by flaunting details of the assassination only an insider could have known. When someone asked if the rumors that General Grant had also been killed were true, Atzerodt spoke up: "If the man that was to follow him followed him, it is likely to be so."[3] One of the other guests was a Union army informant. Atzerodt was arrested at four in the morning a few days later while sleeping at his uncle's nearby house.

Samuel Arnold was quickly marked for arrest. Booth had left a jacket behind in his room at the National Hotel. In the pockets were his bankbook and the letter Arnold had written him on March 27 signed "SAM."[4] Arnold had begged him to destroy the letter. The only motive Booth had for leaving that evidence behind was to implicate Arnold. Booth had not forgiven his desertion.

Arnold soon was arrested at the store he worked in near Fortress Monroe and brought back to Washington in chains aboard an ironclad warship. Mike O'Laughlen had gone to ground in his parents' Baltimore home. Named as an accomplice in the newspapers, he bowed to the inevitable and turned himself in. Dr. Samuel Mudd and the innocent Ford's Theatre handyman, Edman Spangler, were already in custody.

These eight prisoners—the accused conspirators David Edgar Herold, Lewis Thornton Powell, George Andrew Atzerodt, Dr. Samuel Alexander Mudd, Mary Elizabeth Surratt, Samuel Bland Arnold, Michael O'Laughlen, and Edman Spangler—would soon be the defendants in the trial by a military tribunal.

While the search for his killer was still ongoing, Abraham Lincoln was given the most gigantic, prolonged, and elaborate send-off America has ever witnessed. This extravagant, seventeen-hundred-mile, fourteen-day movable funeral has itself been the subject of entire books. The event offered a display of national unity in grief such as the nation had never seen before and would not see again. Lincoln had once joked about the grand funeral given a colleague in the Illinois legislature, saying, "If [he] had known how big a funeral he would have had, he would have died years ago."[5] It's doubtful the president would have felt the same way about his own, far grander, funeral.

After Lincoln's body had lain in state for viewing in both the White House and the Capitol, it was put aboard a special nine-car funeral train for the long, slow journey back to Springfield. (Mary Lincoln had vetoed proposals that her husband be entombed in the Capitol.) In all, more than two weeks passed from Lincoln's death until the time the lid of his coffin was screwed down for good.

There were twelve funerals in twelve cities. At every stop, the body would be taken off the train and conveyed in a magnificently ornate black hearse, a different one built by each city, to the place selected for the viewing, usually a city hall or state capitol. Huge parades escorted the hearse. The silver-trimmed coffin remained open at each viewing, even as the corpse inside continued to deteriorate. Despite all the ministrations of the undertaker who rode in the death car, decomposition proceeded day by day. Profusions of fresh flowers almost covered the smell. Daily applications of chalk and powder disguised the blackened skin. Massive infusions of embalming fluid helped. But nothing could hide the deep-sunk eyes, the severely straight line of the shrunken lips, and the sharp, skeletal look of the fleshless physiognomy.

Absolute hysteria prevailed at these successive leave-takings. Pilgrims were trampled and crushed to death in wild stampedes. As many as one million citizens out of a Northern population of a little over twenty million actually looked on the martyred president's face. Many hundreds of thousands more were turned away, prevented from getting close by the enormous crowds, even after waiting for as much as an entire day. Approximately 1.5 million people lined up to see him in New York City. Only about a third of them got in.[6] The lines of mourners passed the open coffin all night long.

Millions more came out for the mock funerals held in every village, town, and city in the North. Uncountable were the other citizens who stood waiting along the railroad tracks, day and night, in all kinds of weather, to witness the slow passage of the death train, its passing marked by tolling church bells and booming minute guns. Perhaps half of the population of the North took some part personally in the massive collective farewell. The husk of the man who had left Springfield in 1861 came home on May 4, 1865, to be hidden away until a proper tomb could be built. Those who care to follow the bizarre misadventures of Lincoln's corpse between its return to Springfield and the final entombment in a steel cage buried in Portland cement in 1901, thirty-six years after the assassination, will want to consult Michael Kammen's *Digging Up the Dead: A History of Notable American Reburials.*[7]

The trial of Booth's coconspirators took place in Washington, DC, from May 10 until June 29. Identified as "enemy belligerents," the accused were tried by a military tribunal rather than a civil court. The verdict would be decided not by a jury of their peers but by nine Union generals and colonels. All were combat veterans. Not one had any legal training. The defendants were charged with the capital crime of conspiring "maliciously, unlaw-

As many as one million Americans looked on Abraham Lincoln's decaying face as he lay in his open coffin during the twelve-day, seventeen-hundred-mile mobile funeral across the North to Springfield, Illinois.

---

fully, and traitorously . . . to kill and murder" Lincoln and the others. All pleaded not guilty. All were represented by competent attorneys. None had much chance of acquittal. The commission reached a verdict but did not make it public.

On the morning of July 6, an officer visited each of the condemned in his cell to reveal the fate the tribunal had given him. For four of them, it was death. Powell, Atzerodt, Herold, and Mrs. Surratt were to be hanged by the neck until dead. Mudd, Arnold, and O'Laughlen got life in prison. Spangler got six years. President Johnson had approved the sentences. The doomed were shocked to learn that the date of their execution was July 7—tomorrow! The banging they'd been hearing had been the carpenters hammering together the gallows on the grounds of Washington Arsenal, where they were imprisoned.

In regard to Mary Surratt, it was not considered possible that the United States government would actually execute, by hanging, a female, a woman, a lady. It had certainly never happened before. Along with Mrs. Surratt's death sentence, the commission had sent to the president a recommendation that he commute her death sentence to life imprisonment. Andrew Johnson was expected to comply.

On the blazing hot day of the execution, the commanding officer delayed. Everyone was waiting for Mrs. Surratt's reprieve to come from the White House. It never came. Finally, they proceeded. The wretched woman was so weak she had to be half-carried up the gallows' stairs. She had stopped eating days before and was bleeding heavily from some untreated female complaint. They gave her a chair to sit on. To her left stood the unperturbed Lewis Powell. He'd been bantering with the hangman. The nooses were positioned and hoods pulled over the heads of the condemned. "Oh please don't let me fall," Mary Surratt whimpered an instant before the trap dropped. In 1869, President Johnson pardoned Mudd, Arnold, and Spangler. O'Laughlen had died of yellow fever in prison.

Alexander Gardner took a series of four photographs of the hanging of the condemned conspirators. This is the final view. Powell had bantered with the hangman. Mary Surratt had whimpered, "Oh please don't let me fall," an instant before the trap dropped. FROM LEFT TO RIGHT: *Mary Surratt, Lewis Powell, George Atzerodt, David Herold.*

Mary Todd Lincoln survived her murdered husband for seventeen years of misery. She never recovered from the shock she received on Friday, April 14, 1865. Suffering unending grief, further losses and humiliations, widespread unpopularity, irrational fears and a brief confinement in an insane asylum, financial difficulties, and estrangement from her son Robert, she was tortured by migraines and manic depression. One more insupportable loss came when eighteen-year-old Tad died of tuberculosis. She'd lost her husband and three of her four sons and was estranged from the fourth. After years of European exile, the president's widow finally died a desolate recluse in 1882 in a darkened upstairs bedroom of a sister's house in Springfield.

The Lincolns' young theater companions, Major Henry Rathbone and his step-sister Clara Harris, were duly married. His failure to protect his commander in chief continued to haunt the combat veteran. He grew increasingly distraught. Clara became afraid of him. They were living in Hanover, Germany, with their three children when he finally went over the edge. On Christmas morning 1883, he shot Clara dead before stabbing himself deeply in the chest. Like Booth, he had employed both bullet and blade. He survived his self-inflicted wound and spent the rest of his life in a German lunatic asylum, dying there in 1911.

Sergeant Boston Corbett briefly found himself America's most popular hero, celebrated as "Lincoln's Avenger." He was deluged with fan mail and requests for autographs. Admiring maidens and widows of that era were known to proffer matrimonial proposals to unmarried heroes. If Sergeant Corbett was recipient of any such proposition, he would have been hard-pressed to respond. His religious fanaticism had rendered him unfit for marriage. One night before the war, Corbett found himself troubled by impure thoughts after being solicited by a streetwalker. He took bold action to achieve righteous chastity, snipping open his scrotum with scissors and plucking out both his testicles. Along with his fan mail, he also received death threats from Southern sympathizers. He had always been crazy, but now he was a paranoid psychotic who had real enemies. Boston Corbett was last seen armed to the teeth and fleeing across the Kansas prairie to escape a posse intent on returning him to the lunatic asylum from which he'd escaped. He vanished forever.

EPILOGUE

John Wilkes Booth had longed for fame all of his short life. It had to be true historical fame. The fleeting theatrical celebrity he had already won could never satisfy him. He had made it clear that even infamy would be acceptable so long as it brought him lasting remembrance. Infamy he certainly attained. Abraham Lincoln yearned for a different kind of fame. He, too, was successful.

Lincoln long ago took his place as the principal secular saint of America's civic religion. He won such stature by saving the Union and by helping to free four million enslaved Americans while destroying American slavery forever. At the same time, his canonization owed no small part to his death on the pinnacle of triumph at the hands of John Wilkes Booth, for Lincoln was widely regarded, while living, as anything but a saintly person. It was death in the moment of victory that made him a sort of messiah figure who gave his life that the nation might live.

Surely the greatest irony of the assassination must be that John Wilkes Booth did so much to raise Lincoln to the historical immortality the man had always longed for. The assassin had no idea that killing Lincoln would help to fulfill his victim's highest hopes by draping the mantle of martyrdom across his shoulders and exalting him in the company of the republic's greatest heroes. Booth believed Lincoln a guilty tyrant. Yet the unwitting assassin succeeded in projecting the tragic figure of Abraham Lincoln across the firmament of history in an apotheosis perfectly mythic in its grandeur and its symmetry.

In his Second Inaugural, President Lincoln had spoken of the changes brought on by the Civil War as "fundamental and astounding." The vast conflict had, indeed, transformed the founders' little republic. As many historians have noted, before the war, the United States was usually spoken of as a plural entity, a gathering of states. "The United States are . . . ," people said. With the war, that polity had become singular—"the United States is . . ."[1]

The changes had truly been fundamental. After thriving for 250 years, American slavery was dead forever. Although many African Americans would remain impoverished and oppressed, they would never again be slaves. They had escaped the terrible fear that a sale or inheritance might tear their loved ones away from them forever.

Many Americans now will probably agree that the war's suffering and bloodshed was a fair if heavy price to pay for freeing the millions and for the freedom now guaranteed their descendants. At the same time, uncompensated emancipation represented the greatest financial catastrophe in American history. Combined with the conflict's massive destruction of Southern property and infrastructure and the toll of dead and wounded, the enormous loss was enough to reduce the whole South to a state of poverty and stagnation it would not begin to escape for a century.

Secession, too, was dead forever, as dead as slavery. Since the nation's infancy, secession had been debated, predicted, proposed, denounced, and threatened. After 1865, it was never again spoken of as a policy that remained within the realm of possibility.

White supremacy, however, the offspring of slavery that had triggered secession in the first place, remained very much alive in a nation reunited only by resort to catastrophic violence. Defeat had made Southern whites all the more determined never to accept the freed people as fellow citizens. They were unalterably committed to saving white supremacy from the shipwreck of their hopes. They were equally determined to avenge the unendurable insult presented by the US Colored Troops—their own property arrayed for battle against them! The struggles of racial adjustment that followed the Civil War only increased white anger in the South.

President Lincoln had begun proposing plans for the Reconstruction of the Union at the end of 1863. From the beginning, Lincoln's Republican opponents in Congress—the Radical Republicans—fought him every step of the way. The fundamental question was which branch of government had the authority for setting policies for the readmission of former insurgent states to the Union—Congress or the president. Lincoln set to work as if there was no question that the president would take the lead. The Radical Republicans were never able to wrest control from President Lincoln. He outmaneuvered them on most issues. He pocket-vetoed their most important Reconstruction bill, and his veto stood. Some of the radicals hated Abraham Lincoln almost as much as they hated the rebels.

Lincoln's opponents wanted much stricter conditions to readmit to the Union a state formerly in rebellion. Lincoln's terms were lenient, making it relatively easy for a state to rejoin the nation so long as a few conditions were met. When Lincoln laid out his plan in 1863, the outcome of the war was still much in doubt. He hoped his Reconstruction policies could help win the war. He hoped, in vain as it turns out, that by making it easy and attractive to become part of the United States again, he could lure some states away from the rebellion. (There were significant peace movements in parts of the South.) But there were no takers. The white South fought on until it was simply too devastated to continue.

Unlike Lincoln, the Radical Republicans were not much concerned about the war-winning possibilities of their Reconstruction plans. Their goals were to punish the traitors, remake Southern society, and assure the civil and voting rights of Black people in the South. Some of the more advanced proposals even featured the redistribution of land from the wealthy planters to the formerly enslaved. These were laudable goals, and Lincoln himself was growing in his support for Black civil rights, though he was by no means ready to publicly endorse such divisive policies until very near the end.

On the other hand, Lincoln was absolutely opposed to punishing Southern whites or their leaders. His Radical opponents said he was soft on the traitors who had made war against their own country. They said he was besotted with charity and mercy. They also said he was indifferent to the plight of Black Southerners. Lincoln's opponents had tried unsuccessfully to deny him the Republican nomination for a second term in 1864.

So it is hardly surprising that some of the Radical Republicans greeted Abraham Lincoln's assassination with qualified satisfaction. "I believe that the Almighty continued Mr. Lincoln in office as long as he was useful, and then substituted a better man to finish the work," one of them said.[2] They entertained at first the highest hopes for the new president. Andrew Johnson had hated the rich and dominant enslavers with an intensity only possible for a poor Southern white man who had been oppressed by the upper classes.

In the gloomy summer of 1864, when prospects for Lincoln's reelection had appeared so bleak, desperate Republicans scrambled to reverse the slide. They dubbed themselves the "Union" Party. Setting aside Lincoln's invisible first-term vice president, Hannibal Hamlin, an abolitionist from Maine, the convention picked, instead, War Democrat Andrew Johnson, governor of loyal Tennessee, as a sign of their party's national, unionist approach. No one then could have known what a terrible misstep Johnson's selection would prove to be.

Now that he was president, Johnson spoke angrily about imposing the harshest punishments for treason. This was what the Radicals had been yearning for all along. Johnson downplayed his racism. The Radicals even thought they could eventually persuade him to support Black voting rights. The Radicals were deceived. To their most bitter disappointment, Andrew Johnson soon revealed his true, white supremacist colors. He set up new state governments in the South, dominated by defiant former insurgents. He issued many thousands of presidential pardons to those who had been disenfranchised for their treason, including to generals and statesmen. Johnson's new white Southern state governments immediately commenced a blatant campaign to reduce the freed people to a status resembling slavery as closely as possible. Their "Black Codes" did not treat the Black people as US citizens but as members of a subordinate caste under white control.

Johnson, a lifelong Democrat who had never joined the Republican Party despite being Lincoln's running mate, allied himself with the whites in the defeated slave states and with the Democrats in the North. Johnson wanted to readmit the former insurgent states to the Union immediately. All of these Southern state governments were controlled by the Democrats, then as always before the party of white supremacy. That could give the Democratic Party control of the government.

The Republicans fought back and prevailed. Congress was able to wrest control of Reconstruction away from President Johnson. Presidential Reconstruction became Congressional (or Military) Reconstruction. For a time there was progress, if little peace. Legislation in Congress, the work of the federal Freedmen's Bureau, and the bayonets of the occupying US Army managed to win for Black Southerners some of the rights of citizenship, foremost the right to vote. African Americans used their precious franchise to make ambitious steps toward racial equality and social justice. Their progress was but fleeting. As W. E. B. Du Bois would write: "The slave went free; stood a brief moment in the sun; then moved back again toward slavery."[3]

On the national level, the Thirteenth Amendment was ratified at the end of 1865. Two more "Civil War Amendments," the Fourteenth and Fifteenth, affirmed the citizenship of the formerly enslaved and guaranteed African American men the right to vote. After the "redeemer" white supremacist governments took control of the South with the end of Reconstruction, however, the promises of the Civil War amendments would be broken for the better part of a century.

From the beginning, the unreconstructed rebels had clung to the robust hope that someday their chance would come to restore white supremacy to its former place as the guiding principle of Southern society. Historian Martha Hodes has written that the defeated people were "confident that God remained on the side of white people fighting for revolutionary freedom, a freedom that depended on black subjugation."[4]

Southern whites knew that their commitment to white supremacy was stronger and more enduring than the North's commitment to creating a just, biracial society in the former slave states. While white Southerners fought violently against equality from the beginning, they knew that the real battle—and their certain victory—would come only after the North called home its troops.

That came to pass in 1877. President Ulysses S. Grant's administration spanned two terms, 1869 to 1877. His presidency was by no means the failure his detractors have charged. Grant fought valiantly to safeguard the civil rights of African Americans in the South and to protect them from the violence of terrorist white supremacist organizations like the KKK. With the US Army gone, however, the redeemers were free to unleash a savage war of terrorism against Black people and their white Republican allies. It took years to accomplish, but in the end, white supremacy prevailed in a tragic betrayal of the emancipationist aims of the Civil War.

It is tempting to think that the outcome might have been happier had Lincoln lived. The truth is that no one knows what policies Lincoln might have pursued beyond those he had already put in place by the time of his death. He didn't know himself. But unlike the bellicose and stubborn white supremacist Andrew Johnson, Abraham Lincoln was a master politician. Lincoln considered that his ability to forge alliances of expediency between opposing factions was the key to whatever success he had achieved as president. He himself had said, "I may not have made as good a president as some other men, but I believe I have kept these discordant elements together as well as anyone could."[5] To what ends might he have used his unifying abilities during the Reconstruction years?

Could he have tried the political tactic called triangulation? Could Lincoln have made himself the champion of the former insurgents in a shared opposition to the policies of the Radical Republicans? And could he have done this without damaging the prospects of the freed people? Might Lincoln's political genius have allowed him to forge some sort of alliance of class solidarity between poor Southern whites and the even poorer freed people? This seems unlikely given the virulent racism of Southern whites. Yet at one time, Frederick Douglass himself entertained hope for such a realignment. The man's biographer, David Blight, however, implies that Douglass's optimism on this issue was "naive."[6]

All we can know for certain is that the outcome would have been different if Abraham Lincoln had lived. One man who had just gained his freedom may have summed it up best when he said simply, "Things was hurt by Mr. Lincoln gettin' kilt."[7] From what would have been his own point of view, John Wilkes Booth had not died in vain. The blow he struck had not won Southern independence, but it had helped to assure the persistence of white supremacy.

NOTES

PROLOGUE

1. Gene Smith, *American Gothic: The Story of America's Legendary Theatrical Family—Junius, Edwin, and John Wilkes Booth* (New York: Simon and Schuster, 1992), 27.

2. Quoted in Allen C. Guelzo, *Abraham Lincoln: Redeemer President* (Grand Rapids, MI: William B. Eerdmans, 1999), 317.

3. Walt Whitman, "The Death of Abraham Lincoln," in *Prose Works* (Philadelphia: David McKay, 1892), www.bartleby.com/229/2009.html.

4. Carl Sandburg, *Abraham Lincoln: The War Years*, 4 vols. (New York: Harcourt, Brace, 1939), 4:281.

CHAPTER 1. RICHMOND, VIRGINIA, APRIL 4, 1865

1. George S. Bryan, *The Great American Myth* (1940; Chicago: Americana House, 1990), 9.

2. Walt Whitman, "The Death of Abraham Lincoln," in *Prose Works* (Philadelphia: David McKay, 1892), www.bartleby.com/229/2009.html. (Lecture first delivered in 1879.)

3. Quoted in Donald E. Fehrenbacher and Virginia Fehrenbacher, *Recollected Words of Abraham Lincoln* (Stanford, CA: Stanford University Press, 1996), 192.

4. Jay Winik, *April 1865: The Month That Saved America* (New York: HarperCollins, 2001), 118.

5. Charles C. Coffin, *Abraham Lincoln* (New York: Harper and Brothers, 1893), 505.

6. R. M. J. Blackett, ed., *Thomas Morris Chester, Black Civil War Correspondent: His Dispatches from the Virginia Front* (Baton Rouge: Louisiana State University Press, 1989), 297.

7. Blackett, 297.

8. Coffin, *Abraham Lincoln*, 506.

9. Michael Burlingame, *Abraham Lincoln: A Life*, 2 vols. (Baltimore: Johns Hopkins University Press, 2008), 2:790.

10. Charles C. Coffin, "Late Scenes in Richmond," *Atlantic Monthly*, June 15, 1865, 753–55.

11. Coffin, *Abraham Lincoln*, 506.

12. Quoted in Brian R. Dirck, *The Black Heavens: Abraham Lincoln and Death* (Carbondale: Southern Illinois University Press, 2019), 137.

13. Benjamin P. Thomas, *Abraham Lincoln: A Biography* (New York: Knopf, 1952), 268.

14. Quoted in Blackett, *Thomas Morris Chester*, 295.

15. Burlingame, *Abraham Lincoln: A Life*, 2:791.

16. Coffin, *Abraham Lincoln*, 509.

17. John G. Nicolay and John Hay, *Abraham Lincoln: A History*, 10 vols. (New York: Century, 1890), 10:210–11.

18. Blackett, *Thomas Morris Chester*, 290.

19. James M. McPherson, *Battle Cry of Freedom: The Civil War Era* (New York: Oxford University Press, 1988), 565.

20. "Message to Confederate Congress, Jan. 12, 1863," in *Jefferson Davis: The Essential Writings*, ed. William J. Cooper Jr. (New York: Modern Library, 2003), 290.

21. McPherson, *Battle Cry of Freedom*, 835.

22. Charles B. Dew, *Apostles of Disunion* (2001; Charlottesville: University of Virginia Press, 2016), 15.

23. George M. Frederickson, *White Supremacy: A Comparative Study in American and South African History* (New York: Oxford University Press, 1981), 160, 154.

24. Thomas Jefferson, "Notes on the State of Virginia," in *Thomas Jefferson: Writings*, ed. Merrill D. Peterson (New York: Library of America, 1984), 264.

25. John Adams to Louisa Catherine Johnson Adams, Jan. 13, 1820,

Founders Online, https://founders.archives.gov/documents/Adams /99-03-02-3750.

26. "Message to Confederate Congress, Jan. 12, 1863," 290.

27. "Speech in US Senate, March 2, 1859," in *Jefferson Davis: The Essential Writings*, ed. William J. Cooper Jr. (New York: Modern Library, 2003), 159.

28. W. J. Cash, *The Mind of the South* (New York: Knopf, 1941), 66.

29. Quoted in Charles M. Blow, "The Lowest White Man," *New York Times*, Jan. 11, 2018, www.nytimes.com/2018/01/11/opinion/trump -immigration-white-supremacy.html.

30. Fanny Seward, diary entry for April 11, 1865, https://rbscp.lib .rochester.edu/lincoln/fanny-seward-diary/browse.

31. Carl Sandburg, *Abraham Lincoln: The War Years*, 4 vols. (New York: Harcourt, Brace, 1939), 4:195.

CHAPTER 2. "ALL THOSE GODDAMNED BOOTHS"

1. Quoted in Richard Moody, *Edwin Forrest* (New York: Knopf, 1960), 351.

2. See, e.g., Junius Brutus Booth to Mary Ann Holmes Booth, June 23, 1840, transcript of the original letter from the Helen Menkin collection, Peale Center for Baltimore History.

3. Asia Booth Clarke, *Booth Memorials: Passages, Incidents, and Anecdotes in the Life of Junius Brutus Booth, the Elder, by His Daughter* (New York: Carleton, 1866), 64. The younger of the Booths' two surviving daughters, Asia was three years older than John Wilkes. Her father played with the idea of calling her "Ayesha," for one of the Prophet Mohammed's wives. (Junius was a student of the *Koran*.) He finally settled on Asia: "Call the little one Asia in remembrance of that country where God first walked with man," he wrote his wife.

4. Clarke, viii.

5. *Dictionary of American Biography* (1937), s.v. "Booth, Junius Brutus."

6. Clarke, *Booth Memorials*, 15.

7. Stephen M. Archer, *Junius Brutus Booth* (Carbondale: Southern Illinois University Press, 1992), 6.

8. Albert Furtwangler, *Assassin on Stage: Brutus, Hamlet, and the Death of Lincoln* (Urbana: University of Illinois Press, 1991), 58–59.

9. The remarks of John T. Ford, owner of Ford's Theater, were quoted in a letter (signed "A MARYLANDER") to the editor, *Philadelphia Press*, Dec. 27, 1881.

10. Terry Alford, *Fortune's Fool: The Life of John Wilkes Booth* (New York: Oxford University Press, 2015), 11.

11. Stanley Kimmel, *The Mad Booths of Maryland* (New York: Bobbs-Merrill, 1940), 16. See also Eleanor Ruggles, *Prince of Players: Edwin Booth* (New York: Norton, 1953), 7–24.

12. Letter quoted in Frank A. Burr, *New York Press* (Sunday edition), August 9, 1891, 19.

13. Nora Titone, *My Thoughts Be Bloody* (New York: Free Press, 2010), 25.

14. Kimmel, *Mad Booths of Maryland*, 25.

15. James Winston, diary, 1819–27, autograph manuscript in four octavo volumes, Huntington Library, HM 19925. Portions of the diary have been published as *Drury Lane Journal: Selections from James Winston's Diaries, 1817–1827*, ed. Alfred L. Nelson and Gilbert B. Cross (London: Society for Theatre Research, 1974).

16. Clarke, *Booth Memorials*, 64.

17. Archer, *Junius Brutus Booth*, 70.

18. Kimmel, *Mad Booths of Maryland*, 64.

19. Quoted in Justin Kaplan, ed., *Walt Whitman: Complete Poetry and Collected Prose* (New York: Library of America, 1982), 1191–92.

20. Kaplan, 1192.

21. Kaplan, 1187–88.

22. Clarke, *Booth Memorials*, 44.

23. Clarke, 74.

24. The epitaph reads as follows:

> Behold the spot where Genius lies,
> O, drop a tear when talent dies,
> Of Tragedy the mighty chief,
> Thy power to please surpassed belief,
> Hic jacet [here lies] Matchless Booth.

25. "Junius Brutus Booth," *Dictionary of American Biography*, 2:452–56.

26. Alford, *Fortune's Fool*, 16.

27. Asia Booth Clarke, *John Wilkes Booth: A Sister's Memoir*, ed. Terry Alford (Jackson: University Press of Mississippi, 1991), 42.

28. Kimmel, *Mad Booths of Maryland*, 58.

29. James F. Kirkham, Sheldon G. Levy, and William J. Crotty, *Assassination and Political Violence: A Report to the National Commission on the Causes and Prevention of Violence* (New York: Bantam, 1970), 78.

30. Carl Sandburg, *Abraham Lincoln: The War Years*, 4 vols. (New York: Harcourt, Brace, 1939), 4:301. But this passage, while irresistibly quotable, does not accurately reflect Sandburg's approach to the murder of Abraham

Lincoln. As William Hanchett pointed out nearly twenty-five years ago: "More than any other Lincoln biographer to the present, Sandburg made an effort to put Booth and the assassination into their wartime context." William Hanchett to John Rhodehamel, April 22, 1994.

31. Archer, *Junius Brutus Booth*, 112.

32. Otis Skinner, *The Last Tragedian* (New York: Dodd, Mead, 1939), 63.

33. Art Loux, *John Wilkes Booth: Day by Day* (Jefferson, NC: McFarland, 2009), 8.

CHAPTER 3. CASTE

1. Isabel Wilkerson, *Caste: The Origins of Our Discontents* (New York: Random House, 2020), 19–26, and passim.

2. Barbara Jeanne Fields, *Slavery and Freedom in the Middle Ground* (New Haven, CT: Yale University Press, 1985), 1–16.

3. Quoted in Fields, 62.

4. Quoted in John Rhodehamel and Louise Taper, eds., *"Right or Wrong, God Judge Me": The Writings of John Wilkes Booth* (Urbana: University of Illinois Press, 1997), 125. Here and throughout I have retained Booth's punctuation and spelling.

5. Eleanor Ruggles, *Prince of Players: Edwin Booth* (New York: Norton, 1953), 18–20.

6. Junius Brutus Booth to his father, Jan. 28, 1837, quoted in Stephen M. Archer, *Junius Brutus Booth* (Carbondale: Southern Illinois University Press, 1992), 146.

7. William Hanchett, *The Lincoln Murder Conspiracies: Being an Account of the Hatred Felt by Many Americans for President Abraham Lincoln* [. . .] (Urbana: University of Illinois Press, 1983), 152.

8. Quoted in Gene Smith, *American Gothic: The Story of America's Legendary Theatrical Family—Junius, Edwin, and John Wilkes Booth* (New York: Simon and Schuster, 1992), 127.

CHAPTER 4. "THERE ARE NO MORE ACTORS!"

1. Quoted in John Rhodehamel and Louise Taper, eds., *"Right or Wrong, God Judge Me": The Writings of John Wilkes Booth* (Urbana: University of Illinois Press, 1997), 125. Here and throughout I have retained Booth's punctuation and spelling.

2. Drew Gilpin Faust, ed., *The Ideology of Slavery: Proslavery Thought in the*

Antebellum South, 1830–1860 (Baton Rouge: Louisiana State University Press, 1981), 171.

3. Faust, 181.

4. Faust, 181.

5. Faust, 183.

6. Faust, 192.

7. Faust, 192.

8. Barbara Jeanne Fields, *Slavery and Freedom on the Middle Ground* (New Haven, CT: Yale University Press, 1985), 2, 9, 11–13.

9. Frederick Douglass, *Narrative of the Life of Frederick Douglass, an American Slave*, in *Douglass: Autobiographies*, ed. Henry Louis Gates Jr. (New York: Library of America, 1994), 18.

10. David W. Blight, *Frederick Douglass: Prophet of Freedom* (New York: Simon and Schuster, 2018), 14.

11. Quoted in Stanley Kimmel, *The Mad Booths of Maryland* (New York: Bobbs-Merrill, 1940), 64.

12. Kimmel, 72.

13. Michael W. Kauffman, "John Wilkes Booth and the Murder of Abraham Lincoln," *Blue and Gray Magazine*, April 1990, 54.

14. Art Loux, *John Wilkes Booth: Day by Day* (Jefferson, NC: McFarland, 2009), 12.

15. Asia Booth Clarke, *Booth Memorials: Passages, Incidents, and Anecdotes in the Life of Junius Brutus Booth, the Elder, by His Daughter* (New York: Carleton, 1866), 106.

16. Clarke, 106.

17. Remark attributed to Rufus Choate in Kimmel, *Mad Booths of Maryland*, 91.

CHAPTER 5. "I USED TO BE A SLAVE"

1. Roy P. Basler, Marion Dolores Pratt, and Lloyd A. Dunlap, eds., *The Collected Works of Abraham Lincoln*, 8 vols. plus index (New Brunswick, NJ: Rutgers University Press, 1953–55), 1:455–56 (hereafter *CWAL*).

2. Eric Foner, *The Fiery Trial: Abraham Lincoln and American Slavery* (New York: Norton, 2010), 36.

3. Michael Burlingame, *Abraham Lincoln: A Life*, 2 vols. (Baltimore: Johns Hopkins University Press, 2008), 1:42.

4. Michael Burlingame, *The Inner World of Abraham Lincoln* (Urbana: University of Illinois Press, 1994), 42.

5. Burlingame, *Abraham Lincoln: A Life*, 1:48.

6. *CWAL*, 7:281.

7. *CWAL*, 4:60–61.

8. Burlingame, *Abraham Lincoln: A Life*, 1:6–7.

9. Burlingame, 1:8.

10. Burlingame, 1:54n.

11. Douglas L. Wilson and Rodney O. Davis, eds., *Herndon's Informants: Letters, Interviews, and Statements about Abraham Lincoln* (Urbana: University of Illinois Press, 1998), 676.

12. Quoted in Brian Dirck, *Abraham Lincoln and White America* (Lawrence: University Press of Kansas, 2012), 30–31.

13. Burlingame, *Abraham Lincoln: A Life*, 1:10.

14. Burlingame, 1:19.

15. Burlingame, 1:14.

16. Burlingame, 1:13.

17. *CWAL*, 4:61–62.

18. David Herbert Donald, *Lincoln* (New York: Simon and Schuster, 1995), 24.

19. Burlingame, *Inner World of Abraham Lincoln*, 21.

20. "1815 Eruption of Mount Tambora," Wikipedia, last edited Oct. 30, 2020, 01:46, https://en.wikipedia.org/wiki/1815_eruption_of_Mount_Tambora.

21. Burlingame, *Abraham Lincoln: A Life*, 1:22.

22. Burlingame, 1:16.

23. *CWAL*, 4:62.

24. Burlingame, *Abraham Lincoln: A Life*, 1:44.

25. Burlingame, 1:56–57. This account must be regarded with some skepticism since Lincoln said Hanks left the flatboat before the party reached New Orleans. Burlingame, however, judges Hanks's testimony as likely reliable. Burlingame, 1:57n.

26. Burlingame, 1:45.

27. Burlingame, 1:17; 26.

28. *CWAL*, 2:97.

29. *CWAL*, 1:320.

30. *CWAL*, 4:24.

31. *CWAL*, 3:14.

32. *CWAL*, 5:537.

1. Asia Booth Clarke, *John Wilkes Booth: A Sister's Memoir*, ed. Terry Alford (Jackson: University Press of Mississippi, 1991), 40.

2. John Wilkes Booth received his earliest education at day schools near his Baltimore home. His first school was "kept by an old classical scholar named Smith. To this school he was sent while still in breeches, and here he was given the rudiments of an education." David Rankin Barbee, "Lincoln and Booth," unpublished manuscript, Barbee Papers, Georgetown University Library, Special Collections Department, 211. In 1849, at the age of eleven, Booth began three years at Milton Academy, a Quaker boarding school in Cockeysville, Maryland. Located just twelve miles from the Booth farm at Bel Air, the school's three-story stone building contained a dormitory, schoolrooms, and a dining hall. A prospectus of the school survives in the files of the Maryland Historical Society. The Circular of Milton Boarding School states that the school's mission was "by a course of thorough instruction to prepare youths for college, or for a professional or mercantile life." Fees were seventy dollars per term, with an additional ten dollars for Latin and Greek classes. In 1852, John Booth entered another boarding school, St. Timothy's Hall, in Catonsville, Maryland. At St. Timothy's, students wore the steel-gray uniforms of artillery cadets. "The object of . . . St. Timothy's Hall," stated that school's prospectus, a copy of which is preserved in the Maryland Historical Society, "is to make it an institution of strict discipline, of good morals, and, by the grace of God, a religious home for the young. [St. Timothy's was] a literary institution, for the education of young gentlemen whose appreciation of knowledge, and love of order, have made them diligent and patient of restraint."

3. John Rhodehamel and Louise Taper, eds., *"Right or Wrong, God Judge Me": The Writings of John Wilkes Booth* (Urbana: University of Illinois Press, 1997), passim.

4. Clarke, *John Wilkes Booth*, 71.

5. Clarke, 48.

6. Clarke, 49–50.

7. Clarke, 49.

8. Clarke, 49.

9. Clarke, 88.

10. See Bertram Wyatt-Brown, *Honor and Violence in the Old South* (New York: Oxford University Press, 1986), 27–30.

11. Clarke, *John Wilkes Booth*, 71; Rhodehamel and Taper, *"Right or Wrong, God Judge Me,"* 38.

12. George S. Bryan, *The Great American Myth* (1940; Chicago: Americana House, 1990), 32.

13. Terry Alford, *Fortune's Fool: The Life of John Wilkes Booth* (New York: Oxford University Press, 2015), 72.

14. Alford, 66.

15. Quoted in Stanley Kimmel, *The Mad Booths of Maryland* (Indianapolis, IN: Bobbs-Merrill, 1940), 150.

16. Clarke, *John Wilkes Booth*, 77.

17. Bernard Sobel, ed., *The Theatre Handbook and Digest of Plays* (New York: Crown, 1940), 734.

18. George Alfred Townsend, quoted in Kimmel, *Mad Booths of Maryland*, 157.

CHAPTER 7. "I AM MYSELF ALONE!"

1. Art Loux, *John Wilkes Booth: Day by Day* (Jefferson, NC: McFarland, 2009), 32.

2. Terry Alford, *Fortune's Fool: The Life of John Wilkes Booth* (New York: Oxford University Press, 2015), 49–50.

3. Alford, 50.

4. Loux, *John Wilkes Booth*, 37–60.

5. Loux, 47.

6. Asia Booth Clarke, *John Wilkes Booth: A Sister's Memoir*, ed. Terry Alford (Jackson: University Press of Mississippi, 1991), 77.

7. Clara Morris, *Life on the Stage* (New York: McClure, Phillips, 1902), 76.

8. Quoted in William Hanchett, *The Lincoln Murder Conspiracies: Being an Account of the Hatred Felt by Many Americans for President Abraham Lincoln* [. . .] (Urbana: University of Illinois Press, 1983), 37.

9. Francis Wilson, *John Wilkes Booth: Fact and Fiction of Lincoln's Assassination* (New York: Houghton Mifflin, 1929), 15.

10. Loux, *John Wilkes Booth*, 32.

11. Alford, *Fortune's Fool*, 144.

12. E. Lawrence Abel, *John Wilkes Booth and the Women Who Loved Him* (Washington, DC: Regnery History, 2018), 106.

13. Clara Morris interview in the *Boston Herald*, Jan. 10, 1890, quoted in John Rhodehamel and Louise Taper, eds., *"Right or Wrong, God Judge Me":*

The Writings of John Wilkes Booth (Urbana: University of Illinois Press, 1997), 107.

14. Rhodehamel and Taper, 80.

15. Rhodehamel and Taper, 83.

16. Walter Johnson, *River of Dark Dreams: Slavery and Empire in the Cotton Kingdom* (Cambridge, MA: Harvard University Press, 2013), 99.

17. Don B. Wilmeth, "The American Theater in Transition," in *John Wilkes Booth, Actor: The Proceedings of a Conference Weekend in Bel Air, Maryland, May 1988*, ed. Arthur Kincaid (North Leigh, Oxfordshire, UK: Published privately, 1989), 20.

18. Asia Booth Clarke to Jean Anderson, Sept. 10, 1856, Asia Booth Clarke Papers, Maryland Historical Society.

19. Clarke, *John Wilkes Booth*, 77, 88.

20. Clarke, 89.

CHAPTER 8. JOHN BROWN'S BODY

1. "Address at Cooper Institute, 27 Feb. 1860," in Roy P. Basler, Marion Dolores Pratt, and Lloyd A. Dunlap, eds., *The Collected Works of Abraham Lincoln*, 8 vols. plus index (New Brunswick, NJ: Rutgers University Press, 1953–55), 3:541.

2. Herman Melville, *Complete Poems*, ed. Hershel Parker (New York: Library of America, 2019), 288.

3. Tony Horowitz, *Midnight Rising: John Brown and the Raid That Sparked the Civil War* (New York: Henry Holt, 2011), 287.

4. Angela Smythe, "Bound for Glory: John Wilkes Booth and the Richmond Grays," www.antebellumrichmond.com/bound-for-glory, 114.

5. Smythe, 4.

6. Smythe, 18.

7. Smythe, 7.

8. George Alfred Townsend, *The Life, Crime and Capture of John Wilkes Booth* (New York: Dick and Fitzgerald, 1865), 22.

9. "John T. Ford's Recollections," *Baltimore American*, June 8, 1893.

10. Asia Booth Clarke to Jean Anderson, n.d., Record Group ML518, Peale Museum, Baltimore.

11. Terry Alford, *Fortune's Fool: The Life of John Wilkes Booth* (New York: Oxford University Press, 2015), 77.

12. Asia Booth Clarke, *John Wilkes Booth: A Sister's Memoir*, ed. Terry Alford (Jackson: University Press of Mississippi, 1991), 88–89.

13. Horowitz, *Midnight Rising*, 253.

14. Quoted in John Rhodehamel and Louise Taper, eds., *"Right or Wrong, God Judge Me": The Writings of John Wilkes Booth* (Urbana: University of Illinois Press, 1997), 60.

15. Rhodehamel and Taper, 125.

16. For a century, John Wilkes Booth's speech was locked away in the vault of the Hampden-Booth Theatre Library at The Players Club, the institution Edwin Booth had established in his mansion in New York City's Gramercy Park. John Wilkes Booth's 1860 secession crisis speech finally saw the light of day in 1997, when it was published for the first time in Rhodehamel and Taper, *"Right or Wrong, God Judge Me."* The Players sold the manuscript at auction in 2007.

17. Clarke, John Wilkes Booth, 116.

18. E. D. Sander to J. B. Fry, April 24, 1865, in *The Lincoln Assassination: The Evidence*, ed. William C. Edwards and Edward Steers Jr. (Urbana: University of Illinois Press, 2009), 1129.

CHAPTER 9. THE "CORNER-STONE"

1. See *The Works of James Buchanan*, ed. John B. Moore, 12 vols. (Philadelphia: J. P. Lippincott, 1910), 9:7–22.

2. Quoted in John Rhodehamel and Louise Taper, eds., *"Right or Wrong, God Judge Me": The Writings of John Wilkes Booth* (Urbana: University of Illinois Press, 1997), 55. Following quotes from JWB's 1860 speech are from this source and preserve the original spellings and punctuation used by Booth, 55–64.

3. Ellis P. Oberholtzer, *Philadelphia: A History of the City and Its People*, 4 vols. (Philadelphia: S. J. Clarke, 1912), 2:357.

4. Rhodehamel and Taper, *"Right or Wrong, God Judge Me,"* 62.

5. Rhodehamel and Taper, 51.

6. "the secession movement. our telegraphic dispatches. the union meeting in philadelphia. great demonstration the resolutions adopted [. . .]," *New York Times*, Dec. 14, 1860, 1.

7. Asia Booth Clarke, John Wilkes Booth: A Sister's Memoir, ed. Terry Alford (Jackson: University Press of Mississippi, 1991), 71.

8. Quoted in Jonathan Katz, *Resistance at Christiana: The Fugitive Slave Rebellion* (New York: Thomas Crowell, 1974), 90–100.

9. Rhodehamel and Taper, "Right or Wrong, God Judge Me," 56–59.

10. Clarke, *John Wilkes Booth*, 35.

11. Constitution of the Confederate States, March 11, 1861, Yale Law School Avalon Project, avalon.law.yale.edu/19th_century/csa_csa.asp.

12. Articles of Confederation, in *The Debate on the Constitution: Part Two*, ed. Bernard Bailyn (New York: Library of America, 1993), 926–36.

13. Preamble, *Constitution of the Confederate States*.

14. Charles B. Dew, *Apostles of Disunion* (Charlottesville: University of Virginia Press, 2001; reprint 2016), 16.

15. For the full text of Stephen's corner-stone speech see www// teachingamericanhistory.org/library/document/cornerstone-speech.

16. *Hitler's Wartime Conversations: His Personal Thoughts as Recorded by Martin Borman*, ed. Bob Carruthers (South Yorkshire, UK: Pen and Sword Military, 2018), 455–56. This remark was recorded on September 12, 1942.

CHAPTER 10. THE RISE OF ABRAHAM LINCOLN

1. David Herbert Donald, *Lincoln* (New York: Simon and Schuster, 1995), 271.

2. Allen C. Guelzo, *Fateful Lightning: A New History of the Civil War and Reconstruction* (New York: Oxford University Press, 2012), 100.

3. Roy P. Basler, Marion Dolores Pratt, and Lloyd A. Dunlap, eds., *The Collected Works of Abraham Lincoln*, 8 vols. plus index (New Brunswick, NJ: Rutgers University Press, 1953–55), 2:482 (hereafter *CWAL*).

4. *CWAL*, 1:8.

5. Donald, *Lincoln*, 162.

6. Robert V. Bruce, *Lincoln and the Riddle of Death* (Fort Wayne, IN: Louis A. Warren Lincoln Library and Museum, 1981), 23.

7. Bruce, 18.

8. Douglas L. Wilson and Rodney O. Davis, eds., *Herndon's Informants: Letters, Interviews, and Statements about Abraham Lincoln* (Urbana: University of Illinois Press, 1998), 197.

9. James M. McPherson, *Battle Cry of Freedom: The Civil War Era* (New York: Oxford University Press, 1988), 124.

10. *CWAL*, 2:382–83.

11. MeasuringWorth.com, www.measuringworth.com/slavery.php.

12. Charles B. Dew, *Apostles of Disunion* (2001; Charlottesville: University of Virginia Press, 2016), 122.

13. Guelzo, *Fateful Lightning*, 356.

14. Drew Gilpin Faust, *James Henry Hammond and the Old South* (Baton Rouge: Louisiana State University Press, 1982), 280–81.

15. James Henry Hammond, *Remarks of Mr. Hammond, of South Carolina, on the Question of Receiving Petitions for the Abolition of Slavery in the District of Columbia. Delivered in the House of Representatives, February 1, 1836* (Washington City: D. Green, 1836), 11–12, 15.

16. Faust, *James Henry Hammond*, 196.

17. J. David Hacker, "A Census-Based Count of the Civil War Dead," *Civil War History* 57 (2011): 306–47.

18. William W. Freehling, *The South vs. the South: How Anti-Confederate Southerners Shaped the Course of the Civil War* (New York: Oxford University Press, 2001), 34.

19. *CWAL*, 2:255.

20. Phillip Shaw Paludan, "Lincoln and Colonization: Policy or Propaganda?" *Journal of the Abraham Lincoln Association* 25 (Winter 2004): 23–37; Michael Vorenberg, "Abraham Lincoln and the Politics of Black Colonization," *Journal of the Abraham Lincoln Association* 14 (Summer 1993), 22–45.

CHAPTER II. THE TRIUMPH OF THE "BLACK" REPUBLICANS

1. Roy P. Basler, Marion Dolores Pratt, and Lloyd A. Dunlap, eds., *The Collected Works of Abraham Lincoln*, 8 vols plus index (New Brunswick, NJ: Rutgers University Press, 1953–55), 2:482 (hereafter *CWAL*).

2. *CWAL*, 4:67.

3. Eric Foner, *The Fiery Trial: Abraham Lincoln and American Slavery* (New York: Norton, 2010), 65.

4. *CWAL*, 2:282.

5. James M. McPherson, *Abraham Lincoln* (New York: Oxford University Press, 2009), 16.

6. James M. McPherson, *Battle Cry of Freedom: The Civil War Era* (New York: Oxford University Press, 1988), 159.

7. McPherson, 174.

8. McPherson, 174.

9. McPherson, 30–31.

10. McPherson, 182.

11. Brian R. Dirck, *The Black Heavens: Abraham Lincoln and Death* (Carbondale: Southern Illinois University Press, 2019), 70.

12. *CWAL*, 3:326.

13. *CWAL*, 3:16.

14. Foner, *The Fiery Trial*, 97.

15. Quoted in E. N. Elliot, *Cotton Is King, and Pro-slavery Arguments: Comprising the Writings of Hammond, Harper, Christy, Stringfellow, Hodge, Bledsoe, and Cartwright, on This Important Subject* (Augusta, GA: Pritchard, Abbott and Loomis, 1860), 126.

16. McPherson, *Battle Cry of Freedom*, 184.

17. Donald, *Lincoln*, 224.

18. Michael Burlingame, *Abraham Lincoln: A Life*, 2 vols. (Baltimore: Johns Hopkins University Press, 2008), 1:277–79. On Douglas's alcoholism, see 1:478–79.

19. *CWAL*, 3:10.

20. Burlingame, 1:488–89.

21. Burlingame, 1:26.

22. *CWAL*, 4:160–61.

CHAPTER 12. ALTERNATIVE FACTS

1. Quoted in Charles B. Dew, *Apostles of Disunion* (2001; Charlottesville: University of Virginia Press, 2016), 11.

2. Dew, 22.

3. Dew, 120.

4. Quoted in John Rhodehamel and Louise Taper, eds., *"Right or Wrong, God Judge Me": The Writings of John Wilkes Booth* (Urbana: University of Illinois Press, 1997), 130.

5. Dew, *Apostles of Disunion*, 107.

6. Abraham Lincoln, "First Inaugural Address, Monday, March 4, 1861," Atlantic Online, www.theatlantic.com/past/docs/issues/99sep/9909 linc1staddress.htm.

7. James M. McPherson, *Battle Cry of Freedom: The Civil War Era* (New York: Oxford University Press, 1988), 243.

8. McPherson, 224.

9. Michael Burlingame, *Abraham Lincoln: A Life*, 2 vols. (Baltimore: Johns Hopkins University Press, 2008), 2:632.

10. Burlingame, 2:664.

11. Burlingame, 2:633.

12. Edward E. Baptist, *The Half Has Never Been Told: Slavery and the Making of American Capitalism* (New York: Basis Books, 2014), 99.

13. Thomas Jefferson, *Notes on the State of Virginia, in Thomas Jefferson: Writings*, ed. Merrill D. Peterson (New York: Library of America, 1984.), 264.

14. C. Van Woodward, ed., *Mary Chesnut's Civil War* (New Haven, CT: Yale University Press, 1981), 29.

15. Quoted in McPherson, *Battle Cry of Freedom*, 232.

16. Dew, *Apostles of Disunion*, 67.

17. Quoted in Dew, 67.

18. Allan Nevins, *The Emergence of Lincoln: The Ordeal of the Union*, 8 vols. (New York: Scribner's, 1950), 2:217.

19. Nevins, 2:222–23.

20. Quoted in Nevins, 2:227.

CHAPTER 13. FILE UNDER "ASSASSINATION"

1. William H. Seward to John Bigelow, July 15, 1862, in John Bigelow, *Retrospections of an Active Life*, 5 vols. (New York: Baker and Taylor, 1909–13), 1:505.

2. Donald E. Fehrenbacher and Virginia Fehrenbacher, *Recollected Words of Abraham Lincoln* (Stanford, CA: Stanford University Press), 73.

3. Carl Sandburg, *Abraham Lincoln: The Prairie Years*, 2 vols. (New York: Harcourt, Brace, 1926), 2:234.

4. The *Atlanta Southern Confederacy*, quoted in the *New York Times*, quoted in Michael Davis, *The Image of Lincoln in the South* (Knoxville: University of Tennessee Press, 1971), 13.

5. Francis B. Carpenter, *Inner Life of Abraham Lincoln: Six Months in the White House* (New York: Scribners, 1874), 62–63.

6. Fehrenbacher and Fehrenbacher, *Recollected Words*, 17.

7. Joan L. Chaconas, foreword to John C. Fazio, *Decapitating the Union: Jefferson Davis, Judah Benjamin and the Plot to Assassinate Lincoln* (Columbia, SC: Morris Gilbert, 2015), 1.

8. Harold Holzer, ed., *Dear Mr. Lincoln: Letters to the President* (Reading, MA: Addison-Wesley, 1993), 336.

9. Holzer, 341.

10. Holzer, 340.

11. Daniel Stashower, *The Hour of Peril: The Secret Plot to Murder Lincoln before the Civil War* (New York: Minotaur, 2013).

12. Bruce Levin, *The Fall of the House of Dixie: The Civil War and the Social Revolution That Transformed the South* (New York: Random House, 2013), 56.

13. Roy P. Basler, Marion Dolores Pratt, and Lloyd A. Dunlap, eds., *The Collected Works of Abraham Lincoln*, 8 vols. plus index (New Brunswick, NJ: Rutgers University Press, 1953–55), 4:190 (hereafter *CWAL*).

14. Frederick Hatch, *Protecting President Lincoln* (Jefferson, NC: McFarland, 2011), 13.

15. David Herbert Donald, *Lincoln* (New York: Simon and Schuster, 1995), 274.

16. Stashower, *The Hour of Peril*, 181.

17. Michael Burlingame, *Abraham Lincoln: A Life*, 2 vols. (Baltimore: Johns Hopkins University Press, 2008), 2:32.

18. Dorothy Meserve Kunhardt and Philip B. Kunhardt Jr., *Twenty Days* (North Hollywood, CA: Newcastle, 1985), 5.

19. Hatch, *Protecting President Lincoln*, 14.

20. "1860 United States Presidential Election," Wikipedia, last edited Oct. 30, 2020, 13:43, https://en.wikipedia.org/wiki/1860_United_States _presidential_election.

21. Cited in Stashower, *The Hour of Peril*, 182.

22. *CWAL*, 4:236.

23. *CWAL*, 4:240.

24. Fehrenbacher and Fehrenbacher, *Recollected Words*, 18.

25. Stashower, *The Hour of Peril*, 260–63.

26. George S. Bryan, *The Great American Myth* (1940; Chicago: Americana House, 1990), 43.

27. Quoted in Burlingame, *Abraham Lincoln: A Life*, 2:38.

28. Quoted in Bryan, *The Great American Myth*, 48.

29. Quoted in Fehrenbacher and Fehrenbacher, *Recollected Words*, 194.

CHAPTER 14. "THE NEGRO IS NOT EQUAL TO THE WHITE MAN"

1. Art Loux, *John Wilkes Booth: Day by Day* (Jefferson, NC: McFarland, 2009), 74.

2. Roy P. Basler, Marion Dolores Pratt, and Lloyd A. Dunlap, eds., *The Collected Works of Abraham Lincoln*, 8 vols. plus index (New Brunswick, NJ: Rutgers University Press, 1953–55), 4:263. (Hereafter *CWAL*.)

3. Asia Booth Clarke, *John Wilkes Booth: A Sister's Memoir*, ed. Terry Alford (Jackson: University Press of Mississippi, 1991), 116. This is the definitive edition of *The Unlocked Book*.

4. Clarke, 82.

5. Clarke, 96–97.

6. Clarke, 88.

7. Clarke, 82.

8. Clarke, 88–89. Ariston was a sixth century BC tyrant of Byzantium.

"Assanonthine Brown" is a corruption of Osawatomie, Kansas, where Brown fought a famous battle in 1856.

9. Clarke, 84.

10. Francis B. Carpenter, *Six Months at the White House with Abraham Lincoln: The Story of a Picture* (New York: Hurd and Houghton, 1866), 164.

11. Mark E. Neely, *Southern Rights: Political Prisoners and the Myth of Confederate Constitutionalism* (Charlottesville: University Press of Virginia, 1999), 120.

12. Neely, 167.

13. *CWAL*, 4:430.

14. Neely, *Southern Rights*, 75.

15. "1860 United States Presidential Election," Wikipedia, last edited Oct. 30, 2020, 13:43, https://en.wikipedia.org/wiki/1860_United_States_presidential_election.

16. *Richmond Enquirer*, Oct. 1, 1862, quoted in Eric Foner, ed., *Nat Turner* (Englewood Cliffs, NJ: Prentice Hall, 1971), 140.

17. John Rhodehamel and Louise Taper, eds., *"Right or Wrong, God Judge Me": The Writings of John Wilkes Booth* (Urbana: University of Illinois Press, 1997), 124.

18. Clarke, *John Wilkes Booth*, 88.

19. *CWAL*, 4:271.

CHAPTER 15. "I MUST HAVE KENTUCKY"

1. James M. McPherson, *Abraham Lincoln and the Second American Revolution* (New York: Oxford University Press, 1990), 31.

2. David Herbert Donald, *Lincoln* (New York: Simon and Schuster, 1995), 297.

3. Roy P. Basler, Marion Dolores Pratt, and Lloyd A. Dunlap, eds., *The Collected Works of Abraham Lincoln*, 8 vols. plus index (New Brunswick, NJ: Rutgers University Press, 1953–55), 4:532 (hereafter *CWAL*).

4. See "Crittenden-Johnson Resolution," Wikipedia, last edited on July 30, 2020, 22:49, en.wikipedia.org/wiki/Crittenden-Johnson_Resolution.

5. *CWAL*, 5:49.

6. *CWAL*, 5:278–79.

7. Elizabeth R. Varon, *Armies of Deliverance: A New History of the Civil War* (New York: Oxford University Press, 2019), 10.

8. Brion McClanahan, "Is 'White Supremacy' an Exclusively 'Southern' Ideology?" *Abbeville Review*, May 3, 2016, 7.

9. Richard E. Hart, "Springfield's African Americans as a Part of the Lincoln Community," *Journal of the Abraham Lincoln Association* 20 (Winter 1999): 35–54.

10. Northwest Ordinance, July 13, 1787, Avalon Project, Lillian Goldman Law Library, Yale Law School.

11. James M. McPherson, *Battle Cry of Freedom: The Civil War Era* (New York: Oxford University Press, 1988), 55.

12. Quoted in McClanahan, "Is 'White Supremacy' an Exclusively 'Southern' Ideology?," 4.

13. McPherson, *Battle Cry of Freedom*, 159.

14. Quoted in McPherson, 159.

15. Quoted in McPherson, 5.

16. Quoted in Jennifer L. Weber, *Copperheads: The Rise and Fall of Lincoln's Opponents in the North* (Oxford: Oxford University Press, 2006), 161.

17. Donald, *Lincoln*, 305.

18. *CWAL*, 7:54.

19. "General George B. McClellan to President Abraham Lincoln," AmericanCivilWar.com, https://americancivilwar.com/documents/mcclellan_lincoln.html.

20. John Rhodehamel, "American Historical Manuscripts," in *The Huntington Library: Treasures from Ten Centuries* (San Marino, CA: Huntington Library, 2004), 49.

21. *CWAL*, 5:160–61.

22. Quoted in William E. Gienapp and Erica L. Gienapp, eds., *The Civil War Diary of Gideon Welles, Lincoln's Secretary of the Navy: The Original Manuscript Edition* (Urbana: Knox College Lincoln Studies Center and the University of Illinois Press, 2014), 3.

23. Quoted in Donald E. Fehrenbacher and Virginia Fehrenbacher, *Recollected Words of Abraham Lincoln* (Stanford, CA: Stanford University Press, 1996), 288.

24. Fehrenbacher and Fehrenbacher, 245.

25. Fehrenbacher and Fehrenbacher, 440.

26. Donald, *Lincoln*, 448.

27. John C. Fazio, *Decapitating the Union: Jefferson Davis, Judah Benjamin and the Plot to Assassinate Lincoln* (Columbia, SC: Morris Gilbert, 2015), 16.

28. Fazio, 285–86.

29. Frederick Hatch, *Protecting President Lincoln* (Jefferson, NC: McFarland, 2011), 38.

30. *CWAL*, 8:384–85.

CHAPTER 16. "A STAR OF THE FIRST MAGNITUDE"

1. John Rhodehamel and Louise Taper, eds., *"Right or Wrong, God Judge Me": The Writings of John Wilkes Booth* (Urbana: University of Illinois Press, 1997), 126.

2. Asia Booth Clarke, *John Wilkes Booth: A Sister's Memoir*, ed. Terry Alford (Jackson: University Press of Mississippi, 1991), 82.

3. Clarke, 124. During the final months of the Civil War, some defiant insurgents swore they would "die in the last ditch" before surrendering to the hated Yankees and their "nigger allies."

4. Quoted in C. Van Woodward, ed., *Mary Chesnut's Civil War* (New Haven, CT: Yale University Press, 1981), 645, 694.

5. Rhodehamel and Taper, *"Right or Wrong, God Judge Me,"* 126.

6. Art Loux, *John Wilkes Booth: Day by Day* (Jefferson, NC: McFarland, 2009), 77.

7. Loux, 96.

8. Loux, 82.

9. Loux, 80.

10. Quoted in Rhodehamel and Taper, *"Right or Wrong, God Judge Me,"* 125.

11. Rhodehamel and Taper, 125.

12. Frederick Seward, *Reminiscences of a War-Time Statesman and Diplomat, 1830–1915* (New York: Putnam's Sons, 1916), 227.

13. Henry J. Raymond, *Life and Public Services of Abraham Lincoln* (New York: Derby and Miller, 1865), 764.

14. William J. Cooper Jr., ed., *Jefferson Davis: The Essential Writings* (New York: Modern Library, 2003), 290.

15. Brian R. Dirck, *The Black Heavens: Abraham Lincoln and Death* (Carbondale: Southern Illinois University Press, 2019), 128.

16. Alexander H. Stephens, "'Cornerstone' Speech, March 21, 1861," Teaching American History, https://teachingamericanhistory.org/library/document/cornerstone-speech.

17. Abraham Lincoln, "Proclamation of Amnesty and Reconstruction," Dec. 8, 1863, in Roy P. Basler, Marion Dolores Pratt, and Lloyd A. Dunlap, eds., *The Collected Works of Abraham Lincoln*, 8 vols. plus index (New Brunswick, NJ: Rutgers University Press, 1953–55), 7:54 (hereafter *CWAL*).

18. James M. McPherson, *Abraham Lincoln* (New York: Oxford University Press, 1999), 45.

19. *CWAL*, 2:256.

20. *CWAL*, 5:388.

21. Quoted in Donald E. Fehrenbacher and Virginia Fehrenbacher, *Recollected Words of Abraham Lincoln* (Stanford, CA: Stanford University Press, 1996), 441. Scholarly punctiliousness obliges the present writer to note that the Fehrenbachers gave this recollected quote a "D" rating, calling it "a quotation about whose authenticity there is more than average doubt" (liii).

22. Frederick Douglass, "Oration in Memory of Abraham Lincoln, April 14, 1876," Teaching American History, https://teachingamericanhistory.org/library/document/oration-in-memory-of-abraham-lincoln.

CHAPTER 17. "KING ABRAHAM AFRICANUS I"

1. William Hanchett, *The Lincoln Murder Conspiracies: Being an Account of the Hatred Felt by Many Americans for President Abraham Lincoln* [. . .] (Urbana: University of Illinois Press 1983), 129, 130.

2. Hanchett, 13.

3. Robert F. Durden, *The Gray and the Black: The Confederate Debate on Emancipation* (Baton Rouge: Louisiana State University Press, 1972), 109.

4. Edward Steers Jr., *Blood on the Moon: The Assassination of Abraham Lincoln* (Lexington: University of Kentucky Press, 2001), 38.

5. David Herbert Donald, *Lincoln* (New York: Simon and Schuster, 1995), 416.

6. Quoted in Donald, 416.

7. Michael Burlingame, *Abraham Lincoln: A Life*, 2 vols. (Baltimore: Johns Hopkins University Press, 2008), 2:698.

8. Edward Achorn, *Every Drop of Blood: The Momentous Second Inauguration of Abraham Lincoln* (New York: Atlantic Monthly Press, 2020), 157.

9. Frederick Hatch, *Protecting President Lincoln* (Jefferson, NC: McFarland, 2011), 31–32.

10. Thomas Goodrich, *The Darkest Dawn: Lincoln, Booth, and the Great American Tragedy* (Bloomington: Indiana University Press, 2005), 41.

11. Hanchett, *The Lincoln Murder Conspiracies*, 13.

12. Donald, *Lincoln*, 297, 539.

13. Burlingame, *Abraham Lincoln: A Life*, 2:698.

14. Roy P. Basler, Marion Dolores Pratt, and Lloyd A. Dunlap, eds., *The

Collected Works of Abraham Lincoln, 8 vols. plus index (New Brunswick, NJ: Rutgers University Press, 1953–55), 4:263. (Hereafter *CWAL*.)

15. Art Loux, *John Wilkes Booth: Day by Day* (Jefferson, NC: McFarland, 2009), 148.

16. Terry Alford, *Fortune's Fool: The Life of John Wilkes Booth* (New York: Oxford University Press, 2015), 140.

17. Loux, *John Wilkes Booth*, 150.

18. Quoted in John Rhodehamel and Louise Taper, eds., *"Right or Wrong, God Judge Me": The Writings of John Wilkes Booth* (Urbana: University of Illinois Press, 1997), 93. Booth's spelling and punctuation have been preserved.

19. Gordon Samples, *Lust for Fame: The Stage Career of John Wilkes Booth* (Jefferson, NC: McFarland, 1982), 135.

20. John S. Kendall, *The Golden Age of the New Orleans Theater* (Baton Rouge: Louisiana State University Press, 1952), 497.

21. William A. Tidwell, with James O. Hall and David Winfred Gaddy, *Come Retribution: The Confederate Secret Service and the Assassination of Lincoln* (Jackson: University Press of Mississippi, 1988), 261.

22. Alford, *Fortune's Fool*, 168.

23. See Rhodehamel and Taper, *"Right or Wrong, God Judge Me,"* 102.

24. Quoted in Kendall, *The Golden Age*, 502.

25. Kendall, 498.

CHAPTER 18. "WE WORKED TO CAPTURE"

1. Samuel Bland Arnold, *Memoirs of a Lincoln Conspirator*, ed. Michael W. Kauffman (Bowie, MD: Heritage Books, 1995), 42.

2. Art Loux, *John Wilkes Booth: Day by Day* (Jefferson, NC: McFarland, 2009), 176.

3. O'Laughlen's birth year is variously given as 1843 and 1840. The consensus is 1840, providing the age given here.

4. Arnold, *Memoirs*, 39.

5. Testimony of Samuel Street in William C. Edwards and Edward Steers Jr., eds., *The Lincoln Assassination: The Evidence* (Urbana: University of Illinois Press, 2009), 1290; see also William A. Tidwell, with James O. Hall and David Winfrey Gaddy, *Come Retribution: The Confederate Secret Service and the Assassination of Lincoln* (Jackson: University Press of Mississippi, 1988), 262.

6. Edwards and Steers, *The Lincoln Assassination*, 1392.

7. Percy C. Martin, "Samuel Arnold and Michael O'Laughlen," in *The Trial: The Assassination of President Lincoln and the Trial of the Conspirators*, ed. Edward Steers Jr. (Lexington: University Press of Kentucky, 2003), lxxxix–xcv.

8. William J. Cooper Jr., ed., *Jefferson Davis: The Essential Writings* (New York: Modern Library, 2003), 341–43.

9. Testimony of Louis Weichmann, clerk in the War Department's Office of the Commissary General of Prisoners, in Edwards and Steers, *The Lincoln Assassination*, 1329.

10. Edward Achorn, *Every Drop of Blood: The Momentous Second Inauguration of Abraham Lincoln* (New York: Atlantic Monthly Press, 2020), 179.

11. Achorn, 181.

12. James M. McPherson, *Battle Cry of Freedom: The Civil War Era* (New York: Oxford University Press, 1988), 566–67, 650, 792–800.

13. Robert F. Durden, *The Gray and the Black: The Confederate Debate on Emancipation* (Baton Rouge: Louisiana State University Press, 1972), 93.

14. Quoted in John Surratt's Rockville Lecture, 1870, in Louis J. Weichmann, *A True History of the Assassination of Abraham Lincoln and the Conspiracy of 1865* (New York: Knopf, 1975), 430–31.

15. Benn Pitman, comp., *The Assassination of President Lincoln and the Trial of the Conspirators* (New York: Moore, Wilstach and Baldwin, 1865; facsimile edition, ed. Philip Van Doren Stern [New York: Funk and Wagnalls, 1954]), 411.

16. Arnold, *Memoirs*, 43.

17. Terry Alford, *Fortune's Fool: The Life of John Wilkes Booth* (New York: Oxford University Press, 2015), 231.

18. Weichmann, *A True History*, 56–57.

19. *De Bow's Review*, Oct.–Dec. 1861, cited in Michael Davis, *The Image of Lincoln in the South* (Knoxville: University of Tennessee Press, 1971), 66.

20. Anthony S. Pitch, *"They Have Killed Papa Dead!"* (Hanover, NH: Steerford Press, 2008), 28–29.

21. Tidwell, Hall, and Gaddy, *Come Retribution*, 264.

22. Pitman, *Assassination of President Lincoln*, 411.

23. William Hanchett, *The Lincoln Murder Conspiracies: Being an Account of the Hatred Felt by Many Americans for President Abraham Lincoln* [. . .] (Urbana: University of Illinois Press, 1983), 31–32; Edward Steers Jr., *Blood on the Moon: The Assassination of Abraham Lincoln* (Lexington: University Press of Kentucky, 2001), 24–26.

24. McPherson, *Battle Cry of Freedom*, 714.

25. Tidwell, Hall, and Gaddy, *Come Retribution*, 235–36.

26. Tidwell, Hall, and Gaddy, 236.

27. Tidwell, Hall, and Gaddy, 237.

28. Tidwell, Hall, and Gaddy, 283.

29. Edward Steers Jr., ed., *The Lincoln Assassination Encyclopedia* (New York: Harper Perennial, 2010), 119.

30. Duane Schultz, *The Dahlgren Affair: Terror and Conspiracy in the Civil War* (New York: Norton, 1998), 156–57.

31. Roy P. Basler, Marion Dolores Pratt, and Lloyd A. Dunlap, eds., *The Collected Works of Abraham Lincoln*, 8 vols. plus index (New Brunswick, NJ: Rutgers University Press, 1953–55), 6:203.

32. Schultz, *The Dahlgren Affair*, 174.

33. Quoted in Schultz, 175.

34. Schultz, 184.

35. Quoted in John Rhodehamel and Louise Taper, eds., *"Right or Wrong, God Judge Me:" The Writings of John Wilkes Booth* (Urbana: University of Illinois Press, 1997), 130.

CHAPTER 19. "COME RETRIBUTION"

1. See Duane Schultz, *The Dahlgren Affair: Terror and Conspiracy in the Civil War* (New York: Norton, 1998).

2. Quoted in Robert F. Durden, *The Gray and the Black: The Confederate Debate on Emancipation* (Baton Rouge: Louisiana State University Press, 1972), 118.

3. John C. Fazio, *Decapitating the Union: Jefferson Davis, Judah Benjamin and the Plot to Assassinate Lincoln* (Columbia, SC: Morris Gilbert, 2015).

4. William A. Tidwell, with James O. Hall and David Winfrey Gaddy, *Come Retribution: The Confederate Secret Service and the Assassination of Lincoln* (Jackson: University Press of Mississippi, 1988), 157.

5. John Rhodehamel and Louise Taper, eds., *"Right or Wrong, God Judge Me": The Writings of John Wilkes Booth* (Urbana: University of Illinois Press, 1997), 117n.

6. Asia Booth Clarke, *John Wilkes Booth: A Sister's Memoir*, ed. Terry Alford (Jackson: University Press of Mississippi, 1991), 84.

7. Tidwell, Hall, and Gaddy, *Come Retribution*, 263.

8. Testimony of Junius Brutus Booth in William C. Edwards and Edward Steers Jr., eds., *The Lincoln Assassination: The Evidence* (Urbana: University of Illinois Press, 2009), 182.

9. Quoted in Elizabeth R. Varon, *Armies of Deliverance: A New History of the Civil War* (New York: Oxford University Press, 2019), 305.

10. Jane Singer, *The Confederate Dirty War: Arson, Bombings, Assassinations and Plots for Chemical and Germ Warfare Attacks on the Union* (Jefferson, NC: McFarland, 2005), 37–38.

11. Tidwell, Hall, and Gaddy, *Come Retribution*, 331.

12. Tidwell, Hall, and Gaddy, 331.

13. Singer, *The Confederate Dirty War*, 78.

14. This account of Blackburn's career and activities closely follows Jane Singer, *The Confederate Dirty War*, 76–117, passim; and Edward Steers, *Blood on the Moon: The Assassination of Abraham Lincoln* (Lexington: University Press of Kentucky, 2001), 46–55.

15. Terry Alford, *Fortune's Fool: The Life of John Wilkes Booth* (New York: Oxford University Press, 2015), 149.

16. Jane Singer, *The Confederate Dirty War*, 78.

17. Singer, 80.

18. Quoted in Steers, *Blood on the Moon*, 53.

CHAPTER 20. "RIGHT OR WRONG, GOD JUDGE ME"

1. Richard Morcom, "They All Loved Lucy," *American Heritage* 21 (Oct. 1970): 12–15.

2. William A. Tidwell, with James O. Hall and David Winfrey Gaddy, *Come Retribution: The Confederate Secret Service and the Assassination of Lincoln* (Jackson: University Press of Mississippi, 1988), 346.

3. Tidwell, Hall, and Gaddy, 179, 346.

4. Asia Booth Clarke to Jean Anderson, May 22, 1865, Asia Booth Clarke Papers, Maryland Historical Society.

5. Quoted in Terry Alford, *Fortune's Fool: The Life of John Wilkes Booth* (New York: Oxford University Press, 2015), 218.

6. E. Lawrence Abel, *John Wilkes Booth and the Women Who Loved Him* (Washington, DC: Regency, 2018), 185–92.

7. John C. Fazio, *Decapitating the Union: Jefferson Davis, Judah Benjamin and the Plot to Assassinate Lincoln* (Columbia, SC: Morris Gilbert, 2015), 133.

8. John G. Nicolay and John Hay, *Abraham Lincoln: A History*, 10 vols. (New York: Scribners, 1890), 10:221.

9. "Republican Party Platform of 1864," Teaching American History, teachingamericanhistory.org / library / document / the-1864-republican-party -platform.

10. Michael Burlingame, *Abraham Lincoln: A Life*, 2 vols. (Baltimore: Johns Hopkins University Press, 2008), 2:695,

11. Forrest G. Wood, *Black Scare: The Racist Response to Emancipation and Reconstruction* (Berkeley: University of California Press, 1970), Plate 4.

12. John Rhodehamel and Louise Taper, eds., *"Right or Wrong, God Judge Me": The Writings of John Wilkes Booth* (Urbana: University of Illinois Press, 1997), 129.

13. James G. Randall and Richard N. Current, *Lincoln the President: Last Full Measure* (New York: Dodd, Mead, 1955), 156–65; James M. McPherson, *Battle Cry of Freedom: The Civil War Era* (New York: Oxford University Press, 1988), 760–69.

14. McPherson, *Battle Cry of Freedom*, 768–69.

15. Burlingame, *Abraham Lincoln: A Life*, 2:688.

16. Burlingame, 2:688.

17. William C. Edwards and Edward Steers Jr., eds., *The Lincoln Assassination: The Evidence* (Urbana: University of Illinois Press, 2009), 179.

18. Quoted in Adam Badeau, "Dramatic Reminiscences," *St. Paul and Minneapolis Pioneer Press*, February 20, 1887.

19. Edwards and Steers, *The Lincoln Assassination*, 181.

20. Michael W. Kauffman, *American Brutus: John Wilkes Booth and the Lincoln Conspiracies* (New York: Random House, 2004), 150.

21. Jane Singer, *The Confederate Dirty War: Arson, Bombings, Assassinations and Plots for Chemical and Germ Warfare Attacks on the Union* (Jefferson, NC: McFarland, 2005), 63.

22. Alford, *Fortune's Fool*, 196–97.

23. Rhodehamel and Taper, *"Right or Wrong, God Judge Me,"* 124–31. Following quotes from the two letters are from this source. I have preserved Booth's punctuation in these extracts.

CHAPTER 21. COUNTDOWN

1. Michael W. Kauffman, *American Brutus: John Wilkes Booth and the Lincoln Conspiracies* (New York: Random House, 2004), 144; Edward Steers Jr., ed., *The Lincoln Assassination Encyclopedia* (New York: Harper Perennial, 2010), 64.

2. Edward Steers Jr., "Samuel Alexander Mudd," in *The Trial: The Assassination of President Lincoln and the Trial of the Conspirators*, ed. Edward Steers Jr. (Lexington: University Press of Kentucky), lxxxiv–lxxxv.

3. John C. Fazio, *Decapitating the Union: Jefferson Davis, Judah Benjamin and the Plot to Assassinate Lincoln* (Columbia, SC: Morris Gilbert, 2015), 342.

4. Fazio, 50.

5. Fazio, 44.

6. Fazio, 44.

7. George Alfred Townsend, *The Life, Crime, and Capture of John Wilkes Booth* [. . .] (New York: Dick and Fitzgerald, 1865; repr., 1977), 43.

8. David W. Gaddy, "The Surratt Tavern—A Confederate 'Safe House'?" *Surratt Courier* 4, no. 4 (April 1979): 4.

9. Edward Achorn, *Every Drop of Blood: The Momentous Second Inauguration of Abraham Lincoln* (New York: Atlantic Monthly Press, 2020), 179.

10. Fazio, *Decapitating the Union*, 87–90.

11. Terry Alford, *Fortune's Fool: The Life of John Wilkes Booth* (New York: Oxford University Press, 2015), 212.

12. Anthony S. Pitch, *"They Have Killed Papa Dead!"* (Hanover, NH: Steerford Press, 2008), 352.

13. William C. Edwards and Edward Steers Jr., eds., *The Lincoln Assassination: The Evidence* (Urbana: University of Illinois Press, 2009), 828n.

14. Betty Ownsbey, "Lewis Thornton Powell, alias Lewis Payne," in *The Trial: The Assassination of President Lincoln and the Trial of the Conspirators*, ed. Edward Steers Jr. (Lexington: University Press of Kentucky), lxxii.

15. Fazio, Decapitating the Union, 70; Louis J. Weichmann, *A True History of the Assassination of Abraham Lincoln and of the Conspiracy of 1865*, ed. Floyd E. Rivold (New York: Random House, 1975), 80.

16. Ownsbey, "Lewis Thornton Powell," lxxvi.

17. Fazio, *Decapitating the Union*, 69–75.

18. Fazio, 135–36.

19. Edward Steers Jr., *Blood on the Moon: The Assassination of Abraham Lincoln* (Lexington: University Press of Kentucky, 2001), 73–79.

20. John Rhodehamel and Louise Taper, eds., *"Right or Wrong, God Judge Me": The Writings of John Wilkes Booth* (Urbana: University of Illinois Press, 1997), 132.

CHAPTER 22. "EVERY DROP OF BLOOD"

1. Quoted in James M. McPherson, *Abraham Lincoln and the Second American Revolution* (New York: Oxford University Press, 1988), 768.

2. James J. Barnes and Patricia P. Barnes, comps., *The American Civil War*

through British Eyes: Dispatches from British Diplomats, 3 vols. (Kent, OH: Kent State University Press, 2003–5), 3:213.

3. Michael Burlingame, *Abraham Lincoln: A Life*, 2 vols. (Baltimore: Johns Hopkins University Press, 2008), 2:759.

4. The artist Francis Carpenter, recounting a conversation with the president, quoted in Carl Sandburg, *Abraham Lincoln: The War Years*, 4 vols. (New York: Harcourt, Brace, 1939), 4:43. See also James B. Conroy, *Our One Common Country: Abraham Lincoln and the Hampton Roads Peace Conference of 1865* (Guilford, CT: Lyons Press, 2014), 192–93. Rebel Vice President Alexander H. Stephens, who also attended the Hampton Roads Conference, remembered that it was he who told Lincoln of this danger, saying, "I know that negroes will not work, unless forced to, and I tell you that we shall all starve together." Michael Burlingame, *Abraham Lincoln: A Life*, 2:757.

5. Sandburg, *Abraham Lincoln*, 4:43.

6. Sandburg, 4:44.

7. Sandburg, 4:44.

8. Samuel Bland Arnold, *Memoirs of a Lincoln Conspirator*, ed. Michael W. Kauffman (Bowie, MD: Heritage Books, 1995), 45.

9. Art Loux, *John Wilkes Booth: Day by Day* (Jefferson, NC: McFarland, 2009), 201.

10. Arnold, *Memoirs of a Lincoln Conspirator*, 45.

11. Daniel K. Chester, April 28, 1865, testimony quoted in William C. Edwards and Edward Steers Jr., eds., *The Lincoln Assassination: The Evidence* (Urbana: University of Illinois Press, 2009), 345.

12. Robert Pohl, "History: Lost Capitol Hill: John W. Westfall," the-hillishome.com, https://thehillishome.com/2017/01/lost-capitol-hill-john -w-westfall.

13. Benjamin B. French to Francis O. French, April 24 and 30, 1865, quoted in Terry Alford, *Fortune's Fool: The Life of John Wilkes Booth* (New York: Oxford University Press, 2015), 226.

14. Quoted in Don E. Fehrenbacher and Virginia Fehrenbacher, eds., *Recollected Words of Abraham Lincoln* (Stanford, CA: Stanford University Press, 1996), 245.

15. Allen C. Guelzo, *Abraham Lincoln: Redeemer President* (Grand Rapids, MI: William B. Eerdmans, 1999), 153.

16. Douglas L. Wilson and Rodney O. Davis, eds., *Herndon's Informants: Letters, Interviews, and Statements about Lincoln* (Urbana: University of Illinois Press, 1998), 576.

17. Roy P. Basler, Marion Dolores Pratt, and Lloyd A. Dunlap, eds., *The Collected Works of Abraham Lincoln*, 8 vols. plus index (New Brunswick, NJ: Rutgers University Press, 1953–55), 5:403–4. This passage, which Lincoln's secretaries titled "Meditation on Divine Will," has traditionally been dated September 1862, the month of the Preliminary Emancipation Proclamation. More recently, Douglas L. Wilson, a scholar of Lincoln's writings, has argued convincingly, based on parallels with the Second Inaugural Address and other documents of the period, that the piece dates from 1864. See Douglas L. Wilson, *Lincoln's Sword: The Presidency and the Power of Words* (New York: Alfred A. Knopf, 2006), 255–56, 329–30.

18. James Madison to Marie-Joseph-Paul-Yves-Roch-Gibert du Motier, marquis de Lafayette, Nov. 25, 1820, in *The Papers of James Madison, Retirement Series*, vol. 2, *1 Feb. 1820–26 Feb. 1823*, ed. David B. Matten et al. (Charlottesville: University of Virginia Press, 2013), 158–60.

19. George Mason, Philadelphia, August 22, 1787, in Max Farrand, *The Records of the Federal Convention of 1787*, 2:370, 415–17, https://memory.loc.gov/ammem/amlaw/lwusing.html.

20. Quoted in Allan Nevins, *The Ordeal of the Union: The Organized War to Victory, 1864–1865*, 8 vols. (New York: Scribner, 1971; repr. Collier-Macmillan, 1992), 8:216–17.

21. Edward Achorn, *Every Drop of Blood*, 222.

22. Basler, Pratt, and Dunlap, *Collected Works of Abraham Lincoln*, 8:332–33.

23. Alford, *Fortune's Fool*, 218–19.

24. Edwards and Steers, *The Lincoln Assassination*, 620.

25. Loux, *John Wilkes Booth*, 204.

CHAPTER 23. UNHAPPY WITH HISTORY

1. Terry Alford, *Fortune's Fool: The Life of John Wilkes Booth* (New York: Oxford University Press, 2015), 237.

2. Alford, 237.

3. Alford, 239–40.

4. Michael W. Kauffman, *American Brutus: John Wilkes Booth and the Lincoln Conspiracies* (New York: Random House, 2004), 176–85.

5. Samuel Bland Arnold, *Memoirs of a Lincoln Conspirator*, ed. Michael W. Kauffman (Bowie, MD: Heritage Books, 1995), 49.

6. William C. Edwards and Edward Steers Jr., eds., *The Lincoln Assassination: The Evidence* (Urbana: University of Illinois Press, 2009), 160.

7. Louis J. Weichmann, *A True History of the Assassination of Abraham Lincoln and of the Conspiracy of 1865*, ed. Floyd E. Rivold (New York: Random House, 1975), 119.

8. See Alford, *Fortune's Fool*, 242.

9. Arthur F. Loux, *John Wilkes Booth: Day by Day* (Jefferson, NC: MacFarland, 2014), 191.

10. Gene Smith, *American Gothic: The Story of America's Legendary Theatrical Family—Junius, Edwin, and John Wilkes Booth* (New York: Simon and Schuster, 1992), 105–6.

11. Alford, *Fortune's Fool*, 66.

12. Edwards and Steers, *The Lincoln Assassination*, 343.

13. Loux, *John Wilkes Booth*, 256n6.

14. *Surratt Courier* 39, no. 4 (April 2014): 3–6.

15. Ernest C. Miller, *John Wilkes Booth in the Pennsylvania Oil Regions* (Meadville, PA: Crawford County Historical Society, 1987), 17.

16. Miller, 19.

17. George S. Bryan, *The Great American Myth* (1940; repr. Chicago: Americana House, 1990), 141–42.

18. John Rhodehamel and Louise Taper, eds., *"Right or Wrong, God Judge Me": The Writings of John Wilkes Booth* (Urbana: University of Illinois Press, 1997), 142.

19. Surratt Society, *From War Department Files: Statements Made by the Alleged Lincoln Conspirators under Examination, 1865* (Clinton, MD: Surratt Society, 1980), 22.

20. Rhodehamel and Taper, *"Right or Wrong, God Judge Me,"* 143–44.

21. Asia Booth Clarke, *John Wilkes Booth: A Sister's Memoir*, ed. Terry Alford (Jackson: University Press of Mississippi, 1991), 85.

22. Which unit entered Richmond first remains a matter of dispute, but it was widely reported in the North that first on the scene had been the United States Colored Troops. See Nelson Lankford, *Richmond Burning: The Last Days of the Confederate Capital* (New York: Viking, 2002), 130–31.

23. Thomas Goodrich, *The Darkest Dawn* (Bloomington: Indiana University Press, 2005), 59.

24. Carl Sandburg, *Abraham Lincoln: The War Years*, 4 vols. (New York: Harcourt, Brace, 1939), 4:332.

25. Clarke, *John Wilkes Booth*, 85.

26. Clarke, 141.

27. Rhodehamel and Taper, *"Right or Wrong, God Judge Me,"* 130.

28. Weichmann, *A True History*, 131.

29. Rhodehamel and Taper, *"Right or Wrong, God Judge Me,"* 145.

30. John G. Nicolay and John Hay, *Abraham Lincoln: A History*, 10 vols. (New York: Century, 1890), 10:216.

31. Bryan, *The Great American Myth*, 146.

32. Alford, *Fortune's Fool*, 99.

CHAPTER 24. "MIGHT MAKES RIGHT"

1. Noah Brooks, *Lincoln Observed: Civil War Dispatches of Noah Brooks*, ed. Michael Burlingame (Baltimore: Johns Hopkins University Press, 1998), 182.

2. Brooks, 183.

3. Elizabeth Keckley, *Behind the Scenes in the Lincoln White House: Memoirs of an African-American Seamstress* (1868; New York: Dover, 2006), 75.

4. Roy P. Basler, Marion Dolores Pratt, and Lloyd A. Dunlap, eds., *The Collected Works of Abraham Lincoln*, 8 vols. plus index (New Brunswick, NJ: Rutgers University Press, 1953–55), 8:399.

5. Basler, Pratt, and Dunlap, 8:403.

6. William Hanchet, *The Lincoln Murder Conspiracies: Being an Account of the Hatred Felt by Many Americans for President Abraham Lincoln* [. . .] (Urbana: University of Illinois Press 1983), 37.

7. Michael Burlingame, *Abraham Lincoln: A Life*, 2 vols. (Baltimore: Johns Hopkins University Press, 2008), 2:811.

8. Arthur F. Loux, *John Wilkes Booth: Day by Day* (Jefferson, NC: MacFarland, 2014), 188.

9. Shelby Foote, *The Civil War: A Narrative*, 3 vols. (New York: Random House, 1958–74), 3:293.

10. William E. Gienapp and Erica L. Gienapp, eds., *The Civil War Diary of Gideon Welles, Lincoln's Secretary of the Navy: The Original Manuscript Edition* (Urbana: Knox College Lincoln Studies Center and the University of Illinois Press, 2014), 621.

11. Loux, *John Wilkes Booth*, 208; William C. Edwards and Edward Steers Jr., eds., *The Lincoln Assassination: The Evidence* (Urbana: University of Illinois Press, 2009), 739.

12. Allen C. Guelzo, *Fateful Lightning: A New History of the Civil War and Reconstruction* (New York: Oxford University Press, 2012), 469.

13. Elizabeth Brown Pryor, *Reading the Man: A Portrait of Robert E. Lee through His Private Letters* (New York: Viking, 2007), 260–61. For Lee's attitude toward slavery, see chapter 16 of Pryor.

14. Terry Alford, *Fortune's Fool: The Life of John Wilkes Booth* (New York: Oxford University Press, 2015), 224.

15. Quoted in Michael W. Kauffman, *American Brutus: John Wilkes Booth and the Lincoln Conspiracies* (New York: Random House, 2004), 221.

16. Alford, *Fortune's Fool*, 257.

17. Quoted in John Rhodehamel and Louise Taper, eds., *"Right or Wrong, God Judge Me": The Writings of John Wilkes Booth* (Urbana: University of Illinois Press, 1997), 144.

18. Rhodehamel and Taper, 145.

19. Alford, *Fortune's Fool*, 185.

20. Henry Clay Ford testimony, in Edwards and Steers, *The Lincoln Assassination*, 516–24.

21. Edwards and Steers, *The Lincoln Assassination*, 512, 522. In New York City, Edwin Booth had just completed his celebrated, unprecedented run of one hundred nights as Prince Hamlet.

22. Ron Chernow, *Grant* (New York: Simon and Schuster, 2018), 515.

23. James M. McPherson, *Embattled Rebel: Jefferson Davis as Commander in Chief* (New York: Penguin, 2014), 20.

24. Alford, *Fortune's Fool*, 250.

25. Louis J. Weichmann, *A True History of the Assassination of Abraham Lincoln and of the Conspiracy of 1865*, ed. Floyd E. Rivold (New York: Random House, 1975), 138.

26. Cited in William J. Cooper Jr., ed., *Jefferson Davis: The Essential Writings* (New York: Modern Library, 2003), 364–65.

27. John C. Fazio, *Decapitating the Union: Jefferson Davis, Judah Benjamin and the Plot to Assassinate Lincoln* (Columbia, SC: Morris Gilbert, 2015), 30.

28. Burlingame, *Abraham Lincoln: A Life*, 2:778.

29. Quoted in William A. Tidwell, with James O. Hall and David Winfrey Gaddy, *Come Retribution: The Confederate Secret Service and the Assassination of Lincoln* (Jackson: University Press of Mississippi, 1988), 418.

CHAPTER 25. GOOD FRIDAY, 1865

1. Justin G. Turner and Linda Levitt Turner, *Mary Todd Lincoln: Her Life and Letters* (New York: Knopf, 1972), 284–85.

2. W. Emerson Reck, *A. Lincoln: His Last 24 Hours* (Jefferson, NC: McFarland, 1987), 20.

3. Douglas L. Wilson and Rodney O. Davis, eds., *Herndon's Informants:*

Letters, Interviews, and Statements about Abraham Lincoln (Urbana: University of Illinois Press, 1998), 359.

4. Michael Burlingame, ed., *At Lincoln's Side: John Hay's Civil War Correspondence and Selected Writings* (Carbondale: Southern Illinois University Press, 2000), 139.

5. Michael Burlingame, *Abraham Lincoln: A Life*, 2 vols. (Baltimore: Johns Hopkins University Press, 2008), 2:809.

6. Quoted in Thomas Goodrich, *The Darkest Dawn: Lincoln, Booth, and the Great American Tragedy* (Bloomington: Indiana University Press, 2005), 33.

7. Goodrich, 33.

8. Reck, *A. Lincoln*, 32–33.

9. Welles revised his diary extensively after the war. To this passage he added that the strange dream vessel was "moving toward an indefinite shore." William E. Gienapp and Erica L. Gienapp, eds., *The Civil War Diary of Gideon Welles, Lincoln's Secretary of the Navy: The Original Manuscript Edition* (Urbana: Knox College Lincoln Studies Center and the University of Illinois Press, 2014), 621.

10. Carl Sandburg, *Abraham Lincoln: The War Years*, 4 vols. (New York: Harcourt, Brace, 1939), 4:266.

11. Burlingame, *Abraham Lincoln: A Life*, 2:793.

12. Sandburg, *Abraham Lincoln*, 4:264.

13. Burlingame, *Abraham Lincoln: A Life*, 2:805.

14. Michael W. Kauffman, *American Brutus: John Wilkes Booth and the Lincoln Conspiracies* (New York: Random House, 2004), 216.

15. John C. Fazio, *Decapitating the Union: Jefferson Davis, Judah Benjamin and the Plot to Assassinate Lincoln* (Columbia, SC: Morris Gilbert, 2015), 113–17.

16. Kauffman, *American Brutus*, 445, 61n.

17. William C. Edwards and Edward Steers Jr., eds., *The Lincoln Assassination: The Evidence* (Urbana: University of Illinois Press, 2009), 807.

18. Edwards and Steers, 807.

19. Terry Alford, *Fortune's Fool: The Life of John Wilkes Booth* (New York: Oxford University Press, 2015), 212.

20. Burlingame, *Abraham Lincoln: A Life*, 2:779.

21. Burlingame, 2:781–82.

22. Burlingame, 2:782.

23. Quoted in Anthony S. Pitch, *"They Have Killed Papa Dead!"* (Hanover, NH: Steerford Press, 2008), 90.

24. Horace Porter, *Campaigning with Grant* (New York: Century, 1897), 498–99.

25. John Rhodehamel and Louise Taper, eds., "*Right or Wrong, God Judge Me*": *The Writings of John Wilkes Booth* (Urbana: University of Illinois Press, 1997), 146.

26. Mary Todd Lincoln to Sally Orne, March 15, 1866, in Justin G. Turner and Linda Levitt Turner, *Mary Todd Lincoln: Her Life and Letters* (New York: Knopf, 1972), 345.

27. Fazio, *Decapitating the Union*, 258–59.

28. Edwards and Steers, *The Lincoln Assassination*, 63.

29. Alford, *Fortune's Fool*, 262.

30. Fazio, *Decapitating the Union*, 249–53.

CHAPTER 26. BLACK FRIDAY, 1865

1. William C. Edwards and Edward Steers Jr., eds., *The Lincoln Assassination: The Evidence* (Urbana: University of Illinois Press, 2009), 489.

2. Edwards and Steers, 486.

3. Ron Chernow, *Grant* (New York: Penguin, 2017), 522–23.

4. Michael Burlingame, ed., *Lincoln Observed: Civil War Dispatches of Noah Brooks* (Baltimore: Johns Hopkins University Press, 1998), 188.

5. This intriguing story, which has never been taken up by any Lincoln biographer, has a solid provenance but must remain only third-person hearsay. Beckwith, the former owner of Lincoln's pocket pistol and the repository of the family's tradition of its origin, had recounted it to his personal friend James T. Hickey, the respected curator of the Lincoln collections of the Illinois State Historical Library in Springfield. Beckwith said the derringer had been stolen from his home by a confidence man who had befriended him. James T. Hickey, 1923–96, Curator, Lincoln Collection, Illinois State Historical Library, in conversation with John Rhodehamel, February 11, 1989.

6. The contents of Lincoln's pockets on the night of the assassination make up a famous permanent exhibition in the Library of Congress. Included are a pen knife, a watch fob, spectacles, press clippings, and a Confederate five-dollar bill, among other items. If there really was a derringer, it was withheld when Lincoln's descendants donated the items to the government in 1947.

7. Quoted in John C. Fazio, *Decapitating the Union: Jefferson Davis, Judah Benjamin and the Plot to Assassinate Lincoln* (Columbia, SC: Morris Gilbert, 2015), 161.

8. John Rhodehamel and Louise Taper, eds., "*Right or Wrong, God Judge*

Me": The Writings of John Wilkes Booth (Urbana: University of Illinois Press, 1997), 152.

9. Rhodehamel and Taper, 153.

10. Fazio, *Decapitating the Union*, 181–83.

11. Carl Sandburg, *Abraham Lincoln: The War Years*, 4 vols. (New York: Harcourt, Brace, 1939), 4:277.

12. See Art Loux, *John Wilkes Booth: Day by Day* (Jefferson, NC: McFarland, 2009), 37–60.

13. Walt Whitman, "Death of Abraham Lincoln," www.Bartleby.com /229/2009.html.

14. Quoted in Edwards and Steers, *The Lincoln Assassination*, 484.

15. Fazio, *Decapitating the Union*, 200–202.

16. Thomas Goodrich, *The Darkest Dawn: Lincoln, Booth, and the Great American Tragedy* (Bloomington: Indiana University Press, 2005), 98.

17. Goodrich, 99.

18. Whitman, "Death of Abraham Lincoln."

19. Whitman.

CHAPTER 27. A LONG, UGLY NIGHT

1. Dr. Charles A. Leale, *Lincoln's Last Hours: Address Delivered before the Commandery of the State of New York Military Order of the Loyal Legion of the U.S.* (New York: privately printed, 1909), quoted in Thomas Goodrich, *The Darkest Dawn: Lincoln, Booth, and the Great American Tragedy* (Bloomington: Indiana University Press, 2005), 99–101.

2. Quoted in John C. Fazio, *Decapitating the Union: Jefferson Davis, Judah Benjamin and the Plot to Assassinate Lincoln* (Columbia, SC: Morris Gilbert, 2015), 265.

3. Goodrich, *The Darkest Dawn*, 105.

4. Michael W. Kauffman, *American Brutus: John Wilkes Booth and the Lincoln Conspiracies* (New York: Random House, 2004), 183.

5. Fazio, *Decapitating the Union*, 270.

6. William E. Gienapp and Erica L. Gienapp, eds., *The Civil War Diary of Gideon Welles, Lincoln's Secretary of the Navy: The Original Manuscript Edition* (Urbana: Knox College Lincoln Studies Center and the University of Illinois Press, 2014), 626.

7. Gienapp and Gienapp, 627.

8. Gienapp and Gienapp, 627.

9. Gienapp and Gienapp, 629n.

10. James L. Swanson, *Manhunt: The Twelve-Day Chase for Lincoln's Killer* (New York: William Morrow, 2006), 286.

11. Goodrich, *The Darkest Dawn*, 118.

12. Goodrich, 119.

13. Goodrich, 105.

CHAPTER 28. "HUNTED LIKE A DOG"

1. James Swanson gives the number of dead as "more than two hundred" but does not provide documentation. See James L. Swanson, *Bloody Crimes: The Chase for Jefferson Davis and the Death Pageant for Lincoln's Corpse* (New York: William Morrow, 2010), 240.

2. Thomas Goodrich, *The Darkest Dawn: Lincoln, Booth, and the Great American Tragedy* (Bloomington: Indiana University Press, 2005), 141.

3. Asia Booth Clarke to Jean Anderson, May 22, 1865, Record Group ML518, Peale Museum, Baltimore.

4. Caroline Jones, Augusta, Georgia, April 20, 1865, in *The Children of Pride: A True Story of Georgia and the Civil War*, ed. Robert Manson Myers (New Haven, CT: Yale University Press, 1972), 1268.

5. Goodrich, *The Darkest Dawn*,159.

6. Stanley Kimmel, *The Mad Booths of Maryland* (Indianapolis, IN: Bobbs-Merrill, 1940), 150.

7. Martha Hodes, *Mourning Lincoln* (New Haven, CT: Yale University Press, 2015), 70–91.

8. John C. Fazio, *Decapitating the Union: Jefferson Davis, Judah Benjamin and the Plot to Assassinate Lincoln* (Columbia, SC: Morris Gilbert, 2015), 344.

9. Fazio, 345. One of Davis's biographers has maintained that the first statement attributed to him in this paragraph is bogus. See William C. Davis, *An Honorable Defeat: The Last Days of the Confederate Government* (New York: Harcourt, 2001), 173–75.

10. William C. Edwards and Edward Steers Jr., eds., *The Lincoln Assassination: The Evidence* (Urbana: University of Illinois Press, 2009), 816.

11. Edward Steers Jr., *Blood on the Moon: The Assassination of Abraham Lincoln* (Lexington: University Press of Kentucky, 2001), 151.

12. Michael W. Kauffman, *American Brutus: John Wilkes Booth and the Lincoln Conspiracies* (New York: Random House, 2004), 153.

13. Anthony S. Pitch, *"They Have Killed Papa Dead!"* (Hanover, NH: Steerford Press, 2008), 257.

14. Quoted in John Rhodehamel and Louise Taper, eds., *"Right or Wrong,*

God Judge Me": The Writings of John Wilkes Booth (Urbana: University of Illinois Press, 1997), 152.

15. Kauffman, *American Brutus*, 287.

16. Kauffman, 288–89.

17. Rhodehamel and Louise Taper, *"Right or Wrong, God Judge Me,"* 154–55. JWB's hero, Marcus Junius Brutus, was one of the principal assassins of Julius Caesar; William Tell was a fourteenth-century Swiss patriot who killed the Austrian tyrant Albrecht Gessler.

CHAPTER 29. THE LAST ACT

1. Terry Alford, *Fortune's Fool: The Life of John Wilkes Booth* (New York: Oxford University Press, 2015), 290.

2. Alford, 290.

3. William C. Edwards and Edward Steers Jr., eds., *The Lincoln Assassination: The Evidence* (Urbana: University of Illinois Press, 2009), 824–25.

4. Alford, *Fortune's Fool*, 295.

5. Quoted in James L. Swanson, *Manhunt: The Twelve-Day Chase for Lincoln's Killer* (New York: William Morrow, 2006), 274.

6. Alford, *Fortune's Fool*, 296.

7. Alford, 296.

8. Swanson, *Manhunt*, 275.

9. Swanson, 320.

10. Edward Steers Jr., *Blood on the Moon: The Assassination of Abraham Lincoln* (Lexington: University Press of Kentucky, 2001), 192.

11. Edwards and Steers, *The Lincoln Assassination*, 1111–12.

12. Alford, *Fortune's Fool*, 306.

13. Alford, 309.

14. Michael W. Kauffman, *American Brutus: John Wilkes Booth and the Lincoln Conspiracies* (New York: Random House, 2004), 318.

15. Alford, *Fortune's Fool*, 309.

16. Thomas Goodrich, *The Darkest Dawn: Lincoln, Booth, and the Great American Tragedy* (Bloomington: Indiana University Press, 2005), 227.

CHAPTER 30. RECKONINGS

1. James L. Swanson, *Manhunt: The Twelve-Day Chase for Lincoln's Killer* (New York: William Morrow, 2006), 353.

2. John C. Fazio, *Decapitating the Union: Jefferson Davis, Judah Benjamin*

and the *Plot to Assassinate Lincoln* (Columbia, SC: Morris Gilbert, 2015), 98.

3. Fazio, 100.

4. John Rhodehamel and Louise Taper, eds., *"Right or Wrong, God Judge Me": The Writings of John Wilkes Booth* (Urbana: University of Illinois Press, 1997), 143–44.

5. Brian R. Dirck, *The Black Heavens: Abraham Lincoln and Death* (Carbondale: Southern Illinois University Press, 2019), 173.

6. Edward Steers Jr., *Blood on the Moon: The Assassination of Abraham Lincoln* (Lexington: University Press of Kentucky, 2001), 288.

7. Michael Kammen, *Digging Up the Dead: A History of Notable American Reburials* (Chicago: University of Chicago Press, 2009), x, 25, 93–98, 116, 203.

EPILOGUE

1. James M. McPherson, *Battle Cry of Freedom: The Civil War Era* (New York: Oxford University Press, 1988), 859.

2. Eric Foner, *Reconstruction: America's Unfinished Revolution, 1863–1877*, updated ed. (New York: HarperPerennial, 2002), 177–78.

3. W. E. B. Du Bois, *Black Reconstruction in America: An Essay towards a History of the Part Which Black Folk Played in the Attempt to Reconstruct Democracy in America, 1860–1880* (New York: Harcourt Brace, 1935), 60.

4. Martha Hodes, *Mourning Lincoln* (New Haven, CT: Yale University Press, 2015), 266.

5. Quoted in Donald E. Fehrenbacher and Virginia Fehrenbacher, eds., *Recollected Words of Abraham Lincoln* (Stanford, CA: Stanford University Press), 441. Scholarly punctiliousness obliges the present writer to note that the Fehrenbachers assigned this recollected quote a "D" rating given that it is "a quotation about whose authenticity there is more than average doubt" (liii).

6. David W. Blight, *Frederick Douglass: Prophet of Freedom* (New York: Simon and Schuster, 2018), 77.

7. Foner, *Reconstruction*, 184.

INDEX

Page numbers in *italics* indicate images.

Southern cause, 79, 90, 92, 178, 179, 181, 202, 244–48, 295–97; and insanity charge, 31, 91–92; investments of, 81, 291–92; at John Brown hanging, 85, 89–91; meets Andrew Johnson, 200, 335; memo book–diary of, 378–79, 380–81; nativism of, 82–84; in New York, 181, 197, 223, 242–43, 269, 289; personifications by, 100; photos, 78, 250; prostitute visited, 235, 328; secession crisis speech written by, 91, 92, 94, 95–96, 98, 99–100, 429n16; skills of, 79, 286, 292–93; on slavery, 41, 42–44, 49, 246; as Southern gentleman, 69; and Washington victory celebrations, 306, 307–8; white supremacist views, 34, 41, 143, 159–60, 182, 308, 343; and women, 76–77, 79–80, 177, 180, 233–35

Booth, John Wilkes (actor), 55, 76; debut, 71–72; as director, 81; as Hamlet, 1, 153; income, 80, 177, 178; injuries, 180, 198; in *Julius Caesar*, 242–43; last performance, 286; newspaper reviews of, 75, 151–52, 177, 197–98, 201, 260–61; as own manager, 80–81, 151; as Richard III, 1, 151–52, 180, 182, 197, 198; as Romeo, 260–61; star tours by, 74, 80–81, 91, 179–80, 181–82, 197–202; as supporting player, 72–73, 75–76

Booth, John Wilkes (conspirator and assassin): as Confederate spy, 154; dissatisfaction among gang with, 270–71; escape from Ford's Theatre, 349–51; escape from

Washington, 368–69; at Ford's Theatre on assassination day, 340–41, 345–47; funding of, 235, 260, 269; Grant assassination plan, 310–11, 323, 330–31, 332; Johnson assassination plan, 200, 255, 310–11, 323, 326, 337, 338, 401; justifications for Lincoln assassination by, 343–44, 378–79, 380–81; Lincoln kidnapping plots, 210–18, 221; and March 29 possible attempt, 293–94; meetings with conspirators, 281, 283–85, 288, 336–37; and Northwest conspiracy, 223, 224–25, 227; political motives of, 33–34; and presidential succession, 310–12, 323–25; recruitment of conspirators, 221, 249–61; reward for capture of, 374, 375; on run in Maryland, 369, 371–82; on run in Virginia, 382, 383–90; at second Lincoln inauguration, 271–73, 279; and Secret Service Bureau, 235, 249, 260, 325–26; Seventh Street Road abduction plan, 284–86; Seward assassination attempt, 310–11, 323, 325, 326, 337–38, 353–58; shooting of Booth, 395–96; shooting of Lincoln, 3–4, 347–49; troops' hunt for, 363–65, 372, 391–93; troops' surrounding of, 393–95; during Washington victory celebration, 301; weaponry of, 262–63

Booth, Joseph (brother), 66–67, 224, 400

Booth, Junius Brutus (father), 32, 44, 82–83, 421n3; as actor, 1, 23–25, 27–30; as alcoholic, 34–35;

Booth, Junius Brutus (father) (*cont.*)
attacks of insanity, 30–31; as
bigamist, 21, 26; birth of, 22; death
of, 54; financial affairs of, 66; and
first wife Adelaide, 24, 52–53;
grave of, 30, 422n24; home of,
36–37, 204; leaves England, 26–27;
partnership and marriage to Mary
Ann Holmes, 20–21, 53; paternity
suits against, 23; and slavery, 38–39
Booth, Junius Brutus, Jr. (brother),
26, 35, 370; as actor, 66, 242;
arguments with JWB, 242, 244
Booth, Mary Ann (sister), 45
Booth, Mary Ann Holmes (mother),
45, 54, 68, 71–72; background of,
26; at JWB burial, 400; JWB letters
to, 244–48, 307; partnership with
Junius, 20–21, 25–27, 52, 53
Booth, Richard (grandfather), 21–22,
23
Booth, Richard Junius (half-brother),
25, 52, 53
Booth, Rosalie (sister), 67, 224, 400
Booth Delannoy, Adelaide (Junius's
first wife), 24, 26, 51–53
Breckinridge, John C., 125, 139
Britain, 265
Brooks, Noah, 341
Brown, John, 85–86, 87, 88; Booth
on, 99, 156, 246; goal of, 85–86;
hanging of, 90–91; in Kansas, 119;
portrayal of, 86, 144–45
Bruce, Robert V., 108
Brutus, Marcus Junius, 22–23, 381,
454n17
Bryant, William, 384
Bryantown, MD, 249
Buchanan, James, 95, 118, 119, 156–57

Bunyan, John: *Pilgrim's Progress,* 100
Burlingame, Michael, 56–57, 122, 302
Butler, Benjamin, 170

Caesar, Julius, 22
Calhoun, John C., 17, 18, 98, 122
Campbell military hospital, 284
Canada, 224–25, 226, 227, 229
Canning, Matthew, 92–93
Carpenter, Francis, 157, 445n4
Cash, W. J., 18–19
caste system, 38, 41–42
Charleston, SC, 127, 138, 157, 320
Chesnut, Mary, 135, 179
Chester, Samuel Knapp, 289
Chicago Herald, 133–34
Chicago Tribune, 181
cholera, 44–45, 54
Christiana fugitive slave "riot" (1851),
98–99
civil liberties, 157–58
Civil War: battle of Antietam, 170,
188, 241; battle of Gettysburg,
174–75, 241, 263; Black troops in,
12–15, 183, 207–9, 278, 295, 447n22;
Confederate desertions during,
206–7, 305, 309; death toll in,
278–79; escaped slaves during,
170–71; first stage of, 163, 167–70;
killing of Black prisoners in,
207, 209; Lee surrender in, 19,
296–97, 304, 308, 320, 386; Lincoln
policy in, 156–58, 161, 163, 166–67,
168–69, 178–79, 180–81; military
campaigns in, 167–70, 236, 239–41,
319–20; opening of, 153; prisoner
exchanges in, 207, 210, 262;
shelling of Fort Sumter, 128, 152,
153, 298; shift to second stage of,

126; and illegitimacy, 53, 60; as
"King Abraham Africanus I," 156,
194, *195*, 249; as master politician,
190, 267, 416; as mortally
wounded, 359–63; and Niagara
Falls "peace conference," 237, 239;
opposition to slavery itself, 56–57,
61, 62, 65, 96, 127, 138, 162–63, 178–
79, 268–69, 276, 278; opposition to
slavery's spread, 113–14, 116–17, 144;
performances attended by, 198,
280, 330–31; personal bodyguards
for, 7, 173, 175–76, 272, 343, 363;
photos, *10, 124, 275*; physical
strength, 62; pocket pistol of, 342,
451n5; post-presidency plans, 317;
and racial equality issue, 123, 190,
302; racists' hatred of, 191, 192–94,
249; Reconstruction plans, 322–23,
412–13; religious views, 107–8, 273–
74; and secession crisis, 126–27, 152;
Second Inaugural Address, 267,
271, 273–74, 276, 278–79, 322–23, 411,
446n17; as secular saint, 33, 191,
376, 410–11; self-educated, 63, 64;
as Shakespeare admirer, 2–3, 19;
visit to Richmond by, 6–9, 11–15,
19, 297; war's aging of, 317–18; as
Whig, 106–7; White House Civil
War victory speech, 300–302
Lincoln, Captain Abraham
(grandfather), 57–58
Lincoln, Josiah (uncle), 57
Lincoln, Mary Todd (wife), 109,
148, 174–75, 317, 403; Abraham
engagement to, 108; later life of,
408; and Lincoln assassination, 4,
345, 350, 351, 359, 360, 361, 362, 364,
366; as mentally unbalanced, 317,

332, 334
Lincoln, Mordecai (uncle), 57, 58
Lincoln, Nancy Hanks (mother), 60
Lincoln, Robert Todd (son), 233,
362, 364
Lincoln, Sarah (sister), 63
Lincoln, Sarah Bush Johnston
(stepmother), 63
Lincoln, Thomas (father), 57–61,
63–64
Lincoln assassination, 339–41,
344–51, 359–61; Booth escape
from theater following, 349–51;
Booth meeting with henchmen
prior to, 336–37; Booth sneaking
up for, 345–47; Booth written
justifications for, 343–44, 378–79,
380–81; Jefferson Davis on, 371;
deadly shot fired in, 3–4, 347–49;
grief of Blacks following, 371;
hanging of conspirators in, 406,
407; national mourning following,
369–70, 403–4, *405*; political
motives behind, 32–34; reaction in
Washington to, 361–62; response
in South to, 370–71; treatment of
suspects following, 369–70; trial
of conspirators in, 403, 404, 406;
vigilante violence following, 369;
Walt Whitman on, 4, 347–48,
351. *See also* Booth, John Wilkes
(conspirator and assassin)
Lincoln Catechism, The, 194
Lincoln death and kidnapping
threats: Baltimore plot, 143, 145–
50; through biological warfare,
175, 229–32; bodyguards for
protection from, 7, 173, 175–76, 272,
343, 363; Booth's kidnapping

143; Frederick Douglass on, 49–51; and Dred Scott decision, 42–43, 111, 118–19; and escaped slaves, 98–99, 170–71; and Fugitive Slave Act, 97, 98–99, 170; hopes for gradual disappearance of, 102, 110, 116, 121, 162–63, 171; Kansas war over, 119–20; in Kentucky, 57, 61; Lincoln's opposition to, 56–57, 61, 62, 65, 96, 113–14, 116–17, 127, 138, 144, 162–63, 178–79, 268–69, 276, 278; in Maryland, 39–40; Southern justifications for, 47–49, 110–12, 191–92, 267; in Virginia, 40, 57; in Washington, 304–5; and western territories, 108–9, 137, 144, 164–65; and white supremacy, 16–17, 18–19, 134, 267–68. *See also* Emancipation Proclamation

Sons of Liberty, 225, 226

South Carolina, 97, 128, 144, 320

Southern gentlemen, 69–70

Southern Illustrated, 193–94, 195

Spangler, Edman, 402, 403, 406

Spencer Carbines, 262–63

Springfield, IL, 164

Stanton, Edwin, 174, 217, 225, 288, 299, 362, 369–70; and Booth, 392, 398, 399; Booth's plans to assassinate, 310–11, 323, 326–27; on Lincoln, 318, 323, 366–67; Lincoln safety concerns of, 173, 176, 216, 341; takes charge after Lincoln assassination, 363–64

Starr, Ella, 235, 328

Star Saloon, 339, 346

star system in acting, 73, 82

Steers, Edward, Jr., 260

Stephens, Alexander, 103, *104*, 126–27,

136, 185

Stewart, Kensey John, 231–32

Still Waters Run Deep, 284

St. Joseph, MO, 199

St. Louis, MO, 199–200

Strong, George Templeton, 148, 150

St. Timothy's Hall, 66, 67, 98, 203–4

Stuart, Richard H., 384–85

Sumner, Charles, 70, 136

Surratt, Anna, 253

Surratt, John Harrison, 257, 270, 280, 286; about, 251–53; escape following Lincoln assassination, 254, 400; and Lincoln kidnapping plots, 283–84, 285; and Secret Service Bureau, 251–53, 260, 268, 325; and Surratt tavern, 254, 328–29

Surratt, Mary Elizabeth, 253–54, 282, 283, 287, 330; arrest of, 400; trial and hanging of, 288, 328, 403, 406, 407

Surratt tavern, 253–54, 287; Booth at, 328, 372–73; weapons stored at, 328–29

Taney, Roger, 42–43, 119

Taylor, Joseph Walker, 213–14

Tell, William, 381, 454n17

Texas, 129–30

Thirteenth Amendment, 236, 266, 415

Torpedo Bureau, 312–14, 323

triangulation, 416

Trumbull, Lyman, 166

Tudor Hall farm, 36–37, *37*, 68, 72

Unlocked Book, The (Booth Clarke), 153–54